Backroads Pragmatists

POLITICS AND CULTURE IN MODERN AMERICA

Series Editors
Margot Canaday, Glenda Gilmore, Michael Kazin, and Thomas J. Sugrue

Volumes in the series narrate and analyze political and social change in the broadest dimensions from 1865 to the present, including ideas about the ways people have sought and wielded power in the public sphere and the language and institutions of politics at all levels—local, national, and transnational. The series is motivated by a desire to reverse the fragmentation of modern U.S. history and to encourage synthetic perspectives on social movements and the state, on gender, race, and labor, and on intellectual history and popular culture.

Backroads Pragmatists

Mexico's Melting Pot and Civil Rights in the United States

Ruben Flores

PENN

UNIVERSITY OF PENNSYLVANIA PRESS

PHILADELPHIA

Published by
University of Pennsylvania Press
Philadelphia, Pennsylvania 19104-4112
www.upenn.edu/pennpress

Printed in the United States of America
on acid-free paper

10 9 8 7 6 5 4 3 2 1

Library of Congress Cataloging-in-Publication Data
Flores, Ruben, 1967–
   Backroads pragmatists : Mexico's melting pot and civil rights in the United States / Ruben Flores. — 1st ed.
      p.   cm. — (Politics and culture in modern America)
"Published in association with the William B. Clements Center for Southwest Studies at Southern Methodist University."
   Includes bibliographical references and index.
   ISBN 978-0-8122-4620-9 (hardcover : alk. paper)
   1. Mexico—Politics and government—1910–1946. 2. Cultural pluralism—Mexico—History—20th century. 3. Nationalism—Mexico—History—20th century. 4. Education and state—Mexico—History—20th century. 5. Civil rights movements—United States—History—20th century. 6. Social movements—Southwest, New—History—20th century. 7. Social reformers—Mexico—History—20th century. 8. Social reformers—United States—History—20th century. I. William P. Clements Center for Southwest Studies. II. Title. III. Series: Politics and culture in modern America.
F1234.F685   2014
972.08'2—dc23   2014004865

Published in association with the
William B. Clements Center for Southwest Studies at Southern Methodist University

Contents

Introduction

Between 1920 and 1950, a group of influential social scientists who helped build the civil rights movement in the United States believed that a like-minded group from the Republic of Mexico had found the solution to social conflict in the idea of the melting pot. The international conversation the Americans established with the Mexicans transcended the unique histories of their nations, creating a comparative history of state reform that became central to the history of race relations in Mexico, on the one hand, and to the development of civil rights in the United States, on the other. Their exchange showed not merely how America's history of cultural difference influenced the history of pluralism in Mexico, but also how Mexico's own melting pot was integral to the history of democracy in the United States.[1]

This international exchange between social scientists and their belief in the power of schools and government to fuse the peoples of their societies together is the subject of this book. Committed to integrating the immigrant and ethnic enclaves of the American West into a single constituency of citizens, the Americans among them looked on postrevolutionary Mexico as a grand experiment in state reform and cultural fusion that they studied as they struggled to understand diversity and social conflict in American society. They transcended the commonplace wisdom that the United States was a fundamentally different society from Mexico, denying that Mexico's communities of mestizos and Native Americans made its society antithetical to America's culture of immigrants. Like the United States, Mexico for them represented a panethnic republic of multiple ethnicities that struggled to create a national culture from the diverse strands of its various peoples. Other American reformers more often studied the seminal thinkers of early twentieth-century American pluralism like Horace Kallen and Randolph Bourne for ideas about American unity in a time of heavy immigration. Radicals looked to the Soviet Union for ideas about social transformation, and later in the century, to China and Cuba.

But these Americans studied the work of Mexico's integration theorists, instead, including Manuel Gamio's *Forjando patria*, José Vasconcelos's *La raza cósmica*, and Moisés Sáenz's *México íntegro.*[2] They counterposed Mexico's melting pot metaphors—*sinfonía de culturas, crisol de razas y culturas, mosaico de razas*[3]—to America's own "symphony of cultures," "melting pot," and "assimilation." They studied Mexico's state policies (*integración, fusión, incorporación*) for mixing people together into a national body of citizens, imported its educational institutions into the United States in the effort to solve America's race problem, and held Mexico up as the preeminent model of cultural fusion when they had given up on America's rhetoric of equality. Mexico was for them the leading experiment in the relationship between diversity and the nation in the industrial era, a progressive middle way between extremist politics represented by the United States on the one hand and the Soviet Union on the other.

As in much of the modernizing world, industrialization and ethnic conflict were two of the central themes in U.S. and Mexican history at the beginning of the twentieth century. In both places, massive economic and political change had revived old questions about the relationship of the nation's cultural communities to one another. In Mexico between 1920 and 1950, local communities and the state alike struggled to rebuild a united society in the wake of a devastating civil war that killed more than a million people and became the founding event of its twentieth-century history. At the same moment in the United States, early twentieth-century questions about immigration and the expansion of capital merged with the social conflicts generated by the Great Depression and World War II to produce renewed debates about the relationship of America's peoples to one another. The black-white conflict of the New South and the place of the European immigrant in American society were only two major examples of the ethnic tensions in American society that scholars chart as fundamental to American history. By themselves, however, the social transformations taking place simultaneously in Mexico and the United States could not fully explain the conversation in the melting pot that the Americans jointly established with the Mexicans. Industrialization and ethnic conflict were not new in the twentieth century after all, and we are thus left to better comprehend why the Americans and Mexicans established a conversation with one another at this particular juncture in the history of both nations.

The international relationship in books, letters, and personal friend-ships developed not from the structural changes in the Mexican and U.S. economic systems alone, but from the questions that the Americans and Mexicans shared in common as they tried to make sense of those changes. In turn, the ideas of philosopher John Dewey and anthropologist Franz Boas sustained the solutions the Mexicans and the Americans offered in response to those questions, as one of the major revolutions in academic thought was sweeping through the social sciences during the early decades of the twentieth century.[4] Together, the questions and answers that the Americans and Mexicans shared with one another forged an intellectual common ground that mediated their understanding of the place of diversity in the national community at a moment of heavy political and economic change in the United States and Mexico.[5] Mexican educator Moisés Sáenz had studied directly under John Dewey and spread the ideas of experimen-talism throughout rural Mexico in the 1920s alongside his Dewey-inspired colleague Rafael Ramírez. Simultaneously, Americans George I. Sánchez and Loyd L. Tireman were studying pragmatism under professors who had trained with Dewey at Columbia University.[6] When Sánchez and Tireman arrived in Mexico to study reform work there in the early 1930s, they dis-covered a common intellectual ground that drew them close to the integra-tion projects of their Mexican counterparts for the rest of their careers. A similar conversation took place under the ideas of Franz Boas, uniting the Mexicans and Americans in a mutual dialogue of cultural relativism. Together, the cluster of ideas that had revolutionized social science and their corresponding models of social practice in Mexico became fundamen-tal examples for the Americans of how the twentieth-century industrial nation could address the riddles of social and political community pre-sented by ethnic diversity. This international exchange in pragmatist social science and the politics of national integration has not been studied, but its importance to the questions of democracy that the Americans were asking of United States society underscores its importance to U.S. and Mexican history alike.

The Americans who believed that Mexico's social scientists had some-thing to teach the United States about ethnic democracy in the 1930s were transforming pragmatist philosophy and Boasian anthropology into liberal politics in remote provinces of the United States at the same time that historians Arthur Schlesinger, Jr., and Charles Beard were using pragma-tism to build and defend the New Deal.[7] But tired of government inertia in the years before Franklin D. Roosevelt rose to the presidency and of the limits of the New Deal state to transform ethnic relations afterward, these Americans turned to three characteristics of the Mexican state as a successful model of an activist government that was rebalancing the relationship of Mexico's people to one another amid the religious, economic, and political forces of postrevolutionary Mexico.

First, they studied the administrative structure of Mexico's federal government as the postrevolutionary state channeled financial resources into infrastructure programs, arts projects, and reconstituted agencies that were directed at creating a new unified citizenry. Although historians of Mexico have derided the colonialist impulses of Mexico's activist government bureaucracies toward local communities after the Mexican Revolution, for these Americans, Mexico's government interference in the politics of ethnic relations was precisely the catalyst that was needed to accelerate the rate at which Americans were blending themselves into a united group of national citizens.[8] One example was the long campaign to dismantle America's segregated public institutions. In the epic U.S. struggle between the federal and state governments, the failure of the American central state to use its government agencies to dismantle the segregated institutions of the Deep South and the American West was a fundamental theme in U.S. political culture. In the years before they began to see evidence of the federal government's willingness to fight segregation in the United States, these Americans saw postrevolutionary Mexico as an example of government-led reform in ethnic relations.

Second, so impressed were the Americans with the educational models of Mexico's ministry of public education that they replicated them in New Mexico, Texas, and California as the antidote to recalcitrant state governments that refused to expand public education to immigrants from Mexico and rural Americans. Exemplified in the 10,000 public schools Mexico established in the 1920s and the platoons of social reform educators it sent into the remote areas of the nation, those models of education proved fundamental for Americans who had long believed that schools were fundamental to social progress.[9] Linguist Tireman copied the system of rural school supervision that Mexico's ministry of public education had developed in the 1920s, for example, as he tried to centralize the role of the New Mexico state government in managing the state's integration projects. As a supervisor in the system Tireman copied from Mexico, educator Marie Hughes expanded his work in New Mexico during the 1930s, and recreated

Mexico's model in Los Angeles as the postwar civil rights movement was asking new questions about the relationship of the public schools to educational integration a decade later. For founder of UCLA's anthropology department Ralph L. Beals, meanwhile, the policy efforts of the Mexican state had resulted in educational institutions whose role in national integration could be profitably studied by American social scientists concerned to solve the riddles of ethnic conflict at home. When a federal judge asked Beals in 1945 why he was qualified to speak about efforts in southern California to integrate Mexican Americans and whites in the public schools of Orange County, Beals replied with an answer that has always stunned me: "My present personal interest," he told the judge, "is in the problems of cultural change, as they affect the Mexican Indian in relation to the educational and social programs of the Mexican government."[10]

Third, the institutions of scientific research that postrevolutionary Mexican social theory had helped to spawn helped the Americans with questions they had formulated about immigrant assimilation in the United States. Paul S. Taylor, Emory Bogardus, and Herschel T. Manuel began writing the first academic monographs about immigrant Mexicans to the United States in the 1930s, seeking answers to the same questions that had perplexed generations of thinkers before them: the incorporation of the immigrant child in the public schools, the assimilation processes of American communities, and the differences between varieties of immigrant waves to America.[11] But for the American psychologists and social reformers who saw Mexico as the progressive example for the United States, including Montana Hastings and Catherine Vesta Sturges, it was Mexico's postrevolutionary projects in national integration that provided the primary source of social theory as they struggled to understand the immigrant's place in American society. Mexico's postrevolutionary government had institutionalized science as a mechanism for reconstructing Mexican society, yielding new research institutes that gave these Americans the opportunity to examine from inside the Mexican territory the same questions about immigrants that Taylor and Bogardus were asking in universities in California and Texas. Hastings and Sturges realized that Mexico's research institutes were asking the same kinds of questions about the relationship between cultural difference and the nation that academics were asking in the United States. It made as much sense for them to study immigrants at the origin points in Mexico of the migration arc to the United States, as it did to study them from Berkeley, the University of Southern California, and the University of

Texas after the immigrants had arrived in the American West. Mexico's own project in national integration thus allowed Hastings and Sturges to better understand similar questions of mobility, capacity, and character that had historically formed a part of the study of immigrants to the United States.

Together, these institutional contributions by the Mexican state to an understanding of pluralism and social conflict epitomized the critique of the modern social hierarchy that John Dewey had made central to pragmatist thought. Usefully defined as an attack on Western systems of philosophy for defining ideas separately from the experiences people lived every day, pragmatism removed the breach between thought and action that the Americans and their Mexican colleagues believed had plagued nineteenth-century social theory. To pragmatism's insistence that practice had to be brought into a discussion with theory, these Americans held up postrevolutionary Mexico as a province of experimentalism that was challenging outdated notions of social organization with new commitments to policy change.[12] To pragmatism's criticism that nationalism had been idealized by ignoring the texture of local community, these Americans saw possibilities for national reconstruction in the added attention by the Mexican state to rural communities across the republic. "For the true pragmatists—for James and Dewey and all of their tribe—intellectuals played a creative role in history," historian John Higham once wrote. "Ideas were precious tools for attaining practical ends. Consequently, being 'practical' meant continually and deliberately adapting institutions to changing problems."[13] For the Americans, Mexico's policy programs represented the adapting institutions that pragmatism understood to be the fulcrums for translating ideas into social change. Disappointed by the absence of such impulse-generating institutions in the rural American West, the Americans found that postrevolutionary Mexico was acting on the push-and-pull of daily conflict as it sought practical answers to the social challenges of its national community. For the Americans, postrevolutionary Mexico's new state became the practical mechanism that helped them chart the way forward out of the difficulties that separated them from the social justice that they sought in mid-century America. It put them in touch with the deeper values of pragmatism, what Higham described as "an appreciation of the crusading spirit, a responsiveness to indignation, a sense of injustice."[14]

No one exemplified the centrality of Mexico's middle way to the history of American ethnic democracy more than educational philosopher George

I. Sánchez, the long-time champion of American civil rights at the University of Texas, whose overlooked book *Mexico: A Revolution by Education* reflects the crucial influence of Mexican experimentalism on American politics.[15] Sánchez returned to New Mexico in 1934 after earning his Ph.D. at Berkeley for a dissertation that used Dewey's *Democracy and Education* to suggest educational reforms he believed could solve the problem of ethnic conflict in his home state.[16] But several months later a recalcitrant legislature blocked his attempts to create new policies in the state's schools. Crestfallen by the defeat, Sánchez embarked on a research tour of Mexico's postrevolutionary rural schools, which were then in the thirteenth year of Mexico's massive government effort to integrate the white, mestizo, and Indian communities into a unified bloc of citizens, or what anthropologist Manuel Gamio, twenty years earlier, had called "forjando patria" (forging the fatherland).[17] Officials of Mexico's federal ministry of education, the Secretaría de Educación Pública (Secretariat of Public Education, or SEP), escorted Sánchez throughout the country during his nine-month research trip in 1935, where he became close to Mexico's leading Deweyite, Moisés Sáenz. He visited the states of Morelos and Puebla, where he studied the laboratory schools established by the Secretaría de Educación Pública and their relationship to the rural laborers who worked the land that surrounded them. Farther south, he traveled to the states of Guerrero and Oaxaca on the Pacific Coast before swinging north to Tabasco on the Caribbean Sea. Already he had studied Diego Rivera's Mexico City murals of Mexico's new schoolteachers, finding inspiration in them for his integration work in New Mexico. Sánchez also visited the north central and northern provinces of Mexico. He photographed the schools of Chihuahua, and the cultural missionaries of the Mexican state as they performed their outreach work in the state of Zacatecas.

A year later, Sánchez lavishly praised the herculean efforts of the Mexican state to integrate the diverse communities of the nation into a unified group of citizens in his account of Mexico's educational reform efforts, *Mexico: A Revolution by Education*.[18] Through its itinerant platoons of teachers, known as *las misiones culturales*, and centralized administrative control of the rural schools from the national seat of power in Mexico City, Sánchez believed that the Mexican nation was proudly rising from the ashes of civil war and its aftermath. Most important, Sánchez believed, the educational ministry was courageously using John Dewey's philosophy in an attempt to unify the diverse people of Mexico into a single nation through active state intervention in the affairs of local communities. Whereas state government in New Mexico had failed to use its schools to meet the challenges of diversity caused by rapid immigration, the government of Mexico, by contrast, had found the answer for creating Mexico's own national melting pot. The "primary function [of the cultural missions] is that of 'incorporation,'" he wrote in *Mexico: A Revolution by Education*. "They represent the most advanced thinking in Mexico and the actual application of social and educational theories *in situ*, . . . [that] must integrate the Mexican peoples and Mexican practices into a national fold and into a coordinated progressive trend."[19] Sánchez simultaneously leveled a critique of government inaction at President Roosevelt's New Deal state. "The people of the United States have never seriously considered the use of their schools as organs for the propagation of 'new deal' beliefs, for example, nor as active social forces in contemporary reconstruction," he wrote.[20] Not the United States, he argued, but postrevolutionary Mexico was setting the standard for social change. "The front-line place given to the educational missions in the [Mexican] plan of action adds to the importance of these institutions, both in their scholastic functions and in their role of a political New Deal."[21]

Sánchez never stopped celebrating Mexico's use of the public schools to integrate the people of Mexico into a coordinated national constituency, throughout his career in New Mexico and Texas that spanned the New Deal on the one hand and the civil rights movement on the other. In between articles on American education and an active role in the 1940s school integration battles of the ACLU and the NAACP, he wrote new accounts of Mexico's amalgamation projects that complemented the one he had written in 1936, explicitly comparing the challenges of integration in the United States to the challenges of integration in Mexico.[22] Into the 1950s and 1960s, his regard for the Mexican experiments only intensified. "Nothing has affected my thinking and my feelings more than Mexico's experience—redemption by armed Revolution, then Peace by Revolution," he said in 1966. "This latter revolution still goes on, and I associate myself with it vicariously—from afar, and from close-up examination there as often as I can."[23] And he never stopped believing that the United States and Mexico were comparable republics that both had to deal with the challenges of democratic practice amid broad ethnic diversity. "The Mexican people, just like people in many other countries, are not the product of just one culture. In the United States, for example, many cultures have contributed to the

Figure 1. The San Felipe Hidalgo federal rural school, in the state of Tlaxcala, Mexico, in 1930. Mexico's rural schools became the central mechanism used by the state for integrating the nation into a single group of citizens in the thirty years following the Mexican Revolution. Archivo Histórico de la Secretaría de Educación Pública (AHSEP), Mexico City, Mexico, Sección Dirección General de Educación Primaria en los Estados y Territorios, Folder Escuela Federal Rural de San Felipe Hidalgo (Calpulalpan, Tlaxcala).

personality of the United States citizen: Italian, German, English, Polish, Dutch, and many, many others. . . . [I]n Mexico, the same is true: the Mexican is a product of many cultures."[24]

Other westerners who would participate in the civil rights movement mirrored Sánchez's enthusiasm for Mexico's melting pot projects just as sharply. In 1931, Loyd Tireman traveled to Mexico to study the model of progressive education that Mexico's rural schools might become for the state of New Mexico as he sought, as Sánchez would later, the answer to ethnic conflict in the isolated rural hamlets of the state. In the subsequent report that he circulated nationally, *The Rural Schools of Mexico*, Tireman described the institutional models that he soon adapted from Mexico for use in New Mexico's rural north.[25] Mexico's schools "presented a picture that will long linger in my mind," he said in 1932. "This was proof, to me, of what one might expect in our own southwestern states if the people were given a like opportunity."[26] After receiving her MA from Columbia University in 1920, meanwhile, psychologist Montana Hastings found the research programs of Mexico's Secretaría de Educación Pública to be the ideal laboratory for her to examine one of the central questions over which social scientists fought in the early decades of the twentieth century: were immigrant children from Mexico genetically inferior to American children of European extraction, and hence not capable of being integrated into the rural schools of the United States? When Mexico's ministry of education forwarded her report, *Clasificación y estudio estadístico*, to San Diego's Mexican consulate as part of the consulate's support for one of the canonical educational integration lawsuits in the American West, *Lemon Grove v. Alvarez*, in 1931, Hastings became one of the first Americans to attack the rationale that buttressed California's segregated educational system.[27]

As they studied schools in Mexico, these westerners crossed paths with a wider set of iconic reformers whose struggles with race in other provinces of the United States had brought them to study race relations in New Mexico and beyond. Mexico had proved important for the American West because experiments in diversity in New Mexico and California seemed to mirror so many of Mexico's own rural experiments. Mexico remained 80 percent rural as its consolidationist program accelerated to national scale between 1920 and 1930 and did not become primarily metropolitan until 1960. Of the more than 15,000 public schools Mexico constructed in the twenty-year period that ended in 1940, 70 percent were built in the agrarian villages of the nation. The similarity between the rural provinces of Mexico and those of the United States was overwhelming for these western Americans. But Mexico's rural projects resonated similarly among influential Americans who struggled with social conflict in the rural Deep South and rural Midwest. Sánchez had been sent to study the Mexican schools by Chicago's Julius Rosenwald Fund, the Jewish philanthropy that financed the construction of 5,000 public schools in the rural American South between 1912 and 1932 in an effort to solve the original American dilemma, segregation in the Deep South.[28] The Rosenwald schools may have become an influential educational and race relations model in the United States, but simultaneously, it was the Mexican state that had become an educational model for the Rosenwald Fund. In the middle of his Depression-era campaign to solve the problem of white-Indian relations on the rural Great Plains, meanwhile, Bureau of Indian Affairs director John Collier praised Mexico's experiments in race relations as much as anyone ever did. "Mexico has lessons to teach the United States in the matter of schools and Indian administration, lessons which are revolution-ary and which may be epoch-making," he wrote in 1932.[29] John Dewey, too, believed that Mexico's rural practices had a wide range of applicability to the immigrant communities of the United States, both rural and metro-politan. While visiting Mexico's rural schools in 1926, he famously declared his respect for the efforts of the Mexican state. "The most inter-esting as well as the most important educational development is the rural schools," Dewey wrote in the *New Republic*. "This is the cherished preoc-cupation of the present regime; *it signifies a revolution* rather than renais-sance. It is not only a revolution for Mexico, but in some respects one of the most important social experiments undertaken anywhere in the world."[30]

Mexico's influence on American social theorists tells us that the Ameri-can melting pot was part of a larger North American experience of cultural diversity that was shaped by Mexico's efforts to consolidate its peoples into a national bloc of citizens. Mexico's history with polyglot ethnicity served as a philosophical and political platform from which intellectuals in the American West developed their ideas about diversity, and from which oth-ers like the Rosenwald Fund and the Bureau of Indian Affairs sought to repair American democracy as they confronted the legacies of slavery and Indian wars. Seen this way, Mexico's history with diversity is inextricable from the major debates about ethnic pluralism in the twentieth-century United States, and from the political efforts to broaden American democ-racy that followed in their wake. "Imagined communities" is the name Benedict Anderson has given to the development of civic nationalisms in the Americas, while John Dewey once described the search for a more enlightened nation as the quest for the "Great Community."[31] Following a formulation first used by Deweyite and essayist Randolph Bourne in 1916 but still in use today, I shall call the search for a reconstituted nation amid great cultural diversity and social conflict the quest for the "beloved com-munity."[32] And I shall refer to the social scientists who moved between Mexico and the American West as the "backroads pragmatists," in recogni-tion of their use of John Dewey's idea in the rural communities where they struggled to understand the meaning of the modern nation in the context of localism and difference.

Mexico's search for its beloved community provided the Americans with an example of an activist state government whose administrative units were focused on national consolidation amid deep ethnic divisions, at a moment when the role of the state in social welfare and individual political rights was being reformulated in twentieth-century America. As Mexico channeled resources into government relief programs, it provided a sense of possibility for what America's federal government might do in the United States.[33] Its use of social scientists as agents of social transformation provided the Americans with a model for the relationship of academics to public government in the United States. Mexico's distribution of state resources to rural communities provided them an example for how government might intervene in the communities of rural New Mexico, Texas, and California. At a moment in the 1930s when Roosevelt's New Deal state was still an idea and not a policy, these Americans formed intellectual alliances with Mexican social scientists who had been creating an alternative model of activist government different from that of the Soviet Union.[34]

That relationship also became a conduit for the transmission of ideas in progressive education that shaped American efforts to transform ethnic democracy in the U.S. West. Since at least the 1950s, the role of John Dewey in the creation of Mexico's postrevolutionary educational system has been a central theme among scholars of Mexican history.[35] But the reciprocal influence of Mexico's Deweyan experiments on the intellectual development of progressive educators in the United States has never been studied. Likewise, why Mexico's progressive schools became the institutional models for the leading laboratory schools in New Mexico and California is a question that has never received attention. Yet these Americans were deeply impressed by a national state that could establish thousands of new public schools throughout the national territory using ideas that had been transferred there directly from Columbia University. At the height of America's progressive education movement, these scholars visited Mexico's schools, worked for Mexico's ministry of education, and researched ethnic divisions in Mexico as an analogue to ethnic divisions in the United States.

Mexico's postrevolutionary melting pot shaped the American civil rights movement, as well. As the United States transitioned into the postwar civil rights era, the Americans who had first gone to Mexico in the 1930s continued to invoke Mexico's administrative systems, theories of democracy, and scientific institutions as models for desegregation as they became the leading social science actors in the legal campaigns that dismantled the system of segregated public schools in the American West. By analogizing

America's project in desegregation to Mexico's projects in national integration, the Americans used Mexico's melting pot ideas to transition from the
school as a laboratory for social change in the 1930s to the school as an
institution for American integration in the 1940s. Major consequences
follow for our understanding of what Jacqueline Dowd Hall has called the
"long civil rights movement."[36] Scholars have shown us that the social
mobilizations of the Great Depression and World War II, the effects of Nazi
social theory on American servicemen, and the economic boom of the
1940s were major factors in the development of civil rights in the American
West. But none of these influences can account for the place of Mexico in
the civil rights thought of the Americans charted here. Mexico must be
given added attention in the formation of postwar integration movements
in the American West that scholars have described almost exclusively in
domestic terms or have limited internationally to the legal support of Mexico's consulates in the civil rights litigation of the 1930s and 1940s. If it is
also true that those campaigns influenced the work of the NAACP, ACLU,
and American Jewish Congress in the years leading to *Brown v. Board of
Education*, as some scholars of comparative civil rights have argued, then
Mexico's influence in the postwar United States may have even played a
role in the development of civil rights movements in the American Deep
South.[37]

Mexico's history with diversity also tells us that there was a richer source
of ideas beyond Europe from which Americans developed their ideas for
reforming social relationships in American society. When progressive
Americans who were struggling to understand the incorporation of immigrants from Mexico into the public schools of the American West reached
into Mexico for ideas about reconstructing American society, they inter-
jected the history of its southern neighbor into the development of American democracy in ways that became part of the fabric of U.S. political
culture. Great American writers, looking back on the period between 1920
and 1950, were stunned by the enormity of the social dislocations at home
and in Europe that had brought suffering and privation on a massive scale.
Yet what strikes the interested reader about the Americans from Texas and
New Mexico for whom Mexico became the premiere example of integration
in the Western Hemisphere is that none of them considered World War I,
the Great Depression, or World War II to be the signal moment of social
change in the first half of America's twentieth century. These Americans

were instead struck by the inability of the young state governments in Arizona and New Mexico to manage social transformation. They watched the heavy movements of people from Mexico collide with rapid migration from the American East to open deep social fissures in the rural communities of the West to which they claimed allegiance.[38] And they came of age intellectually within the ideological orbit of the twentieth-century ideas that had been spawned by the Mexican Revolution, not by the European or Russian battlegrounds. What strikes the reader is how deeply felt for these Americans were the great cataclysms of Mexico's social changes, in contrast to anything that was happening domestically in the United States or in Europe. Similarly, as many civil rights reformers moved chronologically across mid-century America, they moved geographically to the Soviet Union, Cuba, Ghana, and Europe to find hope and new ideas about the relationship between race and the state in the United States.[39] But these Americans found the analogies between integration in the United States and Mexico to be a defensible basis for sharing policy recommendations across the cultural divide that separated their country from Mexico, instead. Their sympathy for Mexico was rooted not merely in the philosophies that they shared with Mexico's thinkers, but in the viability of Mexico's models for the American West that those philosophies had made possible.

Yet for all the international features of the relationship to Mexico, this history of ideas and institutions was ultimately a narrative of nationalism rather than internationalism. Borderlands scholarship, the growth of international studies between Mexico and the United States in anthropology, sociology, and cultural criticism, and the internationalization and globalization of American history have all offered important reasons to question the national as the normative frame of analytical reference for understanding questions about the social community. But these Americans did not theorize the continuity of social identity between the United States and Mexico that characterizes much recent work on immigrant Mexican communities to the United States or the symbolic attachment to Mexico's many cultures that is often noted as a characteristic of Mexican American communities in the United States. Similarly, the Americans operated in Mexico even as Soviet ideology provided a different model of international community and as Pan-Americanism and Inter-Americanism offered alternative visions of solidarity in the Western Hemisphere. But for them, the border marked a concrete site of difference they willingly reinforced rather than a porous membrane of convergence they sought to soften as the pathway to social reconstruction.[40] Mexico's melting pot may have been an alternative experiment in North American political history, but that fact did not mean that these American scholars had outgrown their nation-state as the political community to which they claimed their allegiance.

These Americans were instead articulate apologists for the United States in the form in which they constructed it—a racist, discriminatory, economically exploitative nation that was only half-formed in its quest for democracy, equality, and justice—who committed their thought and politics to transforming rather than to destroying or replacing it. Like civil rights activists Robert F. Williams and Thurgood Marshall, they looked outside the nation for ideas about social change without abandoning the United States in favor of the nations of Latin America or the internationalism of the Communist party. In short, these Americans were defenders of the U.S. national community who understood the Republic of Mexico as just another nation in the world whose political systems were opportune examples for the United States but not transcendent ones that deserved their political loyalty as contrasted to the systems they had associated themselves with at home.[41] They understood Mexico as a place to be studied and emulated, not a place to be joined or replicated. This allegiance to the United States was not the expression of unbridled faith in the power of the American state to reformulate ethnic relations or to create order from chaos. Instead, like the concept of "doubleness" American studies scholar Leo Marx used to describe abolitionism and women's rights or the Second Reconstruction idea historian C. Vann Woodward used to describe civil rights, their optimism was a guarded hope that the power of the American state could be harnessed to expand opportunities to those who had been denied it and those who searched for the political mechanism by which to change social relationships in the quest for more meaningful forms of social justice.[42]

"Mexico especially offers an unusually good opportunity for studies in the applied field, both for suggesting action programs and for examining the results of programs," anthropologist Ralph Beals once wrote of Mexico's federal government agencies in 1943.[43] He was on the cusp of the civil rights movement in southern California when he wrote those words, yet had been studying federal government policy in Mexico among the Yaqui Indians of Sonora since the early 1930s. Much later, he would recount a Yaqui rampage that had ended with the death of his companions as his first introduction to the indigenous people of Mexico. That murderous episode

had not repulsed him from Mexico, but fascinated him instead to understand the relationship between ethnicity and the modern state. Like the
other Americans profiled here, Beals too would find hope in Mexico's postrevolutionary state for the answers to modern social conflict. He would
carry those solutions into the United States in the 1940s and 1950s, putting
them to use as he struggled with American racial liberalism. Others found
inspiration in other places abroad. But it was in Mexico, the country that
had spawned the first great social revolution of the twentieth century, where
Beals and his fellow Americans found theirs.

PART I

The Beloved Communities

Chapter 1

A Symphony of Cultures

If the essence of comparative history is to find differences rather than to highlight convergences, as Daniel T. Rodgers has argued, then the relationship between the United States and Mexico may be a better case study in comparative history than the transatlantic alliance between the United States and Europe.[1] Scholars have contrasted Mexico's economic underdevelopment to America's industrial leviathan, for example. They have idealized Latin America as a series of politically conservative Catholic societies in contrast to a Protestant United States that they have seen as politically progressive. The Mexican practice of race mixing known as *mestizaje* has been held up as an antithesis to the antimixing politics in the United States regarding *miscegenation*. Political instability has seemed to define Mexico, whereas America is held as the archetype of political stability.

George I. Sánchez and his colleagues in the civil rights movement overcame America's conventional orientalism toward Mexico by comparing three features of postrevolutionary Mexico to the United States.[2] The first was that Mexico represented a country of enormous cultural diversity, not a source of uniform labor for American industry. "It is time now for the revolutionaries of Mexico to take up the hammer and wrap themselves in the blacksmith's apron, in order to fashion the new nation composed of iron and bronze," one of Mexico's eminent twentieth-century public intellectuals, Manuel Gamio, had written of Mexico's diversity in 1916.[3] These Americans concurred, noting the presence of fifty indigenous groups whose distinctive cultures were vibrant contributors to the Mexican national community. The second feature was the central state as the mechanism for blending people into a united bloc of national citizens. Mexico had tried to use its central government to unify its cultural communities every few decades since independence in 1821. But only now, after the devastating Revolution of 1910, had social scientists come to believe that Mexico had finally found the way to national consolidation. As Gamio put it, a "powerful fatherland and a coherent and precisely defined nationality" would be the outcome for Mexico's melting pot democracy, the result of new social sciences that had equipped the enlightened public official with the tools needed to achieve the perfect balance of a united public.[4] The third was Mexico's turn to the theorists at Columbia University to fashion social scientific solutions to the challenges posed by the institutional destruction of the revolution. Faced with an overwhelmingly rural population of extreme cultural diversity, Mexico's state intellectuals faced a militaristic country to the north and the complete destruction of their own state amid ethnic and religious differences of vast proportions. These Mexican thinkers responded by turning to the work of John Dewey and Franz Boas, thus mirroring the responses of the Americans like Sánchez who had turned to Mexico in their search for ethnic consolidation and nation building in the rural American West.

Some of the Americans had come to Mexico in their teens, fleeing the World War I draft. Others came on study trips paid for by private philanthropies in Chicago and New York that saw potential solutions to America's race problem in Mexico's state policy. Yet others were young schoolteachers who backed into Mexico's influence on the life of the American West as a result of youthful enthusiasm to leave homes in Michigan and Iowa for new ones in New Mexico and California. Whatever their trajectories to postrevolutionary Mexico, these Americans became more than tourists to America's southern neighbor. Mexico's own resemblance to pressing questions of social change in the United States made Mexico a lifelong example for them, despite careers that they developed almost exclusively in the American West.

A Symphony of Cultures

It was impressive to watch how much ground of the Mexican countryside George I. Sánchez had covered. Already he had made two trips to Mexico, one to Mexico City in April 1935 to plan his future scope of work there for the Rosenwald Fund and a second in May, marking his first foray outside the national capital. But it was in June that he appeared to encounter his first difficulties, as he followed the rural school officials who escorted him on his trip southward into Mexico's tropics. Guerrero and "Vera Cruz"—he misspelled the name by writing it with two words, not one—came first late in the month, followed by Yucatán, Tabasco, and the remaining southern states in July. The trip to Puebla had been easy and brought him to the federal government's rural teacher-training academy and the Escuela Regional Campesina, the adult magnet school for the region's rural farmers. But the prospect of Yucatán and Campeche was a hard one. "I'm debating on an air trip to Yucatán and Campeche where the problems are quite different due to geography, topography, history, and races," he wrote in June. "By land or sea the trip is prohibitive due to the inclement season, time, poor connections, and cost."[5]

In Zacatecas two months later, he found the architecture stunning but the arrangements horrendous. "I'm taking a two-day field trip with the federal director of education—to contact rural areas," he wrote. But the hotels were flea circuses, the water was contaminated, and the food questionable, Sánchez wrote. "Aside from [this], I really like this town." On this latest trip, he had passed southward from the border with Texas and New Mexico, heading toward Mexico City while stopping in the states in between. He had visited the Tarahumara Indians in Chihuahua, noting the intensive mining and smelting in the state. He was headed for Aguascalientes, San Luis Potosí, and Querétaro thereafter. "If any mail is sent to me before September 20, please address it to me at the Hotel Regis in México, D.F., México. I'll be there through about the 25th on my return trip to the West Coast," he wrote.[6]

Sánchez was on his way to study Mexico's postrevolutionary schools and the rural communities they served. He was twenty-eight, an educator with the state of New Mexico, and at the beginning of a career in education and civil rights that would last until the Vietnam era. Normally not associated with Mexico, Sánchez actually completed nearly half his academic output between 1935 and 1955 on postrevolutionary reform there. In the late 1930s and early 1940s, before his name became synonymous with the American civil rights movement in the American West, he wrote five articles on postrevolutionary reform and published two books. His 1935 trips to Mexico were the first series of forays he made during his career, studying its system of elementary and university education and the cultural diversity of the nation.

When Sánchez published his analysis of Mexico's new revolutionary schools in 1936, he found Diego Rivera's murals the best symbols of the revolutionary policy and social reforms he had gone to Mexico to study. "He is a master of character study—choosing his subjects from among the common people," wrote Sánchez.[7] "He paints them in all their pathos and tragedy, their colour and gaiety, their simplicity." One could criticize Sánchez for his reductionism. Mexico's "common people" shared little in common at all, and his claim about "simplicity" was plain wrong. There was nothing simple about Mexico's peoples, as ten years of civil war two decades earlier had shown. The "simple" peoples of Mexico had helped bring down one government after another, had frustrated church and the civil state alike, and had continued to press their demands for political autonomy from the highlands in the north to the lowlands in the south.

But Sánchez had noted something else in Rivera's work. Rather than just painting a monolithic representation of Mexico's people, Rivera had portrayed the range of Mexico's ethnic diversity. There were the Zapotecs, Mixtecs, Tarascans, Yaqui, and Tarahumara. Rivera had also captured the medium-hued mestizos that made up 60 percent of Mexico's population. In his murals and paintings, he captured the range of Mexico's distinctive ethnic communities using different skin tones, clothing patterns, and bodily features. This variety of people was one of the first observations that Sánchez made about Mexico as he traveled throughout the country for the first time in spring and summer 1935. Much later, as he looked back on a lifetime of visits to Mexico, he would describe the breadth of difference he noted in Mexico's cultural tapestry by analogizing it to that of the United States. "The Mexican people, like people in many other countries, are not the product of just one culture," he wrote. "In the United States . . . many cultures have contributed to the personality of the United States citizen: Italian, German, English, Polish, Dutch, and many, many others. . . . [I]n Mexico, the same is true: the Mexican is the product of many cultures."[8]

Edwin Embree, president of the Julius Rosenwald Fund and committed to white-black relations in the American South, was also captivated by Rivera's murals. He had visited Mexico in 1928, seven years before Sánchez, and his report to the Rosenwald board was especially heavy on the social themes reflected in Rivera's murals. Embree was clearly moved by the open books that Rivera's schoolteachers displayed before their rural pupils in the murals that Rivera had painted at the Ministry of Public Education in Mexico City. One showed "the teacher bringing new light to Mexican peasants," he wrote, while another depicted the "wicked priest and capitalist . . . frowning in the background."[9] And just as Sánchez later noted, Embree, too, noted that there was no cultural uniformity among the Mexican people that Rivera portrayed. "Ethnologically, present day Mexico presents . . . a heterogeneous picture," he wrote. "The indigenous tribes include 49 well distinguished ethnical groups, speaking 100 distinct languages or dialects, and exhibiting markedly different customs and habits of life." These were only part of the many groups, wrote Embree, that composed this single nation.[10]

Rivera's murals reflected the major concerns that had brought two of the central figures of twentieth-century American race relations to study the social reforms of the postrevolutionary Mexican state in the 1920s and 1930s. The first was Mexico's ethnic diversity, which reflected the ethnic diversity of the states in the American West and South where Sánchez and Embree were committed to working. The American West had Mexican-descended mestizos, Indians, and whites, while the Deep South had blacks and whites. But it was the fact of ethnic diversity rather than its specific particularity that made postrevolutionary Mexico important to these Americans. A second was Rivera's representation of the Mexican state. In the Secretaría de Educación Pública murals Rivera captured the state in the form of a federal schoolteacher imparting the wisdom of the nationalist project to indigenous and labor groups arrayed around her, or alternately, as a mounted federal soldier watching over the educational labors of the teacher before rural farmers. For the Americans, Rivera's images of the state symbolized an interested government that saw its responsibilities as extending to the reformulation of ethnic relations in the modern nation. The third concern that Rivera captured was the rural countryside. The teacher and the soldier were portrayed not just anywhere, but in rural Mexico. Since Sánchez and Embree were principally concerned with rural New Mexico and the rural South, they wished to study the labors of Mexico's public officials in the agrarian villages of the nation.

Rivera's art coincided with one of the recognized moments in U.S. history when public discussions about race relations and ethnic diversity in American society seemed to reach a crest. In *The Souls of Black Folk*, for example, W. E. B. Du Bois had declared to America that "the problem of the twentieth century is the problem of the color line."[11] Not long after, Madison Grant's *The Passing of the Great Race* gave Americans a canonical installment in the conservative concern with immigration and nativism.[12] Franz Boas had startled the academy in 1911 with one of the definitive statements of the falsity of racial typologies, *The Mind of Primitive Man*.[13] But it was two images of the American melting pot produced shortly before Rivera painted his representations of ethnic diversity in Mexico City that arguably became even more archetypal in American culture. In 1915, philosopher Horace Kallen announced in *The Nation* that the arrival of non-British immigrants to the United States was creating a federation of peoples whose diversity would destroy the insipid national culture that the heirs of British America had created there.[14] Israel Zangwill had been wrong in his turn-of-the-century play, *The Melting Pot*, that immigrant diversity was destined to collapse into a melting pot that had obliterated the defining features of European immigrants to the United States.[15] Instead, a great moment in American history had been reached at the beginning of the twentieth century, wrote Kallen. The widening of American national character that was happening de facto every day as new immigrants came to the United States represented a "cacophony" that could go one of two ways. It could become a sterile, uniform ethic—what Kallen called a "unison"—if conservative Americans refused to transform the accepted basis for an American national culture. Or it could become a "harmony" of peoples who willingly joined each other's differences to one another to create a richer, more vital American community.[16] In his 1916 "Trans-National America," meanwhile, young New York essayist Randolph Bourne created a second canonical image of American diversity.[17] Kallen had insisted that the American mosaic was to be fashioned from distinctive cultures whose ultimate quality was insularity that emanated from their intrinsic uniqueness. These could not mix, as Kallen insisted, since the individual could never separate himself out of the distinctive history that his ancestors had bequeathed to him. By contrast, Bourne argued that America was becoming "transnational, a weaving back and forth . . . of many threads of all sizes and colors." What made America rich was the impulse toward cultural sharing and the transformation of ethnic cultures that resulted. Kallen stressed the inertial properties of ethnic cultures, arguing that the American federation would be held in place by the pressure of ethnic cultures pushing against one another but never synthesizing. Bourne downplayed the primacy of ethnic cohesion. What mattered was not the intrinsic properties of any one culture, but the decision to share those qualities across cultures. "Any movement which attempts to thwart this weaving, or to dye the fabric any one color, or disentangle the threads of the strands, is false to this cosmopolitan vision," he wrote. Kallen's harmony was rooted in the group, its intrinsic distinctiveness in need of protection because that difference was the root of identity. Bourne was less excited by the vibrancy of particular cultures. For him, the amalgam of borrowed ideas and practices was more important than the cohesion of tradition.

Yet despite their canonical position in the history of American race relations and ethnic diversity, these archetypal metaphors of American pluralism never appeared in the work of the Americans who came of age in the 1920s and helped build the civil rights movement in the American West a generation later. For these far-off western Americans, it was the canonical melting pot images crafted in Mexico in the aftermath of the Mexican Revolution that had instead captured their attention as they tried to understand American pluralism during the 1920s and beyond. Crafted in the aftermath of social conflict in Mexico that rivaled similar episodes of ethnic tension in the United States, images from Mexico like those that Rivera had emblazoned on the walls of the Mexican ministry of education became the primary symbols of national integration in the United States for western Americans whose regional communities in New Mexico, Texas, and California were undergoing the same dramatic demographic changes that Kallen and Bourne had described for the American East. In his 1934 Ph.D. dissertation, for example, New Mexico educational philosopher George I. Sánchez identified the fabled American melting pot as the telos to which state government and public schools should direct their resources. But when he searched for the best example of institutional labors in pursuit of national integration, it was Mexico's melting pot images that he pointed to, not those of the United States. For Carey McWilliams's *North from Mexico*, still considered one the seminal studies of Mexican migration to the United States after sixty years in print, the idea of ethnic fusion created by Mexican intellectual Manuel Gamio in 1916 became the explanatory framework for a narrative of social unity amid the extremes of ethnic tensions that characterized World War II California.[18] For the bureaucrats of the New Deal Office of Education, Mexico's melting pot images provided the template for attempts to reduce social conflict on Western and Great Plains Indian reservations during the Great Depression. For Americans like Sánchez and Embree, it was Mexico's history of diversity that provided the symbols of how the melting pot might be converted into daily politics in the United States, rendering those symbols as politically important in American culture as those that were being created elsewhere by Kallen and Bourne.

Those symbols were constructed in the aftermath of the Mexican Revolution, that great civil war that some progressive Americans had seen as the first salvo in the overthrow of capitalism, whose next installments they believed were represented by World War I and the Russian Revolution.[19] Their cultural history is easy enough to understand. At roughly the same time that the armies of England and Germany were sending 120,000 men to their deaths at the Somme and that the Bolsheviks were destroying the social order of the czar, Mexico was busy destroying the Porfirian state and killing one million of its own people. This was Mexico at the dawn of the twentieth century, a nation in revolution that was doing its own part to destroy the fin de siècle order, wrote Manuel Gamio. Out of that war would rise a new man of steel, continued Gamio, one blended together from the panoply of ethnic cultures that represented Mexico's distinctive peoples. Kallen and Bourne had used musical metaphors to describe the American melting pot. Gamio preferred the symbolism of metal. More than just a crucible where people mixed into one, Mexico was a giant smelter where the future of the nation was being forged by anvil-wielding revolutionaries, Gamio wrote.

It was in the spirit of such rebirth that Diego Rivera had been commissioned by Secretary of Education José Vasconcelos to emblazon the walls of the new secretariat building in Mexico City with murals depicting the postrevolutionary progress of the Mexican nation. Rivera was thirty-six when Vasconcelos hired him in 1922, alongside muralists José Clemente Orozco, David Alfaro Siqueiros, and Rufino Tamayo, on a government-sponsored art project that antedated the WPA murals project by more than a decade. He had recently returned to Mexico from studying art in Europe, and had just painted new murals in various locations throughout Mexico City. No one better captured in visual form the work of the Mexican state as it sought to create Mexico's melting pot ideal from the spectrum of ethnic groups that composed the Mexican nation.

Rivera painted two murals on the walls of the secretariat that captured the relationship of the reconstituted Mexican state to the melting pot ideal. In *Alfabetización: Aprendiendo a leer*, a female schoolteacher looks with pride on a group of students surrounding her whose complexions and dress represent the diverse cultures of the Mexican peoples. A dark-skinned woman with African features sits next to a Maya Indian who is accepting a schoolbook from the teacher. Behind them stand two young men, one a light-skinned resident of the city wearing a gray beret, the other a ruddy-skinned mestizo wearing a straw hat typical of rural Mexico. Above the schoolteacher and her provincials stand three revolutionary soldiers, watching over the process of conversion signified in the textbooks being distributed by the teacher. They wear the bandoliers of the revolution, just recently concluded but still a tangible presence in the life of the country. Rivera painted a more dramatic image of the revolutionary melting pot project at the secretariat headquarters, as well. Whereas the first image of the state's schoolteacher provides no clues about the geographic context for the education lesson that she is imparting, it is clear in *La maestra rural* that the schoolteacher has ventured away from metropolitan Mexico and into the countryside where Mexico's agrarian workers cultivated their fields. Here, the schoolteacher is dressed in red, immediately training the eye on the nine individuals who surround her and the book that she has stretched out before them. They represent three generations, grandparent, parent, and child, sitting in a serene repose as the teacher underscores her latest point with an outstretched hand. But whereas the teacher and her circle had taken up two-thirds of the mural in *Alfabetización*, in the present one, two-thirds of the mural is an agrarian landscape framed by towering mountains in the background, with two teams of horses plowing a field in front of rural laborers who follow them, and an armed federal soldier mounted on horseback who guards the schoolteacher with a carbine rifle that he points at the sky. The state is present in each of the Rivera murals in the form of a teacher and a soldier, but in the latter mural, the melting pot ideal has been transformed from a metaphoric representation of unity into a dynamic panorama where the work that the state has set out for itself is more accurately rendered.

Rivera's murals portrayed Mexico's ethnic communities in their uniqueness as part of the project of national reconciliation that the postrevolutionary state builders had outlined for themselves. Represented quite clearly in his murals are the distinctive clothing, different skin tones, a diverse set of occupational labors, and both men and women as actors in the postrevolutionary drama. Rivera's images suggest that he believed their discrete identities should be allowed to flourish as part of the reconstituted nation. The teacher is positioned as an agent of consolidation, but Rivera did not render consolidation as a threat to the regional cultures that were the constituent elements of the new Mexican nation. Difference abounds and is celebrated, even as books and public officials of the state are portrayed sympathetically. His depiction of the school as an agent of transformation also appears nonthreatening. Although Rivera assigned a centripetal

Figure 2. Alfabetización. Aprendiendo a leer, Diego Rivera, 1929. Secretaría de Educación Pública headquarters, Mexico City. © 2014 Banco de México Diego Rivera Frida Kahlo Museums Trust, Mexico, D.F./ Artists Rights Society (ARS), New York.

function to the school, its task seems limited to creating bonds of citizenship among Mexico's people, not destroying the variety of cultural forms of the twentieth-century republic. For Rivera, nationality seemed to reside above and alongside regional culture, not as a substitute for it or as a superior force to that of the provincial centers.

Three other images crafted by Mexico's leading social theorists proved equally influential to race relations in the American West between 1930 and 1960. Manuel Gamio had crafted his image of cultural heterogeneity in a 1916 text, *Forjando patria*, that originated the phrase that scholars use to this day to describe the postrevolutionary project to rebuild the Mexican nation, *forjar patria*. Gamio opened *Forjando patria* with the image of a giant smelter in which Mexico's diverse cultural communities were being melted into a single synthetic ore. The American continents had always acted as a giant forge in which indigenous Americans mixed with one another to form new communities. Only the arrival of Columbus had prevented a single indigenous superpower aggregated from America's distinct native cultures from forming. That forge had overturned with the arrival of the Europeans, spilling the blend before it had hardened, however. The Europeans—the "men of steel," as Gamio tagged them—refused to mix with the Native Americans—whom Gamio called the "men of bronze"— during the colonial era. Suddenly, however, the independence movements of early nineteenth-century nationalism had presaged a return to a universal mix of peoples. Gamio represented Bolívar, Morelos, and San Martín as Olympic titans, donning the blacksmith's apron and taking up the hammer to forge an original metallic statue that contained all the metals of America's peoples. That statue would have been immense, corresponding to the panhemispheric nation that the liberators would have forged from the ruins of the Spanish empire.[20]

The early idealism of independence was not to be. As the nineteenth century unfolded, smaller national communities had been established across the hemisphere, instead. A new monument had been forged, but rather than containing all Latin America's ores, the statue had been forged out of iron—out of Europeans, in other words—and placed over a pedestal made of bronze—the Native Americans. This was Gamio's way of critiquing the social segregation of Latin America in the national era and its failure to reach toward the equality of its ethnic communities. This era of a stillborn mixture had to an end with the Mexican Revolution, Gamio argued. Now that the revolutionaries of Mexico had deposed Porfirio Díaz and taken up the role of blacksmith, they would consummate the task of blending the iron of Europe and the bronze of America into an indestructible synthetic ore. The new nation would rise to challenge the might of Europe and the power of the United States. "There is the iron . . . and there is the bronze," Gamio wrote in Forjando patria at the halfway point of the Mexican Revolution. "I implore you to mix, my countrymen!" he commanded Mexico's people, hopeful that Mexico's rise to continental prominence after a decade of bloody war was at hand.[21]

Like Bourne and Kallen, Gamio had situated his essay in the context of the attempt by Germany and England to destroy each other in World War I. In "Trans-National America," Bourne had called the United States a "star" wandering between two European antagonists that were trying to blast each other to bits in the Great War. As Bourne put it, America was "a wandering star in a sky dominated by two colossal constellations of states." America would work out her cosmopolitan ethic, "some position of her own. . . . A trans-nationality of all the nations, it is spiritually impossible for her to pass into the orbit of any one," in this colossal tragedy. Gamio, too, believed that World War I was a turning point in history, and like Bourne, believed that the fragments into which Europe was collapsing provided the ideal political moment for the rise of the melting pot in the Western Hemisphere—in Mexico rather than the United States. In *Forjando patria*, Gamio used the example of World War I to chide the presumed superiority that Europeans had historically assumed over Mexico's indigenous cultures, begging the great foreign powers to leave Mexico alone in anticipation of Mexico's postrevolutionary rise to prominence. "Have your last words in Europe," he wrote, "on the occasion of the great battle whose only defense seems to be the will to vanquish the other."[22]

Mexican philosopher José Vasconcelos's vision of the Latin American melting pot arguably became the most enduring image of cultural fusion in twentieth-century Mexican history and the one that has become most prominent in American scholarship.[23] One year before Robert Park added the assimilationist melting pot of the "race relations cycle" to the canonical images of American diversity,[24] Vasconcelos became synonymous with the postrevolutionary melting pot project, an ideal that he captured in a short 1925 essay called *La raza cósmica*.[25] *La raza cósmica* was an aesthetic prophecy of the eventual triumph in the Western Hemisphere of one melting pot civilization, Latin America, over another, British America.[26] The ruins of the great Mesoamerican societies at Chichén Itzá and Palenque were proof that the greatest civilization ever seen had flourished in the Western Hemisphere before being transported—he did not say how—to Egypt, India, China, and Greece. To Greece had fallen the task of reconstructing the once-grand civilizations of Middle America, a project initiated by the migration of Spanish and British whites to America in the fifteenth and sixteenth centuries. Britain's whites had been triumphant through the beginning of the twentieth century owing to Anglo unity amid the challenges of colonization. But Spanish disunity was equally to blame. Incompetent rulers and the rise of provincial nationalisms after Napoleon's invasion of Spain had fractured the once-dominant Iberian peoples into a collection of competitors. While the Protestant descendants of Britain retained their spiritual unity with England, allowing them to expand a hemispheric mission of political dominance, Spain's Catholic tradition had failed before the selfish pursuit of earthly, not transcendent aims.

Vasconcelos's idealized melting pot would rise anew in Latin America as the result of a mortal sin committed by Anglo America, however. Despite its political successes in the hemisphere, England's great weakness in the New World had been the sin of destroying the "dissimilar" races of man that it had encountered there. In the northern half of the Western Hemisphere, British whites had mixed only with other whites, had exterminated the Native Americans they encountered, and had sought physical control of the Chinese and black races, Vasconcelos argued. In the southern half, by contrast, Spanish whites had exhibited an "abundance of love" for Indians and blacks that had resulted in the creation of mixed races. Spain's "greater capacity for sympathy toward strangers" continued to be consummated through the sexual mixture of races that is ongoing through the present day. Vasconcelos switched metaphors at this point, from biology to music. The exclusionary history of white North American represented a vigorous *allegro* march in the direction of the ethics of purity that had been handed to them by their British forebears. By contrast, the Ibero-American path represented the profound *scherzo* of a bottomless symphony that mixed together all the races. Within that symphony could be discerned the faces of the Native American, Chinese Mongol, white European, and Jewish and Muslim. "What is going to emerge there is the definitive race, the synthetical race, the integral race," wrote Vasconcelos. This race, which he termed the cosmic race, would be "possessed of the genius and the blood of all peoples and, for that reason, would be more capable of true human fraternity and a true universal vision."[27]

A mural painted in 1979 by artist Aarón Piña Mora in the deserts far north of Mexico City was a visual reminder that Vasconcelos's vision was not cultural pluralism but a uniform melting pot.[28] As Piña accurately captured by painting a single human archetype emerging from webs of energy that radiated outward from four distinct people, Vasconcelos did not celebrate distinctive cultural communities working in harmony with one another. Instead, Piña Mora captured a synthetic race whose distinctive cultural and biological features had been absorbed into a homogeneous civilization. Vasconcelos's ideal cosmic society was a sexual blend of human beings capped by the cultural forms of classical Greece and Rome and the metaphysics of the Roman Catholic Church. "Love" had produced the mestizo strength of this ideal society, but unlike Randolph Bourne's plea that the United States was to be a cosmopolitan agglomeration of distinct cultures, Vasconcelos did not envision an eclectic mixture of people. *La raza cósmica* represented a melting pot ideal in a destructive sense of the word, as the obliteration of cultural difference as the price of collective strength directed by the Church from above. One of the remarkable ironies of twentieth-century Latin American history is that this autocratic vision posed by a Catholic metaphysician became the institutional foundation for the role of social science in mediating the middle ground between ideas and institutions in postrevolutionary Mexican society.

Musical metaphors were Moisés Sáenz's preferred images for describing Mexico's mixing of peoples into a harmonic assembly of national citizens, as well. At the moment that Kallen was witnessing the heavy movement of European immigrants into the United States that inspired "Democracy Versus the Melting-Pot," Sáenz was studying diversity in New York City at Columbia University and taking deep notice of ethnic democracy in American society as he struggled to make sense of Mexico's own history of ethnic difference. In San Antonio he noted the Mexicans, he wrote, while Nordic whites in Texas seemed to constitute their own race of humanity. In California, those who claimed affiliation to the colonial Spanish empire struck him the most. In Oregon, British Americans, who he argued had been forced out of Boston by the Irish, now lived among Swedes, and Danes. As for metropolitan U.S. society, New York was a Jewish city, Boston an Italian and Irish one, and Chicago a "universe of a thousand races, all built into one."[29] Kallen's analysis had been limited to Europe's ethnic cultures, but as a foreigner, Sáenz noted America's Blacks and Native Americans, as well. These latter groups represented the great problems of the American ethnic order, he wrote, and not the quarrel between British and Jewish America, as Kallen had written. Locked away on reservations or ignored altogether, Blacks and Indians provided the greatest test of the American definition of cultural democracy at the beginning of the twentieth century.

Sáenz's musical metaphors of the Mexican melting pot were written in a series of essays that were published in 1939 under the title *México íntegro*, which given the book's emphasis on national consolidation might be loosely translated as *A Unified Mexico*.[30] As in the writings of both Vasconcelos and Kallen, the image of the symphony orchestra was interspersed throughout the text. Mexico was a grand symphony, he wrote at one point, "where distinctive villages and cultures mix and where the prehistoric lives alongside the feudalism of Europe and the progressivism of the United States."[31] Sáenz also favored the image of a choir organized from all the peoples of the Mexican republic, singing the postrevolutionary songs of nationalism in unison and pride. Each morning as they trained in Mexico City for the task of unification that was at hand, the schoolteachers that

Rivera had painted at the Secretaría de Educación Pública sang the national songs of Mexico alongside the government officials who had hired them. "It seemed as if the entire country was singing," described Sáenz in *México íntegro*. "At the same time, Rivera was painting those strange images on the walls of the public buildings of the capital. . . . We all understood the language of the heart that those images and those songs conveyed. . . . The music was us. . . . We were united."[32]

It was ultimately vernacular rather than foreign images of music, however, that Sáenz favored, a choice that he recorded in *México íntegro* in the form of the mariachi. The mariachis sprang from the rural west of Mexico, especially the state of Jalisco, from individuals who had once spoken the Indian languages but who by 1930 were understood by the people of the nation to represent the hybrid culture of Mexico that had been in the making as a result of the Spanish encounter with the Indian. The mariachis had once been provincial, but now they were interspersed throughout the country. They sang a panoply of song types, not a single one. The music was original, picaresque, and crude all at once. The instruments were European, but the dances they stimulated resembled those of the indigenous communities. The mariachis were, in short, a hybrid art form, neither indigenous nor European, but purely Mexican. They represented the "armies of popular artists in Mexico who had instinctively undertaken the cultural reconstruction of the nation since the advent of the catastrophic conquest."[33] The mariachis symbolized the process of cultural unification that had yet to be fulfilled in postrevolutionary Mexico, argued Sáenz, an art form that had emerged from the originary cultures that had been foreign to one another before the arrival of the Spanish. They represented the task of unification that had yet to be consummated on a national scale.

Nearly a century has elapsed since these melting pot images were introduced to Mexican politics, yet they have remained largely unknown to American scholars interested in Mexico's role in the history of North America. Scholars have more often been interested in Mexico's peoples as laborers and immigrants rather than as members of ethnic cultures with complex relationships to one another and to their national state. Similarly, they have used the term "Mexican" freely, without considering the complicated connotations of that term. But across the twentieth century, the weave of Mexico's peoples was in evidence to a selected range of American scholars who studied Mexico not as an adjunct to the United States, but as a nation unto itself with particularities as rich as those of any nation on the planet. For Lesley Byrd Simpson, the nation to the south of the Rio Grande River was not a single country, but "many Mexicos," a title he gave to his first book.[34] "[W]e must recognize that Mexicans are a brand new people— and that they are the products of tremendously diverse antecedents and circumstances," wrote George I. Sánchez in the early 1940s. "The Mexican and his institutions . . . reflect a kaleidoscopic blending of many peoples, they reflect the coursing of a tortuous stream that is placid here turbid there—where the Moslem, the Jew, the Christian, the Maya, and the Aztec mix to build a new people, and those people new institutions."[35] " 'The Mexican' does not exist," wrote Mexican sociologist Carlos A. Echánove Trujillo in 1946, "because Mexico is constituted from a *mosaic* of diverse ethnic groups and from dissimilar cultural regions."[36]

Some represented twentieth-century Mexico as a solution of peoples waiting to be synthesized into a mixture stronger than the sum of its parts. Others would call Mexico a mosaic, a weave of colored strands brought together on a giant loom. Still others would employ a biological metaphor. Mexico was a crossroads of people where the capacity to love the other translated itself into a sexual power capable of bringing the cosmic energy of the universe to the terrestrial earth. An era of universal harmony was at hand, wrote José Vasconcelos, where the utopian homeland of Latin American prophecy was to be created after two centuries of New World decline and the expansion of Protestant Europe into the Western Hemisphere. Meanwhile, as the postrevolutionary state stabilized later in the century and a government administrative structure had formed, sociologists reduced Gamio's world-historical forge to a laboratory melting pot (*crisol*) where fusion was occurring daily. But the point was clear. Whether it was expressed in the language of biology, the weaver's loom, or as the furnace and smelter, Mexico was a crucible of cultures whose future depended on the idea of blending.

Mestizaje and the Leviathan State

The representations of postrevolutionary national unity created by Gamio, Vasconcelos, and Sáenz have produced a celebration of Mexican *mestizaje* among scholars of the United States as the antithesis to U.S.-based notions of racial purity and what historian David Hollinger has called the "one-drop rule."[37] *Mestizaje* is properly defined as racial amalgamation, or the

biological blend of Spanish and Indian in Latin America, and is conventionally portrayed in contemporary U.S. scholarship as the opposite of the U.S.-
based notion of *miscegenation*.[38] As the argument goes, the historical Mexican porosity to the biological crossing of Spaniard and Indian produced a
social community that defined hybridity as an ethical virtue. Such an ethic
was antithetical to the ethical injunction in U.S. history to avoid racial
mixture, especially across the black-white color line. The contrasts in racial
subjectivity across North America's distinctive national communities are
important to bear in mind historically, of course, especially in the twenty-
first-century context of rapid immigration from Latin America to the
United States.[39]

Yet American scholars have missed the political platforms on which
Sánchez and Embree based their study of Mexican race relations because
they have continued to position *mestizaje* as a biological process rather than
an institutional and cultural one. It is true, clearly, that *mestizaje* included
biological hybridity across the Mexican ethnic spectrum. But in contrast to
many contemporary American interpretations of Mexican racial history, it
was not biological *mestizaje* that Sánchez, Embree, and others celebrated.
Rather, looking horizontally across the bureaucracies of the postrevolutionary Mexican state, these latter scholars were captivated by the institutional
designs the Mexican federal government had created in order to foster cultural exchanges among Mexico's diverse peoples. Such institutional designs
were aimed at new forms of social exchange rather than at biological blending. These broader types of exchanges in Mexican race relations are critical
to bear in mind, for they manifested institutional experiments in ethnic
relations that Gamio, Vasconcelos, and Sáenz created as the analogues to
their teleological visions of the Mexican melting pot.

When Vasconcelos wrote *La raza cósmica*, for example, he was speaking
about racial fusion in Latin America only after three years of government
service with the Secretariat of Public Education, which was attempting to
fuse the peoples of Mexico into a united whole using platoons of schoolteachers called cultural missionaries. Gamio's image of the smelter as a
metaphor for postrevolutionary history in *Forjando patria* was an injunction to mix, but his text was one of the founding statements of twentieth-
century Mexican statecraft for its argument about the application of social
science to twentieth-century government in the interest of national unity.
Moisés Sáenz described Mexico as a mosaic, a mariachi, and a choir, but
he had done so on the leeward side of a ten-year career with the Mexican

central state, spent trying to reconcile Mexico's cultural diversity via a centralized political structure capable of addressing Mexico's social ills through the institution of the public school.[40] Thus, while U.S. scholars have emphasized the visual and linguistic metaphors of Mexico's integrated community as evidence for the ethical superiority of biological *mestizaje*, it is in fact more important to underscore *mestizaje* as the policy outcome shaped by public intellectuals who are recognized in Mexican national history as the architects of Mexico's postrevolutionary state. In contrast to romantic portrayals of biological *mestizaje* in Mexico among contemporary U.S. scholars, then, it is important to understand the careers of the civil rights Americans in the 1930s as more than the wanderings of orientalist intellectuals who imbued a foreign society with dreams of race mixture. Mexico came to represent for the Americans as much a province of policy work as a source of ethnic imagery as, beginning in 1920, Mexico mobilized its public policy resources and harnessed the power of the central state to fuse the nation culturally into a unified citizenry.

The same set of documents in which Sánchez and Embree discussed Rivera's mural images also captured their interest in Mexico's state-led policy projects for achieving the harmonious society. Sánchez had come to Mexico in 1935, two years into the massive reorganization of government Franklin D. Roosevelt initiated in 1932. And yet, during the quintessential episode in the growth of the American federal state, it was not the New Deal that represented the archetype of the activist state for George Sánchez. When he returned from Mexico in 1935, it was Mexico's central state growth after 1920 that he celebrated for its postrevolutionary 'new deal' efforts, not that of the United States.[41] Edwin Embree had long been involved in the Rosenwald Fund project to build schools for Blacks in the American Deep South. But Mexico's public mechanism for constructing educational institutions in rural Mexico provided a novel model for thinking about the role of public government in modern society rather than that of private philanthropy.[42] For these Americans, Rivera's images had provided proof that the United States was not alone in conceiving of itself as a society of disparate cultures needing to be fused into a common whole. But those images functioned primarily as symbols of a monumental government attempt to harness the power of the central state in the pursuit of social reform, not as images of the romantic racial utopia.

The history of state involvement in the relationship between the Europeans who colonized Mexico and the native Americans they encountered there was not original to the postrevolutionary writings of Vasconcelos, Gamio, and Sáenz. Such thought has always been one of the dominant strands in Mexican intellectual history. In his assessment of the differences between social projects that came before and after the revolution, for example, Mexican philosopher Luis Villoro traced a line of antecedent projects that had attempted to merge Mexico's indigenous cultures into the life of the nation-state as far back as the sixteenth century.[43] Hernán Cortés, Fray Bernardino de Sahagún, Francisco Javier Clavijero, Fray Servando Teresa de Mier, and Manuel Orozco y Berra—these and more had all attempted to reformulate the relationship of Mexico's native Americans to the European power structures established by the Spanish invaders.[44] These ideas about the relationship between the Indian and the European were a broad spectrum of models that stretched as far back in Mexican history as one cared to look, Villoro argued. One important precursor to postrevolutionary thought about the relationship of Mexico's peoples to one another that had been reached in the late nineteenth century, for example, when the Porfirian era work of Francisco Pimentel, Francisco Bulnes, and Andrés Molina Enríquez had reformulated the Native American from a novelty to an integral sociological unit of the Mexican nation. "Before we were interested in the Indian as a relic of the past, as a tradition. But now he has been configured as a vital element of our national character," wrote Villoro. "The Indian is now considered to be a living, breathing factor in our social life, an input into our nation whose efficient contribution we are all now in search of."[45] Operating from the vantage point of 1900, when the view of Mexican history seemed only to magnify Mexico's military and economic weaknesses before the growth of the United States, Villoro wrote, Pimentel and others had accepted the assumption that only a reconfigured relationship of Mexico's people to one another could produce a strong nation capable of withstanding foreign military power. While they stopped short of giving Indians autonomy within the nation, they nonetheless triumphed Native Americans as integral to fin de siècle Mexico. "A nation is an assemblage of men who share a common set of beliefs, who are guided by a single idea, and who labor toward the same goal," wrote Pimentel in 1864. "So long as our Indians are segregated as they are today, Mexico cannot reach the rank of true nationhood."[46]

But it was the heavy growth of the postrevolutionary federal state after 1920 that dramatically transformed the relationship of Mexico's people to one another. The expansion of the postrevolutionary state was so rapid, in fact, that an important historiography dating to the 1970s began referring to the postrevolutionary Mexican government as the "Leviathan state." The state had transformed itself into a top-down behemoth that imposed its will on the people of the nation, these scholars argued, as represented by the PRI party's seventy-year dominance of Mexican politics across the twentieth century. Subsequent scholarship argued strongly that postrevolutionary state growth was real but not necessarily evidence in itself of an increasingly powerful federal government.[47] But even those scholars who disputed the strength of Mexico's central state agreed that the period 1920–1940 represented a moment of radical reformulation for the Mexican melting pot. The institutional state became the site of social transformation via policy work that sought to rebalance Mexican society in the aftermath of its terrible civil war. As Alan Knight has argued, "The revolutionaries' discovery of the Indian . . . was paralleled by their commitment to state- and nation-building."[48] This was the institutional state from which Vasconcelos, Gamio, and Sáenz launched their policy projects in social fusion.

The generation who built Mexico's central state in the years following the Mexican Revolution spoke of building a harmonic national symphony from a triptych of peoples. In the context of the United States, the U.S. Census Bureau and others have condensed America's diverse ethnic and racial communities into what David Hollinger has called the twentieth-century racial pentagon.[49] That formation is characterized by symbolic red, black, brown, yellow, and white hues, corresponding to the distinctive communities in North America, Africa, South America, Asia, and Europe from which America's people are descended. In Mexico, the analogue consisted of the *criollos*, *mestizos*, and *indígenas*.[50] Of a total population of 14 million persons the year before the beginning of the Mexican Revolution (1909), 2.25 million were criollos, or white foreigners born in Spain or to Spanish parents living in Mexico. These were Mexicans who had never intermarried with either the *indígenas* or the *mestizos*.[51] The *indígenas* (Indians) numbered a total of 4.75 million persons, roughly 35 percent of the population, while 7 million persons representing 50 percent of the population were of mixed white and Indian blood, or mestizos. In the work of postrevolutionary social theorists, mid-century Mexican sociologists and anthropologists, and historians of twentieth-century Mexico, this triptych became the standard shorthand representation of Mexico's peoples.

No one had identified the ethnic range of Mexico's indigenous cultures, the *indígenas*, perhaps more than Andrés Molina Enríquez, who had once printed a list of 752 distinct tribes who he argued had left anthropological records of their presence in Mexico at the moment of the Spanish conquest.[52] But the smaller number of fifty or so Indian groups became the conventional number for Mexico's Indian cultures in the century of scholarship that followed after the revolution. No one could agree on precisely what constituted the definition of "indigenous." Early in the century, affiliation based on phenotype was common, but as biological arguments for race became less defensible after 1900, cultural characteristics such as language and dress became more common markers. Statistics could fluctuate widely at any one moment as well, depending on the definition of language ability. The 1930 census counted 2.6 million speakers of indigenous languages, for example, 17 percent of a population base of 16.5 million people, but half of these were monolingual in one indigenous language and the other half bilingual in combination with Spanish.[53] Indians could be reduced to 8.5 percent of the population, in other words, if monolingualism was the defining characteristic of *indígena* society.

Less in dispute in postrevolutionary society was the social distance that separated Mexico's indigenous groups from the metropolis that had emerged as the agent of national consolidation. The Maya Indians of the Yucatán peninsula had managed to sustain a forty-year low-intensity conflict against the Porfirian state that had not ended until 1890, and these Maya, after the triumph of the revolutionary armies, remained dominant across a vast expanse of mountain and jungle that remains forbidding even today. In the far north, in the states of Sonora and Sinaloa immediately south of Arizona, the Yaqui Indians remained a marauding presence whose war parties continued to disrupt the economic projects of the national state. The Otomí people lived in the mountains of Hidalgo state, less than one hundred miles from Mexico City, yet they were largely independent from the political and economic projects of the state. Around Mexico City proper were the Aztec peoples, descendants of the original settlers of Tenochtitlán, while in eastern Michoacán, surrounding the vastness of Lake Pátzcuaro, were the Tarascan Indians. Each of the communities had a different relationship to the national state, just as individual Indian nations did to the federal government in the United States, yet in general they were characterized by independent economic and political systems that remained in place alongside the accelerating projects in nation building that surrounded them.

The mestizos were noteworthy for the sheer volume as a percentage of Mexico's population that they represented. At a moment in U.S. history when the social distance between those people configured as white and those configured as Native American and Black was rigid, Mexico's mixed population represented half or more of the country's entire population base. Vasconcelos called them the integral race of hybridized people whose birth in Mexico had been made possible by the fecund love of the Spanish. As descendants of both the Indian and European peoples of Mexico, Mexico's state-builders designated them the mythic carriers of postrevolutionary Mexican nationalism and imbued them with the project of leading the reconstruction of the twentieth-century nation. As representatives of both the European and the Native American lineages of twentieth-century Mexico, it is they who were believed to contain each of the originary strands out of which postrevolutionary nationalism was to be constructed.

At the top of the racial hierarchy were the criollos, or whites, who lived mostly in the large cities of the nation, including Mexico City, Guadalajara, Monterrey, and Puebla. The historical blending between Europeans and Indians in Mexico meant that whiteness had become less of a marker of elite society by the twentieth century than was membership in the country's plutocracy. But those who claimed descent strictly from European society continued to wield cultural power in a nation where indigeneity had become a despised mark of identity. Whites were the smallest of Mexico's ethnic groups, yet the sense of superior European civilization with which they were associated became a social marker that defined much of Mexico's Porfirian era culture. French-inspired architecture and art, for example, were prominent in nineteenth-century Mexico, and the golden era of colonial Spain remained a large touchstone for those who believed that Mexico should develop its European heritage rather than its indigenous ethnicities as a marker of progress.

Mestizaje has been a perennial theme in the sociology of Mexico, just as amalgamation has been a perennial concern in the United States. As Milton Gordon pointed out many years ago, however, many variables can contribute to the centripetal acceleration of one group toward another. Peoples can be joined by marriage and sexual contact, but they may also be directed toward one another through the reorientation of cultural patterns, entrance into new organizations, and government efforts to control conflict toward one another.[54] At stake in postrevolutionary Mexico was not merely the presumed endpoint of new experiments in cultural and political mixing, but the question of who was to provide the motor for such transformation. In Mexico, that motor became the postrevolutionary state, whose attempts to reorganize its people paralleled a similar interest by American reformers in the United States. In both places, at the same time, intellectuals and social scientists were widely debating the role of the federal state as a mediator of ethnic conflict.[55] The Americans came to Mexico to study these debates beginning in the 1920s, and would continue to do so through the era of civil rights change in the United States that followed the end of World War II.

Pragmatism in Mexico and the United States

While businessmen and government officials in Mexico City and Washington, D.C., fretted over Mexico's nationalist stance toward American capitalists in the 1930s, a different relationship between the United States and Mexico was evident as Embree, Sánchez, and other Americans came to Mexico at that time. For some Americans, periodic ruptures in diplomatic relations seemed to presage war if Mexico could not convince the United States that it would not expropriate American property in the aftermath of the Querétaro Constitution of 1917. But elsewhere, intellectuals from both sides were simultaneously engaging one another on philosophical common ground, representing an important moment in an intellectual rapprochement that became the discursive platform for the later entry of the American westerners into Mexico in the 1930s. That philosophical common ground was adequately represented by the visit by José Manuel Puig Casauranc, Mexico's Minister of Education between 1924 and 1933, to Columbia University in 1926.

It is unclear how Puig Casauranc forged a friendship with Nicholas Butler Murray, president of Columbia University, but as the *New York Times* reported in March 1926, Casauranc had spoken at Teachers College to warm applause about Mexico's efforts to expand public education to the peoples of Mexico.[56] William F. Russell of Teachers College spoke of Mexico's great educational advances since the end of the revolution, from which would flow economic prosperity for the peoples of the nation, as Samuel M. Vauclain, president of the Baldwin Locomotive Works, had already explained. It was in such myriad ways that Mexico was reconstituting itself in the shadow of the United States. For some, Mexico was consolidating the nation through the expansion of the workforce. For others, it was through the schools. Yet others saw a new nation taking hold through the diminution of the Church's power.

Casauranc's meeting at Columbia was deeply symbolic, for it marked the beginning of a new wave of research collaboration between the Mexican state and Columbia University that reinforced the intellectual links that had become part of the institutional culture of Mexico's postrevolutionary government ministries after 1920. Those links had started earlier, and though they were small, they were powerfully influential. Manuel Gamio himself, whose image of the smelter in *Forjando patria* had become a metaphor for Mexico's assimilation projects, had earned a Ph.D. in anthropology at Columbia under Franz Boas in 1911. Manuel Gamio was explicit about the importance of the ideas he had learned in New York in *Forjando patria*. "In the interesting text *The Mind of Primitive Man*, in which Dr. Franz Boas published the summary of conferences he had delivered at Harvard and in Mexico, the chapter entitled 'Racial Prejudices' is of particular note. There [Boas] proves that there does not exist any innate inferiority that is sometimes attributed to some human groups relative to others," he wrote. "The general statement of such logical ideas is indispensable among the Mexican people, who constitute a panoply of ethnically diverse social groups whose social evolution has been dissimilar and which continue to develop along divergent, not parallel paths."[57] On his return to Mexico, Gamio had begun applying Boas's theory of cultural relativism to the case of Mexico's indigenous peoples as an instrument for rebuilding the Mexican nation. Under the continuing tutelage of Boas, meanwhile, he developed Mexico's twentieth-century institutions of anthropology. Scholars of Mexican anthropology still disagree over the extent to which Gamio truly abandoned the formalism of nineteenth-century anthropology, but they all agree that his scientific and administrative career marked the integration of Boasian relativism into the agencies of the Mexican state that had targeted ethnic relations as an arena of social transformation.

Moisés Sáenz, meanwhile, had been heavily influenced by the development at Columbia University of one of the central movements in American philosophical history, pragmatism. At its broadest, pragmatism was a critique of the abstract principles of Western philosophy for their detachment from the everyday experiences that shaped social life. Thinkers had turned ideas into rationalizations that bore little resemblance to what people were living, it argued, a dualism that had separated life into abstract principles on the one hand and social experience on the other. Sáenz used pragmatism as an intellectual wedge to reshape the deterministic ideas that had presided over Mexican social theory under Porfirio Díaz toward the more fluid, experimentalist tenets that came to characterize postrevolutionary social ethics after 1920. For him, pragmatism closed the breach between the old idealisms of Comte and Spencer and the use of lived experience as the test of ethics that he adopted in postrevolutionary society. Sáenz studied at Columbia between 1919 and 1921 directly under one of pragmatism's central theorists, John Dewey, before going on to become Dewey's most important Mexican student. When Puig Casauranc hired Sáenz in 1924 to assume supervision of the SEP rural school campaign Vasconcelos had originally established three years earlier, Sáenz began a career that would spread Dewey's ideas throughout the Mexican countryside. Sáenz spoke of Dewey's influence in Mexico before an audience of sociologists and anthropologists at the University of Chicago in 1926, for example. "John Dewey has gone to Mexico. He was first carried there by his pupils at Columbia; he went later in his books—*School and Society* is a book we know and love in Mexico."[58] But Sáenz's pragmatist approach was most evident in his 1939 collection of essays, *México íntegro*, in which he spoke about the difficulties Dewey's emphasis on experience had made for his attempt to reformulate Mexico's postrevolutionary social contract:

> For those who live here, the task is not so simple. Our emotions occlude our vision; we become confused by the complexity of experience; our accomplishments contradict one another at every turn; they seem to put the most obvious and the most profound into war with one another. At the end of three weeks of studying my country you may now feel that you are prepared to write an authoritative text on Mexico; we, on the other hand, may have to wait another three years, maybe thirty years, and still we will not have written our Baedeker.[59]

Some will interpret Sáenz's statement as a criticism of the orientalist American mind that Mexican intellectuals often felt occluded an understanding of Mexican history and society. Yet when it is reframed in the context of Deweyan philosophy, it is impossible not to be riveted by Sáenz's allusion to the "complexity of experience." As philosopher Gregory Pappas has underscored, "experience" was the fulcrum of Deweyan philosophy, and Sáenz, in choosing to use that precise term, turned the ethical complexity of postrevolutionary Mexico back onto itself, as he confessed the difficulty of arriving at the practical solutions to the challenges of nationalism

Figure 3. Moisés Sáenz Garza at Long Beach, New York, 1922, just after graduating from study with John Dewey at Columbia University. New York was a Jewish city, Boston an Italian and Irish one, and Chicago, a "universe of a thousand races, all built into one," Sáenz later wrote. Personal collection of the author.

posed by a society that was diverse, pluralistic, and historically complex.[60] Sáenz would similarly underscore the difficulty of creating Mexico's beloved community in the context of Deweyan philosophy in 1933, when he titled his analysis of Michoacán's Tarascan Indians with a similar signifier, *Carapan: The Outlines of an Experience.*[61] "We are walking on the edge of a knife," Sáenz wrote there. "We must choose between excessive empiricism and excessive speculation."[62]

Similarly, psychologists and teachers who, like Gamio and Sáenz, had also came under the spell of Columbia University now worked in Mexico's Secretaría de Educación Pública. Rafael Ramírez, a long-time collaborator of Sáenz, lectured on Dewey's understanding of psychology to audiences of young schoolteachers being trained to work in Sáenz's corps of rural educators, for example.[63] As the education ministry developed its capacity in anthropology as part of the attempt to organize historical narratives of

Mexico's indigenous groups, Mexico's anthropologists reached toward Boas's department of anthropology at Columbia for training in understanding "culture," helping in the process to create the anthropological tradition of twentieth-century Mexican social science. It was the growing relationship between Columbia University and the postrevolutionary Mexican state that Puig Casauranc's 1926 visit to Columbia University symbolized, even as public officials elsewhere seemed to pay more attention to Mexico's economic relationship to the United States. After 1926, the links between Mexico City and Columbia University became more public, transformed by government administrators in Mexico from philosophical platforms for integrating the ethnic groups of the nation into political celebrations of administrative collaboration across North America. In the aftermath of Puig Casauranc's visit to Columbia in 1926, John Dewey would lecture at UNAM in a summer tour that the Mexican ministry of education celebrated in its official propaganda. Famed Columbia University education theorist Isaac Leon Kandel would study Mexico's educational system beginning in 1927 for a series of new articles on secondary education in Latin America and Europe. Nicholas Butler Murray would fete Casauranc in New York, initiating a correspondence that would last more than twenty years. Columbia University's relationship with Mexico extended beyond these immediate personal links, as well, to scholarly associations that were themselves trying to extend the ideas at work in Teachers College throughout the continent. The Progressive Education Association maintained a relationship with Mexico's ministry of education, for example, based on Dewey's growing influence in Mexico's rural provinces.[64]

One important corollary effect of Columbia's influence on Mexico has gone unnoticed in the scholarship on the postrevolutionary state. While scholars of Mexican history have long known that Franz Boas and John Dewey were large influences on postrevolutionary Mexican statecraft, they have not noted that it was from the career of pragmatism in Mexico that Sánchez and other Americans fashioned their experiments in assimilation for the 1930s United States.[65] It was from the Mexican pole of pragmatist ideas that assimilation projects in the American West took many of their important clues about the role of the state and education in social change. This relationship was not accidental, but a by-product of the fact that the Americans had themselves trained in the public universities of the American West in the same set of ideas the Mexicans had learned at Columbia University. Sánchez's dissertation had depended on Dewey's *Democracy and*

Figure 4. John Dewey (third from right) in Mexico City in 1926, when he lectured at UNAM at the behest of his former student, SEP subsecretary Moisés Sáenz (standing, second from left). Dewey's visit symbolized the transmission of pragmatist ideas from Columbia University to Mexico City's government ministries in the twenty years after the Mexican Revolution. Archivo General de la Nación, Centro de Información Gráfica, Archivo Fotográfico Enrique Díaz, Delgado y García, Curso de verano de 1926.

Education, for example, while New Mexican Loyd Tireman, who traveled to Mexico in 1931, had depended on Dewey's *How We Think.*[66] Both sets of scholars, not only the Mexicans, were using pragmatism as a platform for social reform. Americans and Mexicans made an important intellectual connection with one another in the 1930s that made a difference to American political history because they were each wrestling with the challenge of translating Deweyan and Boasian ideas from the world of philosophy to the world of politics.[67]

This link in social science between Mexico's state builders and the Americans who would go on to help shape the American civil rights movement was more than a curiosity of modernist ideas. Instead, it converted Gamio's and Sáenz's application of science to social philosophy in postrevolutionary Mexico into a fulcrum of institutional experimentation for rural Americans who had sought the solutions to modern ethical conflict in *The*

Mind of Primitive Man and *Democracy and Education*. As the Americans took note of the political projects that Gamio and Sáenz had designed, they used them to engender a political relationship with the Mexicans. And as they helped to spread pragmatism's reach into the back alleys and dirt roads of the American West, Mexico's experiments shaped the American response to ethnic conflict in the United States. In the context of the United States, New Deal advocates like Arthur Schlesinger, Jr., and Rexford Tugwell would later argue that pragmatism had become a philosophical basis for the New Deal state.[68] But because the transfer of Deweyan ideas for use by the state came a decade earlier in Mexico, it was a foreign pole of administrative activity from which American intellectuals in the American West took their cue for the transformation of American society in the 1930s. Not pragmatism in the United States but pragmatism in Mexico became the model for institutional experimentalism in the American West.

The Mexican social scientists reflected the thrill of discovering that the Americans had recognized their philosophical departures in social reconstruction when the Americans returned home to write about the postrevolutionary state. "[George Sánchez] places in the hands of the spectator the eyeglasses of history, to the end that the reader may perceive with full clarity all the scenes as they succeed one another on the Mexican stage," wrote one Mexican official who followed Deweyan philosophy after the Mexican Revolution.[69] Here was an allusion to the importance of history and context as the guiding rationale of the modernist movement of ideas of which pragmatism was a part.[70] Meanwhile, the Americans most often recorded their appreciation for Mexico's use of those ideas through allusions in their work to the institutional implications of the social analyses that the Mexicans had produced. "As one looks back on [Mexico's rural] experiments," wrote Loyd Tireman, "he is impressed with the ways in which the Mexican government has attacked [its social] problems."[71] Ralph Beals was more explicit:

Mexico especially offers an unusually good opportunity for studies in the applied field, both for suggesting action programs and for examining the results of programs. The active interference of governmental agencies in Mexico in the native mixed culture has of late often been in accordance with definite concepts of social problem and structure. Study of the effects of government programs should be fruitful both in testing theories and formulating programs.[72]

Sánchez, meanwhile, compared Mexico's reform projects to the missionary zeal of the sixteenth-century mendicant friars. "Their function and methods of procedure have varied from time to time, owing to their exploratory character and their ability to adapt to changing conditions."[73] Dewey himself had been impressed with Mexico's schools as institutions of social transformation during his 1926 visit there: "there is no educational movement in the world which exhibits more of the spirit of intimate union of school activities with those of the community than is found in [Mexico]," he wrote.[74]

The link in Dewey and Boas between the Americans and the Mexicans extended beyond the period of the 1930s and into the civil rights era after World War II. It attuned the Americans to Mexico's postrevolutionary experiments not for a period of one or two years, but for decades, making Mexico an example for renewed social relations in the United States that extended into the late 1950s. It connected the rural experiments in progressive education in Mexico to rural experiments in progressive education in the United States, providing the Americans with models of interethnic relations that became a canonical part of their construction of the American melting pot. And it provided one of the most visceral examples of a long-held tenet of Deweyan pragmatism. Rather than being an arcane set of experiments in academic social science, the connection to Mexico represented Dewey's maxim that the role of philosophy in the modern era was instrumental. If the role of philosophy represented, as Dewey believed, the use of lived experience as part of the search for ways to transform the violence, contradictions, and destructiveness of industrial society, no one was trying harder to institutionalize those ideas than the circle of Americans and Mexicans who found commonality with one another for the three decades between 1920 and 1950 across the international boundary that separated their nations.[75]

The philosophical shift in Mexico that Gamio and Sáenz represented broadens our understanding of the transatlantic geography of progressive statecraft. Recent work in American intellectual history has illuminated the philosophical and political relationships that connected modernist American thinkers to their European counterparts in the late nineteenth and early twentieth centuries. The via media of James Kloppenberg, for example, brought Americans into a transatlantic circulation of philosophical ideas that shaped American reform movements. Daniel T. Rodgers, meanwhile, has charted the institutional examples that progressive European social reform became for American intellectuals.[76] Gamio and Sáenz show us that exchanges in progressive statecraft were not endemic to the United States and Europe alone, but flowed simultaneously across the United States and Mexico at the same moment that pragmatism was bringing intellectuals into contact with one another across the Atlantic Ocean. Mexico was part of the expansion of a web of ideas that had spread across Europe and North America at the beginning of the twentieth century, showing us that the international political conversation about the role of the state in modern industrial society was not unique to the transatlatlantic alliance. It enveloped Latin America, as well, in ways that shaped political practice in the United States.

Convergence in Comparative History

Juxtaposing the Republic of Mexico and the United States of America as melting pot societies, nations searching for unity through the instrument of the state, and homes to social science thinkers who were using pragmatism to reconstruct their national communities does not mean denying the radical differences between the two societies at the beginning of the twentieth century. Mexico was a prostrate country economically even as the United States was fast rising to superpower status in the decades following the Spanish-American War.[77] The Mexican state had been destroyed after the revolution, whereas the aftermath of the American Civil War had enabled the consolidation of federal power in the United States. The United States remained a country primarily of immigrants from Europe, whereas Mexico was primarily a country of indigenous-descended Americans. National consolidation in Mexico emanated from the top down under the tangible fear of American imperialism, whereas consolidation in the United States emanated from the bottom up by marginalized citizens seeking to expand the privileges of citizenship.

But we do not have to insist that the United States and Mexico were equivalent societies in order to juxtapose them alongside each other. Instead, we must merely recognize that intellectuals in two distinctive national traditions were simultaneously reconstructing their social contracts by remolding the state's relationship to the distinct peoples of their societies using the same sets of ideas. These nationalist projects did not imply equivalent visions of the nation, but rather, distinctive ones that were

nonetheless shaped by similar policy debates about blending distinct cultural communities into unified blocs of citizens. These policy juxtapositions
underscore a point Daniel Rodgers has made. Convergences between
nations get left out of historiography, Rodgers has argued, because comparative history deepens differences in the act of placing nations alongside
one another. But while similarities get left behind and unremembered, the
contingent convergences in ideas and social policy they represented are as
important to underscore as the differences.[78]

The term *melting pot* was one point of convergence. *Melting pot* appears
less frequently in the historical record of twentieth-century Mexico than it
does in that of the United States. While *crisol* (melting pot, or crucible)
does not appear often, however, *mestizaje, fusión, batir, asimilación,* and
conglomerado social were all prominent in postrevolutionary scholarship.
For Manuel Gamio and José Vasconcelos, for example, the terms *batir* (to
mix) and *fusión* (fusion) implied cultural and biological blending under the
direction of public institutions. For Moisés Sáenz, meanwhile, the term
integración implied a greater attention to the blending of distinct cultural
structures without the necessity of amalgamation across the color and race
line. Mexico's social scientists, moreover, used metaphors and descriptions
that would have been easily recognizable to the theorists of the U.S. melting
pot. Moisés Sáenz described his ideal society as a *sinfonía de culturas* (symphony of cultures), for example, using a term that is easily recognizable to
American scholars as one of Horace Kallen's central metaphors for the
blending of cultures in the twentieth-century United States.[79] Similarly, Luis
Villoro reprised a variant of the debate between Kallen and Randolph
Bourne over the ideal character the American melting pot should assume
when he reviewed the long history of Mexico's relationship to its indigenous cultures. Just as Kallen and Bourne had debated the relative merits of
pluralism versus cosmopolitanism, so did Villoro see the same debate at
work in postrevolutionary Mexico. Some, he argued, would have created a
society in which the Indians maintained the characteristics of their individual cultures as part of a larger society, while others preferred a more synthetic ideal.[80] Thus, while the term *melting pot* is less frequently used in
Mexico's twentieth-century debates, the ideas behind it were found just as
readily there as they were in the United States. One can find many of the
same ideas about the melting pot in Gonzalo Aguirre Beltrán's survey of
integration in twentieth-century Mexican society that one can find in Russell Kazal's treatment of the subject in the context of U.S. society.[81]

The use of state policy to achieve social integration was another point of convergence. Vasconcelos's aesthetic vision was one of the canonical romances of postrevolutionary Mexico, shaped by cultural communities different from those of the United States, but the the Americans who came to Mexico to study his tenure with the Secretaría de Educación Pública were not primarily interested in his portrayal of the Latin American paradise. They wrote far more about the platoons of educators that he hired to translate his vision into the Mexican political scene than they wrote about *La raza cósmica*. Whatever they believed about Vasconcelos's ideal world, the Americans understood that it meant little until it had been translated into political action. This was, of course, a much harder bargain to achieve than was the writing of a millenarian prophecy that was more metaphoric than institutional. But there existed no ideal worlds for the Americans, and they never considered the rhetorical constructions lying on the surface of society without also considering the structure of society's institutions.

The state policies of Vasconcelos, Gamio, and Sáenz mattered because analogous policies were already the subject of much debate in the United States. The Secretaría de Educación Pública was not the only educational agency to produce new policies about integrating society, but only one of many government agencies around the world that were similarly struggling with the costs generated by industrialization amid the forces of local communities. There was, in other words, *context*. Had the Americans not already been wrestling with educational policy at home before they plunged into postrevolutionary Mexico, they could have been hypnotized by the SEP's educators. They were not so taken, precisely because they were already immersed in the difficulties of achieving change via the institution of the school and the agencies of government. Intellectuals in the United States had been fighting since at least the mid-nineteenth century over the quality and goals of the public schools amid the horrific history of segregation and violence. For this reason, the Americans who studied in Mexico had little reason to believe in utopias.

A third point of convergence was the modernist understanding of the primacy of institutions rather than biology in determining social values and social hierarchy. In this, the Mexicans and the Americans agreed with Franz Boas that biology did not make people different from one another in any meaningful way, and with Dewey that the challenge of modern society was the moral question of how to reconcile modern technological advances with communities that suffered their costs as much as they experienced their benefits. In the United States, men and women may not have come to believe that all people were intrinsically equal until after World War II. But in this belief, they lagged far behind the Americans profiled here. Sánchez, Beals, Sturges, and others had been convinced of the fact as graduate students in the 1920s and as they pursued their political projects in the two decades before World War II. They never escaped the essentialisms of race altogether, but they were acting out of the impulse that increasingly sought to marginalize natural definitions of race in favor of social constructions of race that they knew were reflections of particular arrangements of power and wealth.

Comparative history's urgency to draw distinctions rather than convergences is one argument for scrutinizing the ideas of cultural blending from two distinct national traditions as part of two separate historical contexts. But while no exact comparison can be made between the use of the phrase *melting pot* in two distinctive national traditions, it is my intention to show that two groups of thinkers saw enough similarity with one another despite those differences to claim that they could speak to one another about the relationship of ethnic pluralism to the nation-state. Scholars have shown us the weaknesses of the thought of these individuals within their particular national contexts. But they have not shown us why these thinkers believed they could speak to one another across their nations about a phenomenon as filled with the possibilities of failure as the mixing of people under the aegis of government. Yet these thinkers believed that they shared similar questions about the relationship of ethnic difference to the institutions of the state, and thereby created a dialogue that transcended the differences that separated their countries. Moreover, they built long-lasting relationships based on those assumptions. When the Mexican ministry of education argued that the desegregation movement in the United States represented the same political project in *incorporación* that it had been embarked on since 1920, they explicitly compared two distinct national projects in integration to one another.[82] Similarly, when George I. Sánchez argued in 1940 that the United States and Mexico both represented synthetic cultures composed of distinct cultural communities, he made a comparative claim about two nations that should be taken seriously by scholars. Whether they were right or wrong in drawing the analogies between concepts of cultural fusion in one nation with concepts from the other is a question to be examined. But that these scientists believed those comparisons could be made does not mean that an absolute convergence must be established by scholars today between the ideas of the melting pot in one tradition with ideas of the melting pot in the other.

It was the Americans profiled here who originally juxtaposed the structures of ethnic diversity from the United States and Mexico in the 1920s and 1930s in the first place. Had the Americans never traveled to Mexico before I insisted on a parallel analysis of U.S. and Mexican societies, scholars could rightly criticize my comparison as wrong-headed. But Sánchez went to Mexico and continued going there for the rest of his life. Beals became important in the legal segregation cases of the United States, but his understanding of race and ethnicity was born from a fifty-year career dedicated to understanding Mexico, not the United States. I am not alone in making the comparison, for these American intellectuals made it at an earlier moment in the twentieth century. *Their* juxtaposition is a historical artifact that needs debate and analysis, whatever conclusions we might come to today about its philosophical and political validity.

Chapter 2

Shock Troops

The Mexican state attempted to integrate the peoples of Mexico into a single bloc of citizens not through a timeless process of biological *mestizaje*, but through instruments of statecraft that included patronage of the arts, a new infrastructure network, and a renewed focus on national symbols like the flag, the Indian, and folkloric dress.[1] However, it was three institutions of the Secretaría de Educación Pública (SEP), institutions symbolized by the schoolteacher depicted in Rivera's murals, that the Americans found amenable to the work of integration and civil rights in the American West. When the Americans returned home, they duplicated the intellectual and political labor of these institutions. They wrote of them as models for the United States in the aftermath of institutional failures that had led them to Mexico in the first place. They took photographs of them, juxtaposed them to their own schools in New Mexico and Texas, and described them as the agents of cultural regeneration for a Mexican nation on the move. These institutions became the policy units through which the Americans refracted their pragmatism-inspired experiments in the United States.

The first was the cultural mission. As the name suggested, *la misión cultural* (cultural mission) was an adaptation of the sixteenth-century practice through which the mendicant orders had attempted to proselytize the indigenous communities of Mexico to the Spanish Catholic Church. The mendicants learned the language of the Indian nations to which they had been assigned, then moved into their communities during temporary journeys of exile from their Catholic monasteries as they sought to transform indigenous Mexico into Catholic Mexico. José Vasconcelos adapted this model as the outreach campaign of the postrevolutionary Mexican state when he became secretary of public education in

1921. Under Vasconcelos, the cultural mission became a secular organ of the state, not a religious one, although the millenarian project on which it was embarked shared the hallmarks of the erstwhile projects of the Spanish mendicant orders. Vasconcelos organized libraries of classical European texts that he sent into the provinces of the nation via cultural missionaries who were tasked with social reform work in the form of formal seminars conducted in the rural countryside. Schoolteachers from the rural schools were obligated to attend the seminars for three weeks at a time, where they were introduced to the pedagogical techniques that Mexico City had directed them to try.

The second was the *escuela normal rural* (rural normal school), which was a permanent teacher training academy at which the rural schoolteacher trained to be an educator in the service of the state. The normal school was the centerpiece of rural education, for it was there that first-time teachers were introduced to the pedagogy of the state. As a central repository of state resources directed from Mexico City, its physical plant sometimes became the location at which the cultural mission performed its three-week seminars for rural schoolteachers. But the rural normal school provided the original imprint of what the postrevolutionary educator was supposed to be, a role that was enriched thereafter by the cultural missions.

The third was the rural school. Forming the base of a pyramid whose apex was represented by the federal secretariat in Mexico City, it was the closest institution to the young schoolchildren and their parents whose lives were the targets of reform work by the postrevolutionary state. Beautiful images taken by photographers of the SEP while accompanying federal inspectors detail the discrete acts of labor through which the rural schools resocialized their students into the revolutionary nationalism Diego Rivera had captured in his Mexico City murals. There are students marching through small towns in remote areas while carrying the Mexican flag that had become the symbol of regeneration across the country. Primary school students are shown playing basketball as rural schoolteachers work to instill athletic games imported from the United States. In other photographs, young men and women stand in front of school buildings as they read from schoolbooks brought to them from Mexico City, or they offload bricks from trucks brought in to help with village construction projects. The rural school was what the Americans came to call the "House of the People," after the nickname the Secretariat of Public Education had given to the school, *la casa del pueblo*. From the 1930s until the 1950s, the Mexican rural school would provide the primary model for the Americans of what the public school in rural America should be.

Together, the personnel of these three institutions were the shock troops of the postrevolutionary Mexican state. They were schoolteachers and school administrators, inspectors and vocational experts whose labors in education may have appeared docile and beneficent. But in the photographs that captured their work, they appear as nothing so much as Green Beret soldiers who had been sent to resocialize the rural communities of the nation into the policy platform of the state. They operated as platoons of teachers, trained in a variety of skills that were put to use in the service of creating a new economy and a new relationship of the individual to the school. They operated in remote communities where schools had been built for the first time in the history of the country. They traveled to municipal seats of power at regular intervals, where they were greeted by federal inspectors who monitored their work and advised them on the newest advances in science and pedagogy. For the Americans, they came to represent the caring state. In the federal government's interest in moving the villages of the nation toward national integration, the Americans saw a central state that cared enough to bring the promises of the public school to the remotest areas of the country.

The Cultural Missions

Of Mexico's federal institutions for integrating the nation into one, the *misión cultural* was the model that the Americans found most practical to replicate at home. The excitement for the Americans resided in the metaphor that the mission represented. The mission was not merely attached to the metropolitan center of the nation. It was that the center of the nation had flung itself outward toward the provinces, like some giant exhalation of energy that was the embodiment of social change itself. In the mission's centrifugal movement outward, the Americans detected the promise of state responsibility to cultural frontiers that had long been forgotten. My own attempt to translate the institution of the mission to the American scene always returns to the institution of the Freedman's Bureau after the American Civil War, for it was there that the American state took responsibility for redefining the relationship to cultural communities that had been locked out of the American political experiment. Something similar in both its promise and its failures was at work in the Mexican terrain after the revolution. For Americans looking to multiply the resources of the state in the effort to create an integrated society, the effects of the *misión cultural* were irresistible. Loyd Tireman immediately copied the *misión cultural* when he returned home to New Mexico from Mexico in 1931, flinging out his own cultural mission from Albuquerque in a bid to tether the rural communities of New Mexico to the melting pot project that he was building there. George Sánchez experimented with the *misión cultural* in Louisiana, where he replicated it among the black communities of the American South in an institutional experiment that became part of the founding history of Grambling State University. It was only in the aftermath of this experiment that he returned to New Mexico, Texas, and civil rights fame.

Institutionally, the Mexican cultural missions acted as platoons of metropolitan intellectuals who traveled to rural communities in the provinces in the attempt to proselytize their members to the integrationist project of the state. Pictures show them radiating outward from the capital by truck or by donkey, laden with the equipment needed to establish a new political beachhead in former monasteries expropriated from the Catholic Church. As a unit of the state, the missionaries were entrusted to organize the local school in each community to which they came, with the assistance of the local inhabitants. They were the organizers of the rural schools that would perform the work of pedagogy and indoctrination in pursuit of the postrevolutionary republic's integration project. At first, the missionaries moved from community to community at three-week intervals. The missionaries organized the school, helped to recruit a schoolteacher from the local community who had been trained in one of the state's normal schools, and regularized an academic pattern of instruction that was formalized through the succeeding years of operation. As the work of the cultural missionaries expanded and the rural schools became a formal part of the rural environment, the work of the missions was modified to increase the efficiency of the government's labors. The cultural missions were given permanent seats at the rural normal schools, for example, out of which they now radiated rather than returning to Mexico City each time. They began to journey repeatedly to each village for multiple trainings each year rather than a single one. And they modified their curriculum in accordance with the labor needs of the local community.

The *misión cultural* was one of the mythical institutions of twentieth-century Mexican history, in part because it seemed to be a reworking of an organic institution that dated to sixteenth-century Mexico. As the Spanish continued their conquest of Mexico in the aftermath of the Aztec defeat in 1521, they turned to the Spanish Catholic Church to aid in the cultural transformation of Mexico's indigenous societies. It was then that the mendicant priests, dressed in their robes and carrying the Catholic cross, spread across central Mexico in the effort to proselytize the Native Americans to the Christian faith. In their twentieth-century guise, however, the cultural missions received their great institutional impulse in the state from José Vasconcelos, the conservative melting pot theorist who would offer his *raza cósmica* vision of Mexican society in 1925.[2] Beginning in 1921, Vasconcelos launched a series of grand experiments within the federal Secretariat of Public Education that included itinerant platoons of educators whose role was to establish rural public schools under the direction of the federal government. Vasconcelos may indeed have been acting out of respect for the Spanish Catholic mendicant tradition, given his lifelong devotion to the Mexican Catholic Church. Historians have argued vigorously about whether the ministry's ultimate aim was to create a democratic polity or to rebuild a national economy under the supervision of capitalist elites, just as they have argued about the relationship of the SEP to the communities where the *misiones* did their work. They disagree less over the character of that project, which Vasconcelos rooted in Catholic metaphysics and the classical education associated with ancient Greece and Rome.

But the centralizing work of José Manuel Puig Casauranc and Moisés Sáenz after 1924 was of greater importance to the history of integration in the American West. Vasconcelos provided the initial burst of institutional energy out of which emerged the cultural missions, but it was between 1924 and 1935 that the specific configuration of institutions, policy framework, and management structure emerged that won the accolades of the Americans. In my own estimation, the Americans would not have been nearly as impressed with the integrationist work of the Mexican state at any other moment after 1920. Prior to the centralizing work of Casauranc and Sáenz between 1924 and 1935, Vasconcelos's emphasis on the classical curriculum impeded the Deweyan philosophy to which the Americans had committed themselves in the United States. After the departure of Casauranc in 1931 and Sáenz in 1933 and the subsequent accession of the socialist-inspired Narciso Bassols to the Secretariat of Public Education, experimentalism in progressive education was diluted in favor of socialist doctrine whose determinisms were every bit as unattractive to pragmatists as nineteenth-century *científico* science. And beginning in 1940, the increasingly conservative tone of the presidential administrations deflated the institutional enthusiasm that had given the postrevolutionary period its definition. It was only during the narrow moment of educational changes between 1924 and 1935 when the American westerners were swept away by Mexican reform. What occurred under Casauranc and Sáenz drew them to Mexico for the rest of their careers.

The greatest transformation was the profound philosophical shift of the *misión cultural* toward pragmatism under Moisés Sáenz after 1924. When he became SEP secretary in 1924, Puig Casauranc had hired Sáenz to assume supervision for the rural school campaign Vasconcelos had initiated three years earlier. Sáenz had trained to be a schoolteacher at Jalapa Normal School in the state of Veracruz, graduating there in 1915 before being elevated to the directorship of Mexico's Escuela Nacional Preparatoria, the prominent preparatory academy that educated the children of Mexico's elite.[3] Then, at twenty-five, he left Mexico to study with Dewey at Columbia Teachers College in New York City, for reasons that remain unclear. The decision may have resulted from his immersion in the Protestant missionary circles of Mexico, part of a long tradition of Protestantism in his family. As children, he and his sister had attended Protestant schools in Mexico City and Laredo, Texas, for example, and Protestant preacher Isaac Boyce was among the family's closest friends. These ties to Protestantism carried into his professional career. Even as he was directing the Escuela Nacional Preparatoria, he was simultaneously helping to widen the influence of liberal Christianity in revolutionary Mexico. In 1918, the American missionary organization whose efforts were directed at proselytizing Mexicans to evangelical Christianity, the Protestant Cooperating Committee, had turned to Sáenz to edit its monthly newsletter *El mundo cristiano*. It is through the editorship of *El mundo* that Sáenz may have first been exposed to Dewey, for it regularly published articles on pedagogical practice in the United States. The translations of Dewey and work of American progressive educators would have reinforced the pedagogical training Sáenz had already received at Jalapa.

Sáenz expanded Mexico's rural education system to new areas of the Mexican countryside by increasing the number of schoolteachers in the field and, alongside fellow Deweyite Rafael Ramírez, by instituting normal training academies to supervise schoolteacher fieldwork. But it was in Sáenz's attention to pedagogy where the influence of Dewey was felt most deeply. Sáenz remolded Vasconcelos's platoons of educators to emphasize Dewey's experimentalist ethics rather than Christian metaphysics as the guiding philosophy of rural education. By replacing a classical curriculum with an experimentalist project in pragmatist education, Sáenz elevated local experience to a primary role in the public schools and imbued them with the opportunity to transform postrevolutionary society. How quickly Sáenz transformed Vasconcelos's work is indicated by the enthusiasm Dewey noted for Mexico's schools during a summer research trip to Mexico City in 1926, only two years after Sáenz had assumed control of the rural schools. Dewey famously declared his admiration for the efforts of the Mexican schools, concluding that Mexico's education efforts were providing a model of rural education for the rest of the world. "The most interesting as well as the most important educational development is the rural schools," he wrote: "This is the cherished preoccupation of the present regime; *it signifies a revolution* rather than renaissance. It is not only a revolution for Mexico, but in some respects one of the most important social experiments undertaken anywhere in the world."[4]

The fiscal and philosophical investment away from the metropolitan centers that the cultural mission represented made it the most exciting institutional development for the Americans during this time. The financial commitment the central government needed to maintain the platoons drew much attention. The scale of that work was not immense, but given that it operated in the rural arena where resources from the state were historically low, the consistent funding pattern was not unimpressive. Three years into Casauranc's tenure with the SEP, in 1927, the Mexican state was providing support for six platoons of educators who had conducted a total of forty-five itinerant seminars lasting three weeks each over a terrain that included twenty of Mexico's thirty-one states. The division of labor represented by these missions was not haphazard, but discrete and standardized. There were standardized duties for a platoon director, a social worker, a physical education teacher, an agricultural specialist, an animal technician, and a vocational arts instructor. There were the usual necessities for instruction, but also included had been agricultural implements and means of transportation to get the instructors into the field.

That a centrally coordinated effort was responsible for the division of labor of the cultural missions was another of its impressive features. It was not merely the large scale of each of the cultural missions that was worth noting, but that the fiscal resources for the missions were provided by the central government of the Mexican republic. The importance of central state financing is best understood not in the context of Mexican history, but in that of the historical tension in American history between the federal government and the various state governments. The Americans had been historical antagonists of states' rights philosophies, since state control of educational resources had been a major historical impediment to the expansion of schools to the ethnic communities in whose name they fought. Thus, when the central coordination of the *misión cultural* out of Mexico City became evident to them, the Americans celebrated the different role of the central state in Mexico from that which they traditionally associated with the federal state in the United States. The presence of the *misión cultural* was the proof that the state was willing to place its institutional energy behind political transformation in an aggressive pursuit of a new moral vision. That the effort of the Mexican state was directed at the nation's poorest and most ethnically marginalized communities only underscored the transformative moral vision to which the power of government had been harnessed. Such a vision seemed to validate a philosophy of government based on social welfare in an era that Daniel T. Rodgers has called the age of social politics.[5]

In the cultural mission the Americans saw a system that could be adapted to the Deweyan principles that made a new integrationist ethics possible. Loyd Tireman had only just moved from northern Iowa to New Mexico when, in the process of opening his laboratory school at the University of New Mexico, he was faced with the task of extending the results of his experimental labors to rural New Mexico's 600 villages. To achieve the pedagogical outcome promised by Dewey's philosophy was one of the labors he set for himself in 1927. But to replicate those results throughout the provinces of rural New Mexico was equally important. For him, the cultural missions in Mexico became the administrative platform for extending the reach of his ideas, just as extending the reach of the Mexican ministry of education had become the task Moisés Sáenz and Rafael Ramírez had assigned to the cultural missions in Michoacán and Tlaxcala. For George Sánchez, the missions became the instrument to create the community school in rural Louisiana from a seat of administrative power at Grambling University. After leaving his home state of New Mexico in 1937, but before starting his famed career at the University of Texas in 1940, he stopped in the Deep South to experiment in the rural schools of Louisiana. Under the philosophical gaze of John Dewey, it was there that he created Grambling's

Figure 5. Cultural missionaries in the field at El Nith, one of the rural communities served by the normal school of Actopan, Hidalgo, 1932. Archivo Histórico de la Secretaría de Educación Pública (AHSEP), Mexico City, Mexico, Sección Dirección de Misiones Culturales, Serie Misión Cultural Permanente en Ixmiquilpan, Box 45, Folder 34 (Hidalgo).

equivalent of the cultural mission, radiating to the rural villages still residing in the long reach of Huey Long's populist politics.

Hundreds of communities became the objects of SEP attention, representing a chronological and geographical relationship of spectacular breadth beginning in 1921 that had no match anywhere in the hemisphere. The diversity of ethnic communities, the variations in the regional economies, the spectrum of political ideologies from supporters of the state to supporters of the Catholic Church, and the orientation of the SEP educators were some of the many factors that determined the fate of the state's project in national consolidation via the instrument of the cultural mission. In the state of Chiapas, for example, the cultural missionaries were welcomed as agents of a moral order that promised to protect new agrarian rights against the landed *hacendados* whose power had been curtailed by the state. In Michoacán, the cultural missionaries represented a moral threat to the power of the church, whose authority had been confined and narrowed by the rise of the Sonoran Dynasty. Given such dramatic differences, the relationship of the cultural mission to the local community in Mexico was descriptive rather than normative, a matter of local experience and negotiation rather than distant control and top-down absolutes.

Under such differential conditions, the Americans witnessed missionary programs in Mexico that worked with the support of the local community when the federal state deliberately avoided places that were physically hostile to the presence of Mexico's shock troops. This success explains the enthusiasm the Americans noted in the communities where the cultural mission was present, for there the community had been vetted and approved. The cultural missions became, in other words, a malleable instrument for rethinking the administrative power of the school and government's relationship to rural communities in the United States. Tireman found residents eager to use the outreach power of the state government to improve the soil of their rural New Mexico communities. Likewise, rural residents in New Mexico were eager to use the school to learn English for their children, a task considered necessary to participate in the changing economy. In 1940s California, meanwhile, the cultural mission became the mechanism for assimilating immigrant children to a national culture of the United States that was being reformulated in the aftermath of the Great Depression and World War II.

Actopan, or the Rural Normal School

Sixty miles northeast of Mexico City, as one moves out of the historical core where the SEP established its headquarters in 1921, Mexico's highway system collapses from a pattern of north-south tributaries radiating out of the capital into an east-west federal interstate that veers sharply around the southern periphery of the Las Cruces Mountains. Follow the interstate east to the city of Puebla, eighty miles away; follow it west, and Querétaro can be reached one hundred miles away. But directly to the north, the Las Cruces Mountains remain largely impenetrable even today, effectively helping frame the northern tier of mountain ranges that give Mexico City its shape as a bowl.

It is on the flat plain that drops out of the northern side of the Las Cruces Mountains that the postrevolutionary Mexican state located the educational institution that received more commentary by the Americans than any other. Here, in the geographic center of the homeland where the indigenous Otomí people have lived for more than one thousand years, the SEP established the teacher training academy, or *escuela normal rural*, known as Actopan, in a converted Catholic monastery the Mexican government had stripped away from the Catholic Church. Rural normal schools as physically close to Mexico City as Actopan had also been located in the states of Tlaxcala, Puebla, and Morelos, part of a system of normal academies that had been established throughout the republic.[6] But the density of indigenous communities so close to Mexico City made the state of Hidalgo a prime target for Mexico's educational integration work. It was the site of the oldest *misión cultural*, for example, and SEP officials frequently steered American visitors who came to Mexico in the 1930s toward Actopan. It was here that child psychologist Loyd Tireman visited in 1931 and wrote of several months later. Educator George Sánchez visited here and showcased Actopan in his 1936 book on Mexico's schools. Social worker and teacher Catherine Vesta Sturges worked at Actopan for four years beginning in 1928 before becoming a protégé of John Collier at the BIA during the New Deal.

This premier showcase of the Mexican government won accolades from the Americans for its attempts to systematize the training of the schoolteachers to whom the Mexican state had given primary responsibility for ensuring the success of the postrevolutionary integration project. If the *misiones culturales* launched the postrevolutionary project out of Mexico City in the early years when local communities did not yet have federal schools, it was the role of the *escuela normal rural* to indoctrinate the cadre of schoolteachers into the state's melting pot project after those rural schools had been established. Much like a normal school in the United States, the federal normal school was a teacher training college for young adults, and it received lavish resources from Mexico City. In the early years of the SEP, the *escuela normal rural* was absent from the educational landscape. But as the number of elementary schools grew in the years after 1921, it became the hub of teacher training. It took on the responsibility of training the teachers who went to work in the new public schools, and it provided the primary institutional footprint out of which radiated the cultural missions on the training sojourns to the rural communities of the nation. Teachers migrated from their home villages to the normal school for extended seasons of classroom instruction, after which they were certified to teach in the rural schools of the various provinces. Once they returned home to their villages, they were visited by the instructors of the cultural missions, whose duty was to reinforce the original instruction that the teachers had received from the state.

Since normal schools like Actopan were expected to operate indefinitely in remote areas of the nation, they depended almost entirely on federal outlays from the SEP budget. Education professors were assigned to the normal school, where they often remained in place for three years or more. Pupils at the normal school were adolescents and young adults, many with only rudimentary reading and writing skills, yet they were much older than the four- to ten-year-olds who attended the federal rural schools, and they were expected, as a result, to maintain much higher degrees of discipline and attention to their studies as representatives of the new state. The *escuela anexa* (annex school) was attached to each federal normal school and served as the laboratory school for these young teachers. The normal school and annex school are sometimes mistaken for one another, but they were distinct institutions. Much as a laboratory school served as a teacher train-ing elementary school in schools of education in the United States, the *escuela anexa* was the laboratory school where normal students trained to be classroom instructors under the supervision of the normal school profes-sors. It was in the *escuela anexa* where theory hit the road. Ideas in learning were transformed into the practice of learning, in preparation for the ulti-mate test of the new nation: instruction and social reconstruction from within the federal rural school where the new teachers would find them-selves in trial-by-fire situations within a few months. If things went well, the teachers would find a happy medium with the community to which they had gone. If things went poorly, they would be killed and their bodies dumped on the outskirts of the village.[7]

For the Americans, the most important characteristic of the rural nor-mal schools was the system of supervision through which the Mexican fed-eral state attempted to indoctrinate its normal school students into the regimen prescribed by the Secretariat of Public Education. The rural nor-mal school of Oaxtepec, Morelos, was typical. Along with Anenecuilco, both Oaxtepec and Cuautla—the first city to fall to Zapata during the Mexi-can Revolution—lie on the same flat plain in Morelos fifty miles south of Mexico City, bounded by mountains on all sides. When inspector Higinio Vázquez Santa Ana was tasked with preparing an inspection report for the SEP headquarters in 1933, he left a description of Oaxtepec's training poli-cies. Vázquez left out the exact number of students enrolled at the school,

Figures 6 and 7. Two photographs of the normal rural school at Erongícuaro,
Michoacán. At bottom, a teacher in training guides his students at Erongarícuaro's
annex school. Archivo Histórico de la Secretaría de Educación Pública (AHSEP),
Mexico City, Mexico, Sección Dirección de Misiones Culturales, Serie Escuelas
Normales Rurales, Box 77, Folder 9 (Michoacán) and Box 40, Folder 1 (Michoacán).

but they had come from the states of Guerrero, Puebla, and Mexico, and from Mexico City. He reported that 50 percent were men and 50 percent women. Students had to be sixteen or older to enroll, and they were subsequently arranged in classes of instruction that corresponded to the first-, third-, and fifth-grade classrooms to which they would be assigned on graduation. Some students were deficient in primary skills, including reading and writing, and required an additional year of primary school instruction before they could return to their studies at Oaxtepec. Of those found to need an extra year, two-thirds were members of Mexico's Native American communities.[8]

The teaching corps at Oaxtepec was one of its greatest strengths, according to Vázquez. "They are all actively involved in the school, enthusiastic, and come with good training." They were primarily responsible for giving classes in the traditional curriculum, including arithmetic and geometry, algebra, Spanish literature and language, social science, and music and singing. But they also demonstrated specializations in other domains that had been deemed central to the integration project of the state. They were expected to study the native languages of the indigenous communities of Morelos, since, as Vázquez reported, a majority of schoolchildren still spoke only their native language rather than Spanish. He was even surprised to find that Spanish was being spoken in one location in the jurisdiction of the rural normal school. "It is important to take note of the fact that in the region of Oaxtepec there is to be found one school whose students speak Spanish," Vázquez wrote. "That village is Tetelcingo. It is for this reason that we must endeavor to teach this language not only there, but in other communities of Morelos state, where it is more common to find the languages of the native Americans." There were classes in psychology of education, rural sociology, Native American languages, and a broad range of manual arts that included carpentry, toolmaking, introduction to the manual trades, the domestic household, and basic drawing. Normal school students were expected to attend six forty-five-minute sessions of instruction every day from Monday through Friday every month between January and June, with added sessions dedicated to physical activity and rural economic production at night.[9]

The state maintained its leverage through the relationship between the cultural missions and the rural normal school. Programming at the normal school was modified through the cultural missions, which functioned as the network through which instruction from Mexico City could be modified in the field. "The normal school professors put into place those programs that had been sent to the school in 1931 from the Office of the Cultural Missions [in Mexico City]," wrote Vázquez. The cultural missions continued to function as a centralizing agency whose role was to standardize pedagogy as it radiated out from Mexico City. Still, local conditions often tempered this centralizing function. "These directions from the Office of Cultural Missions are always modified by the particularities dictated by the region in question," wrote Vázquez. "We must put them to work in the context of the cultures that our students bring to them." Meanwhile, the normal school was open to whoever wanted to visit, including the parents of the normal school students. "Some parents of the students at the school visit Oaxtepec and even live at the school themselves," Vázquez reported. Oaxtepec was also the subject of frequent visits by cultural missionaries from other states and dignitaries out of Mexico City. "I was also there during the visit by one of our congressmen from Mexico City and when several visitors were escorted to the school," wrote Vázquez. Another visit was made by Alfredo Basurto. "Professor Alfredo Basurto, Chief of the Cultural Mission, also visited the school while I was there. . . . His visit was beneficial for both the teachers and students of the school, since Basurto was interested in the technical progress being made in the methods of instruction and spoke with them about the refinements that had to be made to their chosen methods. He finished after consulting with several of the teachers and students of the school."[10]

The House of the People

In a photograph taken in Zacatecas in August 1935, New Mexican George Sánchez began capturing the visual record of the analogy in integration he made between rural Mexico and the rural American West during the 1930s. Already he had captured images of instruction in regional dancing, waterworks, and manual labor that was happening at the *escuela normal rural* in Oaxtepec, Morelos.[11] Sánchez had captured scenes from the annex schools attached to the other normal academies he had already visited, as well. There was a community park with a new fountain in one photograph. In another, there was a collection of farm animals taken in the company of a trainee learning animal husbandry in the state of Puebla. He also recorded his impressions of daily life. In one, he recorded the thatch huts of Morelos's peasants, under a canopy of sky that was framed by the volcanos Popocatépetl and Ixtaccihuatl in the background.[12] Here, in Anenecuilco twenty-five years earlier, Zapata had begun the revolutionary movement of sugar workers whose rebellion against the state became a central component of armed confrontation in Mexico between 1911 and 1920. In these photographs taken in Mexico's rural valleys, away from the metropolitan centers of the postrevolutionary nation, one can see Sánchez's impressions of rural Mexico.

But it was after he arrived in the state of Zacatecas in the desert north that Sánchez took the photograph that provided the finest visual metaphor for the integrationist work of the Mexican state he had come to study. Sánchez was making an inspection tour of Mexico's northern schools in the company of one of the regional directors of federal education. He had already visited Chihuahua, and was headed next to Aguascalientes, San Luis Potosí, and Querétaro before turning east toward Yucatán.[13] In front of an adobe structure with a single door and two large windows, he arranged a group of Zacatecan elementary school students in front of their rural school. They were arranged by gender and size, with women to the left, men to the right, and smaller children to the front. At the far left, Sánchez placed the schoolteacher. As adobe structures go, the school was an impressive achievement. The large adobe bricks depend on stone arches for support. The style is territorial as New Mexicans understood it, with rock lining the edges of the roof for architectural display. This was a building into which some resources had been devoted, indicating that it must have functioned ceremoniously in the high deserts of the Mexican altiplano.

Sánchez had collected a similar group of photographs in New Mexico one year earlier. He had embarked on a study tour of northern New Mexico's own rural schools, and just as he would later do in Zacatecas, he arranged the students of northern New Mexico's rural schools into the same pattern he would later follow in Mexico. In the New Mexico photographs, as well, Sánchez lined up the schoolchildren in front of their own school, with the schoolteacher to their immediate left. Behind them towers the rural school, while in the background one can detect something of the environmental isolation in which these communities were located. The New Mexico schools are more modest than those in the Mexican photographs. But the larger statement is the same as the one at work in the Zacatecas photo. Here is the rural school as an instrument of national integration. The children are arrayed close together, as if in some statement of unity. The teacher and the school watch over the group, as if to protect them and guide them toward the social ideal of the progressive reformer. That one would have difficulty separating the photos taken in New Mexico from those taken in Mexico is perhaps the greatest statement of the single project in unification that united Sánchez's career across Mexico and the United States.

What George Sánchez had photographed in Zacatecas was the rural school, *la casa del pueblo*. It was at the bottom of the SEP's institutional pyramid, or, depending on one's point of view, at the top. In the SEP archives in Mexico City, no institutions built during the 1920s have received less attention than the rural schools. Their paper trail to Mexico City is far thinner than it is for the cultural missions and the rural normal schools, with large gaps in the chronological sequences of the documents collected. The information gathered is sporadic and haphazard. One finds little evidence of the high officials of the SEP, and little attention devoted to the questions of pedagogy that one finds among the records of the rural normal schools. Such inattention is perhaps to be expected, given that some 10,000 of these rural schools had been established in the decade of the 1920s. With so many schools operating in such a small span of time, it is easy to see why any particular one did not receive much attention. Yet Sánchez's photographs indicate that he understood the heavy responsibility of the rural school in Mexico's integration project. The cultural missions and rural normal schools were tactically important as the platforms for the delivery of ideologies and resources through which the melting pot was to create itself in the Mexican territory. They received the most resources and attention from foreigners and state officials alike. But the central state had aimed the cultural missions and the rural normal schools at the rural school. It was through the rural school that hundreds of thousands of Mexico's schoolchildren were to be fused together into a united society. It was there where the nation was to be forged. A recent book by one of Mexico's leading scholars of postrevolutionary education has adequately captured the hope that was infused into the rural school: *To Build the School, To Build the State*.[14] Sánchez implicitly recognized the true import of the rural school in the Mexican hierarchy of power and social transformation. It was the rural school that was to carry the heaviest burden of Mexico's integration project, and in this sense, it was the most important institution of the state after 1920, just as Sánchez's photographs reflect.

In theory, the purpose of *la casa del pueblo* was to close the political gap between Mexico City and the thousands of rural villages that composed the

Figures 8 and 9. George I. Sánchez's photographs of rural public schools in Mexico and New Mexico. While the discursive framework of integration across Mexico and the American West was made possible by the pragmatist ideas Mexican and American social scientists shared, the political movements toward integration were reflected in the institution of the elementary school as a site of cultural consolidation across distinctive cultural communities. At the top, for instance, Indian and mestizo schoolchildren attended postrevolutionary Mexico's new public schools after 1921; at the bottom, Mexico-descended and European immigrant children went to school together in the schools of rural New Mexico. These projects in national consolidation did not occur independently of one another. Top: George I. Sánchez, *Mexico: A Revolution by Education* (New York: Viking, 1936), 202; Bottom: Nettie Lee Benson Latin American Collection, University of Texas Libraries, The University of Texas at Austin.

postrevolutionary nation. The extent to which the state was promoting the cultural life of the villages as part of the reconstituted nation has been the topic of some of the finest scholarship in Latin American history over the last thirty years. Some forty years ago, Josefina Zoraida Vázquez noted that the textbooks used by the federal state promoted a vision of Mexico that favored the dictates of the SEP over the cultural practices of the local communities.[15] A large body of important scholarship subsequently argued that Mexico's state builders, including the Columbia University graduates Manuel Gamio and Moisés Sáenz, sometimes failed to uphold the designs of local communities in establishing the new equilibrium between the local and the national during the process of national consolidation. Even if no transcendent ethical platform existed on which to construct the new nation, as pragmatism and cultural relativism held, it did not matter anyhow, these scholars have argued, since public officials in Mexico City were unwilling to modify their presumptions to align themselves more closely with the wishes of the local community. More recently, new scholarship has deepened our understanding of the local experiments in nation building from which the Mexican melting pot was forged. Local communities often supported the state schools, thereby establishing new avenues for social movement that became important for social mobility in later generations. And the melting pot project may have witnessed its first hesitant movement toward cultural pluralism during the 1930s under the banner of the SEP schools.[16]

A universal statement about these petit projects within *la casa del pueblo* is elusive given the diversity of postrevolutionary Mexico's rural communities, but there can be no doubt of the enormous scope of the work they performed. Looking back on the years between 1920 and 1940, one could see the establishment of thousands of new schools in the Republic of Mexico at the hands of the federal government and the local community alike. Like the Rosenwald schools of the American Deep South and the progressive education movement in the United States, this institutional project was one of the grandest educational chapters in the twentieth-century history of the Western Hemisphere. In every state of the Mexican republic, new rural schools were constructed by the hundreds. Whereas prior to 1910 and the downfall of Porfirio Díaz, schooling had taken place exclusively in the metropolitan centers of the republic, by 1940 nearly every community in the country could claim a rural school of its own. The French state took notice and replicated Mexico's efforts by 1960.[17] Nicaragua, El Salvador, Guatemala, and Bolivia also copied the example. This international example may have reached its apogee in the late 1940s, when UNESCO turned to Mexico's revolutionary schools as models for development in many parts of the world.

Ultimately, however, it is less important that we come to a universal resolution on the quality of Mexico's schools than it is to understand why the rural schools became a powerful example off which Americans reflected their spectrum of thought as they wrestled with the place of the public school in the rural American West. First, the relationship between the local community and the national government in Mexico was an example for the Americans of how to rethink the relationship between the state and rural America in the 1930s. Nothing drew their attention more than the willingness of some communities to use their resource bases to construct public schools and provide for the maintenance of the local schoolteachers. Such a funding mechanism for the rural schools was an example, the Americans thought, for the system of schools in the American West, where village schoolhouses still operated without the financial support of state government and outside the supervision of state boards of education. Second, the Americans were interested in the comprehensiveness and uniformity with which pedagogical instruction was carried out away from the metropolitan centers of the nation. The communities that they had come from in the United States were not merely minority communities, but, more important, rural communities whose relationship to the metropole was uncertain and underfinanced. In the context of the small size of the federal state before President Roosevelt and state resources that failed to protect the educational resources of the rural American West, the question of implementing reform was among the most important topics of concern for these Americans. As we shall see, they had committed their careers to the public school as an instrument of ethnic democracy. But such ethical commitments meant almost nothing if institutions could not be produced to carry forth the rejuvenation of industrial society that they imagined. Third, Mexico's use of the local natural environment as an adjunct space of pedagogy that could be harnessed to the classroom was an important model of instruction. Agriculture, ravines, mountains, flora, animals—all these and more formed a part of the organic environment the Americans surveyed as they journeyed through the provinces of the Mexican countryside. It should be remembered that they had been trained in the pedagogy of pragmatism, and so were constantly on the lookout for methods in learning that they could put into practice in the context of the rural American West.

John Dewey and the Mexican State

Moisés Sáenz had imported pragmatist education to Mexico from Columbia University at the height of John Dewey's influence in North America. He had studied with Dewey only three years after the publication of *Democracy and Education*, and he began studying at Columbia the same year, 1919, as the founding of the Progressive Education Association. When he helped to create a province of experimentalist schools for the postrevolutionary state, then, Sáenz transformed the thousands of new schools that began operating in Mexico into a new province of experimentalist education in North America at the very moment new schools inspired by Dewey were simultaneously opening in the United States. Yet timing alone cannot explain the attraction Mexico's institutions had for the Americans.

The use of Deweyan pragmatism as a system of social transformation in Mexico suffered from important shortcomings, moreover. The expansion of modernist ideas on Mexican soil appears to have been unsystematic, applied across a variety of institutions in various forms rather than on any single level of the federal system, and not limited to any single theory of new education or any single theorist. Pragmatist theory appeared more prominently in the curriculum units of the *escuelas normales regionales* and the *misiones culturales* than it did a level below, in the rural elementary schools where the children were attending school. Even in the normal school, however, one is struck by small evidence of direct discussions of pragmatism in comparison to the room given to matters of hygiene, the agricultural economy, and rudimentary pedagogy in mathematics, language instruction, history, and physical science. Similarly, it is difficult to measure systematically the extent to which normal school teachers translated their theoretical training into experiential learning techniques, and to what end. One cannot gauge comprehensively, therefore, whether the outcomes of pragmatism reached Mexico's schoolchildren, or in what form. Similarly, if one of the ultimate values of Deweyan theory lay in its moral critique of political and economic intransigence in Western society, then we are still left short from understanding without much further work whether children

Figure 10. A cultural missionary in the state of Tlaxcala delivering a lesson in educational pedagogy in 1928. John Dewey was received with warm praise and the public honors attending to a foreign diplomat of large stature during a 1926 visit here. Archivo Histórico de la Secretaría de Educación Pública (AHSEP), Mexico City, Mexico, Sección Dirección de Misiones Culturales, Serie Institutos Sociales, Box 20, Folder 3 (Tlaxcala).

in rural villages like San Miguel Nocutzepo, Michoacán, or Santa Cruz, Hidalgo, were being given the opportunity to think creatively and independently about the relationship of their communities to the new nation that was being reformulated after 1920.

Dewey himself had noted the shortcomings of Mexico's nascent education system. Famously, he had celebrated Mexico's rural schools in a series of articles for the *New Republic* after Sáenz had invited him to Mexico City in 1926. Yet in a little-known article in the *New York Times* on his return to the United States, Dewey revealed his skepticism that Mexico had produced a system of education that reflected the particular needs of Mexico's peoples. "[T]he Mexican peon, like the Russian mujik, could do with a quarter of a century of intensive drill in reading, writing, spelling, and playing with ideas," he told the newspaper.[18] Although some would indict Dewey as assuming that U.S. democracy was the normative model to which postrevolutionary Mexico should aspire, Dewey's own view of the importance of diversity to the development of the good community had actually led him to underscore the differences between social organization in the United States and Mexico. Social conditions in Mexico were different, he was arguing, and those particularities deserved deeper considerations from the schools there than they had received. A comment to a group of rural schoolteachers while visiting the normal school of Tlaxcala underscored his skepticism to the *New York Times* that Mexico had established schools designed for its own needs instead of copying those of other countries. "Dewey wanted the rural schoolteachers to remember the urgency and necessity of avoiding imitation, even if the model originated in the advanced countries, because each nation organizes its own system of education in accordance with its unique history, tradition, racial past, and economic and social institutions," wrote cultural missionary Primitivo Alvarez during Dewey's visit to Tlaxcala. "He told us never to look dismally upon the surroundings in which we worked, because once education was reduced to mere imitation, we would lose our unique personality and those things that we could contribute to world civilization."[19] As James Gouinlock has argued, what was noteworthy about Dewey's observations about Mexico's schools was Dewey's "insistence that historical change of all sorts be governed by ideas appropriate to the respective cultures. As in any problematic circumstance, plans should not be imposed a priori and from without."[20]

Why, then, did the *misión cultural,* the *escuela normal rural,* and *casa del pueblo* become institutional examples of progressive change for the U.S. social scientists if neither the timing nor pragmatism's ambivalent career in Mexico suffices to explain the turn? Like Dewey, they noted important shortcomings in Mexico's schools, including a heavy-handed state bureaucracy that did not always live up to the highest hopes of Deweyan philosophy and the unevenness of educational reform policies across the expanse of the nation. These Americans may have been foreign observers, but they were not intellectuals blind to the weaknesses of Mexican reform. They may have been optimistic, but they were not naive social scientists who saw redemptionist possibilities for the postrevolutionary educational system where there were none.[21]

For the Americans, Mexico's educational institutions were a realm of contingent possibilities rather than a model example of politics that had been successfully achieved. First, the evidence of pragmatist theory at the level of the rural normal school—however attenuated it may have been—represented an experiment in potential transformation via the school they tested for use in the United States. Second, Mexico provided a source of experimental ideas about educational administration in the rural scene. Third, because they placed experience and practice alongside theory, Mexico's schools provided the Americans with useful evidence for the questions of psychology that Dewey asked in the wake of the educational revolution that he helped to usher in. Taken collectively, these broader interpretations of Dewey provided three strong reasons the Americans found institutional experimentation in Mexico constructive for their discrete projects at home rather than a superficial confirmation of the spontaneous emergence of ethnic democracy in postrevolutionary society.[22]

Documentary evidence from the rural normal schools, for example, shows that some of the essential characteristics that defined pragmatist theory were being used in rural Mexico. In a series of handwritten exams completed by schoolteachers-in-training in the state of Michoacán, for example, young men and women in residence at the *escuelas normales* left evidence that what they were being taught was something more than top-down management techniques designed to create a tractable labor force. Félix Gómez was one case in point. "The child has a divine right to a life of enjoyment, to an abundance of room carved out for play, to shape his labors at school in a manner that conforms to the distinct stages of his life and to express his efforts through activities of immediate interest," he wrote in his final exam. "It is the case, then, that to impose on the child is to stifle his spontaneity; it is fatal to his free choice; that work subverts play and the execution of labor to his own proper initiative." He continued: "Under the inspiration of a good schoolteacher and with a developed sense of initiative, the innate interests of the child are sufficient for him to carry out his daily labors." There are many questions raised by this small passage buried in the final exam of a young schoolteacher in training as it was recorded in the educational records of a nascent normal school in the mountains of central Michoacán state. What was the precise source of these ideas? To what extent were these ideas practiced at the annex school among four- and five-year-old children rather than merely left at the level of theoretical instruction in the normal school? Were Gómez's ideas edited by his normal school professors? We may never know the answers to these questions. But the very presence of these ideas in modern education, written just three months after John Dewey's 1926 study trip to Mexico, opens up the possibility that some of the tenets of pragmatist thought were infiltrating the minds of the young schoolteachers of the nation.[23]

Félix Gómez was not alone. Another handwritten document by a young schoolteacher from the rural normal school at Tacámbaro, Michoacán, supports the role of the pragmatist critique of formalistic education in the educational institutions of Mexico's still evolving nation: In the old school "it was simply understood that the students would work, like the teeth of the wheel of a grand machine without enjoying any of the benefits of their excessive labors, by force of the teacher who would give loud orders or harsh punishments. . . . But today this method no longer exists in the schools. It is not the teacher who obligates one to work, but love itself, or interest in the thing that the student is dedicated to learning." Like a divine wind, the student wrote, a new school had been created. "The day came when the winds of progress came and broke apart the walls of the old school, leaving it clear to everyone in general, that, like the dictum that is repeated in the Decalogue of *El Maestro Rural*, 'My school in the true house of the people.' "[24] In a different example, schoolteacher-in-training María Chávez exhibited the new philosophical principles as they had been introduced in rural Mexico in a celebration of the career of the sixteenth-century Catholic bishop Vasco de Quiroga. Among the episodes in Mexican history that the Americans celebrated when they began arriving in Mexico in the early 1930s were the open-air academies of Vasco de Quiroga, whose sixteenth-century policies in education and self-government among the Tarascan Indians of Michoacán continue to be honored by some in Michoacán today. Often counterposed to the scorched-earth policies of Nuño Beltrán de Guzmán, Quiroga's policies of vernacular-language instruction and autonomy in learning practices were used by the Americans as a precursor to twentieth-century postrevolutionary government policy. Chávez agreed, as her 1926 final exam at the Tacámbaro rural normal school reflected: "The theme that was recommended to me has convinced me of the large similarity that exists between the pedagogy imparted by a group of benefactors after the conquest and the present-day rural schools," she wrote. "Don Vasco de Quiroga . . . said that the Indian is a rational human being and a younger brother who waits for an education and who is worthy of it like anyone else. . . . Quiroga formed the rural schools whose trajectory to better the conditions of the Indians was very great. That tendency cannot be reduced to the social life of the Indians, but to Quiroga's move to release them from the slavery in which they found themselves."[25]

The monthly newspapers published by the rural normal schools displayed testimonials to potential social change, meanwhile. In Erongarícuaro, Michoacán, for example, a young fourth-grade student named Jesús published a short editorial consisting of the ten maxims that expressed the social ethics he was developing at the rural normal school there. "Our country cries for citizens who fight to be free. It is good to be independent," he wrote. In a space left blank, he invited his readers to express their hopes for self-fulfillment as the administrators of the SEP in Mexico City attempted to build a national system of schools. "If you would create a brilliant career, fulfill your responsibility as student and you shall end by becoming a (fill-in-the-blank-as-you-choose)." In a third comment, Jesús directly targeted the Indians of Michoacán: "You [the Indian] have fought to liberate your race and died [for that cause] so that others later could defend their rights, thereby becoming free like the lion of the mountain and free like the birds of the skies."[26] A second example comes from the monthly newspaper of the rural normal school at Xocoyucan, Tlaxcala. In December 1926, the young student identified only as "A.G.A." described the importance of paying attention to the interests of the child as the central consideration of the schoolteacher under whose supervision she would fall. "To study the talents of a child is fundamental and requires continuous and close observation of his spontaneous activities. One must watch the child at play and during her assigned tasks, where one can measure the satisfaction that occurs when she experiments with a difficult labor," he wrote. Such work, wrote the student, was a labor of many years, since oftentimes one's interests did not emerge until age twelve or fourteen. Yet such difficult labor was necessary because the world needed people of all types. "We take great notice of our mission, which is steadfastly opposed to transform our classrooms into warehouses for our students. Many students who were called good-for-nothings, stubborn, dense, dumb, or crazy were simply misunderstood; we tried to force square pegs into round holes." Earlier in his essay, he had elaborated on just this very point. "It is well known that there are no two individuals who are exactly alike. That is why we say that nature breaks the mold each time that a new child is born."[27]

These postrevolutionary challenges to traditional power structures do not invalidate contemporary historical criticism that Mexico's postrevolutionary educational projects were efforts at social control. In Chávez's own words is the evidence that the state could be a paternalistic influence on rural Mexico via education policies that rationalized the Indian as a member of the human race in the attempt merely to subvert his freedom anew. Chávez states that it was her schoolteacher who had recommended the topic of Vasco de Quiroga to her, for example. Quiroga was a Catholic priest who, as Chávez writes, was attempting to convert Mexico's Native Americans to the Catholic faith rather than trying to increase their level of freedom to some precursor condition that antedated the Spanish conquest.[28] Similar clues of control are found throughout the essays in the files of Tacámbaro, Michoacán. In the words of Agripina Magaña J., for example, the Indian was alcoholic, dirty, and lazy.[29] According to Catalina Medina César, life in rural Mexico was a decayed civilization where new light had to be introduced as part of the postrevolutionary moral order.[30] The rural normal school newspapers sometimes argued that the new Mexican school should become an arbiter of power no matter what the local community desired. These examples clearly confirm what scholars like Mary Kay Vaughan, Susana Quintanilla, and Josefina Zoraida Vázquez have argued about postrevolutionary Mexico: through such instruments as *El Maestro Rural*, the state represented a heavy hand of authority that constrained the possibilities for rural people into prescribed channels rather than increasing the chances for lives free of authoritarian control.[31]

Yet as historian of Mexico Alexander Dawson has pointed out, emphasizing paternalistic control without underscoring the simultaneous presence of ideas that can be interpreted as challenges to authority structures is a good story that "relies on a vision of the past that distorts as much as it reveals."[32] Félix Gómez emphasized free choice in his essay, for example. Salvador León y Ortiz was clear that the SEP's new education models emphasized interest in the task at hand rather than obligation as the source of work. And even as Chávez romanticized the career of a sixteenth-century priest whose politics was not neutral, she underscored the critique of the conventional view of the Indian that John Dewey and Franz Boas had helped to make central to twentieth-century social theory. The Indian was rational in the context of his own culture, and fitted to ideas just like anyone else, she wrote.[33] Quiroga was a model not merely because he emphasized the expansion of freedom in the realm of civic intercourse, but because he emphasized political freedom as part of the hierarchy of power. One eminent historian of postrevolutionary education in Mexico, Elsie Rockwell, has put the spread of modernist ideas in the following way. "The

SEP's bulletins and journals carried the new educational philosophy into the states of the nation. The echo of those ideas is to be found in the texts and the discussions in the schools of Tlaxcala. Those ideas did not enter without much subsequent commentary, but at the very least, the educators of the SEP created new spaces in which these debates could take place."[34] These examples do not suggest Mexico had been transformed into a democratic nation. They support the more modest claim that new philosophical ideas were entering the provinces of the Mexican state through the influence of John Dewey and others, where they were recognized by the Americans who visited Mexico in the 1930s. The Americans who came to Mexico later were astonished to find such ideas at work there, because they were struggling to bring those same ideas to bear on the difficult social conditions of the rural American West where they worked.

Mexico's schools also represented important experimental models of administrative practice for the Americans. Such concerns may seem quotidian, but the flow of resources from Mexico City to the rural normal schools required methodical planning, good communication between SEP headquarters and rural schools in the provinces, and a system for supervising the mandates directed by the state. Cultural missionaries had to find ways to organize rural students into discrete grades and classrooms, integrate teaching methodologies into the daily rituals of rural villagers, and convince supportive villages that new methods of instruction would prove beneficial to the economic and political inclinations of local families. None of these measures could be taken for granted, the Americans knew. Faced with metropolitan political bureaucracies at home that had little experience in managing new educational techniques in rural communities, the Americans were amazed by the extent to which Mexico's central state had unfolded its educational projects in the provinces of the postrevolutionary republic. The expenditure of resources was deeply inadequate by Mexico's own standard, covering only a fraction of the national territory. But to the Americans, those resources represented a formidable administrative project in the rural scene whose components could be profitably modified for use in the American West.

Third, Dewey in Mexico had currency for the Americans because he had succeeded in moving the understanding of the school in the direction of the study of psychology. Contextualizing Dewey within psychology is not an easy move to make in twentieth-century Mexican history, since debates about psychology and the school are not antiseptic discussions to be considered outside the deep political stakes involved in the decades following the Mexican Revolution. Yet any review of Dewey's role in educational reform, political transformation, aesthetics, and ethics is not merely incomplete, but fundamentally flawed, if it does not first take into account his interest in how the mind creates knowledge out of experience in order to transform how knowledge is used politically. Psychology was central to Dewey's transformational project, but it was not its handmaiden, as it is typically treated in the historiography of the Mexican Revolution.[35]

Mexico's emphasis on psychology in education sensitized the Americans to rural education in Mexico as a system that was attempting to make the apprehension of meaning more transparent and tangible. In this regard, nothing was more important than the process that in Mexican historiography has come to be called "action-centered education." In the tradition of Mexican historiography, the rituals of practice in Mexico's rural schools have been widely condemned for their presumptions and attempts at labor control. Teaching such manual skills as gardening, sewing, furniture design, and basket making has been rightly critiqued as a means of emphasizing specific labor practices in the interest of promoting a particular form of economic production in postrevolutionary Mexico. Yet for the Americans, manual practice was more than mere production for the economy. It was, instead, the measure of an idea. It was what distinguished one thought from another, the link between an impression residing in the mind and a specific object, process, or relationship in the world that surrounded the human being. As Greg Grandin has recently pointed out in the case of Brazil, it is right to see experience in the progressive educational universe as amenable to labor control and the dictates of the teacher.[36] But such a view does not exhaust what practice represented. If viewed though the language of psychology that was under development during the first half of the twentieth century, it also represented a way to comprehend how human beings made associations between thought and world. As such, practice was an inescapable component of knowing, a process that needed to be studied and refined in all the circumstances in which it took place. Such experiential practice was fundamental to Deweyan thought. For making associations in the world was a fundamental step in transforming the physical and social conditions in which human communities were enmeshed.[37]

Psychologist Loyd Tireman was the consummate example of the window into practice and action that rural education in Mexico represented when the Americans arrived to study state policy there. He had long been interested in the psychology of language as a process of thinking. In the laboratory schools of the American Midwest and American West where he had trained, the concern with drawing associations between word and object was the fundamental concern of a forty-year career in education. When he arrived in Mexico in 1931, he was quickly drawn to the use of guitars as instruments of practice in the rural schools of Hidalgo, as well as plays and skits as instruments for teaching history and cultural tradition. Such practices, he knew, had long been a staple of Deweyan laboratory schools across the American landscape, as John and Evelyn Dewey's 1915 *Schools of Tomorrow* attested.[38] Yet such techniques for understanding how the mind apprehends data routinely came up against a problem in psychology that remains a large stumbling block in social science work into the twenty-first century: how were educators and psychologists to design systems of learning for children whose native language was not English? In the context of New Mexico where Tireman worked, the dominant language was Spanish, a language for which he found a ready analog in postrevolutionary Mexico. Not labor control, but the fit between ideas in Spanish and practice in Mexico and New Mexico became the object of his search within the institutions of the Mexican state in the 1930s. Such minute observations by Tireman may seem otherworldly for scholars searching to tell the political history of twentieth-century Mexico. Yet the fact that such minuscule work was central to the Americans only underscores how important it is to interpret Deweyan pragmatism as something other than a defense of Fordist political economy.

The set of policy experiments that postrevolutionary Mexico represented made its cultural missions, rural normal academies, and rural schools institutions the Americans could profitably study as potential new instruments for social reconstruction in the United States. As practitioners of modernist ideas who had studied the thickness of Dewey's wide-ranging thought, the Americans searched for clues about Dewey in Mexico that were broader than most contemporary scholars have assigned to them. The evidence suggests that some elements of Deweyan theory were being applied in the Mexican field to the wider spectrum of instruments that Dewey understood to be a part of social change. And it suggests that Mexican policy experimentation was useful to the Americans because it was a working system of interdependent institutions that represented the complicated relationship between education and the modern state rather than a complacent ethical pronouncement about local communities in a rapidly changing North America. The teacher, the importance of experience in learning, and the relationship of the student to the larger community were all instruments to be studied closely, the Americans knew. Given the large framework into which Dewey developed his philosophy, it makes sense to evaluate the presence of Dewey in Mexico by splintering the elements of education into its multiple parts and testing each one, rather than reducing Dewey to an unbreakable whole that must stand as a single test of ethics in the modern nation. It was not hope alone that had brought the Americans to study Mexico's *misiones culturales* and *casas del pueblo*. In the face of a political project that was still unfolding, the Americans saw reform impulses of potential change in Mexico's educational institutions that they adapted for their racial liberalism work in the United States. It was these impulses that attracted their attention, even as they acknowledged that transforming the social hierarchy was neither an instantaneous process nor one for which success was ever guaranteed.

The Convergence of Pragmatism and *Indigenismo*

If John Dewey's ideas had helped to enable discrete social policy convergences between the United States and Mexico, the Americans and Mexicans also manifested an ethical convergence between two of the fundamental intellectual movements in North American history, *indigenismo* and pragmatism.[39] While this convergence remains tenuous, it is underscored by recent scholarship noting small-scale changes that moved in the direction of pluralism as integral to the new postrevolutionary Mexican nation. Among those changes was a Mexican state that created new possibilities for Indians in Mexico's postrevolutionary society. These new possibilities do not mean that liberationist trajectories were dominant in the state's experiments in social change. Neither do they suggest that such possibilities became permanent fixtures of the political landscape, or that intellectuals continued to support them beyond the initial ventures when they took place. It does, mean, however, that Americans in Mexico were attuned to contingent political projects whose possibilities for liberationist reform were opening up in Mexico in the 1930s. And they suggest some possibilities in Mexican institutional history that the American pragmatists, as pragmatists, were sensitive to at a moment when the *indigenista* intellectuals of the Mexican state were actively debating the merits of the state's education projects.

Whether treated as knowledge about the Indian by non-Indians or as the institutional projects designed to incorporate them into the political life of the nation, the *indigenista* project of the Mexican state has been rightly criticized since the 1960s for the orientalist guise of social science toward the Indian and the projects in social hierarchy that it masked. And yet, Estelle Tarica has noted that three characteristics of *indigenista* thought over the twentieth century make it a more complicated and even puzzling set of ideas.[40] First, even after *indigenismo* has been widely condemned as destructive to Indian communities, it has continued to maintain a powerful oppositional hold on Mexican intellectuals seeking to reform the federal state. Subcomandante Marcos and Cuauhtémoc Cárdenas are two Latin American intellectuals who have recently invoked the Indian to argue for the reformation of state power in contemporary Mexico, for example, continuing in the process to keep alive an oppositional trajectory within *indigenismo* whose history in Latin American political discourse stretches back for hundreds of years. Rather than simply being a colonialist discourse through which to control Indians by orientalizing them, the oppositional characteristics of *indigenismo* have made it a powerful intellectual movement that has historically opposed the state's claim to the legitimacy of power.[41] Second, Tarica agrees with Martin Stabb's observation many years ago that *indigenismo* has always promoted a "sympathetic awareness of the Indian."[42] Thus, while recent historiography has emphasized the destructive capacities of postrevolutionary thought about the Indian, *indigenismo* has also been in the paradoxical position of producing representations of the Indians that have humanized them before the national community. Third, Tarica has pointed out that *indigenismo* has always been more than a regional oppositional voice. Rather than being a marginal voice aimed at breaking local power relations, it has provided a counterexample of how Indian/non-Indian relationships might be universally reimagined across the expanse of the entire national community. As Tarica has argued, such a "discourse aims, quite sincerely, to listen to an Indian voice rather than to silence it, and to evoke the affiliations between Indians and non-Indians rather than to assert a hierarchical difference between the two."[43] The sympathetic characteristics of *indigenismo* that Tarica has identified do not mitigate the destructive projects that *indigenista* discourse helped to create in postrevolutionary Mexico. But they do show that *indigenismo* was a spectrum of ideas that contained a liberationist thread within it, not a monolithic ideology whose consequences for Mexican society can be rendered in negative terms alone. That broader envelope of ideas pointed to new configurations of ethnic relations in Mexico that *indigenismo* made possible, so it need not be seen only as a destructive state project.

Tarica's reminder about the wider possibilities of *indigenismo* is partially grounded in the ethical transformation of Mexico's prominent twentieth-century novelist Rosario Castellanos, who became a functionary of the Mexican state's melting pot projects in the 1950s. Castellanos worked in the 1950s in the same state educational agencies that Manuel Gamio and Moisés Sáenz had established in the 1920s, thus representing a generation of scientists who followed in the wake of the SEP institutionalization after the Mexican Revolution. According to Tarica, Castellanos embodied in her novels and poems the renewal of ethnic relations in postrevolutionary Mexico via a new articulation of the relationship between Indians and non-Indians. In her famous novel of ethnic strife in 1930s Chiapas, *Balún-Canán*, Castellanos narrated the emergence of a new social consciousness in which the Indian in Mexican society is transformed from a servant in the Mexican social hierarchy to an equal member of the national community to whom non-Indians owed a moral debt.[44] Castellanos later attempted to translate into institutional practice the new vision of ethnic relations in Mexico that she had synthesized during the writing of her novel, becoming a public official of the state in the wake of her novel. In capturing this relationship between the renewed social consciousness of Castellanos's novel and the institutional work that Castellanos performed with the federal government, Tarica has provided a model for comprehending the liberationist characteristics of the institutional labors of the Mexican public officials on whom the Americans depended when they traveled to Mexico in the 1930s. Just as Tarica argues that Castellanos had arrived at a renewed social consciousness about the Indian through her writing and institutional work, I maintain that the Americans noted the analogous use of the ideas of Dewey and Boas by Sáenz and Gamio to achieve a measure of institutional transformation during an earlier moment in postrevolutionary ethnic relations.

One cannot equate the transformation of Castellanos's subjectivity with the institutional transformation of postrevolutionary ethnic relations in twentieth-century Mexico, of course. Any casual glimpse at Mexico, whether in 1930, 1950, or 1980, would show the significant failures of those institutional projects that claimed to work in the service of new ethnic relations. Indeed, Tarica herself notes that the *indigenista* philosophy that allowed Castellanos to imagine a new relationship to the Indians of Chiapas was ultimately not favorable to the subaltern actors who served as the servile caste of southern Mexico. Castellanos ended *Balún-Canán* by returning to the voice of a centered, rational narrator, Tarica argues, thus abandoning the marginal positionality that marked the early sections of the novel. The abandonment corresponds to Castellanos's view, Tarica argues, that the only way to reconcile the alternative epistemologies of the master class and the Indians was through the force of postrevolutionary state law. Only by forcing the Indians to abandon their view of history in favor of the state's nationalist project could two utterly incompatible lifeways be reconciled. Law's role as the ultimate and coercive mediator in a society of distinct ethnic affiliations was Castellanos's way of signaling what so many progressive intellectuals ultimately believed about the Indian in Mexico: that only by killing the Indian's culture could true national integration be achieved. This was one of the perennial tragedies of *indigenismo*, in fact. While it may have allowed non-Indians to reimagine ethnic relations, Indians themselves were left out of the conversation.

But one does not have to indict the *indigenista* project for failing to transform ethnic relations in twentieth-century Mexico in order to claim that *indigenismo* included a spectrum of liberationist ideas in addition to the colonialist ones with which it is more conventionally associated. As Tarica argues, *indigenista* novels allow the reader to figuratively transform the nation into "a redemptive, egalitarian space of inner self-encounter, one that counteracts and overwhelms the oppressive, hierarchical space of oligarchical daily life, marked by slavery, injustice, self-repudiation, and shame."[45] That function is a critical act along the road to institutional change, just as, for example, Harriet Beecher Stowe's consideration of U.S. Black-white relations in *Uncle Tom's Cabin* represented an analogous political moment in American race relations. While some *indigenista* intellectuals ultimately submitted to a nationalist project that did not free the Indians, the act of *indigenista* submission to the nation cannot mask the corollary effects of *indigenista* discourse. As Tarica has written, one corollary effect of *indigenismo* has been to "challenge the racial status quo in the first half of the twentieth century in Mexico, Bolivia, and Peru."[46]

The production of new social relationships that was a central characteristic of the liberationist strains of *indigenismo* provides the clue to understanding why Deweyan pragmatism complemented the ethical reformulation of ethnic relations in Mexico. What pragmatism shared with *indigenista* thought was the goal of transformed social relationships, or what philosopher of pragmatism Gregory F. Pappas has recently called the "amelioration of experience."[47] But rather than accepting a complacent, predetermined social transformation of the historical relationship between the Indians, mestizos, and whites who made up the Mexican melting pot, "amelioration" underscores Dewey's belief that new alignments of interethnic affiliation and wide-scale social change could be created only if prolonged effort, institutional struggle, and introspection were brought to bear on the challenges of social organization. Seen as an incremental intervention for the creation of new social relationships rather than as a predetermined prescription for reordering Mexican society by fiat, Deweyan pragmatism did not contemplate the instantaneous reordering of social organization as a foregone conclusion. Instead, as Pappas argues, Dewey saw social change as a contingent, tenuous process that could result in institutional change only from tireless effort. Transformation required constant intervention and a hope of possibility rather than a summary teleology of fixed ends approved unilaterally from the high agencies of the Mexican state. It also required the "transformation of [personal] character," Pappas has written, something that "can be a slow and arduous process requiring the indirect change of environmental conditions."[48] Contemporary scholarship has often given us a view of Deweyan social scientists as hardened colonialists bent on shaping the social body into a preconceived hierarchy. While many state intellectuals no doubt functioned this way in postrevolutionary Mexico, there were others whose efforts contained attempts at amelioration that pragmatist Americans recognized while they traveled in the postrevolutionary republic. We should be wary of putting on rose-colored glasses that give the best possible hue to social scientists whose state projects sometimes had disastrous consequences for local communities. But misconstruing pragmatism's insistence on the difficulty of process as a teleological justification for top-down social experimentation has been one of the largest mistakes in the scholarship on Dewey's relationship to the postrevolutionary melting pot project. John Dewey himself responded to this same misreading that social scientists and public officials had given to his philosophy in his 1938 *Education and Experience*.[49] It is a mistake that scholars continue to repeat today, making it impossible to see the liberationist possibilities that the Americans found in the institutions of the postrevolutionary state.

How the small changes in ethical subjectivity that Tarica noted for postrevolutionary Mexico could be converted into institutional practice has been shown by Alexander Dawson's recent analysis of Mexican state policy in the 1930s. Like Tarica, Dawson has argued that the conventional critique of *indigenista* orientalism obscures as much as it illuminates by focusing too exclusively on the destructive consequences of *indigenista* thought rather than its more contradictory capacities. As he explains, the orientalist critique of *indigenista* thought in Mexico distorts as much as it illuminates our understanding of postrevolutionary change.[50] While Tarica was focused on the transformation of *indigenista* subjectivity rather than on the subaltern communities that became the objects of *indigenista* labor, Dawson charts the opportunities for the renewal of ethnic relations that thirty years of institutional innovation yielded in postrevolutionary Mexico. The *indigenista* intellectuals were guilty of racialist overtones, writes Dawson, yet simply dismissing them "risks interpreting them too narrowly."[51] More often than not, they argued that the Mexican Indian was in no way inferior to Europeans and criollos in Mexico. Their labors not only helped to undermine race as an essential category of identity, but by reconstructing those institutions that were failing, they also took "the federal state's first halting steps toward recognizing Mexico as a plural nation."[52] Mexico's federal state provided the initial education that allowed villagers to attain the status of attorneys, doctors, teachers, and engineers, argues Dawson, career positions that allowed them to ascend to local political hierarchies and to transform the power relations of their villages to the national state. Support for the state's schools was so intense in some communities that villagers quarreled with one another for control of local schools out of a commitment to "the opportunities they offered . . . to make a better life for the Indian."[53] Mexico's *indigenistas* also modified the definition of what integration meant as they worked within scientific organizations that sought new answers to the question of achieving the Mexican melting pot. Whereas for some it had once meant the cultural transformation of the Indian to a cultural ideal associated with Europe, others argued for a new philosophy that transformed the European into the Indian, or the protection of a vibrant Indian society as a part of the national community. In short, Dawson has noted a trajectory of postrevolutionary nationalism in which the state made room for the particularities of local communities as a part of an integrated community.

The reconceptualization of postrevolutionary ethnic relations that Tarica calls "the reimagination of the nation" and that Dawson sees at work in the institutions of the postrevolutionary state was not something that the

Americans imagined. It represented the new contingent moral and institutional possibilities that the crafters of the Mexican melting pot project were engaged in producing via the liberationist side of *indigenista* thought in the immediate three decades after the Mexican Revolution. The haunting work of Fernando Benítez and Francisco Rojas González has shown us that releasing the Mexican Indian from a status of Mexico's pariah class was not an unqualified success in postrevolutionary Mexico.[54] Yet there is no necessity to establish that Mexico's federal schools had created a supreme model of pluralistic democracy in the short span of ten to fifteen years they had been operating on Mexican soil at the time Sánchez and Embree came to Michoacán and Hidalgo. Like believers who knew the slow pace of social change and worked hard to achieve it, the American pragmatists were looking for cracks in the old systems rather than new monuments achieved. Dewey and pragmatist analysis were no less optimistic in Mexico than in the United States, but for Americans searching for evidence of change rather than a new utopia, there was plenty of experimentation to justify their belief that rural Mexico was doing something that the rural American West was not. They were not romanticizing the achievement of a utopia in Mexico or underestimating the forces of institutional inertia against which they struggled all their lives. Instead, they were guarded believers in a racial project whose success remains unachieved even today.

In the United States, too, social change occurred by inches rather than miles, a process that every American intellectual has had to contend with since the end of the American Civil War. Along the way, such writers as Walt Whitman, Mark Twain, and Edward Bellamy, as Castellanos did in Mexico, crafted alternative moral universes that looked toward a reimagined future of American institutional change. But while building an institutional democracy was clearly a working endpoint for the Americans, they were not so naïve as to believe that it could be produced quickly, easily, and without continuing struggle. It is for this reason that the Americans were more interested in whether a political impulse operated in Mexico in the 1930s that could be interpreted as a modest but practical experiment in reformulating ethnic relations than in the immediate transformation of the social hierarchy. The Americans, like the Mexicans, stressed the small possibilities of social science to produce new social relationships. And just as Deweyan theory guided these Americans toward the restructuring of American society without believing that democracy was right around the corner in the United States, so too, does one not need to establish that democracy succeeded in Mexico in order to believe that Mexican pragmatism contained ideas for revolutionary reform within its own matrix of ideas.

The reform-minded political sensibilities that set the Americans apart from the more radical political actors that surrounded them fits perfectly well with Pappas's sense that the Americans were "meliorists." Ralph Beals, for example, came from a socialist-inspired family that also spawned the radical journalist Carleton Beals, yet unlike his brother Carleton, Ralph committed his career to gradual change through the instruments of the state rather than revolutionary change through labor activism and Marxist critique. George I. Sánchez fought for civil rights through the mechanism of the federal courts and the public school systems, whereas Mexican American laborites like Emma Tenayuca fought through workers' alliances and labor strikes in Texas. In a career spent almost entirely in the academy, Loyd Tireman was inspired by the political traditions of Midwestern populism, not the Bolshevik example in Moscow or the Popular Front politics of the radical New South. The relative conservatism that marked the reformist politics of these Americans should not, moreover, obscure the outsider status that they claimed for themselves. We could assume that they defined themselves primarily as elite social scientists, or as white intellectuals with a claim on the privileges of social power and authority. But this would be a mistake. Sánchez saw himself as a minority citizen, fighting to widen the privileges of liberal society against the presumptions of white Americans. Beals had fled the industrial west of California, seeking respite in the farms of Mexico and Southern California from the industrial destruction of Harry Bridges era California. And Tireman sought to defend the agrarian towns of the Midwest as they succumbed to the power of corporations based in the eastern United States. These Americans saw themselves as the losers of history, and this sensitized them to Mexico's small-scale political changes and the Deweyan experiments of the SEP's schools. If some people believed that they were conservative in their defense for reforming the system rather than destroying it, they were conservative from the outside looking in.[55] What they sought was to transform the system, not destroy it, for the benefit of those in Mexico whom Mariano Azuela had once referred to as *los de abajo*, those of the rural American West that George Sánchez once called the "forgotten people," and those of Winesburg, Ohio, whom Sherwood Anderson had once called *the grotesques*.[56]

The Scientific State

Chapter 3

The Language of Experience

The difference Mexico's postrevolutionary state made to American integration history becomes evident when we examine the encounters of American social scientists with the policy experiments of the Mexican government. These Americans retreated into postrevolutionary Mexico when government in the United States could not provide solutions to the problems of racial conflict in the American West. In Mexico, they found a central state using Dewey's ideas to reconstruct the Mexican melting pot across the rural provinces of the republic. Mexico's scientific state became the most important model of social change for them during the New Deal and World War II. As Gregory Pappas has argued, science became a metaphor for them, a way of searching for new possibilities rather than prescribing set truths for social action in the United States.[1] Their resulting attempts to integrate the West in the aftermath of their time in Mexico were among the most creative social science experiments in the nation. Some championed language reform as an instrument toward the lessening of social conflict across ethnic difference. Others built the most successful laboratory schools in the American West, hoping to understand the role of the school in shaping ethnic democracy. For others, anthropology became a way to study the process of "acculturation," or how people from one culture absorbed the lifeways of people from another culture. Was it possible, they wondered, to manage that process as part of an administrative attempt to create the beloved community in the United States?

Montana Hastings and Psychology in Mexico City

The relationship of Mexican integration policy to the integration movements of the American West started to become evident in one of California's canonical legal battles in the early 1930s, just at the moment that school experimentation in Mexico was about to reach the height of reform. It was late 1931, and Mexico's state department, the Secretaría de Relaciones Exteriores (Secretariat of Foreign Affairs; SRE), had just reported that widespread segregationist practices in the United States had begun to draw the attention of Mexico's consular officials in California, Arizona, and Texas. Just to the east of San Diego, the public school separation of immigrant Mexicans and white Americans had brought immigrant Mexicans into conflict with school officials. The superintendent had directed immigrant schoolchildren to enroll in "Mexican-only schools" located outside the neighborhoods where they would have otherwise attended school, but they had revolted. "The San Diego consulate," reported the SRE, "protested to district officials, and sought out a larger rationale for the actions of the school district."[2] Lemon Grove would become one of the canonical flashpoints of racial conflict in the twentieth-century American West, but from the perspective of the Mexican state there was nothing especially compelling about the Lemon Grove incident. Many other incidents stretching from California to Texas had been described by the SRE. In South San Antonio, an Americanization academy for Mexican immigrants had been burned to the ground. Mexican pupils had been denied access to the elementary schools of Mission, Texas. In Del Rio (Texas), Carpinteria (California), and Somerton (Arizona), students who had come to the United States from Mexico had been denied entry into the public schools or placed in segregated academies whose facilities did not match those provided to non-Mexican youth. Racial hostility seemed to have become a normal part of social organization everywhere that immigrants from Mexico had recently arrived in the United States.

That Mexico's broader scientific state, rather than its consulate alone, was interested in the Lemon Grove case was evident in the joint policy reports Mexico's federal government issued in response in 1931. In one, the SRE reported that Mexico's diplomatic corps had commissioned its sister ministry, the Secretariat of Public Education, to study the arc of conflict from California to Texas that was becoming a central feature of immigration from Mexico to the United States. "In view of the plethora of racist incidents, the Secretariat of Foreign Affairs saw fit to solicit from the SEP that the question of segregation in the public schools of the United States be submitted for special consideration by a corpus of Mexican experts on the matter," the memo read. The SEP was the same ministry that had institutionalized Mexico's melting pot projects beginning in 1921 with José

Vasconcelos's *raza cósmica* vision. "Such a body was to determine the legitimate reasons that could be invoked in favor of, or against, school segregation in the United States, for what was needed, given the nature of the problem, was a scientific basis on which the SRE could proceed in its work. Only in consonance with such scientific reason could we hope to communicate adequate instructions to our diplomats in the United States," the SRE memo continued.[3] In response, the SEP issued a report on discrimination in the United States prepared by a team of internal investigators (*comisión técnica consultiva*) specially convened by its administration.

The SEP report collected two decades of scientific work by its agencies to provide an independent analysis of the problem of segregation in American public schools. These agencies included the national university in Mexico City, the federal government's educational psychology department, and the secondary schools division of the Mexico City public schools. American educators argue, wrote the SEP, "that school progress of students from Mexico is impossible because immigrants do not speak English, and further, that they act as a retardant to English-speaking children who go to school alongside them." The Americans argued, it said, that there is not sufficient room in the local schools for immigrant Mexican children, or that Mexican schoolchildren pose a hygiene threat to American-born students. But the SEP found these reasons to be subterfuges. "Seen from the point of view of the technical aspects surrounding the reasons that the Americans have given for the exclusion of Mexican students from their schools, this Commission does not find those to be valid," the SEP reported to the SRE. "As a result, we believe that all steps should be taken to suspend the segregation policy that is in question."[4]

In its own policy report, the Secretariat of Foreign Affairs juxtaposed the opinions of prominent American and Mexican pedagogues to reinforce the SEP findings. Ezequiel A. Chávez was one of the grand old men of Mexican education, a secretary of education during the revolutionary war years, and president of UNAM in the early 1920s. "There are no countries anywhere on the earth in which considerable differences are not to be found among the numerous social classes of society," Chávez wrote in the SRE report as he analogized Mexico's multiethnic society to the multiethnic society of the United States where Mexicans had begun to migrate. "The only means, furthermore, by which to assure that these differences should not come to create great antagonisms is to create a common consensus across all of the social classes of the community," he continued. "The best instrument to achieve this consensus is a public school that is universally accessible to all, whether that school is to be found in the United States or in the Republic of Mexico. From this it follows that it is indispensable for the purpose of avoiding the emergence of irreconcilable antagonism that would follow by making the public school exclusionary, which would necessarily hurt those who would be excluded."[5] To complete the analogy between the United States and postrevolutionary Mexico, the SRE juxtaposed University of Texas psychologist and early student of Mexican American education Hershel T. Manuel alongside Chávez. Using a speech Manuel had recently delivered to the League of United Latin American Citizens (LULAC), the SRE came to the same conclusion the SEP had arrived at. "Segregation is a dangerous procedure to attempt; and when it is necessary, it must be applied only as a means by which to arrive at a beneficial good," Manuel had told LULAC. "Even then, adverse consequences will follow which must be reduced to the extent possible." Manuel had even followed Chávez's logic with regard to the question of social antagonisms, the SRE wrote. "Segregation runs counter to one of the fundamental goals of education, which is to create student citizens who know how to live in harmony with those around them. Children learn to live in peace and harmony not when they are separated from one another, but when they participate alongside in joint adventures. Americanization will naturally follow if we merely give Mexican youth those opportunities that they need for their social success. But Americanization without justice is a lost hope. Injustice creates antagonism, not loyalty."[6]

The result of these joint policy reports was a set of recommendations by the SRE to its consulates abroad for responding to educational segregation in the United States. Segregation could not be justified when it was ultimately based on racial factors since children had to be evaluated individually. Segregation based on language proficiency might be acceptable, but only in reading classes and only until such time as students developed their English skills under the guidance of English language specialists. Government had the duty to avoid segregated schools, since segregation produced animosities among children and national communities alike. Finally, while Americanization centers might be properly provided for adults, it was the public school that was best equipped to provide similar assimilation techniques in the case of schoolchildren. Implementation of these guidelines was to be accomplished with "an eye to preserving the maximum harmony with school officials in the United States," the SRE concluded: "But with a view toward demonstrating that the ideals of justice that they represented were the means by which to properly determine the best solutions to the question of Mexican children who were being educated abroad."[7]

Already the connections between Mexico's integrationist state and American civil rights were clear in the joint reports, but no one dramatized them better than Montana Hastings. "Ms. Montana Hastings, an American specialist in intelligence testing of children who is today a resident of Mexico City, observed with her own eyes in 1921 and 1922 that those Mexican schoolchildren who attended the schools of San Diego, California, could easily learn to speak English when given the opportunity," the SEP had written in its policy report to the SRE. "After a few months in special instruction to learn English, and after it had been determined that they had developed facility in English, those children were incorporated into the larger units of the school and thereafter they made rapid progress in their studies."[8]

Montana Hastings had been a schoolteacher in Missouri before developing an expertise in mental intelligence testing as a graduate student under psychologist Edward Thorndike at Columbia University. After subsequently relocating to New Mexico, she became director of the state's child welfare agency, where she led efforts to assimilate immigrant Mexican schoolchildren into 1920s New Mexico society. In a report on the duties of the welfare bureau whose completion had been among her first duties, *The Organization of the State Child Welfare Work*, she clarified the relationship between New Mexico's public schools and her training in child psychology. "The constant purpose of the psychologist of the Child Welfare Service will be to assist in the more intelligent adjustment of school world to life needs of boys and girls," she wrote. "It means that guidance . . . must rely primarily on research principles, and that guidance is not merely what can be advised for an individual child after mental and physical examinations have been made, but in addition, there must be a complete follow-up plan whereby the child's progress may be observed daily and adjustments made at any time."[9] As historian Lawrence Cremin once commented, psychologists like Hastings were using techniques developed in the psychological sciences in the 1920s to sharpen the fit between public schools that were undergoing dramatic change and schoolchildren whose differential abilities had become the focus of modern educational philosophy.[10] Shortly after Hastings published her study, however, an oddity appeared in her career. Her documentary record in the United States was quiet for the next eighteen years and did not appear again until her death in Missouri during World War II. In its place, her career trajectory began to appear in the files of the Secretariat of Public Education in Mexico City.

Fifteen hundred miles south of San Diego, the SEP personnel files in Mexico City show that Hastings had relocated from New Mexico sometime between 1920 and 1922 to begin working with immigrant Mexicans in San Diego County. In a major research study she published in Mexico City for the Secretariat of Public Education in 1929, Hastings described this move herself. "I think it opportune at this moment to make mention here of the work that the author has completed on the subject of the mental capacities of Mexican schoolchildren," she wrote. "That study originated in California, as a consequence of the practical problem of classifying the Mexican schoolchildren who had enrolled in the public schools of San Diego, California. I completed a small scientific study there under the direction of the Psychology Department at the University of California."[11] Hastings's comments explained why her work had been present in the SEP 1931 Lemon Grove report. From New Mexico, where she had used mental examinations to categorize the immigrant pupils who were beginning to arrive in the state from Mexico, she had relocated to California to pursue the same line of investigation in San Diego. But her comments added more. She had relocated a second time, this time to Mexico City, to begin studying the mental capacity of Mexico's students from within the testing agency of the Secretaría de Educación Pública. Her work in San Diego had focused on Mexican immigrants in the public schools, just as it had in New Mexico, "but as interest in the subject would surely only grow, much broader investigations were required that finally led me to relocate to Mexico City in 1922," she wrote.[12] We cannot fill in all the gaps without some guesswork, but at the precise moment that the migration of Mexico's peoples to the United States had begun to accelerate after the Mexican Revolution, the SEP records captured the career trajectory that Hastings had made from New Mexico to California and Mexico City as she studied an immigrant group that was appearing on the radar scope of educational officials for the first time in the history of the American West. As early as 1920, even before the seminal work of Emory Bogardus and Thomas Garth had taken notice of immigrant Mexicans to the United States, Hastings had developed an expertise in an immigrant population whose location within the American nation would increasingly occupy social scientists for the next thirty years.

More important than the fact that Hastings was one of the first scientists to pursue the study of immigrant children from Mexico to the United States was the improbable rationale that had guided her career into postrevolutionary Mexico. Hastings's movement across the continent appeared in the archival records of the Mexican state rather than archives in the United States, in Spanish rather than English, because she spent the majority of a professional career trying to understand the melting pot in the American West from within the postrevolutionary bureaucracies in Mexico City. Hastings had become an employee of the Secretaría de Educación Pública in April 1923 after relocating to Mexico City in late 1922. In that month, she was named a research professor at UNAM School of Graduate Studies, with responsibility to teach classes in mental intelligence testing within the university. "Her studies are of great novelty," wrote UNAM's rector to José Vasconcelos, "and she has experience in teaching mental intelligence testing as a result of similar classes she has imparted at the San Diego Normal School. . . . Various of our professors have also expressed an interest in her analysis and lectures."[13] After serving as a research specialist for the SEP rural schools administration, she became permanently connected for the rest of her career to the SEP Department of Psychopedagogy and Hygiene and to the new secondary schools Moisés Sáenz was establishing in Mexico City. It was in the latter two roles that Hastings completed the remarkable 1929 study, *Clasificación y estudio estadístico*, in which she revealed the relationship between her work in the United States and her work in the Republic of Mexico. Even though scholars of cultural relations have long known that Americans and Mexicans were moving back and forth across the continent to study one another's countries, this was still a remarkable episode in the history of social science.[14] From the United States, an American social scientist had relocated to the agencies of the Mexican state to study a research question that was being investigated abroad as much as it was at home. Remarkably, by the time that the SEP had referenced Hastings's work in its 1931 Lemon Grove report, Hastings had been an employee of the Secretaría de Educación Pública for nearly ten years. As her personnel file in the archives in Mexico City testifies, her tenure with the SEP did not end until 1938.[15]

Why Hastings had found common ground with the psychologists of the SEP is explained by a short look at the history of psychology in postrevolutionary Mexico.[16] In the same year that the initial battles of the Mexican Revolution toppled Porfirio Díaz in 1911, Alfred Binet published the last

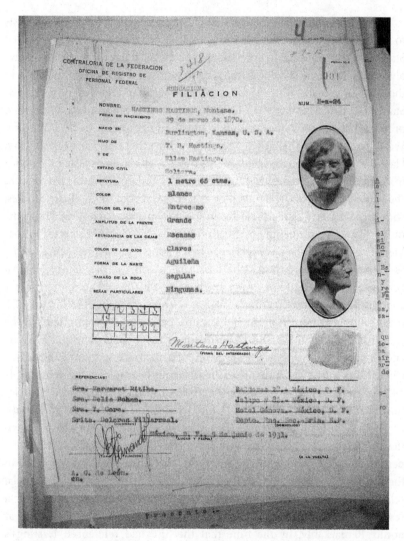

Figure 11. Montana Hastings's personnel file at the Secretaría de Educación Pública in Mexico City. Archivo Histórico de la Secretaría de Educación Pública (AHSEP), Mexico City, Mexico, Sección Dirección General de Administración de Personal del Sector Central, Serie 4.3, Referencia D 131, Expediente 3418.

edition of his Simon-Binet intelligence test in Paris, only months before his death. Mexican psychologist and educator Rafael Santamarina had used previous editions of the test in the asylums of Mexico City, and by the time of the founding of the Secretariat of Public Education after the revolution in 1921, he had become the leading proponent for the diffusion of the updated Simon-Binet in Mexico's postrevolutionary education institutes. When the SEP subsequently established an educational psychology institute as part of its millenarian project in national integration, it chose Santamarina to head the new agency. Santamarina lodged the new institute in Mexico's national university, UNAM, where he had worked for most of his life and which had been placed under the SEP by the revolutionary government. When Santamarina's psychology bureau expanded its work, among its first hires was Montana Hastings, who had developed expertise in the updated Simon-Binet independently in the United States. Beginning in 1922, when she first relocated to Mexico City, until 1928, Hastings administered the Simon-Binet exam Santamarina had imported from France to students of Mexico City's newly institutionalized secondary schools. The results of the 3,719 mental intelligence exams Hastings captured in *Clasificación* was the first large-scale investigation of the mental capacities of Mexico's schoolchildren in the aftermath of the Mexican Revolution.

The larger intellectual history of mental intelligence testing had been bracketed by Hastings at the front and back ends of her 1929 study. The chapter "Mediciones mentales," in *Clasificación*, provided a genealogy of the use of mental exams beginning in France and moving west to the United States and the Republic of Mexico in the early twentieth century. Psychologists in Paris had grown concerned with the apparent inability of some pupils in the schools to advance in their grammar school studies. This had triggered the development of new exams that could be applied outside the confined laboratory studies that previous research had developed. By 1911, Alfred Binet's exams had begun to circulate around the world, including Stanford, Columbia, and UNAM in North America. Progressive education theory in the United States marked a new expansion of mental testing by 1915, primarily at Columbia University, though its practical application was sidetracked from schoolchildren to soldiers by the onset of World War I. It was after the war that intelligence testing exploded in the United States, she wrote. "The schoolchildren that each teacher now had responsibility for had become voluminous and heterogeneous," wrote Hastings, "because immigration had each year produced millions of new schoolchildren, and compulsory education laws had now brought new pupils into the schools who were not capable of making regular progress through the schools." Among those who were tested for the first time were the foreign-born, who, Hastings argued, had been left out of previous work because of the language barrier. Her concluding chapter gave her defense of mental testing as part of the history of progressive education, meanwhile. "The 'New Education' or 'Progressive Education' that is so widely heralded today certainly under-scores the importance of giving to each student the opportunity to develop his mind and talents in a proper and worthy direction," she wrote. In Mex-ico City, she continued, there were at least 8,900 students who had com-pleted elementary school studies the previous year. "It would be a great loss for society and for Mexico's educational future, if for whatever reason, these children were not given the educational advantages that they were worthy of." Psychologists had to continue their current line of work, she argued, if the presumptions of progressive education were still accepted by social scientists. "If it is true that the first proposition of the school is to help each student to discover himself or herself and then to put himself at the service of his society, [we must continue]."[17]

John Dewey's student Moisés Sáenz had provided the direct link between Hastings and Santamarina, meanwhile. His correspondence with Teachers College graduates who might be valuable to the SEP's new post-revolutionary mission was evident in the Mexico City reports that Hastings produced during a career with the SEP that lasted from her initial travel to Mexico in 1922 until her employment ended in 1938. In *Clasificación*, for example, Hastings acknowledged her thanks to both the SEP and the Teach-ers College mentors who had made her work possible in Mexico City. "I wish to thank professor Moisés Sáenz, subsecretary of Public Education, who is responsible for establishing my line of work within the secondary schools. . . . Because this book makes ample use of statistics, I also wish to thank the professors who instructed me while in graduate school, including Professors Thorndike, Whipple, Frazier, and Hollingworth of Columbia University."[18] More than just reflecting the personal career of a single edu-cator, Hastings's Mexico City work reflected the institutional relationships between Mexico's central state and Columbia University that became one basis for the comparative history of the melting pot in the United States and Mexico that Hastings's career represented.

The melting pot concerns that connected her work in New Mexico to Mexico's postrevolutionary state were clearly represented in *Clasificación*.

Between 1926 and 1928, she wrote there, she had analyzed the mental capacities of the Native American students who lived at the Casa del Estudiante Indígena. The Casa was one of the most radical experiments of the Mexican state. It had been designed to test the acculturative advantages of instruction in the urban environment by removing Mexico's *indígenas* from their rural homelands and transplanting them to metropolitan Mexico City. It was among the clearest manifestations of the interethnic schooling Diego Rivera had captured in his SEP murals, with the teacher sitting at the center of the state's political program. In a small appendix to *Clasificación*, Hastings listed the representative Native American cultures the Mexican state had relocated to Mexico City. The Huichol from Jalisco and the Mexicana from Guerrero and Hidalgo were the most numerous, followed by the Tarahumara from Chihuahua, Huaxteca and Zapotec from Veracruz, and Maya from Yucatán. In all, tribes speaking twenty-one dialects had been assembled from nineteen of Mexico's thirty-one states.[19] The Mexican melting pot the Casa del Estudiante Indígena was attempting to create was one of the clearest analogies to the melting pot in the American West that had brought Hastings to Mexico in 1922. In both New Mexico and California, Hastings had been involved in assimilationist efforts through the school designed to transform the immigrant peoples of Mexico into new American citizens.

Mental intelligence exams such as the Simon-Binet reflected middle-class anxieties over the presence of schoolchildren who did not fit the usual profile of secondary school students, some have argued. Rather than merely charting the differential capacities of brain function, intelligence tests also became social documents that showed the attempts by some educators to channel the life outcomes of the community's spectrum of ethnic groups into a priori conceptions of hierarchy and control. But we risk missing the larger historical convergence that was represented in the Mexican state's recruitment of an American psychologist by focusing on the Simon-Binet exams in Mexico as a misguided episode in social science. In describing her history in Mexico at the time postrevolutionary Mexico's state educational institutions were rapidly expanding, Hastings underscored the pinpoint possibilities for scientific research that Mexico's postrevolutionary institutions had presented for Americans when the scientific study of immigrant Mexicans in the United States was just beginning. Her career in Mexico City was a metaphor for the deep and sustained relationship that civil rights Americans had begun building with Mexico's scientific state just at the moment that Mexico reached the most intense period of its twentieth-century public school movement in the two decades after 1920.

That relationship had three parts. First, these assimilationist Americans had begun to study a central state apparatus whose units worked in tandem as they tried to integrate Mexico's various peoples into a unitary whole. Consulates in San Diego, San Antonio, and El Paso may have seemed to be the locus of integration discourses of the postrevolutionary Mexican state, but these were only one small part of a much larger state policy framework that was expanding its integrationist reach throughout the republic between 1920 and 1940. Along the entire length of the U.S.-Mexico border where the SRE had flagged racial segregation in U.S. schools, for example, a related project in racial integration was taking place in the Republic of Mexico. In El Sásabe, Nacozari, and Nogales, Sonora, new schools had been built by the Mexican state to integrate students into the state's nationalistic project.[20] Farther inland, in the states of Baja California and Sonora, rural normal academies were sending platoons of educators to the rural countryside for the same reason.[21] Not until the arrival of immigrant Mexicans in the United States beginning in the 1920s did Mexico's policy framework start to become important in the context of the United States, with the advent of the organized efforts that would coalesce into the American civil rights movement. But that larger framework is central to recognize for the effects that it had on the American individuals who would participate in America's "long civil rights movement." Second, for Americans concerned with the role of the schools in American integration, Mexico's scientific institutions were poised equally with those of the United States to begin answering empirical questions of social integration. Just as we shall see for the American civil righters who would visit the rural institutions of the Mexican state, urban Mexico City was possessed of an educational infrastructure program that permitted American researchers to study questions of common importance from within the Mexican territory. The SEP had established an institute of psychological research, for example, where it studied learning behavior and questions of cross-cultural mental capacity among the various ethnic groups of the nation. It had established secondary schools in Mexico City, all of which required new specialties in child psychology, educational administration, curricular development, and learning instruction. And the ultimate end of the SEP's project, to create an integrated nation, raised substantial philosophical questions of the relationship of the state to ethnic groups in Mexico City that were not unlike those with which the United States was dealing in Los Angeles, Albuquerque, San Antonio, and beyond.

The third was the ethical analogy that Mexico's integration projects provided for the American civil rights movement. It would be difficult for some to reconcile Hastings's expertise in mental intelligence testing in Mexico City with the ethics of the American civil rights movement. Mental intelligence testing was often used to create new categories of students from a general population and to isolate them from one another in the name of efficiency and hierarchy. And yet, looking closely, what becomes apparent is that Hastings's ideas reflected the second-wave social science progressives who, according to civil rights scholars like Carlos Blanton, Guadalupe San Miguel, Jr., and Charles Wollenberg, used intelligence testing to develop new civil rights critiques of American segregationist practices.[22] As Carlos Blanton has noted, these second-wave social science progressives did not change school segregation or the presumed hierarchy of peoples, despite their shift toward culture rather than biology as the root of human behavior. Yet, he observes, "the implications of this shift within the testing community were potentially revolutionary."[23] In the line of scientific thought from World War I to World War II, Hastings was a thinker who was moving away from the defensive bulwarks eugenicists had used to justify the separation of cultural communities from one another in California and Texas. Mexico was central to the move away from biology, providing policy answers to questions of pluralism that became organic to her work. Her career in assimilation practices unfolded from within the policy choices the Mexican state made, before becoming part of the arguments that emerged in one the canonical civil rights cases of the American West in 1930.

Language and Experience in New Mexico

If Montana Hastings's research in Mexico City had come from her interest in the relationship between intelligence testing and assimilation in the United States, Loyd Tireman's trajectory toward Mexico's scientific state hinged on the relationship of assimilation in New Mexico to one of the turning points of twentieth-century psychology. While the use of language to read and write seemed like ordinary experiences in industrial society, language first required a mastery of the thousands of associations between words and the objects to which they corresponded. The process through which the mind apprehended words, furthermore, involved both the brain as a physical organ and the environment in which an individual acted. How did the mind make such associations from the raw stuff of biology and the environment that surrounded the person, researchers wondered. And if language acquisition required repetitive, cumulative, and ongoing training throughout the human lifespan, could human beings intervene to make comprehension faster and more meaningful?[24]

Tireman and the psychologists who had trained him had shifted their answers to these questions in light of the radical new way in how they perceived the mind. Scientists had previously believed the mind was a fixed reservoir of dormant power. Language then occurred when stimuli in the world activated meaning that was presumed to reside latently there. But such an explanation failed, Tireman and his colleagues believed, because it did not explain how meaning had found its way into the mind in the first place. With Dewey and other pragmatist psychologists, Tireman and his cohort of similarly minded scientists instead began popularizing the idea that the brain was not a vessel that had been filled beforehand, but an organ that created associations gradually, through repeated use. Words corresponded to objects and people who existed in the physical realm outside the body, but the association between symbol and object quickened over time only when an action made that association unique among all other associations in the environment. Such associations were formed through repetition, when experiences in the world presented new situations that needed explanation. Those associations were not curious artifacts of the social scientific mind, either. They were also central to the way that people communicated with one another across the cultural boundaries that separated them.

Tireman came into contact with Dewey's ideas as this transformation in the understanding of the mind converged with his study of language in the public schools. He was training in child psychology at the University of Missouri's University School at the same time that Dewey was profiling it as one of America's top experimental schools in *Schools of Tomorrow*.[25] His advisor, Ernest Horn, had studied under Dewey at Columbia's Teachers College. It was at the laboratory school that Horn subsequently established at the University of Iowa, where Tireman received his own Ph.D. in psychology.[26] Under the influences of these laboratory schools, Tireman's career culminated when he established a laboratory school of his own at the University of New Mexico in Albuquerque in 1927.

Tireman's New Mexico school has never attracted as much attention as the nation's most famous laboratory schools, but alongside the Francis Parker School of San Diego, it was one of the most remarkable training schools ever established in the American West. Beginning in 1930 as he opened the San José Experimental School in the rural community of San José, five miles from the University of New Mexico in Albuquerque, and continuing through 1937 amid financial difficulties and imperfect test results, Tireman experimented with language and the ethics of assimilation during the decade of the 1930s.[27] San José became one node in the loose network of schools in the American West influenced by Columbia University, applying the same theories in psychology and language acquisition in New Mexico that Mexico's scientists were working on as they sought to craft a new relationship between cultural difference and the state in postrevolutionary Mexico. San José's concerns with language and social cohesion catapulted Tireman to postrevolutionary Mexico's school reform movements. And it became the platform for experiments in rural conflict that led Tireman to the integrationist campaigns of the civil rights movement. Scholars have sometimes portrayed San José as a bilingual academy analogous to others in contemporary U.S. society. But it is better understood as an experimental school that fused the study of psychology with the study of language in an era when foreign-language students rarely benefited from the insights of the school models Dewey had helped to pioneer.

Tireman's notes at the University of New Mexico preserved the new understandings of language and the mind that he had brought with him to the American West from the universities of the east where they had been developed. On file at the University of New Mexico Southwest Research Center are thirty years of explanations that reflected the changed understanding of the mind's relationship to language. He often emphasized in his lectures that language acquisition had once been wrongly attributed to a haphazard process:

> Not so many years ago we used the alphabet method in teaching beginners to read. The child had to start from the printed symbol; from this he was led to the spelling of the word; from the spelling to [the word-sounds that are familiar to him]; from this point, having the ability to pronounce the word, he was taken directly to "oral reading"—that is he was taught to pronounce the words in the

sequence in which they were printed in his book. There was occa-
sionally some connection between the oral symbol and its meaning,
but this was left more or less to chance. If the pupil pronounced his
words well, he was considered a good reader. Reading meant to call
words.[28]

What was missing in this outdated model, he told his students, was the
importance of felt experience. A child might spell the symbol "radio," but
until one had the experience of the radio its meaning remained unfulfilled.
To know what a radio was required that one first hear it as it linked people
together in communication across empty space. Any comprehension of the
idea latent in the symbol was otherwise left to chance. It remained an
abstraction whose meaning had no content. Tireman's papers also reflected
the work of theorists at Columbia University who had provided the intellectual bridge for his work. Montana Hastings's own teacher, Edward Thorndike, was prominent in Tireman's library of language studies, and Tireman
made frequent references to related work in psychology by John Dewey,
William James, and G. Stanley Hall. Tireman also preserved those publications marking the movement of the new psychology into the domains of
America's educational psychologists and progressive educators. "No information can be gained from the printed page, no pleasure shared, and no
adequate emotional response felt by a reader who does not first get the
thought," one piece read.[29] *Reading is thinking. All other things that have
attached themselves to the name are imposters. That is the New Viewpoint.*"[30] Another pamphlet concurred. "Reading is not a subject but
instead is a process of thinking, reasoning, or experiencing."[31]

The studies in experience that connected his work in New Mexico to
Columbia University did not prevent Tireman's arrival in Albuquerque
from being a frustrating one. A long history of immigration from Germany,
Wales, and Norway to northeastern Iowa had provided the ethnic diversity
out of which his original interest in the relationship between language and
social ethics had been formed in Iowa, as evidenced by one of his earlier
writings, "The Immigration Problem."[32] Much later, these Iowa immigrant
communities where Tireman worked would make national headlines, when
immigrant Mexican laborers in Postville would be kicked out of the United
States while in the employ of Hassidic Jews who had built a kosher meat
industry for the domestic Jewish market.[33] Still, despite his experience with
immigrants in the Midwest, he found 1930s New Mexico otherworldly, a

cultural province he once equated to taking a magic carpet ride to Baghdad.[34] At the root of his discomfort was the strong presence of Spanish as the dominant language of rural New Mexico. Spanish was foreign to him, just as English was foreign to rural New Mexico, and Tireman had never trained to teach children who communicated in Spanish. Given his training in the new psychology, Tireman was also confronted by systems of experience that were alien to him. To call words in Spanish was one thing, he knew; to learn the experiences they reflected was quite another.

Still, New Mexico's progressive impulse made the state the most fertile ground in the American West for the melting pot questions that later pushed Tireman and his colleagues into the World War II integration movement. It was in New Mexico that Montana Hastings had experimented with the American melting pot before heading for California and Mexico City. It was in New Mexico where Tireman built the only laboratory school in the nation to focus on the Spanish-speaking students who were entering America's schools. It was in New Mexico where Sánchez first theorized the ideas of desegregation that characterized his later civil rights work in Texas, as we shall see. Much later, scholars would configure California, Texas, and Arizona as the provinces that framed the legal debates over segregated schooling in the American West. But of the states in the American West, it was New Mexico, where no civil rights lawsuit ever took place, where the social scientists of the West's desegregation cases performed the intellectual labor on which the legal campaigns of the civil rights movement were based. Sánchez and Tireman would remain friends and colleagues long after their mutual tenure studying integration in New Mexico had ended, alongside other intellectuals with whom they forged professional relationships in New Mexico. Few scholars would recognize it, but the work they had performed together in New Mexico became the basis for their joint endeavors in civil rights as late as 1950.

As early as 1920, university president James Zimmerman had rebuilt the University of New Mexico academic foundations along progressive currents in political science, psychology, and history. He was a Columbia University-trained political scientist whose familiarity with the laboratory schools there and at the University of Missouri prior to his arrival in New Mexico mirrored Tireman's experience with the new education models with which John Dewey became synonymous.[35] Without Zimmerman's support or that of his predecessor, Spence Hill, San José Experimental School would not have succeeded financially.[36] Zimmerman was central to the support from the General Education Board (GEB) that made the San José operation feasible through the 1930s. The GEB had long been interested in elementary schools in rural Black America, but it was Zimmerman who helped convince the GEB that it could learn from New Mexico's experience to better understand the challenges of Black-white relations in the New South:

> In recommending aid . . . , the officers point out that this is something of a departure from the present policy of the Board, since New Mexico is not classed as a Southern State. . . . Although New Mexico is not usually regarded as one of the Southern States, the officers are of the opinion that the similarity of its problems with a large backward Spanish-American population and its lack of resources justifies this grant.[37]

At his remarkable laboratory school, Tireman investigated the psychology of language among American citizens who spoke Spanish at home. Among his largest concerns was the question of how students used experience in their surroundings to draw associations to words in English. Another concern was the rapidity of language acquisition through elementary school. How quickly did non-English-speakers learn English in the context of the public school, and did language ability accelerate as students continued through school? Another series of questions revolved around the role of government in rural education. What was the responsibility of the state government for educating children of Spanish-speaking families who had never attended school? One is stunned by the scope of concerns that Tireman addressed simultaneously as he struggled with the psychology of language in New Mexico.

Tireman's goals were always more ambitious, however. In view of social conflict among Protestant whites and Catholic Hispanos in New Mexico, Tireman sought to use language as a harmonizing instrument for solving the conflicts of rural New Mexico society. "In a word," he wrote in 1933, "the [San José] project is an attempt, not only to find a satisfactory solution of a real educational problem, but aspires, through educational channels, to solve the broader bi-racial problem of the Southwest."[38] There were no melting pot metaphors in Tireman's formulation of New Mexico's "bi-racial problem," but the concern with assimilationist ethics that would characterize his study of language throughout his career was clear nonetheless. Tireman's concern with the role of language in solving social conflict provided one early clue to his political role in the civil rights movement of the American West after World War II. Many years later, as the legal campaigns of the desegregation movements were underway in the American West, Tireman would make clear the philosophical link between his study of experience in language in the 1930s and the American integration movement in the 1940s. When Sánchez asked him in 1948 to testify in the legal case that desegregated the elementary schools of Texas for Mexican Americans, *Delgado v. Bastrop* (1948), Tireman responded with an answer that scholars of civil rights in the West would have easily understood. "I do believe that children who do not speak English should be grouped in separate classes within the same building from those who do speak English until they have acquired an English vocabulary of from three hundred to five hundred words," he wrote to Sánchez. "Then I favor their incorporation in the regular classes of the school."[39] Tireman's response reflected what scholars of civil rights have long underscored. The study of language was a central component of 1940s integration battles because school officials justified segregation on the basis of language deficiencies even as integrationist lawyers argued that race or ethnicity was the guiding rationale around which state officials had acted. But Tireman's observations about language in the civil rights cases did not emerge overnight. It came from twenty years of language study at San José.

The ethics that guided Tireman as he struggled with assimilation reflected those of the laboratory schools Dewey represented during his early career rather than those of the efficiency educators and child-centered theorists like William Kilpatrick, George Counts, and Edward Thorndike who also influenced him. Like Dewey, these other thinkers were firmly rooted in the scientific tradition. But like Dewey, Tireman avoided extremes of interpretation in favor of an approach that emphasized experimental skepticism. Where Counts expected that the school would transform national society through teachers acting as a vanguard of radical change, Tireman, like Dewey, believed in small adjustments created by a plurality rather than instantaneous change commanded by phalanxes of educators.[40] Where Thorndike created a mechanistic model of human knowledge that made little room for contingency in the development of comprehension, Tireman, like Dewey, interpreted knowledge as subject to will and value.[41] Where Kilpatrick developed a project method of pedagogy that Dewey later criticized, Tireman refused to create a one size fits all solution to the challenges of language acquisition.[42] Herbert Kliebard has argued that John Dewey's ideas "hovered" above the thinkers of progressive education, serving as a benchmark from which social scientists and educators took their cues for social and educational reform rather than as a ready-made portfolio of commitments that others adopted wholesale.[43] Following Kliebard, Tireman was not a carbon copy of Dewey's own mind, but Dewey's sense of ethics hovered over Tireman all his life.

Tireman was always more interested than his integrationist colleagues in the relationship between immediate experience and psychology as the primary gateway to social ethics. As San José was entering its third year in 1933, for instance, Tireman underscored the importance of experience to thought when he copied Dewey's 1910 text on the psychology of the mind, *How We Think*, into his notes:

Felt difficulty
Location and definition
Suggestions of possible solutions
Development by reasoning
Further observation and experience leading to its acceptance or
    rejection[44]

Yet Tireman's deep concern with the relationship between experience and the psychology of language should not obscure his concern with moral values, just as it is impossible to separate Dewey's psychology from his concern with the formation of social ethics. Dewey hovered above Tireman all his life, beginning with the Deweyan mentorship of his teachers in the Midwest, to the ethics and experimentalism that guided his work at San José, to the Dewey-inspired community school that Tireman would later establish in New Mexico in the 1940s. Throughout, his pedagogy and ethics reflected Dewey's understanding of the acquisition of knowledge in the modern world, including the cultivation of science for the development of contingent truth and the belief in social consensus as the platform for the elimination of social conflict in industrial society. These beliefs were in full display at the San José school. New Mexico's social challenges required creative, vibrant thought, articulated across the social communities that manifested the problem, and San José represented Tireman's attempts to craft a participatory curriculum that attempted to take advantage of the importance of experience to the cultivation of social and physical knowledge. It was Tireman's immersion in Dewey's thought, furthermore, that would also explain the connections to postrevolutionary Mexican education that Tireman made beginning in 1931.

Actopan in Tireman's *The Rural Schools of Mexico*

Tireman's plunge into Mexico's rural schools in 1931 resulted from the frustrations at San José. Tireman had become convinced of the broad approach he had set for himself after he had familiarized himself with the schools of New Mexico. Despite the skepticism of most, the confidence others had expressed in his institutionalist approach to the ethical challenges of modern New Mexico society had made him optimistic: "[Tireman] is director of a project which will do more to bring the Spanish-American and the Anglo-American together than any other thing that is being done in the state," the county superintendent in Albuquerque had said of his work in late 1930. "You will be glad to know that the people of the community where San José is located are becoming prouder of their school every day," he told Leo Favrot of the GEB.[45] "We are trying to build up this sentiment so that if we wish to do any radical experimenting in the years to come, they will have confidence in us," Tireman told the GEB.[46] His tenacity and that of his staff were striking.

Yet even as he charged forward at San José there were mounting concerns. Rural New Mexico was thousands of square miles of isolated terrain where rural teachers worked alone for long periods of time, but the scholarship system he had designed to eliminate the wide distances between New Mexico's rural villages and the San José Laboratory School by bringing young teachers to Albuquerque was not working: "we had some young teachers who were rather poorly prepared," he wrote. "At times we were quite at a loss as to how to proceed."[47] Within six months, Tireman had grown skeptical that the scholarship program could produce the right corps of teachers his project required. "We are not satisfied with this phase of the work and plan changes. . . . The thing we are trying to do may be impossible. To take relatively untrained people and give them sufficient training in three months to make an observable change in their method of conducting school may prove to be too big a task," he wrote. "The difficulties must be faced and a careful check made as the years pass."[48]

Other difficulties multiplied. Board members of the San José school had begun questioning the utility of intelligence tests Tireman had begun using, and the project budget had not included funds to maintain rural school-teachers while they were in Albuquerque for training.[49] Tireman was spending too much time educating his board members in the principles of the new psychology, and too little time on establishing a research agenda. And he was being pushed to produce results by the General Education Board. They wanted to know what plans were being formulated to attack similar problems in remote parts of the state. The GEB also wanted Tireman to introduce control schools against which to measure the results of his San José testing program. And he was asked to begin thinking of testing students in primarily Spanish-speaking schools against those in mixed English- and Spanish-speaking ones. His frustrations only mounted. There was already the problem of translating his curriculum from English to Spanish. And no instruments had ever been developed to measure the language characteristics of his Spanish-speaking students.[50]

How long Tireman had known of Mexico's postrevolutionary schools is unknown, but the influence Mexican state reform had begun to make on American scholars was evident in his board correspondence. "Dr. Tireman has felt that a visit to Mexico City might be of some service to him in working out [the direction of a school that is experimenting in the most desirable methods of teaching in American schools the Spanish-speaking pupils of the state]," one GEB official wrote.[51] Tireman was grateful. "The Board was kind enough (perhaps I should say enlightened enough) to suggest that I take the small surplus from this year's budget to finance a trip to Mexico City. . . . This, of course, was very pleasing to me as I have long wanted to do this very thing."[52] His visit to a broad sweep of institutions in Mexico City and its rural environments indicates that he spent eight weeks in Mexico, commencing in late July or early August 1931.[53] It was through the pragmatist philosophy that had been imported into Mexico's schools that Tireman developed his comprehension of the SEP projects. "My linguistic ability is about zero. . . . I must rely upon my knowledge of the procedure in elementary education. When I visited the schools of Mexico I had no difficulty in judging the work because of my intimate understanding of the work at that level," he wrote to the GEB.[54]

In the report he published after his return, *The Rural Schools of Mexico*, Tireman made careful note of the spectrum of rural programs that the Secretaría de Educación Pública had implemented after the revolution, including the rural normal schools, the cultural missions, and the metro-politan language academies.[55] Tireman visited the same institution where Montana Hastings had performed her experiments in mental intelligence testing in 1928, the Casa del Estudiante Indígena in Mexico City. He visited native communities at the base of the volcano Ixtaccihuatl, forty miles southeast of Mexico City. His longest visits were to the rural institutions of the states that bordered on the national capital. He visited the *escuela normal rural* at Oaxtepec, Morelos, forty miles south of Mexico City, where he studied the Mexican state programs to train school teachers in rural communities. And he visited Actopan in Hidalgo, sixty miles north of Mexico City, where he studied the work of the *misión cultural* among the Otomí Indians. Some guesswork is required to complete the schedule of rural schools, normal academies, and cultural missions he visited, but he indi-cated trips to numerous institutions across various states, sometimes on more than one occasion.[56] Everywhere he went, he was escorted by adminis-trators of the Secretaría de Educación Pública, where Sáenz was still working.

Tireman ultimately celebrated Mexico's school reforms as models for the United States, as had Dewey in 1926, but he, too, expressed partial skepticism about Mexico's school-based efforts. His experience with labora-tory schools in Missouri, Iowa, and New Mexico led him to conclude that Mexico's faithfulness to pragmatist theory in *las casas del pueblo*—the rural schools where Mexico's schoolchildren were receiving their elementary education—was uneven and sometimes completely absent. In some rural schools, Tireman reported that "the academic work of the schools [was] chiefly confined to reading and arithmetic, and [was] of a conventional nature."[57] Tireman's complaint was as sharp an indictment of the failures of conventional education as could be had from the principles of Deweyan pragmatism. Many of Mexico's rural schools were failing, Tireman argued, because rote methods of education there replicated the worst fea-tures of conventional math and reading instruction. They were not using experience-based education to test principles taught in the classroom, and were thus failing to institutionalize into action the tenets of experience-based instruction that were a hallmark of Dewey's critique of conventional schooling. Hundreds of rural schools had been established, yet a majority of schools did not seem to be succeeding in fielding the new ideas in educa-tion that he had learned in the United States, he wrote. Instead, reform seemed to have been confined to a narrow band of rural schools. "Since I was not attempting to make a survey of Mexican education, I asked to be taken only to the better rural school," he reported. "My comments, therefore, should not be considered as describing typical Mexican schools, but rather the better type of rural school."[58]

Yet in spite of the lapses in *las casas del pueblo*, some features of Mexico's integration projects were working exceedingly well, he believed. The comprehensiveness of the state's administrative approach to rural education was deeply impressive to him. Taken together, the *escuela normal rural*, the *misión cultural*, and the *casa del pueblo* represented an integrated platform of school reform whose relationship to one another had been thoughtfully planned. Tireman had no familiarity with the longer evolutionary history of these institutions, from the early cultural missions to the rural schools, and thus, of the deficiencies in the postrevolutionary system that had been identified from the vantage point of Mexico City. But for him, Mexico seemed to be building a successful system within the context of a rural geography that multiplied the difficulties of launching new schools. Mexico City had correctly identified that such success depended on skilled teachers who had been previously trained in psychology, for example. It had recognized the necessity of an administrative structure to carry out the successful operation of the normal academies. And neither the training of teachers nor the logistical support of the normal academies could work without a central authority that could coordinate the efforts of the *casas del pueblo* in the countryside. Tireman was also struck by the willingness of public government to support multiple types of institutions that complemented one another and from which successful pedagogy might eventually emerge. In New Mexico, by contrast, the Albuquerque state government had no coordinating mechanisms for reaching New Mexico's six hundred rural schools, and no effort to institutionalize the progressive education theory radiating from the San José school.

The extravagant resources represented in Mexico's schools contrasted with the absence of resources for rural schools in New Mexico, meanwhile. Nothing had been more apparent to Tireman during his tenure in New Mexico than the absence of political support for a system of schools that could facilitate the regeneration of the relationships of New Mexico's people to one another. Tireman had depended on the General Education Board to fund the San José Project because the state of New Mexico had been unwilling to finance the experimentalist philosophy that guided the policy work of the school, for example. Even after the school was established, the lack of funds was reflected everywhere in the system, from rural teachers who had to support themselves while in residence in Albuquerque to lack of basic supplies in the rural schools. There were no expenditures to meet the specialized challenges of New Mexico's rural areas. There was no federal involvement in the education of the state's people. In contrast to these New Mexico shortcomings, Tireman's report on Mexico's education system read like a schedule of lavish expenditures by the Mexican federal state. There was not one field worker within the *misiones culturales*, but fourteen different platoons of teachers each composed of seven educators. Mexico had developed a system of normal schools that operated in various provinces throughout the country, which rural schoolteachers were asked to attend multiple times on an annual basis. Mexico had developed the permanent cultural mission and bilingual boarding schools in Mexico City, two institutions that rounded out the already impressive array of interventions that the state had deemed important for the nation. "As one looks back on these experiments, he is impressed with the way in which the Mexican government has attacked these problems," he wrote. "The federal government maintains fourteen Cultural Missions for the training of teachers. . . . Each mission is staffed by seven instructors and continues for one month. It meets in each state bi-annually, and is attended by all the federal teachers," he wrote.[59] His surprise at the voluntary cooperation of the teachers and their students in Mexico became a source of his celebration of postrevolutionary Mexican society. In one village, his visit coincided with the closing ceremonies of the cultural mission's training regimen, events that included a grand fiesta to which the governor of Michoacán—future president Lázaro Cárdenas—was invited. Tireman was impressed. "Such a [fiesta] generated a tremendous amount of enthusiasm and gave both the student teachers and villagers a psychological impetus," he argued, "which could not be denied."[60]

But nothing impressed Tireman more than the psychology of experience that was at work in Mexico's *escuelas normales rurales* and *misiones culturales.* From his earliest immersion in the laboratory school movement in Missouri and Iowa, restoring experience to the study of language had been his fundamental goal. Action in the physical world was an intrinsic element of how people acquired the meaning that corresponded to the symbols they created in language. But if Mexico's rural schools had not impressed Tireman in this regard, its normal schools were a different story. There, he found teachers who had not only integrated physical action into teaching as an essential component of the formation of knowledge, but who had made such techniques systematic. At Oaxtepec, for example, Tireman documented rural teachers involved in farming and knitting. These teachers presented original mathematics problems they had composed themselves rather than copied from textbooks. They performed skits prepared on the spot, and strengthened vocabulary by singing songs to the accompaniment of guitars.[61] The most impressive techniques at Oaxtepec concerned foreign language instruction, a concern that had deepened as a result of his move to Spanish-speaking New Mexico after graduate school. If New Mexico faced the challenge of training English-speaking teachers to guide Spanish-speaking students, Mexico faced the challenge of training Spanish-speaking teachers to guide Tarascan-speaking students.[62] Tireman found Mexico's answer to be brilliant. The normal schools had integrated action-based learning into their curriculum units to reinforce the meaning of words. Students composed stories that moved back and forth between indigenous and European languages. They kept notebooks in which they illustrated their words with pictures and diagrams, a task that seems simple beyond description but was a central tenet in the reassessment of the psychology of language that Tireman had studied. Nowhere did students use textbooks during instruction, but rather, the raw ingredients that were found in the immediate environment. It was a system whose simplicity was as impressive as its connection to the regional community was organic. Tireman was similarly impressed with the efforts of the cultural missionaries from Moisés Sáenz's teaching corps to reinforce theory with practice. "Each of the professors of the Mission took his group [of teachers] and started out to investigate the needs of [a] particular village," he wrote. The missions completed their lessons by drawing their students into practical activities that reinforced the intellectual work at hand: "I visited the Mission again and found that the work [I had earlier seen] was being crystallized. The teacher of music had formed an orchestra of some thirty pieces. He also had a class of children organized and was planning to visit nearby towns searching for folk dances."[63]

The Progressive Education Association underscored Tireman's sense that "experience" was being used to strengthen the fabric of local community when they studied the cultural missions in 1932. Since 1926, American Catherine Vesta Sturges had traveled out of Mexico City to the provinces of the republic alongside the six other teachers who made up the platoon of one of Mexico's cultural missions. Like Montana Hastings before her,

Sturges had become an employee of the Mexican state in 1926, when Moisés Sáenz had offered her the position of social worker in the first cultural mission that he supervised out of Mexico City. In Mexico, she appeared often in the photographs of the annual reports that the SEP presented to the congress of the republic, alongside her colleagues in the cultural mission to which she had been assigned. One remarkable photo shows her in the company of a rural schoolteacher on a hillside in the state of Oaxaca, while she towers over the students who surround her in the landscape of southern Mexico. By 1929, Sturges had been elevated to the directorship of the first Permanent Cultural Mission at Actopan, and she was still there when Tireman traveled to Mexico in summer 1931. Her exchanges with Mexico City show that American educators had begun coming to Mexico systematically to study school reform there. "I wish to apprise you that frequently from now on we shall have groups of American and Cuban professors who are visiting Mexico City to visit our various educational institutions and who have demonstrated an interest in the work that our social missions are beginning to realize in our rural communities," Deweyite Rafael Ramírez wrote her.[64] Sturges would eventually leave Mexico to become John Collier's protégé at the U.S. Bureau of Indian Affairs in the 1930s.

Like Tireman, Sturges underscored the central role experience had come to play in the cultural mission at Actopan. "Swoop down now over the tiny village of Bathi Baji in the region which was taken into the jurisdiction of the great Augustinian convent of Actopan," she wrote for the Progressive Education Association in 1932, and one would find that practical activity defined the meaning of education. Three years of great effort had been invested by the community to build the rural school, whose activities were characterized by what one did rather than what one read. A school garden and kiln were being used, for example, in the collective effort to add to the original building. "We find ourselves in the presence of a sudden demand for a new instrument of education," she wrote. "We look at the books in our hand and quail with a sense of inadequacy. We see at once that, to use them, is not what we want to do first." She added: "creative activity, including the day's work, is a more adequate instrument than books in the functioning of education."[65]

The goal of "experience" in Hidalgo was an educational process consonant with the daily lives of the people, Sturges reported in her director's reports to Ramírez.[66] The intent was to liberate the interest of the rural

citizen in a manner that was symmetrical with what she called "the conscience of the community" and "the continuity of community life." Such
goals were also accepted by every member of the SEP team that worked in
Actopan. "Those of us who are here [as part of the mission] are feeling our
way through our labors, even though we are all of the same mind that our
concept of education involves something that is integrated into the life of
the people."[67] Sturges could not yet identify a method of attack for her
labors. How one actually arrived at a convergence between the process of
learning and the mystical concept that encapsulated the "way of the people"
was something that was not particularly clear to her. But she had adopted
the "project method" associated with Columbia University professor William Kilpatrick, as it had been described in the journals of the SEP, because
it was fully in keeping with the "conscience of the people" in a manner that
could be used to support the daily labors of the rural villages of Hidalgo,
she reported to Ramírez. Turning to the same rationale of Dewey's *How
We Think* that Tireman would copy into his San José notes, Vesta Sturges
argued that the emphasis on self-interest and independent thought had
made the project method an important instrument for the work of the
cultural mission in Actopan. Everyone alike, whether one was a child, an
adolescent, or an adult, passed through similar stages of thought: "the identification of interests that came from within the individual; the search for
the best means through which to achieve those interests; the necessary
action or thought that followed."[68] "I have engaged in this type of abstract
thought," Vesta Sturges told Ramírez, "because three years of labor spent
working with the SEP's cultural missions have led me to reflect on the
search for an educational process integrated with daily life that preserves
the continuity of life."[69]

Tireman's interpretation of Mexico's rural communities could sometimes be romantic. He remembered the collective enthusiasm of the people
as he struggled to make sense of the state's efforts in building community
that were taking place in the countryside, for example. "It is almost impossible to portray adequately the attitude of the Mexican people toward education. Everywhere, I saw them building or repairing school buildings,
making a home for the teacher and helping in other ways."[70] The people
were ambitious, he said, despite the poverty in which they lived. Men and
women in tattered clothing obviously suffered from a poor economic situation, but they were communally united in building new rural schools and
providing for their new teachers. Tireman's sense that some of the rural

communities he visited were excited about the postrevolutionary state was accurate for many villages in the states of Hidalgo and Michoacán.[71] There, postrevolutionary support for the national state had been transformed into local enthusiasm for the village school as rural communities took advantage of its possibilities for the local economy. Yet Tireman seemed to assume such support was universal in Mexico rather than based on local conditions and historical relationships to the state.

Still, Mexico's normal schools had reinforced Tireman's belief that experience-based experimentation was a productive mechanism for a psychology of learning rooted in the relationship between action and ideas. The contrast between such practices in the Mexican schools and the system of rural instruction in New Mexico deserved much further study. "I could not help but notice how different was the attitude here than in many American classes," he commented.[72] And despite the uneven and conventional pedagogy in *las casas del pueblo*, such failure did not undermine the broad strength that Tireman believed Mexico's rural system of education represented. Fifteen years later, amid the legal campaigns of the civil rights movement, Tireman continued to recall Mexico's practice-based education as an example that had much to offer the American educator. "Much can be learned from a study of the rural schools of Mexico," he wrote in 1948, "often called the 'people's houses' ":[73]

> Little by little, without being aware of it, the teachers have come to realize that the rural school has ceased to be a place where children and adults learn the alphabet, and has been converted into a broader thing of transcendent social importance which embraces the entire community—young and old, men and women—and which teaches all people not only the rudiments of knowledge, but also . . . how to lead a better life. Henceforth, the rural schools of Mexico will work for the advent of a better society, a more equitable and juster society than anywhere else, so that nowhere shall the disproportion common in capitalistic societies be very great.[74]

Tireman received an enthusiastic response from the General Education Board when he published *The Rural Schools of Mexico* in December 1931. "Your study of the rural schools of Mexico is excellent," wrote Leo Favrot to Tireman. "I wonder if you could send me two dozen copies for distribution among our state agents of negro schools and to such important persons as Doctor Thomas Jesse Jones, Doctor J. H. Dillard, Arthur D. Wright,

Figure 12. Catherine Vesta Sturges at Tututepec, Oaxaca, as portrayed in the SEP annual report to the Mexican Congress for 1926. For five years she continued to serve alongside the platoon of colleagues who comprised the cultural missions in the states of Veracruz and Hidalgo. Vesta Sturges would be at Actopan, Hidalgo at the same time that Loyd Tireman visited the rural normal school there in 1931. Like Tireman, she underscored the importance of experience in the cultural mission curriculum. *El sistema de escuelas rurales en México* (Mexico City: Talleres Gráficos de la Nación, 1927), 248.

Jackson Davis, and Dr. C. J. Loram." Favrot identified why Mexico was so important to the American South. "We certainly need a redirection of our rural school program in all of the states," he wrote. "What distresses me is that notwithstanding the large number of small rural schools in this country, there is relatively so little emphasis placed on the suitable preparation of teachers for them."[75] Coming between his enthusiastic visit in 1931 and the reforms to San José he was to make in summer 1932, it must have been a triumphant moment for Tireman to watch his report circulate across the country.

The Backroad Pragmatists

Mexico's schools "presented a picture that will long linger in my mind," Tireman said after he returned to the United States. "This was proof, to me, of what one might expect in our own southwestern states if the people were given a like opportunity."[76] Frank Angel, Jr., captured Mexico's influence on him in stronger terms. Angel would later become president of New Mexico Highlands University, but he had started as Tireman's graduate student at the San José school. "In 1931, he went to Mexico under a program financed by the U.S. Government," wrote Angel in 1959. "His visit to Mexico proved to be one of the most stimulating and idea-generating of his career. Mexico, at that time, was developing educational programs for the education of the native Indian population. The Mission School Movement was just beginning."[77] Angel recognized what historians of American integration have missed: that the SEP's policies had made a sharp turnaround in Tireman's skepticism about San José within months of his return to rural New Mexico. "By this plan," he commented as he imported Mexico's ideas into the United States, "we will really get our findings into the school system of the state."[78] Months earlier, Tireman had seemed perplexed by the size of his challenges at San José. But by spring 1932, Tireman's visit to Mexico had ushered in the highest optimism for the San José Project that Tireman ever enjoyed. So great was the change resulting from Mexico's cultural missions and rural normal schools that Tireman even began issuing challenges to the U.S. government.

In view of the magnitude of the problem and the number of people involved we are entirely justified in directing the attention of our

educational forces in this part of the country to this pertinent problem. And since the Spanish-speaking people, excluding the strictly
Mexican immigrant, are as indigenous to this part of our national
territory as the Indians, there is no logical reason why the federal
government should not give some attention to this matter. It is
within the last few years that a specialist in negro education had
been added to the federal bureau. It is quite possible that, if the
Southwest would make a sufficiently strong presentation to their
claims, a specialist in the problems of the Spanish-speaking people
could be added to our federal bureau of education.[79]

Tireman jumped on the example that the *escuela normal rural* and the
misión cultural presented for the San José Project by integrating them into
his laboratory school beginning in January 1932, just after he had published
The Rural Schools of Mexico. Tireman found two principles underlying
Mexico's integration policies especially adaptable to the case of New Mexico. The first was a mechanism for maintaining supervision over teaching
in New Mexico's remote rural communities, away from Albuquerque where
pedagogy was usually taught. Given that the San José school was only five
miles from the University of New Mexico, one of his chief problems was
how to expand the lessons of the school to the six hundred remote villages
of the state.[80] This was a problem of huge proportions, given the factors
under which San José operated. There was already little money for administrative support of the project. Albuquerque was not representative of rural
New Mexico, meanwhile, however removed from the city the village of San
José itself was. Tireman could not count on a connection from the University of New Mexico to New Mexico's rural schools in his attempt to develop
his programs for the rest of the state. And Tireman needed to ensure that
regular inspections were being conducted of the experimental work that
was to occur in the remote areas of the state. The second principle was the
importance of delivering ongoing training at regular intervals to reinforce
the pedagogy that teachers had received while training in Albuquerque. In
the remote villages of New Mexico, regular courses of instruction were
needed in order to maintain the talents of the rural teacher. But how could
that be accomplished? He had noted to the state superintendent the promise that Mexico's cultural missionary program might mean for his project.
To this, he had received a promising reply. "The first of this week I had a

long conference with the State Superintendent and the State Board of Education, and it seems extremely probable that they will hire a field agent for San Jose," he wrote to the GEB in early 1932. "There has been such a divergence in the type of work in the various counties that it would seem good business to have one coordinating agent."[81]

Officially called the County Extension Program of the San José Project, Tireman's outreach system was a hybrid of the *misiones culturales* and *escuelas normales rurales* that he established after his return from Mexico to supervise the work of New Mexico's rural schools and reinforce his system of pedagogy.[82] Following Mexico's lead, Tireman catapulted a field worker to the rural schools throughout New Mexico, where she would function as did Mexico's cultural missionaries. Under his new plan, the field agent was charged with establishing a model school in each rural county of the state and with conducting rural seminars in local communities. Instead of once-a-year training in Albuquerque, the field worker would now deliver instruction directly multiple times each year. Meanwhile, the new model schools that would follow would act in the same capacity as Mexico's rural normal schools. Graduates of the San José school would use the new model schools as a platform for future work, under the guidance of the field agent, who would move from county to county to standardize the school program. "The natural geographic divisions within the counties were utilized for the selection of centrally located schools designated as Key Schools," he wrote.[83] "Our general plan of procedure will be to use the San José cadets in these counties as sort of model schools and bring in all the teachers around to this teacher for demonstration work," he wrote to Leo Favrot. "Periodic visits are [then] made to the Key Schools [by the Field Worker]. This time the Field Worker advises with and directs the work of the teacher, [and] each county school superintendent is encouraged to call other teachers in the county to the Key School for this meeting."[84]

What Tireman's trip to Mexico's schools in 1931 had shown him was that he had to reverse his modus operandi to extend control over education in the distant rural communities of New Mexico. Tireman copied the normal school system of Mexico to which the field worker was attached, helping him regularize teacher training in the field for novice school teachers who had been attached to the state government. "This organization of the counties into Key Schools (1) Represents a definite effort on the part of the county to improve instruction. (2) Sets a standard for other schools in the county. (3) Provides a group of teachers publicly pledged to work for the improvement of rural schools," he wrote as he replicated the central models of the SEP's system of rural education.[85] Tireman articulated his intentions for the new outreach program in his San José reports and academic papers in the year following his return from Mexico. In this way, "we may gradually build up a group of rural teachers who will plan to make this work their life occupation," he described in one.[86] "It is [the field agent's] duty to visit the former cadets and assist them in their adjusting their work to the principles they had seen demonstrated at the [San José] Training School," he wrote in another. "[This] work is confined to centers where Spanish-speaking pupils predominate, [allowing] an extension of the San Jose service."[87]

The influence of Mexico's *misiones culturales* and *escuelas normales rurales* on Tireman was perfectly evident in the visual representation he drew of his new supervision system in the report he prepared describing the administrative rationale behind his adoption of his new field agent system.[88] Overlaid on the state map of New Mexico that he subdivided by county, Tireman drew seven tangents radiating outward from the University of New Mexico in Albuquerque to the seven rural counties where the field agent was to begin her work among the state's one-room schoolhouses. Tireman identified "Key Schools" in each county on the map, representing rural schools where instruction in pedagogy and planning techniques were to be conducted by the field agent on a rotating basis, just as he had seen the cultural missionaries of the Mexican rural schools doing in Mexico. Operating on a much smaller and far more precarious scale than those in Mexico, the Key Schools and field agent would nonetheless function in the same capacities as the Mexican normal schools and cultural missions he had seen only a few months earlier. Five years earlier, the Secretaría de Educación Pública had printed its own map to represent the work of the cultural missionaries in the Mexican states of Querétaro and Hidalgo.[89] Except for the geography in question, remarkably, one could not tell the difference between Tireman's map and that of the SEP.

There is no evidence that Tireman had read the SEP reports during his 1931 study of the Mexican state, but the similarity between the Mexican and New Mexican maps was clear. For Tireman, Mexico had fashioned a skillful administrative solution to the challenges of rural education, and when juxtaposed, the maps reflected how closely aligned were the ideas about rural integration that were operating simultaneously in two distinct parts of North America. As had Montana Hastings, Loyd

Tireman had used Mexico's scientific state to reformulate his understanding of American race relations. At a moment when his idealism for San José was still vibrant, postrevolutionary Mexico had shown Tireman how government agencies could be put to use in rural New Mexico, and helped convince him to adapt his project along the Mexican models he saw in 1931. We shall later see that he would put experiential learning in Mexico to work in the American West beginning in 1937, but things had changed for San José enormously after his visit to Mexico's scientific state. "In fact, I think that this is an important a step as the original founding of the school," Tireman wrote in 1932.[90]

Many years later, as she testified in the civil rights case that desegregated the public schools of the American West, the field agent Loyd Tireman had hired as he replicated Mexico's school models in New Mexico recounted the long imprint San José had made on her political work. Just after Japan's surrender to the American Navy, and in the federal courtroom of Judge Paul John McCormick, Marie H. Hughes described her experience with education in New Mexico for the lawyers in one of the canonical school desegregation cases of the American West, *Mendez v. Westminster*. The *Mendez* lawsuit would desegregate California's schools in 1947, but two years earlier, when the witnesses had been called to make their case, it was New Mexico Hughes had underscored for the court. "I have worked in the State of New Mexico as principal and curricular director, and so on, for a period of some 19 years, and worked in Los Angeles County for the past 5 years," she told Judge McCormick and the *Mendez* courtroom in 1945.[91] Between 1920 and 1940, she had worked in the rural villages of New Mexico, obtaining skills she transplanted to California after the end of Tireman's San José experiment. When she was prodded by the *Mendez* court to describe her expertise in assimilation and the language-acquisition capabilities of the Spanish-speaking schoolchildren of California, Hughes rattled off the long line of projects at San José that had only recently culminated in her Southern California tenure with the Los Angeles County Schools. "Have you made any special study of research to children of Mexican descent?" the court asked. "Yes," Hughes replied. "I was field worker and principal of the San José Experimental School of the University of New Mexico, where we studied the problem of the Spanish children, with the help of a graduate from the General Education Board."[92] Here was one manifestation of postrevolutionary Mexico's reach into the American civil rights movement that followed after World War II. There would be other

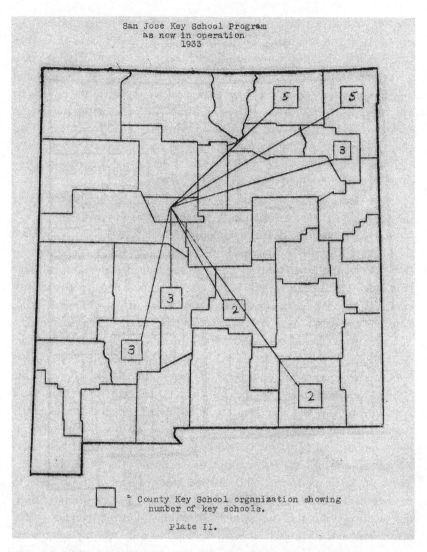

= County Key School organization showing
number of key schools.

Plate II.

Figure 13. Map of the field agent and Key Schools program Loyd Tireman
implemented in New Mexico, six months after his return from Mexico's revolutionary
schools, as a mechanism to extend the reach and efficiency of the San José
Experimental School throughout the 600 rural communities of New Mexico. Tireman
was intent on fostering new language capacities in New Mexico's rural youth, and in
creating cultural communities of cooperation out of the immigrant Mexican, Hispano,
and Protestant communities of the state. © Courtesy of the Rockefeller Archive
Center, Loyd Tireman and Marie M. Hughes, "The County Extension Program of the
San Jose Project," 1933, General Education Board Archives, Box 599, Folder 6361.

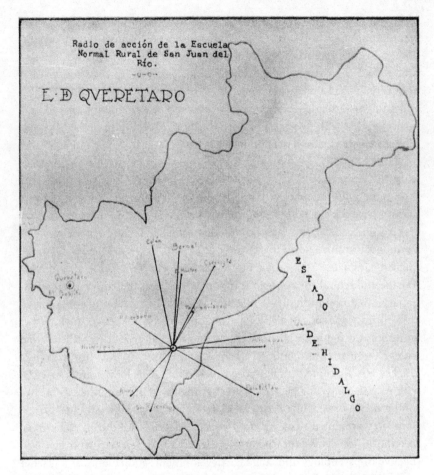

Figure 14. Map of the operation of the cultural missions and rural normal schools in the states of Querétaro and Hidalgo, north of Mexico City. The Mexican Congress required the Secretaría de Educación Pública to report each year on the accomplishments of the cultural missions toward the projects in *incorporación* Gamio and Sáenz had been tasked with completing. *Las misiones culturales en 1927* (Mexico City: SEP, 1928), 306.

links, as we shall see later, but it was the deep research conducted in New Mexico, with its links to Mexico in the 1930s, that became the legal rationale for the testimony that Hughes provided to the federal court in 1945.

Marie Hughes had worked alongside Tireman to resolve the puzzles of ethnic difference in rural New Mexico for the better part of the 1930s. She had come to New Mexico from Michigan in 1920 to work in the master-planned mining community called Tyrone that the Phelps Dodge Corporation had organized according to a new industrial ideal. Elaborate sums of money had been spent on the town, which profited by the World War I need for silver and other precious ores. No school had been built, however, and students attended one in nearby Leopold when Hughes arrived as a novice teacher with two years of normal school preparation in the Midwest. Most of her students were later described as "Mexican-American" children of Tyrone's employees, though it is uncertain whether they claimed descent from the colonial settlers of New Mexico, Mexicans who had transferred their nationality to the United States in the nineteenth century, or were recent arrivals from postrevolutionary Mexico. Later, in far southern New Mexico, she gained wide attention for adapting her Tyrone experiences into a sympathetic curriculum that introduced Spanish-speaking students to the English language. Her curriculum was one of the earliest attempts to reshape the school for immigrants from Mexico in the era of postrevolutionary migration to the United States. Quickly, her system of songs, plays, and stories was replicated throughout southern New Mexico, making her an important figure in New Mexico schooling whose work paralleled that which Tireman was conducting in Albuquerque to the north. When Hughes was appointed rural school supervisor for the local county in 1929, with responsibility for pedagogical experimentation among the teachers of southern New Mexico, an interested Tireman began following her career. Both later presented work on rural educational practice during the annual meeting of the state educational agencies in 1930, Tireman from his perspective in psychology and language development, and Hughes as a teacher of English who had created a new curriculum. Then, in the wake of Tireman's trip to Mexico, he invited Hughes to visit the San José Laboratory School in 1931. By 1932, she had accepted the field worker position that Tireman had created at San José. Her labor for the next five years was outreach service to the novice teachers who had returned to rural New Mexico after training at San José. By the time she joined Tireman, she had been working among New Mexico's Spanish-speaking communities for twelve years. It was from this position that she went to California and a role in American civil rights in 1941.

"Field worker" was too prosaic a description of Hughes's job, for what Tireman had done in bringing Hughes into the San José Project was to make her the linchpin in the cultural missionary program that he had replicated from the Mexican state. No one who has ever studied Hughes and Tireman has ever noted that Hughes was stepping into an analogous role in New Mexico that Tireman had adapted from the cultural missions in Mexico when she moved to Albuquerque.[93] But even in his description of Hughes's job, Tireman replicated the chief tasks Mexico's federal government had assigned to its cultural missionaries. "Through the cooperation of the State Board of Education, a field worker was added to the San José staff in July, 1932," he described in a 1932 report to the General Education Board. "The duties of Field Worker were outlined as visiting those teachers who had received training at San José, interviewing possible scholarship candidates, and assisting county school superintendents in the improvement of classroom teaching."[94] Hughes would continue to work in New Mexico through the end of the 1930s. But beginning in 1941, as she moved on to Los Angeles County, California, she would perform the same missionary efforts as those in New Mexico, eventually using her expertise in support of the rural villages of Orange County that would file the legal lawsuit that would desegregate California's public schools in 1947. When she was asked by the federal judge to detail her experience, she would cite her time in New Mexico with Tireman's laboratory school as the chief basis for her experience in integration.

If there was an upside to the policy reform Loyd Tireman had imported from the Secretaría de Educación Pública in 1932, however, Marie Hughes could not yet see it in New Mexico. Rather than seeing a noble experiment in social ethics that John Dewey would have wished for in the interest of social reconstruction, Hughes saw only the frustrations of a Sisyphean task of converting theory into practical reforms in the six hundred rural communities to which Tireman hoped to expand the scope of his laboratory school. Hughes found terrible living conditions among the schoolteachers whom she visited. Some lived in one-room shacks, four by ten feet in size, rather than homes where they could build a life, while others lived with nearby families in crowded conditions. The travel distances between homes and schools sometimes left no time for planning the day's curriculum, a serious shortfall in a career that required meticulous strategy. "[T]he teacher has no time at school to make preparations for the next day's work," Hughes reported. There was also a recidivism problem. "Returning to a county where certain recommended teaching procedures were not the rule, it was easy to slip back into their former method of doing things," Hughes reported to Tireman. "The attitude of the principal and teachers with whom they were working also acted to prevent them from making changes in their classroom work." Not least of the problems was the lack of equipment and supplies. Hughes carried a typewriter, reading charts, paper, primers, workbooks, crayons, pencils, and thumbtacks with her, but she could not make up for all the supplies that were missing at the schools. "Reading charts made by the teachers play a most important part in teaching in the primary grades but the cadets couldn't make the charts because chart papers and ink was not furnished by the county office," she wrote. John Dewey's theoretical concerns had included the location of the desk in the classroom and the skill level of the teacher in preparation for teaching.[95] But in back-roads New Mexico, Hughes found there weren't even any schools. And where there were, the teachers sometimes could not reach them. "The geographic positions of the other schools made it impossible to use them," she reported at one point. "One is reached by fording three creeks and opening six gates. When one arrives, he finds a place so small there is scarcely standing room. Incidentally, seven of the eleven enrolled belong to one family, therefore, an average public school situation is not present."[96]

Hughes's work as a fieldworker shows us how microscopic were the inflows of capital into rural northern New Mexico in comparison to the much larger resource base that was necessary for the schools to carry out the program of a more just society through the mechanism of education. In Hughes's reports on the Key School program, any mention of an enlarged democratic politics across culture and ethnicity got drowned out because the ordinary components needed for such an experiment to take place were never close to being adequately channeled into rural New Mexico. Following the photographs of the successful laboratory schools that Dewey had provided in *Schools of Tomorrow* at the time that Tireman was training in Missouri, one might imagine the expansive possibilities in New Mexico of schoolchildren speaking to one another in English and Spanish across large work tables, sharing experiences with one another that helped them to bridge the Catholic and Protestant, white and brown, and rural and urban divides of New Deal era New Mexico.[97] Such experiments in ethics did not seem so far out of reach theoretically, given the commitment to consensus and practical experience of these pragmatist reformers. Yet the world in which Hughes operated precluded a quick moral renewal from the outset.

Hughes recommended that San José's cadet teachers should be outfitted with permanent supplies with which they could supervise rural teachers. She believed better teachers had to be found, more money had to be paid them, and closer supervision had to be instituted between field worker and school. New texts had to be acquired for the schools, and the mundane physical difficulties that impeded tangible progress had to be overcome. The distances between the Key Schools and rural schools had to be reduced, the home of the teacher had to be located closer to the school, and more time had to be built into the day to allow for adequate teacher planning. All of these could have made a difference to the New Mexico melting pot. San José's focus on supervision, planning, and control did not represent narrow-minded value systems or an efficiency-minded philosophy. Instead, it represented an attempt with meager resources to accomplish the enormous logistical task of organizing a teaching space where ethics could be reformulated. Hughes herself was committed to an enlarged public sphere in New Mexico, yet her work in Tireman's system left her little room to breathe. How could she remold the outcome of assimilation toward a new ethical ideal, one wonders, when she could not even get to the rural schools where the needed discussions were to take place?

It is ironic, then, that the desegregation of the public schools in the American West in the 1940s could in part trace its philosophical lineage to this system that Tireman had imported from the postrevolutionary Mexican state. For some, the beginnings of the civil rights movement go back to the labor conflicts of the 1930s. For others, civil rights emerged from mutual aid organizations established in the American West to provide community solidarity and social welfare benefits before the emergence of the New Deal state. Others remembered radical ideologies from experiments in the Soviet Union as the catalyst for new formulations of ethnic democracy in the United States. And after World War II, servicemen cited the racial hatreds of Europe and the entitlements provided by the G.I. Bill as reasons for the civil rights movement. Yet for the reformist social scientists of the American West, it was Tireman's cultural missionary system that became one of the pillars in the birth of American civil rights, many years before the desegregation battles had started in the southern California lawsuits. Not for another fifteen years would the importance of Tireman's field agent system become apparent for the integration history of the American West, as we shall see. But when the American federal courts turned to social scientists to marshal the evidence against segregated public schools, it was the same Marie Hughes that Tireman fitted into a missionary system that had been copied from Mexico's scientific state who provided the social science testimony in one of the most important cases in American West legal history, *Mendez v. Westminster*. Tireman would provide his own defense of civil rights, based on work he had copied from Mexico, too. It was in these ways that Mexico's integrationist legacy would resonate beyond the 1930s into postwar America of the 1940s.

Chapter 4

The School and Society

Mexico's scientific state was central to the civil rights career of educational philosopher George Isidore Sánchez as well. Long known as one of the prominent figures of the civil rights movement in the American West for his work alongside such luminaries of racial liberalism as Carey McWilliams, Loren Miller, and Hector Garcia, Sánchez grew to regional stature as a result of forty years of political activism in New Mexico and Texas from his position as a professor of philosophy and education at the University of Texas at Austin. But although he has been principally associated with the American West, Sánchez once wrote that Mexico's scientific state had been the single most important influence on his intellectual and political career. Deweyan philosophy, meanwhile, was pivotal to his political activism. Not only did John Dewey's *Democracy and Education* became the foundation on which Sánchez constructed his critique of public education in the 1930s, but pragmatism in Mexico's public schools continued to be the model of progressive change that he celebrated through the 1940s. These important episodes in his career become evident only when we analyze the influence of Mexico's postrevolutionary institutions on his understanding of the role of the state in fostering social change. That influence becomes obvious when we look at his travel to Mexico's rural villages in 1935 and consider the social and intellectual connections he made to Mexico's *misiones culturales* as a result of Moisés Sáenz's own immersion in the ideas of Dewey. Mexican postrevolutionary reform practices, these considerations show, became his primary filter for understanding social conflict in the American West.

The New Mexico Melting Pot

Little in George Sánchez's early life suggested that he would study policy reform in Mexico's scientific state. He lived in the industrial mining centers of Arizona before settling with his parents in the agricultural villages that surrounded Albuquerque in the years before World War I. He was raised in Barelas, one such community, from age six before working as a menial laborer during adolescence to provide for his mother. When an opportunity presented itself to work as a teacher in a village school in the Sandia Mountains that block the approach to Albuquerque from the east, he embarked on a career in education and philosophy that lasted until his death in 1972. But he continued to work as a laborer on the side and to attend night school at the University of New Mexico, where he graduated with a bachelor's degree in education in 1930. At the University of Texas at Austin, he subsequently earned a master's degree for an educational study of New Mexico's rural schools prepared under Hershel T. Manuel, the American professor whose work had been cited by Mexico's diplomatic service during the *Lemon Grove* desegregation case in 1931. In Austin, Sánchez began to make political connections that reflected his growing understanding of the role of social policy in structuring New Mexico society, even as those connections helped launch a career of some acclaim. In a series of memos to the state superintendent of New Mexico's schools, he urged the New Mexico state government to establish a statistical agency that could track the educational attainment of the state's pupils. The superintendent immediately sent memoranda to the same philanthropy that had underwritten Loyd Tireman's San José Laboratory School, the General Education Board. "The work of the General Education Board in providing for the establishment of divisions of information and statistics in state departments of education in several Southern states has come to the attention of the leaders of education in New Mexico," Georgia Lusk wrote to the Rockefeller philanthropies in March 1931. "After a careful study of the peculiar needs of public education in this state, we have decided to request the General Education Board to establish a division in the State Department of Education here."[1]

Within three years the census bureau Sánchez had suggested was drawing the attention of progressive educators throughout the nation for its studies in educational theory and rural education. As he considered the opportunity four years later to study state policy in Mexico, the officers of the GEB praised his reformist work. "As you doubtless know, I am not only sold on the Division from the standpoint of the excellent work which had been done in the field of keeping records and studying scientifically our public educational set-up in the state," wrote one GEB officer to President Zimmerman of the University of New Mexico, "but I am further convinced that the progressive legislation which we have secured in New Mexico is due almost entirely to the earnest and determined efforts of Sánchez. He has worked like a beaver for four years, and has accomplished more than many men have been able to accomplish in a lifetime. It is my sincere belief that when temporary political considerations have passed, there will be a much clearer recognition of the fundamental work which George has done for New Mexico."[2]

Success in New Mexico led to doctoral work to study the relationship of the school to rural life and lent additional credibility to the statistics agency that had quickly developed a reputation for scientific excellence. In 1933, Sánchez took a one-year sabbatical from New Mexico to attend graduate school at the University of California, Berkeley.[3] There, his work had attracted the attention of Professors Frank William Hart and Fletcher Harper Swift, both of whom had studied at Columbia University with the two leading theorists of American educational philosophy, John Dewey and William Kilpatrick.[4] The decision to attend graduate school propelled Sánchez into conversations with the theorists of progressive education in the United States whose work would anchor his political commitments for the rest of his life, across both Mexico and the American West. When he arrived at Berkeley in 1933, his career was unfolding in three directions. He was building a career in educational policy. His intellectual influences were moving outward from the village school where he had taught to the principles of Deweyan pragmatism. Most important for our understanding of his turn to the Mexican state, he was formulating a system of ethics that permitted him to delineate a relationship between New Mexico's rural villages where he had lived and the public schools to which he was committing his career.

That system began to emerge in the Berkeley dissertation that he completed in 1934, "The Education of Bilinguals in a State School System."[5] The dissertation is studded with empirical tables showing the enrollment rates of Hispanic and white pupils in public schools as a rough measure of cultural mixing in rural New Mexico.[6] Because 50 of the text's 161 pages are comprised of nothing but charts, Sánchez's biographers have overlooked the evidence of an ethical system.[7] In fact, however, how far he had

developed the ethical concerns that would lead to his study of rural education in postrevolutionary Mexico is evident from a comparison to his master's thesis, which also contained a statistical analysis of the performance of
the pupils of Mexican descent in the schools of the American West.[8] Where
he failed to frame the master's thesis as a philosophical project, his dissertation contained a 21-page argument about the American melting pot that
reflected the ethics that would take him to postrevolutionary Mexico.[9]

Sánchez used a mythical assumption about unity in U.S. society to
frame a perceived social problem that he never directly defined. "Looking
back on the history of the United States, the amalgamation which has been
taking place in the 'melting pot' of the democratic education process can be
visioned."[10] It was a cryptic statement. But he seemed to say that a historical
analysis of cultural mixing in the United States would show that the educational process had created a blended unity of peoples. Sánchez provided no
defense, or even a definition, of "amalgamation."[11] How the process of
education had historically functioned as a "melting pot" was similarly not
scrutinized. But this unexamined presumption, bearing a concern with
unity amid multiple cultural geographies within the context of a single society, was the bedrock on which his dissertation was constructed. The social
problem that he never directly defined, fragmentation, sprang from the
premise of the "melting pot," meanwhile. Though American society had
historically created a "blended unity" of people out of diverse cultural
communities, Sánchez argued that contemporary industrial society had
produced an unprecedented scale of immigration that was disruptive of
American social unity. Thus, he wrote, in recent years "the problem of
educating large numbers of children from foreign-language homes" had
become a concern for thinkers and social scientists, since recently "significant increases in the numbers of [immigrant] children in the schools" had
produced a "challenge to educational thought."[12] These increases "demand
solution if our educational system is to function efficiently in the attainment of those desirable aims and ideals toward which its process is
directed."[13] Like "fragmentation," Sánchez did not define beyond "amalgamation" what the "desirable aims and ideals" of education were. After his
return from studying Mexico's schools several years later he would define
spiritual freedom, voluntary cultural affiliation, and cooperative brotherhood as the ethics to which society should strive, but here he danced
around these ideas, reflecting a process of intellectual maturation that he
would not complete for another two years.

Sánchez began at this point to connect the histories of the rural communities where he had worked to the ethical engagements that concerned him. The dissertation had thus far been a universal argument revolving around the dialectic of unity and fragmentation and the importance of education to social reconciliation in the context of industrial-era immigration to America. But he now inserted New Mexico as one of a number of cultural provinces that posed a contemporary threat to American social unity. "There is the Oriental problem in California, the Mexican problem in the Southwest, and the Italian and Hebrew problem of some of the large cities of the East."[14] If education had once made it possible for America to absorb new people and maintain a uniform social blend, he argued, Catholic and Jewish immigrants to America's eastern cities from Europe, Asian immigrants to the West Coast from China and Japan, and immigrant Mexicans to the Southwest were today challenging the ability of the United States to contain the centrifugal cultural forces represented in more recent arrivals to the nation. The turn to immigrant Mexicans as one example of the various cultural provinces that tended toward contemporary social fragmentation was partly utilitarian. He was introducing the case of immigrant Mexicans in the American West to his mentors as a recent social phenomenon that had become new terrain for academic study. Like Paul Taylor's work on Mexican labor at Berkeley's economics department, Sánchez's dissertation represented a new field of academic endeavor for academics who were discovering that the movement of immigrant Mexicans to the United States after the Mexican Revolution was not a temporary effect. In 1930, Mexican social scientists were likewise waking to the new phenomenon: in that year, Manuel Gamio published his celebrated study, *Mexican Immigration to the United States*.[15] Others who had followed a similar trajectory of study included Montana Hastings and Loyd Tireman.

But Sánchez's turn to the history of New Mexico's rural communities was ultimately personal, and here his life experiences and progressive faith became critical analytical lenses for understanding his logic. The concern he had articulated in the dissertation with immigration and the wages of industrial capital in twentieth-century America was not a novel formulation of a new social problem. Instead, it repeated what historians of progressive America have long identified as a central concern of the reformist liberals of late nineteenth- and early twentieth-century American society. Disruption by industrial processes and the movement of new peoples into the nation had helped to define the Progressive era. But while Sánchez framed his dissertation in the Progressive era texts and discourses he had become familiar with through the scholars with whom he studied, both industrial destruction and immigration had deeply intimate resonances for him. Of those resonances none was more important than the destruction he witnessed of New Mexico's cultural communities via the incorporation of the territory into the industrial order of the American capitalist system. His childhood years spent in the industrialized mining centrs of Arizona before moving to rural New Mexico were formative experiences that became the source of his lifelong concern with American culture. He did not provide in his dissertation even a rudimentary outline of how industrialization had affected New Mexico's home villages. But in 1940, when he set down on paper his recollections of life in rural New Mexico in his *Forgotten People: A Study of New Mexicans*, he recorded thoughts he had first had a decade earlier in a forlorn idiom that marked the sense of loss he felt for the destructive trajectories that capital had taken, without response from government, in the places he had once claimed as his primary communities of allegiance.[16] "Bewildered by their failure [New Mexicans] have developed a defeatism that contrasts with their proud past," he wrote there, "a past in which they knew self-reliance and success under tremendous unfavorable circumstances. Unwittingly, they struggle against circumstances that are too much for their efforts."[17]

The rapid transformation of New Mexico's social demography was another source of conflict that resonated deeply with Sánchez. Traditionally, progressives had defined the immigration threat that characterized their political commitments along an East Coast axis, as a process of European Catholics, Slavs, and Jews moving across the Atlantic Ocean into a northeastern America whose cultural hegemony was the province of English, Scots, and to some extent Germans. Sánchez flipped that interpretation on its head. Not Europeans to New York and Boston, he noted in *Forgotten People*, but the incursion of white ethnics from the East and Midwest to New Mexico represented the original immigrant threat, as English-speaking immigrants had overtaken the cultural patrimony of the Spanish-descended colonists of the Rio Grande Valley after the Mexican-American War (1846–1848). Meanwhile, immigrant Mexicans leaving the Republic of Mexico after 1910 compounded the contemporary threat to New Mexico's rural villages.

If his life experiences gave critical meaning to the turn he had made in the dissertation to the relationship between the particularistic history of his home villages and his universal assumptions, Sánchez's faith in the schools animated the solution he provided to the problems of industry and immigration. Transforming the public schools was the solution to both problems, he argued in "Bilinguals," for it promised that students of disparate cultural backgrounds could begin to comprehend the costs that capital growth and the movement of people had exacted on New Mexico's social geography. His answer represented a thoroughly progressive solution to the twin challenges of industry and immigration. Sánchez did not go as far as identifying the specific pedagogical practices, in the context of the classroom, that should be used to remedy the social problems with which he was concerned, but there is no doubt that he believed it was within the educational process that the disruptions of cultural conflict and economic dislocation would be minimized. A blended unity of peoples within a democratic society would once again be the result. "Amalgamation" would spring anew from the fabric of the American community.

One could see what Sánchez's ethical system looked like when the dynamics of his dissertation were considered as a whole. The good society was marked by the social unity of "amalgamation," which he implied was a blend of America's cultural enclaves into a synthetic whole. While the challenge of the immigrant existed in multiple settings across the nation— among the Spanish, the Oriental, the Italian, and the Hebrew—the "melting pot" could be achieved by an educational system that was sensitive to cultural difference yet dedicated to civic discourse and cultural understanding. He left out the question of who should be responsible for compelling such unity, but in the context of his career, it was clear who would be responsible for the opportunity for social freedom to emerge from the tumult of difference. The state commanded the rural schools of New Mexico, and such responsibility should fall to its institutions.

Democracy and Education in the American West

For the first generation of scholars who analyzed Sánchez's career, his defense of social reform via the schools of American society was striking for its promise of ethnic solidarity. For Jesús Chavarría, then a history professor at the University of California at Santa Barbara, and Juan Gómez-Quiñones, today at UCLA, for example, Sánchez was an early hero in the struggle for cultural affirmation. The title of Sánchez's dissertation included "bilinguals," for instance, a term that fit what the new generation defined as "bilingualism"—the right of immigrant Mexican and Chicano pupils to preserve their original language.[18] But the New Left generation conflated Sánchez's approach to pluralism in American society with the ethnic ideologies and antigovernment critiques of the Vietnam era. His 1930s construction of cultural difference as an instrumental problem of polyglot ethnicities in a democratic society was clearly different from later emphasis on bilingualism as a moral right to maintain one's original language. Sánchez did not use "bilingualism" in his dissertation as a noun referring to instruction conducted in a foreign language, for example. Instead, "bilinguals" meant pupils, and "bilingual" was used as an adjective to designate a misfit between the language spoken at home and the language spoken at school. Later scholars interpreted instructional policy in foreign languages to be the central concern of Sánchez's work, but in fact, for all of its discussion about American education, his dissertation is better understood as an essay in democratic theory rather than in language policy.

This generational contrast in the historiographical interpretation of Sánchez's life is important to bear in mind, because it is easy to overlook that his approach to the Chinese, Hebrew, and Spanish enclaves of his dissertation had been framed not by 1960s political ideologies, but by early twentieth-century social scientific discourses in philosophy and psychology that had transformed social science. Even a cursory review of the footnotes in Sánchez's dissertation shows the strong influence the work of the leading psychologists, educators, and philosophers of the Progressive era had made on his intellectual development. Among others, for example, he cited George S. Counts, G. Stanley Hall, and William Kilpatrick, all three of whose work was concerned with the effects of the industrial order on the cultural complexity of American society.[19] We must not overlook these academic discourses of an earlier age as their participants sought to restore an American society unbalanced by accelerating industrial change to social equilibrium, for doing so means missing an important influence on the emergence of civil rights in mid-century America. These discourses explain why Sánchez reached out to John Dewey to eliminate the central obstacle that stood in the way of his pursuit of amalgamation in New Mexico. They help explain his later celebration of Mexico's scientific state as the supreme example of social reform in North America. And they make the history of ethnic pluralism in the American West as much a part of the historical expansion of pragmatism in North America as it was a history of local community in the U.S.-Mexico borderlands. Seen from the vantage point of these earlier ideas, integration and civil rights in the American West developed as much out of pragmatist discourses in North America as it did out of labor struggles and radical political ideologies that historians have elsewhere charted.

To unlock the premise of his dissertation that "the 'melting pot' of the democratic education process" was responsible for "amalgamation," Sánchez turned to Dewey's pragmatism. He had realized that a paralyzing barrier had to be dismantled if educational reform among the rural cultures of New Mexico was to work as an instrument of the melting pot. If some progressive educators like Sánchez were looking to institutional reform to solve the nation's social challenges, other progressive thinkers had reached a consensus, beginning immediately before World War I and then increasingly as immigrants from Mexico arrived in the United States in large numbers after 1920, that the students of the American West's Spanish-speaking communities were innately incapable of reaching the goals of participation in U.S. democracy. "[I]nvestigators as a rule have sought to *find in the child* the cause of his educational failure," is how Sánchez phrased this conclusion in his dissertation.[20] He had to prove that the Spanish-speaking pupils of New Mexico's rural schools were not intrinsically deficient as a first step in affirming that a social process contained the solutions to the ethic of amalgamation. As he put it in his dissertation, "Factors other than innate abilities function in deficiencies observed in the achievement of Spanish-speaking children in New Mexico. . . . It is possible that the low standard of scholarship observed among bilinguals reflects a function of the school."[21] One way to challenge the theory of innate deficiency, Sánchez calculated, was to show that it was New Mexico's schools that hindered the learning process within the state's rural communities, not the students themselves. "The school," he wrote, "[is not relieved] of its responsibility in promoting the fullest development of the child in relation to self, to the world of nature, to organized society, and to the force of law and love."[22]

Sánchez deployed one of the two classical texts on educational theory that John Dewey wrote during his career, *Democracy and Education*, to elevate institutions above biology as the linchpin of amalgamation.[23] Dewey's text was then at the height of its discursive influence in America, and it is certain that his Berkeley professors Frank William Hart and Fletcher Harper Swift, both of whom had trained under Dewey at Columbia, had introduced him to a book that counts among the most important artifacts of twentieth-century American thought. Like *Reconstruction in Philosophy*, it counts among the most important statements of Dewey's understanding of the importance of human intervention in social transformation in pursuit of social justice.[24] For Sánchez, it was Dewey's argument for the place of social consensus, and not transcendent moral codes, as the standard for the resolution of social conflict in industrial society that became important.

Sánchez cited *Democracy and Education* in one paragraph of inelegant prose: "the aims of education in a democracy arise within the process itself and by so doing are sanctioned by and become the measure of the educative process."[25] It was a confusing statement for those not immersed in Dewey's challenge to the nineteenth-century belief in fixed moral principles and metaphysical authority. He was arguing that the measure of educational attainment for New Mexico's rural pupils was not to be determined as it had conventionally been: a priori, based on a fixed standard that had been established beforehand, without reference to the social conditions of New Mexico's institutional evolution or a consideration of the experiential capacities that New Mexico's rural pupils brought to the classroom. Educational authorities, he argued, had wrongfully measured educational attainment using a standard that had been designed for English-speaking pupils in the industrial communities of the eastern United States. Those standards could not be useful in rural New Mexico, however, where formal schooling had never been considered significantly necessary to the social structure. There, students spoke only Spanish. And few had been exposed to the industrial processes of larger scales of trade and industry that had made the school an institutional necessity elsewhere. Sánchez's criticism was another way of stating Dewey's attack in *Reconstruction in Philosophy* on "remote" knowledge.[26] Rather than setting a standard that accorded well with the social ends cultural practices in New Mexico's rural communities had established as important to the immediate needs of its people, the standard had been fixed from without. This was problematical, for there was no relationship between what the community did in practice and what others expected it should know. This was the same logic Dewey had used to measure the value of Mexico's rural schools in Tlaxcala in 1926. As cultural missionary Primitivo Alvarez had described then, Dewey had reminded Mexico's teachers that systems of education had to reflect local histories and local conditions. They could not be imposed a priori and from the outside.[27]

Like the political authority that Dewey had argued philosophy claimed for itself in order to hide its isolation from social institutions and human relationships, Sánchez argued that educational standards in New Mexico were cut off from the communities they were intended to serve. School authorities had elevated a social standard that had been transplanted from geographies of the nation remote to New Mexico into a transcendent standard that did not fit the rural life of New Mexico's Spanish-speaking provinces. These ethical shortcomings were exacerbated by the institutional barriers to social consensus that ill-informed state officials had erected, he argued: "What evidences are there that the major aspects of the theory of education in a democracy have been infringed on in the education of the Spanish-speaking child?"[28] Beyond an ill-fitting educational standard, his answer was a list of institutional deficiencies whose correction was a necessary platform for New Mexico's rural communities to participate in the search for social consensus that pragmatist ethics demanded. The absence of educational opportunity open to all, the failure to use the wealth of the state to finance public education, administrative indifference, and public segregation represented "infringements of theory" that barred New Mexico's cultural provinces from bringing their truth claims to the national culture of the United States. Because the state refused to establish the institutional environment necessary for rural pupils to explore their relationship to society, unencumbered by expectations dictated to them by officials unfamiliar with their capacities, rural pupils were foreclosed from pursuing the social consensus that was at the heart of pragmatism's construction of public ethics.

Sánchez was not a philosopher, and one can make a case that he used Dewey's ideas selectively, not systematically, in pursuit of a political project in the American West. Sáenz, by contrast, spent the better part of a decade wrestling intensely with Dewey's ideas; so, too, did Tireman, as we shall see. It is also true that any number of teachers, educational administrators, and philosophers used Dewey in the years before World War II for limitless numbers of reasons and limitless numbers of projects. Dewey became so prevalent in the 1930s and 1940s that the intellectual counterattack he inspired drove his ideas into the academic closet for thirty years, until their return in the 1970s in the work of political scientists and philosophers.

Yet missing the relationship between Sánchez's defense of amalgamation and Dewey's commitment to social reconstruction means missing the importance of a central pillar of American thought to a corner of North American social history where individuals were struggling to understand social change on a scale that had overwhelmed them. Sánchez returned to

Dewey over and over throughout his career, reflecting for the rest of his life the imprint Dewey had left on his understanding of the role of institutions in social reconstruction. He would return to Dewey in the study of Mexico's rural education program that he would complete two years after his dissertation, as he was struggling to find the meaning of Mexico's scientific state in the rural villages of the Mexican countryside. In 1938, he would publish an essay driven by Dewey's ideas examining the concept of the "community school," a model of education whose intellectual genesis was Dewey's laboratory school at Chicago, in an anthology that included contributions by one of the most intense advocates of Dewey's ideas in education, William Kilpatrick.[29] Sánchez's institutional criticisms of America's public institutions sprang from his pragmatist critique of social ethics in rural New Mexico and represent, as such, the genesis of his political commitments to civil rights in the 1940s and 1950s.[30]

By using Dewey, Sánchez had opened up the central ethical concern of his dissertation, unity from fragmentation, to the realm of New Mexico's institutions. Immigrant Mexicans were not innately deficient, but merely one set of participants within institutions that represented the primary levers in the development of community. As Frank Angel, Jr., correctly put it, "Sánchez showed that cultural and environmental influences were responsible for low scores on tests and not inherent lack of intelligence as had been shown by investigation."[31] Furthermore, pragmatism's antipathy to fixed and timeless ends implied the possibility of a renegotiated educational goal for New Mexico's schools, not an a priori standard implemented by fiat. New Mexico rural communities would necessarily take part in the redefined standard for social unity, because social consensus rather than metaphysical authority or abstract logic would be the measure of social ethics. Dewey had fundamentally reshaped Sánchez's view of society. Just as Dewey had argued that diversity was natural to the social and physical universe, so, too, did Sánchez now see diversity as a characteristic of the New Mexico social landscape that could be harnessed to consensual ends. Rather than a centrifugal force that threatened to destroy communal unity, difference could become the new basis of social consensus. And institutions such as the schools could be transformed into instruments of that social contract, rather than functioning as monitors of preconceived notions of biology or ethics.

But Sánchez's ethical project in amalgamation was only half complete. The theoretical impression of the study had been crafted, but just as Dewey argued that the abstract systems of philosophical thought were often ideal, not real—unconnected to the social world rather than intrinsic to it—his experiment had to be tested in the world of action. This attempt was what Dewey called *experimentalism*, though colloquially it has often been termed "the scientific method." "Process," "experience," "practice"—these action nouns were fundamentally important in Dewey's thought, because testing an idea in the world of practice was the only way to arrive at a conclusion about its meaningfulness. Converted into the realm of education, Dewey often referred to the necessary relationship between ideas and action as *theory and practice*: "The science and philosophy of education can and should work together in overcoming the split between knowledge and action, between theory and practice, which now affects both education and society so seriously and harmfully," he had written in *School and Society*, for instance. "Indeed, it is not too much to say that institution of a happy marriage between theory and practice is in the end the chief meaning of a science and a philosophy of education that works together for common ends."[32] No one recognized this essential component of Dewey's thought more than Sánchez himself. "The test of democratic theories is in their practice, and educational ideas must be evaluated on the proving ground of the educational process," he wrote in 1936. "If these ideas cannot be subjected to the test, or if they are found wanting, it is hypocritical to accept them as goals for the schools."[33]

The split between *theory* and *practice* in Sánchez's analysis of New Mexico's rural schools is the backdrop against which to understand why Mexico's postrevolutionary experiments in social reform became important to his understanding of social transformation in the American West. Despite New Mexico's hostility to progressive change, Sánchez was at the height of his optimism when he completed his dissertation in 1934. And not without reason. He had grown accustomed as a young scholar, fresh out of the University of Texas at Austin and then the University of California, Berkeley, to the optimistic hope resulting from two by-products of the studied mind. First, he relished the attention that a graduate education had brought to him. He was only twenty-five when he left Austin to head the state census bureau in New Mexico, when all his life before then he had worked as a menial laborer and as an apprentice schoolteacher in remote rural villages no one had ever heard of. And again, he was only twenty-eight when Frank William Hart and Fletcher Harper Swift had accepted him to study with them at Berkeley, the Athens of the West. Even Sánchez's understudies at the New Mexico census agency he directed were impressed by his rapid ascent in the professional world of the academy, which had brought the attention of the far-off Rockefeller philanthropies to rural communities in New Mexico. Even more than the acclaim an academic career brought to him, however, Sánchez relished the idea that he was a scientist. He believed himself to be immune from the politics of coercion, because the unending quest for perfection to which he had committed himself as a scientist would safeguard him from the politics of the daily world. Naively, he believed science would triumph, because his faith in "experience" was stronger than the polemics of partisan politics. No cabal of public officials, when made to understand the import of pragmatist ideas for New Mexico society, could interfere with the clear mandate toward social amelioration that the scientific ethic demanded.

At the height of his optimism Sánchez learned the greatest lesson of his life. The Rockefeller philanthropies had already funded the New Mexico census bureau he had directed for four years, beginning in 1931. By 1935, Rockefeller expected the state of New Mexico, as a public body whose responsibility was the amelioration of social conflict, to assume complete financial support of the educational bureau Sánchez had built to national prominence. And, in fact, the state legislature and governor indicated their approval of Sánchez's work, the acclaim it had brought to the state, and the useful reform projects it seemed to herald in the years ahead. Fresh on the heels of his dissertation and with his growing faith in the scientific method, he returned to New Mexico from Berkeley, a freshly minted Ed.D., ready to resume control of the census bureau from which he had taken a leave of absence. He was prepared to lobby for the passage of a state funding bill that would allow him to convert into practice the ideas he had laid out in his dissertation. New Mexico would become a laboratory in social transformation in which he would test in the world of action the ideas that he had equipped himself with in graduate school.

The funding bill on which Sánchez based his hopes, however, never made it out of committee, representing an unexpected development that dashed his hopes of testing practice against theory in his home state. The reformist efforts of the Berkeley dissertation he was intent on converting into action had drawn a counterreaction from legislators aligned with the Taxpayer's Association, a powerful New Mexico lobby financed by railroad and mining corporations that were threatened by the potential costs of projects intended to reform the educational system of rural New Mexico.

The Association was ill disposed to projects in institutional change, and it succeeded through its legislative allies in killing the funding on which Sánchez's scientific enterprise depended. Sánchez was distraught. He could not understand how a scientific enterprise could be so suddenly stripped of its promise. It was not simply that his faith was implicated here. It was that the political forces that had stopped his project knew nothing of his bureau's scientific promise. He poured his vitriol into a series of articles to Albuquerque newspapers that did nothing to bolster whatever political capital he had in the state. In them, he outlined the difference between the "scientist" and the "politician" that he had first charted in 1932, though it is reasonably certain that not one in a hundred persons either read or cared about his formulation of the scientific enterprise.[34]

Sánchez was crestfallen. By spring 1935, he had accepted an assignment to study rural education in postrevolutionary Mexico. Angered, bitter, hurt, he retreated into Mexico full of doubt about the role of government in the reformation of society that a decade of study and practice in Albuquerque, Austin, and Berkeley had taught him to believe in. The Mexico project was a bittersweet assignment, a good compromise to a situation that had deprived him of his hope. He embarked in 1935 on the nine-month assignment that culminated in the publication of his study of the postrevolutionary schools that Mexican integrationists Manuel Gamio and Moisés Sáenz were actively building. "I'd be much happier and, I think, more effective if I were doing this same sort of work in the Southwest," he wrote to the Rockefeller philanthropies after his New Mexico defeat. "Maybe some day (not too late, I hope) I'll discover the way of connecting! . . . Well, you can see that I am thinking about it—with no results so far. It worries me constantly to find that I cannot do what I set out to do—what the GEB helped prepare me to do—even though the things I'm now engaged in are very attractive and are receiving some recognition and success."[35]

Sánchez in Mexico

Mexico's influence on American social relations was never deeper than in the rural American West, but its geography of influence over other communities of racial transformation was central to George Sánchez's turn to Mexico's scientific state. Among Mexico's geography of influence was American

Indian Country, for whom Mexico's scientific state became a clarion call of institutional policy in the guise of John Collier and the young social worker Collier would later hire to work at the Bureau of Indian Affairs, Actopan cultural missionary Catherine Vesta Sturges. For the Progressive Education Association, Mexico's rural schools represented novel institutional experimentation at the very moment that educational progressivism was reaching its zenith in the United States. But for George Sánchez, no geography of influence was more important than Mexico's influence on the American South, home of the original "American dilemma."

For the Julius Rosenwald Fund of Chicago, Mexico's policy reforms had provided a means by which to rethink education in the Deep South in an era that was heading toward the civil rights movement. Rosenwald was a philanthropic foundation remarkable for its dedication to black schools in the Deep South and a particular attraction for international models in education that might prove of value to the United States. By 1935, for example, it had funded studies of education in the West Indies and American Samoa, and it had provided funding for 5,000 schools in the rural south.[36] The Rosenwald Fund had independently become interested in the education experiments of the Mexican state as a result of 1928 invitations to visit there from Dwight Morrow and Samuel Guy Inman to Rosenwald president Edwin Embree. Embree agreed to visit, and quickly it became apparent how much he had been struck by Mexico's experimental schools. His report to the Rosenwald Fund is little known, but it captured the scale of Mexico's school reform efforts in short, precise language.[37] "I was particularly impressed by the very practical programs being carried out in the rural schools and in connection with the normal institutions and cultural missions," he wrote to Moisés Sáenz's brother, Aarón, in 1928.[38] When he visited Mexico, Embree benefited from close attention by the Secretaría de Educación Pública as he visited the variety of institutions set up by the Mexican state in the vicinity of Mexico City. "With Mr. Rafael Ramírez, Chief of the Department of Cultural Missions, I made a two-day excursion to the rural sections of Tlaxcala and Puebla, visiting a rural school, a primary school, a normal school and one of the Cultural Missions," he later told U.S. embassy officials in the aftermath of his visit.[39] He had visited several of Mexico's other experimentalist institutions, too, including the open-air school at Balbuena park, the Central Indian School, and the Institute for Hygiene. The federal government was to be commended, Embree wrote, for the extent to which it had attacked the problems of education and economic development. He had also been struck by Diego Rivera's SEP murals, which he copied into his report. Mexico's attempts to integrate its variety of ethnic groups into the Mexican melting pot quickly became one of the most important influences on Embree's career in the Deep South.

Yet any notion that Embree's intent was to import Mexico's ideas for use in the American South was laid to rest at the next meeting of the Rosenwald Board of Directors. It was not Mexico's scientific state that would help Rosenwald, but Rosenwald that would help Mexico. "The question that has been raised is should the Julius Rosenwald Fund try to cooperate in making possible the application and extension of this school work [in Mexico]."[40] Embree's answer was in the affirmative, which he defended by invoking Rosenwald's work in the American South. "Our aid in Mexico would of course not work miracles. But the effect of international good will expressed in substantial aid to this well-conceived school program might do much to improve the schools and through them to alter in significant ways general conditions throughout that country. . . . The Fund has had a successful experience in supporting rural schools for one needy group—the negroes in the South. . . . While the problems in Mexico are different from those in our South, an experience with schools in one area should make it easier for us successfully to aid a school program in another country."[41]

The formation of Rosenwald's Council on Rural Education in late 1934 revealed how dramatically Embree had changed his mind about Rosenwald's relationship to Mexico. Six years after Embree had suggested Rosenwald assistance to Mexico's federal state, he redefined his position toward the Secretaría de Educación Pública from patron to beneficiary as a result of the increasing difficulties that Rosenwald programs were experiencing in the American South. "In May, 1934, the trustees of the Julius Rosenwald Fund decided to undertake a program of study of rural schools and rural life. This decision was the result of a sharp realization that the traditional activity of the Fund—that of assisting in the building of rural schools for Negroes—was not enough."[42] Rosenwald had historically emphasized the physical structure of the school, but it had now added the components within the school as more important to reform in the South. "Obviously, one of the essentials of adequate education is the schoolhouse. The physical housing of education, however, is only the barest of beginnings. Far more important, and infinitely more difficult of accomplishment, is effective and proper use of this schoolhouse. The teachers, the children, the materials and programs of instruction are in the last analysis the elements which

Figure 15. Edwin Embree's photograph of Diego Rivera's Secretaría de Educación Pública murals, as depicted in his 1928 report to the Julius Rosenwald Fund Board of Directors. © 2014 Banco de México Diego Rivera Frida Kahlo Museums Trust, Mexico, D.F./Artists Rights Society (ARS), New York; and Edwin Embree, "Schools in Mexico: A Report to the Trustees of the Julius Rosenwald Fund," May 1928, Fisk University, John Hope and Aurelia Franklin Library, Special Collections, Julius Rosenwald Fund Archives, Box 537, Folder 4.

make education."[43] It was in the aftermath of its new attention to the philosophical dimensions of education that Rosenwald began its pursuit of Frank Tannenbaum, the remarkable American progressive who Latin Americanist historian Charles A. Hale once called "the first major foreign interpreter of the [Mexican] Revolution of 1910," to write a study of the national integration project that Mexico was pursuing through its schools.[44] Tannenbaum was still fresh off his Great Depression era books on Mexico, *The Mexican Agrarian Revolution* (1929) and *Peace by Revolution* (1933), in which he had analyzed Mexico's schools as one instrument of national integration that also included agrarian reform.[45] He had drawn the attention of the Rosenwald Fund not merely for his expertise on Mexico, but for his social critique of labor conditions in the New South, published in 1924 as *Darker Phases of the South.*[46] For Rosenwald, Tannenbaum's experience studying labor reform in Mexico and the American South made him a prime candidate to write their project book on Mexico's schools.

The General Education Board recommended Sánchez as an adequate replacement for Rosenwald's Mexico study when Tannenbaum was called into national service by Roosevelt's New Deal state in 1935. The discursive connections between American philanthropies like the Julius Rosenwald Fund, the Laura Spelman Rockefeller Memorial, and the GEB with Mexico's Secretaría de Educación Pública deserve more treatment than they can receive here. For now, it is enough to signal that Sánchez went to Mexico as an agent of the Rosenwald philanthropy, whose archives in Nashville, Tennessee contain the records of Sánchez's work in Mexico. He was a research fellow of the Rosenwald Fund in 1935–1938, and it was under that sponsorship that he published his interpretation of integration in Mexico, *Mexico: A Revolution by Education*, from the Rosenwald offices in Chicago. He went to Mexico not as a lone individual but as an agent of an American philanthropy that was attempting to solve the economic and social problems of the New South.

Sánchez traveled extensively throughout Mexico during the ninth-month assignment with the Rosenwald Fund that he completed in 1935 and 1936.[47] In central and south Mexico, he traveled to the state of Oaxaca, Vasconcelos's home province, and its neighbor, Guerrero, where he documented the rural homes of the workers who tilled the land and the federal schools the consolidationist campaigns by Vasconcelos, Gamio, and Sáenz had helped establish. In the immediate vicinity of Mexico City, he visited the states of Morelos and Puebla, documenting community parks established by the federal agencies of the Mexican central government and the craft industries of their rural residents. Farther south, in the state of Tabasco, he noted the patterns of agriculture of local villagers and the varieties of elementary schools they had constructed with the assistance of the government. Meanwhile, beginning with the states to the immediate west of Mexico City, Sánchez visited the north central and northern provinces of Mexico, as far north as the Mexican boundary with Texas. In Zacatecas, he photographed the teachers of a *misión cultural*. In the state of Chihuahua, just south of Texas, he photographed the federal schools in the harsh environment of Mexico's northern deserts.

Sánchez published *Mexico: A Revolution by Education* in 1936, one year after returning to the United States. It was 192 pages long, divided except for a final capitulatory chapter into three parts. First, he critiqued four centuries of political unrest in a sixty-page review of Mexico's history before announcing that the Revolution of 1910 had succeeded in establishing a progressive government. By far the longest section was the next one. Reflecting his own training in the philosophy of education and the emphasis the Rosenwald Fund had assigned to the pedagogy of rural education, part two was a 120-page institutional analysis of Mexico's national education system, which Vasconcelos, Gamio, and Sáenz had been attempting to institutionalize since 1921. It was in this section that Sánchez documented the social reconstruction work, based on Dewey's thought, that Sáenz had established. The final section was a short collection of photographs taken during Sánchez's research forays throughout Mexico. He photographed public markets in Querétaro, as well as the personnel of a Zacatecan *misión cultural* standing in a line in front of the van in which they carried their educational materials to remote villages. He also favored Indians. Among the photos were pictures of Huicholes in Zacatecas and Tarahumaras in Chihuahua.

The history Sánchez told of the Mexican nation was a teleology in which every episode was a prelude to the awakening of freedom for the cultures of Mexico, with which he associated the revolution.[48] As he recorded it in the first section of the Rosenwald study, four centuries of Mexican history, from the conquest of the Aztecs in 1521 to the revolution, could be reduced to a desperate, yet futile, attempt to establish national unity and spiritual freedom out of what Sánchez termed "intolerance, ignorance, fanaticism, and racial and geographic provincialism."[49] The exact word he used was "melee," which he incorporated into the title of his opening chapter on Mexican history, "Mexican Melee."[50] "Through the strife there has been

Figure 16. Photograph of a *misión cultural* George I. Sánchez took on his research trip throughout Mexico in 1935. Dewey student Moisés Sáenz had amplified the cultural missions to their greatest size in the late 1920s, and they continued to develop through the 1930s and beyond. The sign on the truck reads "Misión ambulante de cultura campesina, Estado de Zacatecas" (Itinerant Mission for Agrarian Life, State of Zacatecas). George I. Sánchez, *Mexico: A Revolution by Education* (New York: Viking, 1936), 198.

evidence only of unrest, of uncertainty, of vague hopes, and of the unfulfilled wish to be free," he wrote.[51] The "melee" was attributable to cultural difference that emanated from what Sánchez called the problem of Mexico's human diversity, three stock types of which had clashed incessantly before the recent triumph of the revolution: "the Indian masses," "the mestizo movement," and the "Spanish influence."[52]

Sánchez estimated that Mexico's Indians composed a quarter of the nation's seventeen million inhabitants, divided into thirteen linguistic classes and forty-nine ethnic groups who spoke "many strange tongues and dialects."[53] Indian society had never been idyllic, he argued, since even before the conquest the Indian cultures of Mexico had fought mercilessly against one another. But one fortunate result was the survival of Indian cultural forms. In the villages removed from the seats of Spanish power,

Mexico's Indians had "turned into [themselves]," thus preserving their customs, traditions, philosophy, and language. If Indians were the epitome of cultural preservation, the second archetype of Mexican history, the mestizos, were the epitome of "cultural confusion." The mestizos were "confused," because they had never been able to adapt themselves to the institutions of either the colonial European or Mexico's Indians. One mark of that confusion was the mestizos' existential suspension in Mexican society. The Indians "possessed a place in the order of things," by virtue of their cultural vitality, Sánchez wrote, while the Spaniards, "through a brilliant and courageous conquest," could lead. The mestizo was a bastard child, however, "an unwelcome interloper—[who] did not belong to either of his parents," the Indian or the Spanish. "He was Sánchez in a limbo of social, political, and economic insecurity." But it was because of cultural confusion that the mestizos had become the driving force of Mexican history. Their "spirit of unrest and rebellion" had (1) "contributed largely to the struggles that resulted in independence;" (2) "provoked the reform movement [La Reforma] of the nineteenth century;" and (3) "found rabid expression in the Revolution of 1910 . . . [to carry] through the agrarian revolution which we witness today." Precisely because social institutions had never been molded to alleviate their existential plight, the mestizos had found it necessary to create institutional change in an attempt to establish their cultural stability.[54] The third archetype was the Spaniard, the representative of "a dominant nation [encountering] a weaker culture." The Spaniards had enslaved and exploited during the conquest, but Sánchez found this eminently forgivable, since the Spanish government had pursued an enlightenment project of social unity, or what he described as the "lofty ends [of conquest] 'for God and King.'" "Apologies to the Mayas, the Aztecs, the Incas and the Pueblos," he wrote, because "for whatever it is worth, the Spaniard introduced Western civilization to a New World."[55] That enlightenment project had been the importation of the humanistic scholarship of the Catholic Church. Despite the atrocities of the conquest—"it is true that there were shameless exploiters, brutal and iniquitous men whose sway of power spread like a terrible plague over the land of Mexico," he wrote—the work of the Church to establish political unity for Indians and mestizos alike ultimately exonerated the Spanish conquest. He especially celebrated the kindness of the mendicant orders: "It should be recognized that there were also large numbers of benevolent and humble individuals who were daily sacrificing themselves to instruct, to elevate, and in fact to 'redeem' the masses."[56]

The Franciscans, Augustinians, and Dominicans formed "an inspiring chapter" in Mexican history, Sánchez argued, because their educational efforts were empathetic to the strange lifeways of the Native Americans while dedicated to political unification.[57] "The teachers in the colonial schools in large measure unfettered the hands and the soul of the Indian who, from prehistoric times, had lived in a state of subjugation, oppression, and misery."[58] They also established schools for the growing population of mestizos who were beginning to assert a social presence in the seventeenth century. The colonial schools of the mendicant orders had functioned comprehensively, to educate and uplift in a wide array of social spheres. They taught pupils to read and write; to prepare for civic life; to teach good customs; to introduce the fine arts to the "masses"; to engage in a large number of "successful ventures that was indicative of a general progressive trend."[59] Here he used an allusion that marked the current of American philosophy from which he was drawing inspiration. "Almost four hundred years before John Dewey," he wrote, Fray Pedro de Gante had in Texcoco an "activity school, a school based on current life."[60]

Though he celebrated their goal of social unity, Sánchez was ultimately critical of the Spanish. By the end of the eighteenth century, he argued, subsequent secular officials had allowed the promise of the Church's educational project to plummet, by virtue of greed and neglect of the cultures of the Indian and the mestizo. Ultimate failure had occurred because the colonial government had failed to strengthen the institutions of society, whose primary duty was to reduce social conflict. Despite the best efforts of the mendicant orders, the colonial schools had not had the power to overcome the "indifference" of the colonial government.[61] "Indifference" was key. Government had failed because it had abrogated its institutional responsibility to the cultures of the nation. As a consequence, Mexican civilization had never risen "above the level of past and present practices of Western nations."[62] Rather than attempting to continue to uplift the Indian, for example, the failure of secular officials had resulted in the Indian's being robbed of his lands, driven from his "traditional home," and oppressed "by his masters, by disease, by hunger, and by social and cultural ostracism."[63]

The failure of political unity emblematic of the colony was exacerbated by Mexican independence from Spain in 1821. The nadir of Mexican history had come with independence, because the new Mexican nation did not expand the reach of education that the mendicant orders had established—thus, "colonial education may well be thought of as extending until 1910," he wrote.[64] Social conflict was worsened by the incipient conflict between the Church and state, war with the United States (1846–48), and internecine fighting among state and federal officials that "required all the energies and financial resources that the new nation had at its command."[65] Despite the enlightened work of Benito Juárez and Porfirio Diáz, Mexico on the eve of the revolution "did not exist as a unified nation but rather as a conglomeration of almost independent provinces, state, and feudal subdivisions."[66] Mexicans were, in fact, "no better off [in 1910] than they were one hundred years before. *Los de abajo*"—he invoked the title of one of the famous novels of the Mexican Revolution, written in 1915[67]—"the masses, were still in a condition of oppression and subjugation."[68] Enslavement of Indians still existed; the "thirst for spiritual freedom and land hunger of the people had not been appeased. It had failed because to all intents and purposes it had not arisen from its medieval stage of feudalism."[69]

The Revolution of 1910 marked what Sánchez joyously called the "Mexican Renascence."[70] Like a phoenix, "the cultural qualities that had lain dormant for centuries" were being set free.[71] Even during Independence, Mexico had "submerged native talent and obscured it in the mad rush for the superficial polish of European forms."[72] But now that the revolution had triumphed, a growing number of criollos were coming to understand that "the privilege of the few [had to give] way to the welfare of the many."[73] Indian and mestizo retribution for past injustice had not yet ended completely, but Sánchez thought it clear that with the revolution, old enmities among Mexico's archetype peoples were giving way to a unified social order. He celebrated the revolution, because a forward-thinking government was uniting the cultures of Mexico into a cohesive society, after four centuries of racial and political conflict. One critical result was that "culture" was being allowed to spread for the first time, the product of enlightened progressive leaders whose finest expression was to be found in the rural school that Vasconcelos and Sáenz had created. "Unencumbered by the restrictions imposed by an artificial society and an unresponsive government, [the Mexican] could now look upon the Mexican scene in its true colors."[74] Native art, literature, regional music, painting—all were being liberated for the first time. It was, indeed, in the context of the rural school that Sánchez first used the phrase that spawned the title of the Rosenwald study. "The redeeming qualities of popular education," he wrote, "form the very bases upon which Mexico is waging a revolution by education."[75]

Dewey and the Comparative Melting Pot

The report Sánchez completed of his research in Mexico reflected the intellectual influence Mexico's revolutionary experiments in rural education had on his understanding of the problem of pluralism and political reform in the United States. His defense of the revolutionary Mexican state reflected the reformist themes and social ethics that he had defined in his Berkeley dissertation for the cultures of rural New Mexico. Social unity was permitted by the institutions of Mexico's central state, underscoring the influence enlightened leadership could have on rural cultures. Strong government could centralize, yet still help people preserve their cultures. It could assure the vitality of the individual, whose creativity, talent, and self-fulfillment would help install the vibrant democratic practice that was central to Sánchez's political identity. Unity; amalgamation; the importance of education to the process of incorporation; the role of public institutions in reducing social conflict—this was the vision that he read into *Mexico: A Revolution by Education*, only months after retreating from the home province that had not permitted him to test the ethic of amalgamation in New Mexico. His interpretation of Mexico's history marked the role he assigned to the consolidation projects of the revolution in activating Mexican society toward the cultural stability demanded by the commitment to reform he had cultivated during his graduate career.

The difference between Sánchez's two studies underscored the importance of pragmatism to his work. The Berkeley dissertation had been a theoretical statement that remained untried in action. But *Mexico: A Revolution by Education* was a statement about theory and action, in which he argued that Mexico, in contrast to New Mexico, was establishing modes of rural transformation that complemented the theory of education that John Dewey had praised when he had gone to Mexico in 1926. In the context of his defeat in New Mexico, Sánchez discovered Deweyan-inspired social reconstruction in a province of North America outside the United States. He had made Mexico an adjunct province to Deweyan experimentation in the United States, in effect, by converting the cultural missions into examples of Deweyan laboratory schools that blended *theory* and *practice* into a synthetic dialectic.[76] "The Cultural Missions of the SEP," Sánchez wrote in *Mexico: A Revolution by Education*, "serve not only as teacher-training and social welfare agencies, but in the much more important capacity of *bridging the gap between theory and practice*."[77] This was the most important quality of Mexican experimentalism, he noted. It brought the realm of social action in line with the realm of philosophical speculation, the two working in tandem as part of a reformist effort to recreate the institutions of a nation that was still struggling to redefine itself after the military conflict represented by the Mexican Revolution.

Here was the guiding spirit of John Dewey's theory of knowledge Sánchez had not found in New Mexico. If New Mexico had prevented him from drawing theory into a dialectic with practice, he found in the revolutionary Mexican state evidence that delivered on the mystical promise of "amalgamation" that had been the founding premise of his Berkeley dissertation. "Large numbers of children from foreign-language homes" had become a concern in the United States, he had argued in his dissertation, because they raised the specter of destroying social unity in a country where migration from Europe, Latin America, and Asia posed an unanswered "challenge to educational thought."[78] But Moisés Sáenz had solved this problem in Mexico. "[The] primary function [of the cultural missions] is that of 'incorporation,'" Sánchez wrote in *Mexico: A Revolution by Education.* "They represent the most advanced thinking in Mexico and the actual application of social and educational theories *in situ,* . . . [that] must integrate the Mexican peoples and Mexican practices into a national fold and into a coordinated progressive trend."[79]

The Deweyan "revolution by education" that Sánchez recorded in *Mexico: A Revolution by Education* remained a permanent part of the intellectual framework that shaped his career in educational reform in the United States until the 1970s. First, in consequence of his philosophical interest to create a broader democratic society in New Mexico through the instrument of the public schools, Sánchez's great appreciation for Mexico stemmed from the work he assigned to the *misiones culturales* of the Secretaría de Educación Pública as the levers of social unity in a society struggling to define itself amidst rapid social change. Sánchez had already given evidence in *Mexico: A Revolution by Education* that his thought was still being guided by Dewey, as it had been in graduate school, in his historical review of the ethical antecedents of the twentieth-century Mexican state. "The first school in the New World was established by Fray Pedro de Gante in 1523 at the village of Texcoco," he wrote. "Here the Indian children, Mexico, and the world were introduced to a true 'school of action.' . . . Two hundred years before Froebel, and almost four hundred years before John Dewey, he had an activity school, a school based on current life."[80] Sánchez underscored the importance of the American philosopher to his intellectual development by analogizing the sixteenth-century enlightenment project of the Spanish mendicant orders, whose unification project he believed represented Mexico's earliest attempts at amalgamation, to the Dewey-inspired schools of action Sáenz had established in the twentieth century. But it was the itinerant platoons of teachers that Dewey's Mexican student Sáenz had sent from the normal schools of the nation to the remote rural communities of revolutionary Mexico, in an effort to bridge the cultural differences separating the republic's cultural enclaves from one another, that represented for Sánchez the epitome of educational process that melded the realm of ideas with the realm of practice at the core of his commitment to Deweyan experimentalism.

Sánchez also celebrated the activist state. In contrast to the passive work of government in New Mexico, he praised the Mexican central state as the agent of transformation in postrevolutionary society. The work of the Mexican state defined the difference between social reconstruction in Mexico and social reconstruction in the United States. He made this contrast explicit when he described in *Mexico: A Revolution by Education* the dismal role of the school's relationship to social change in New Mexico: "those of us who are accustomed to schools with more limited responsibilities find it difficult to think of state educational agencies that are actively involved in revolutionary, social, and economic reforms," he wrote.[81] He captured this contrast in the criticism that he directed at President Roosevelt's New Deal program, as well. In contrast to some liberals, Sánchez would have none of the celebratory rhetoric that followed in the wake of the expansion of the New Deal state, finding it shameful, instead, that the American schools had not been brought into the arena of social change. "The people of the United States have never seriously considered the use of their schools as organs for the propagation of "new deal" beliefs, for example, nor as active social forces in contemporary reconstruction."[82] Not the United States, he argued, but postrevolutionary Mexico, was setting the standard for social change. "The front-line place given to the educational missions in the [Mexican] plan of action adds to the importance of these institutions, both in their scholastic functions and in their role of a political New Deal."[83] His deliberate capitalization of the term "New Deal" when referring to Mexico would have been lost on no one in the 1930s United States.

Sánchez's reading of Mexico had deep elements of romance, but it was something more than the imperialist gesture of a foreign observer seeking relief from his political projects at home. When he transplanted to Mexico the dialectic between theory and practice that Dewey had helped him to generate in New Mexico, he was not merely replacing the history of Mexico's rural communities with his own subjective representation of social transformation. Moisés Sáenz, too, had followed the example of John Dewey's ideas about social transformation in rural society, beginning at Columbia University in 1919. In the wake of his attempt to transform New Mexico society, Sánchez thus bore witness to the domestic reform projects that Mexico's Deweyans were attempting to convert into practice at the moment he himself went to Mexico. Moisés Sáenz had already left the Secretaría de Educación Pública, and was preparing to publish the last of the trio of books in which he expanded Dewey's theory of education to rural Michoacán, Peru, and Ecuador.[84] But Sáenz's efforts in defense of rural community and the pursuit of national consolidation were still being widely felt throughout the Mexican countryside, as Sánchez's eyewitness account of the *misiones culturales* indicated:

> While one might speak of the rural school *program* it would be more apt to think of this program as a *movement* for, because of their political inception and their militant nature, the rural schools have an emotional and missionary aspect firmly grounded in the spirit of the Revolution and whole-heartedly dedicated to the Reformation. The words of Dr. Moisés Sáenz probably give the most fitting and colorful impression of the new education in Mexico: "This is the human scene upon which the rural school must act: an abrupt and forbidding land . . . a people learned in the wisdom of many races with the memory of many traditions, tired at times, more often with virginal strength; a confused murmuring of strange tongues, kaleidoscopic coursing of lives and customs; a fluid race, flowing constantly . . . a country of many peoples, united in sentiment, divided in ideas."[85]

Sánchez's travel through Mexico and subsequent publication of the Rosenwald study represented an installment in the career of pragmatism in North America that had been created as much by the Mexicans as it had by the Americans.

Another of the discrete moments in the history of the pragmatist discourse the Mexicans and Americans shared was found in Rafael Ramírez's introduction to Sánchez's *Mexico: A Revolution by Education*. Ramírez had been for more than a decade one of Dewey's strongest acolytes in Mexico as Sánchez was preparing to go to Mexico in 1935. His earliest analysis of pragmatism came during his teaching career in the *misiones*, when he outlined the relationship of pragmatism to rural education in two pamphlets he prepared for teachers and administrators of the Mexican federal school system, *La escuela de la acción dentro de la enseñanza rural* and *El pragmatismo y la escuela de la acción*.[86] Ramírez noted his respect for Sánchez's interpretation of the Mexican rural schools with the most lavish words of congratulations Sánchez ever received.[87] "The Julius Rosenwald Fund could not have done better than to choose Dr. George I. Sánchez to make the investigation," he wrote. "A distinguished educator, of wide general culture and of a solid professional preparation, Dr. Sánchez is also a man of penetrating social vision and of an enormous capacity for work."[88] It was in Ramírez's praise for Sánchez's historical sensibility where we can see the philosophical connection that the Mexican and American Deweyans were making across the boundaries of their nations. Historicism, Ramírez argued, had allowed Sánchez to look beyond the superficial analyses of the Mexican Revolution that marked most contemporary interpretations of Mexico's twentieth-century civil war. It had allowed Sánchez to champion the social changes wrought by the Revolution, instead of merely equating Mexico with the military destruction of the war. Ramírez was pointing to Sánchez's appreciation for the role of history that Dewey had argued was central to pragmatism's search for moral enlightenment. History was not just a record of the past, Dewey had argued. It was a record of experiences to be brought to bear instrumentally in fashioning institutional attempts to reduce social conflict. As Morton White once pointed out, history was central to the social philosophy that marked Dewey and the other thinkers who had revolutionized American thought at the beginning of the twentieth century.[89] Manuel Gamio had similarly underscored history as central to social analysis in *Forjando patria* and *Teotihuacán*.[90]

Historians cannot overlook the simultaneous implementation of Deweyan thought in two nations that were dealing with the pressures of industrial change and ethnic difference at the same moment in the twentieth century. Pragmatism brought the histories of two nations usually drawn in contradistinction to one another into convergent relief. And the dialogue between Ramírez and Sánchez underscored not only that Dewey's thought became central to rural projects that simultaneously unfolded in two North

American republics struggling to define the meaning of social change in twentieth-century industrial society, but that the rural reform projects in Mexico and the United States did not occur independently of one another. Rather, they mutually reinforced one another as thinkers in both nations were defining the role of government in the reorganization of society. Sáenz had traveled in 1919 to the United States, from which he transplanted ideas of reform to Mexico as he sought to transform the rural communities of his postrevolutionary nation. Sixteen years later, Sánchez traveled to Mexico, from which he transplanted the practice of social reform as he sought to integrate New Mexico's rural communities in the American West. The circle was a dialectic, *theory* going one way, *practice* coming another, and the two together represented something larger than either one was by itself.

Sánchez celebrated Dewey's role in Mexico for the rest of his career and never stopped thinking of pragmatist-inspired reform there as an ethical example for the educational reform movements of the American West in which he participated after 1940. "Gante and Quiroga were operating schools of experience . . . a century before Comenius and Bacon's *Novum Organum*, and were showing that their interest was not in knowledge per se but as a tool for the utilization of the forces of nature in the interests of human welfare—precursors of the scientific method and of pragmatism," he wrote in 1942.[91] A year later, Sánchez underscored the influence of Mexico's schools on the United States as he considered his own involvement in the educational reform movements of New Mexico and Texas. "In the United States . . . some of our efforts in developing community schools, the education of rural teachers, and Indian education have been influenced by ideas and procedures which Mexico has applied to related problems with resounding success," he wrote in 1943.[92] In 1959, he invited historian Oscar Handlin to speak at the University of Texas at Austin on Dewey's role in educational reform, following the recent publication of Handlin's *John Dewey's Challenge to Education*.[93] And in the 1960s, he continued to maintain an allegiance to postrevolutionary Mexican reform as he examined the historical roots of the Mexican American public school integration campaigns of the 1940s and '50s in which he had participated. "Nothing has affected my thinking and my feelings more than Mexico's experience— redemption by armed Revolution, then Peace by Revolution," he said in 1966. "This latter revolution still goes on, and I associate myself with it vicariously—from afar, and from closeup examination there as often as I can."[94] These remarks came during a conference on civil rights held in El

Paso, Texas, in 1966, some thirty years after Sánchez's initial research trip to Mexico for the Rosenwald Fund. But they symbolize the importance of Mexico to the political commitments for which Sánchez is best known. He here affirmed the continuing influence that postrevolutionary Mexico had been on his intellectual formation, in the context of a forum on American civil rights. For him, the consolidation projects of the Mexican state bore a clear relationship to the consolidationist projects that he pursued throughout his professional career in the United States. Indeed, though he is primarily known as an American civil rights activist, Sánchez continued to write frequently about Mexico into the 1960s. Throughout his lifetime, Mexico's Dewey-inspired educational projects remained a forceful example for American society that he never forgot.[95]

The Cultural Mission in Louisiana

Sánchez would never again attain the analytical strength that he reached in the three years after he published *Mexico: A Revolution by Education*. He had invoked Dewey only haltingly in a badly written dissertation, using *Democracy and Education* to provide a lone theoretical insight about democracy in the American West. Institutions there had failed democracy because they had failed to place the New Mexican in the webs of meaning through which he had structured his life. But stimulated to the heights of his optimism in the aftermath of his study of Mexico's rural schools, Sánchez reached into the connecting threads of Deweyan philosophy to reconstruct the institutional platforms for American education beginning with two remarkable pieces on the rural school in America and ending with the cultural missions in Louisiana that he replicated for the Rosenwald Fund. He would not feel the day-to-day frustrations of Marie Hughes and Loyd Tireman in New Mexico. Instead, as the Rosenwald Fund put his indignation to work in the Deep South after his return from Mexico, he would feel the triumph of social innovation amid the original "American dilemma." It was the height of his pragmatist career. In his wake, Grambling University would send out its own educational platoons throughout Louisiana, hoping to close the breach between black and white Southerners, just as Sánchez was attempting to close his own racial gap in New Mexico. Looking back on this important interim step in his career in relation to what came later in the American West, Sánchez's time in Louisiana showed how his study of the postrevolutionary Mexican state accelerated a liberationist project grounded in pragmatism that carried him until the beginning of his civil rights career in Texas in the 1940s.

Sánchez's initial philosophical salvo after his return from Mexico came in a piece written for *Progressive Education* in 1936, where he adopted a radical cultural relativist position to attack two errors progressive education had made about the school in the rural scene.[96] The first weakness was the metaphysical character of the educational ideals that had been accepted for rural America. In *Reconstruction in Philosophy*, Dewey had identified the breach between the abstractness of moral systems and the observable needs of human communities as the most pressing problem in philosophy. Sánchez reasoned analogously, accusing progressive education theory of assuming the rightness of urban schooling models without consideration for the vastly different needs that typified the rural village: "The devices utilized in urban schools—characterized by their applicability to large concentrations of pupils and by a high degree of professional specialization—have been, in a manner of speaking, forced upon [rural schools] and are not necessarily an indispensable part of the process of education."[97] A large measure of this misfit was attributable to the lack of resources Marie Hughes had discovered in her rural work as a cultural missionary in New Mexico. Rural areas did not have expensive buildings, elaborate classroom materials, or the specialized activities of the urban school. But such instruments only avoided the question, reasoned Sánchez: why were such instruments assumed to be important in the rural scene in the first place, when, in fact, the standards of life there were different from the urban scene? Progressive education had not pushed hard enough in the direction of its own principles. "While we have expected the schools to fit their procedures to the requirements of their respective communities, we accomplished little . . . in the light of the changed requirements of a new program of rural education."[98] Rural schools were often accused of being resource poor, but, in fact, argued Sánchez, they were stocked with attributes of rural life that were perfectly amenable to the designs of those who had sympathetic expectations for their students. "The rural schools have at their very doorstep a wealth of educational situations which the urban school can experience only vicariously or can approach only through makeshift and artificial means," he argued. The assumptions that progressives had made about the rural school had to be modified before theorists could take seriously any proposed model of school for rural America, he maintained.

The second weakness lay in the government systems that had been orga-nized to carry out the goals of the rural school. At the very top, the adminis-trative systems had to be reoriented away from the measures that had conventionally defined success in the school. "It seems to be in order to weigh such matters as consolidation and academic specialization, not in terms of economic considerations or on the grounds of mass production and factory-like efficiency, but in the light of their intrinsic value to the fundamental function of the school—education."[99] Progressive administra-tive practice may have produced better academic achievement or tighter economic efficiency in school organization and management, but why were such outcomes desirable in the first place, Sánchez wondered. Instead, suc-cess had to be measured from within the social context, not from outside it: "the final measure of the success of these practices must be found in their feasibility and in the effects which they have produced upon the life of the people whom they have influenced."[100] The need for administrative reform included the necessity for new models of teacher education: "it is sophistry to think that teacher-education should fail to take into account those knowledges, attitudes, and experiences which are essential to active participation in the life of rural people." Here was the complement to the work of the administrator. If the right teacher could not be put into the school, administrative reform would mean nothing at all.

Sánchez had just made the strongest case he would ever make for understanding the role of the school as a defense of local culture before the nation. In contrast to the morally condescending tone to local practice that typified many understandings of rural education, Sánchez in the wake of his trip to Mexico made a case for the rural school as an instrument of the preservation of local community in the encounter between the state and the rural village. Over and over, his article constructed a relationship of the nation to local culture that elevated the values of the rural community to an equal position with those of the urban progressive school. Not efficiency and economic production were paramount, but the "cultural, social, and economic standards of life in rural areas."[101] The measures of school success ultimately depended on the "effects which they have produced upon the life of the peoples whom they have influenced." And even though the fun-damental principles of education were "nation-wide," he defended the local community as a part of some larger national community. "Rural teachers must be fitted to live a rural life fully, so that, by so living they will almost of necessity cooperate with country people in improving that life and the materials which it involves," he wrote. This was Sánchez acting as some-thing more than a theoretician bent on destroying the local as part of a moral presumption of rural unfittedness for the modern nation. This was Sánchez as a young pragmatist, seeking a way to redefine the American national community by making room for people who had continued to be left out of it. Assimilation of some sort was implied here, but it was not to come at the price of local destruction of culture. Instead, it was the local that was paramount.

Sánchez's address to the Progressive Education Association that same year provided a more emphatic retort to the claim that progressive educa-tion had succeeded in creating a superior moral ideal for the nation.[102] Here, he used metaphors from classical Greece to return to the presump-tions of philosophy that Dewey had criticized. "The rural school had no oracular message to carry to country people," he argued. "It does not bring culture into rural life, nor should it propose to teach rural children as if those children were existing in a cultural limbo—untouched by the agricul-tural economy of their communities and by the practical necessities of a very real social life."[103] He was more explicit in his defense of cultural rela-tivism, and more specific on the factors that had historically produced vari-ations in culture in American society. "The problem of rural education is not so much a question of developing a cultural readiness in children, as it is that of coming to grips with the necessity of instilling the school with a readiness to belong in the social realities of rural people."[104] The rural school, moreover, was not a singular institution for a singular people. "If the rural school is to belong in its various environments in the American rural societies, it must first be flexible and plastic—it must first become rural in terms of the total rurality of its patrons." Such variation was not haphazard, he argued, but the product of long-standing features of Ameri-can life. "The American school has sought to adapt itself to the various stages of intellectual and physical growth of children," he wrote, "but it has rarely attempted to adapt itself to the environmental socio-economic variations in culture occasioned by such far-reaching atypical elements as race, foreign-language, agriculture, climate, unemployment, public health, etc." Sánchez's defense that local communities were not to be fitted to the school, but rather, that the school was to be fitted to the local community, was among the strongest defenses that he ever gave for rethinking the basis of American pluralism. In his 1934 dissertation only two years earlier, he had written about the school as an instrument of the American melting pot in a manner that suggested a destructive synthesis of culture. But after his time in Mexico, he began writing of the school as a means to protect cultural particularity as part of the process of national integration.

Sánchez's speech was a less synthetic indictment of progressive education than his earlier piece in *Progressive Education*. He did not allude to the metaphysical presumptions of American education, nor did he divide his critique into a statement of philosophical shortcomings, on the one hand, and policy failures, on the other. Instead, by resorting to a description of the lives and complex environment of the rural village, he succeeded brilliantly in showing the absence of thought that had gone into the American rural school. Rural schoolchildren were not deficient inhabitants of a morally inferior America, he implied, but "constantly developing" human beings for whom "horses and cows, town meetings and civic affairs, planting seasons and gardens" were vital and pressing concerns of everyday life.[105] This complex relationship between the child and the environment had been forgotten, resulting in "make-shift, artificial substitutes utilized to arouse interest in the fundamentals of education [that had made] the rural school a stereotyped, lifeless, and unnatural phenomenon."[106] What was needed was a new educator who recognized that there was no hypothetical child in a purified environment, but human beings who understood their relationship to the environment in which they resided. School activities had no "oracular sanction or authority," he wrote, but arose spontaneously "only as they are worth-while in themselves in the given environment."[107] The problem of the progressive educator had been a school "as we would have it be," rather than a "school [that] should be grounded in rural soil as it is."[108] But a new educator could close the gap between theory and practice by accepting that the rural environment was actually real rather than a generalized obstacle to be eliminated. "The function of the teacher is not to change the rural community, but rather to help that community grow through the natural improvement of rural process."[109] What strikes the reader is the pragmatist argument here for the preservation of the local as part of the new attempt to activate democracy in all spheres of the American experience. This was not pragmatism as destruction. This was pragmatism as construction.

Sánchez's post-Mexico pieces on rural education climaxed politically in the cultural missionary program that he designed in the United States in 1937. His study of Mexico's schools had been one phase of the Rosenwald Fund's redesign of its rural education programs in the American South, but the second step had been a redirection of its work toward improved teacher training rather than new school construction. In 1937, Rosenwald redirected him from Mexico to rural Louisiana, where he reinvented the teacher education program at Grambling University. The result was another installment of the Secretaría de Educación Pública's cultural missionary program in the United States, a model known as the "Louisiana Plan."

In New Mexico, Loyd Tireman's efforts to replicate the cultural missions had produced one field worker who traveled alone in the state's rural counties. Working a thousand miles to the east at the same time that Tireman was working in New Mexico, however, Sánchez replicated the entire platoon of cultural missionaries that he had seen in Mexico. Where Mexico had generally sent seven missionaries at a time, in Louisiana, five outreach workers used a station wagon to visit rural schools whose curricula were the responsibility of the state normal school at Grambling University. Sánchez molded the Grambling missionaries to complement the teacher education programs and supervising responsibility of Louisiana's black colleges, working in tandem with the Louisiana government agency for Negro education that the Rosenwald Fund had been recruited to support many years earlier. Grambling cultural missionary Jane McAllister referred to Sánchez's role in the design of the project when she analyzed the Louisiana Plan for the *Journal of Negro Education* in 1938: "representatives of the State Department [of Education] with the aid of a representative of the Rosenwald Fund started cooperative planning and thinking with the faculty at the Grambling center to inaugurate a program for coordinating teacher-education, curriculum development, and supervision."[110] But it was Edwin Embree who best triangulated the relationship to Mexico represented in the Grambling experiment. "George Sánchez had first been employed for a study of rural education in Mexico, and contributed his knowledge of rural schools in that country and the American Southwest," wrote Embree in 1949 as he discussed Rosenwald's role in the development of the missionary program at Grambling.[111] When Sánchez himself described the Louisiana Plan in 1938, he pushed beyond his earlier pieces to one of the strongest statements of Deweyan pragmatism that he would ever write.[112]

Sánchez began by offering the basic assumptions that united progressive education theorists. Perhaps no unanimity existed in the definition of the "community school," but all agreed that "education" included the attempt to draw relationships between the environment in which people lived and the daily interests of pupils. It could not be limited to the classroom, since such relationships went far beyond the "mental discipline theories" that progressives had thrown out in favor of the "sum total of relevant stimuli" in the environment, physical and mental, material and social.[113] Because this definition of education was so expansive, he argued, there existed no easy boundary between the classroom and the environment that surrounded it. In fact, every institution in the community, from the classroom to the social welfare agencies of the rising New Deal state, from the library to the museums, and from the CCC to trade and industry, was an element in the complex of stimuli that represented the new education.[114] It was here that Sánchez nested the themes of his earlier pieces for the Progressive Education Association in the context of the Deep South. Contemporary rural education had been wrongly organized by values that emanated from outside rural communities, not ones that responded to their needs and interests. But "elementary education in a rural society should respond to the vital forces in that society, to the social and economic factors upon which the society is founded," he argued. This did not mean vocational education, but something far broader: "the outcomes of the school's processes should tend to enhance rural life values and to develop the potentialities of rural society for a richer and more wholesome existence."[115] There was not much attention to the cultural relativism and metaphysical critique of his earlier pieces, but his defense of education as a connection between the larger society and the priorities that rural communities established for themselves was the same. Not abstract principles unconnected from daily life were to be the organizing rationale for the school, but sympathy for the social texture of the local community as it performed in the ordinary conduct of its own values and relationships.

Substituting the American South as a particular environment in place of the generalized theoretical environment that had characterized his earlier defenses of pragmatist theory, Sánchez then crafted a disturbing picture of the results of unsympathetic thought in the Deep South where the rural school was expected to enter the field of battle. By any measure, the Southern states of the Union were the poorest, most deteriorated, and most badly mismanaged provinces of the nation. Infant mortality was higher than anywhere else. A peasant class of tenant farmers and sharecroppers had been produced that could not feed its own population. The typical rural home lacked adequate housing, clothing, and diet, while the schools had the lowest per capita wealth in the nation. Homicide rates were higher than anywhere else, and evidence of political demagoguery, racial hatred, and unprepared leadership was everywhere. "Suffice it to say, in summary, that in no other large area of the country is there so great a need for the rehabilitation of a people, socially and physically, culturally and materially, as exists in the South to-day," he argued.[116] The Deep South had produced a society of human misery by virtue of the social obstacles that politics had established there over the decades and centuries.

To some it might have seemed that Sánchez was orientalizing the Deep South as part of a master plan to justify the reform techniques of the social scientist. But a look back on the articles he had produced immediately after returning from Mexico gives a different view. Instead, Sánchez had created a picture of the social forces of the Deep South with which the pragmatist school had to come into a relationship. Following the same argument he had made in his Progressive Education Association address, he attacked education in the South for being unsuited to the needs and interests that defined rural Louisiana. "It is a sad commentary on our science of education that . . . the South has had to pattern its schools after urban practices," he wrote, a state of affairs that reflected the "astonishing indifference to rural conditions" that typified teacher preparation programs across the nation.[117] The failure to accept the cultural texture of the South, with all its deficiencies and strengths alike, as the de facto context for the rural school repeated the breach between idealism in education and the pragmatist realities to which the school had to be tailored. Again he attacked the structures of administration for their own failures. Welfare agencies tasked with improving rural life had failed to coordinate their efforts and provided obsolete analysis, instead. There was too much concern with control and not enough with constructive leadership. Teachers were badly trained. Underneath it all was an economic structure that made country agents unable to help the rural farmers that they had been assigned to help.

Like the experience of the cultural missionaries in Mexico, Grambling's experience with the missions in Louisiana was mixed. Commentators have had different reactions to those efforts, just as they have with the rural missions in postrevolutionary Mexico. But we should not underestimate what the Louisiana Plan tells us about Sánchez's politics in the late 1930s. Already it had reflected the continuing hold of Dewey's thought on his understanding of the rural school. More important, it tells us something about the character of pluralism he had crafted as a direct result of his time in postrevolutionary Mexico. Sánchez had defended the rural community for its particularistic characteristics, not as something to be destroyed. He had fought for the school as an instrument of consensus, not as an instrument of top-down politics. And he had argued for the importance of a sympathetic state that delivered on the promise of human beings who had been left out of democratic politics. In his pieces on the rural scene, we see the constructive link that Mexico's scientific state had made to Sánchez's politics in the United States, immediately before the social protest movements that would draw him into the desegregation campaigns in the American West. Mexico's state policies had brought him to the strongest defense of the local he would ever give, just as they had transformed Tireman's own politics several years earlier.

Chapter 5

The Yaqui Way of Life

During the same moments that Hastings, Tireman, and Sánchez studied there, Ralph L. Beals studied central state policy toward ethnic communities in postrevolutionary Mexico. Many of Beals's observations of life in post-revolutionary Mexico were comments on the importance of government capacity to foster political stability in an ethnically diverse country. The recent "period begins with the era of violent revolutionary change in Mexico," he wrote in 1943, "often causing great dislocation in the lives of Indian groups."[1] But whereas others might have emphasized the destruction of Indian culture, Beals underscored the state's efforts to modify Mexico's social relationships constructively, instead. "It [has] subsided into the period of peaceful revolutionary change, with government directed efforts to modify Indian culture."[2]

It was the influence the postrevolutionary Mexican state had on his understanding of the relationship between ethnic cultures and the modern nation through which Beals formed his view of the productive capacity of the U.S. central state to transform American race relations. Beals's understanding of the possibilities of U.S. government intervention in the Southern California civil rights campaigns was shaped by the efforts of the Mexican state to intervene in the interest of *forjando patria* in the years after the Mexican Revolution. Why Mexico helped to frame the context of racial change in World War II America for Beals is easy to see if we interpret the American civil rights movement sociologically rather than through its moral role in American political history alone. For Beals, the assimilation projects of the Mexican state were the sociological equivalent of integrating the public schools of the American West. The power of the state was being mobilized by social scientists in both cases to produce new sociological relationships within the public schools of agrarian communities.

Like those of Hastings and Sánchez, Beals's career illuminates a fundamental influence on the origins of civil rights struggles in the United States. Both the notion of acculturation as he had developed it from within his specialization in cultural transformation in Mexico and the integrationist movement in the United States known as civil rights were concerned with the state's role in reformulating the relationship of distinct cultural communities to one another. Beals found his career studying the Mexican central state's work in the aftermath of the revolution not merely amenable to his political support of American civil rights, but an intrinsic intellectual foundation for the political goals he pursued after World War II. Using social science as the platform to understand cultural change in Mexico, he put twenty years of scholarship on postrevolutionary society to work in the service of the Southern California civil rights movement.

The Yaqui and the Pursuit of Anthropology

It was an encounter with the Yaqui Indians in the Mexican state of Sonora that changed Ralph Beals's life forever. On a particular Sunday morning in 1917, Beals and his brother Carleton traveled thirty miles outside Guaymas with two American companions looking for land on which to raise melons. Moving northeast into the alluvial floodplain of the Yaqui River, they were taking the chance that they would not encounter the Yaqui Indians who inhabited the area, though residents of Guaymas had warned them not to go. Suddenly, just as they had been warned, the Americans ran into the Yaqui. As they crested a hill, the four men witnessed a Yaqui war party destroying a railroad trestle directly in front of them. Alarmed by the harm that could come if they attempted to approach a party of Yaqui on the march, Ralph warned the others not to venture toward the Indians.[3]

The Yaqui became famous to American readers in the 1970s when one of Beals's later students, Carlos Castañeda, memorialized their desert cultures in *The Teachings of Don Juan: A Yaqui Way of Knowledge*.[4] But in Mexico they needed no introduction. Known for their repeated defeats of the Mexican army across the expanse of terrain that marked the northwestern provinces of Mexico, the Yaqui had waged a war for fifty years against

the Mexican government to protect their homelands. Their ongoing griev-
ances against the Mexican state did not directly bear on the events that had
produced the Mexican Revolution in 1910. But the Yaqui did remain the
most combative and intractable indigenous community in the Republic of
Mexico during the period of the revolution. In *Forjando patria*, Manuel
Gamio had featured the Yaqui warriors as an example of the regional cultures of Mexico that he believed had yet to be integrated into a synthetic
nation.[5] Not until 1930, ten years after the end of the revolution, would
they be subdued by the Mexican state. At the moment that Ralph and
Carleton encountered them in the Yaqui River basin, they still roamed
freely in the vicinity of Guaymas, attacking government installations, transportation infrastructure, and revolutionary troops.

At fifteen, with his brother, Beals had fled San José, California, in an
old Ford truck to escape the World War I draft. The United States was
fighting Germany in Europe by now, but Ralph and Carleton headed south
for Mexico because of their political opposition to a war they considered
immoral. Once they reached the international boundary, Mexico would be
a safe haven from inquisitive American officials eager to bolster troop
strength in Europe. One might have guessed that the Beals brothers would
have opposed the war. Ralph had been born to leftist parents from the
American Midwest who had left Kansas after his district attorney father had
run afoul of constituents who opposed his antiliquor politics. Beals had
never remembered a time when talk of politics was not prominent in his
household, he later told colleagues. Friends also said that the activism of
his socialist mother and progressive father helped shape the concern with
the social order that Ralph carried with him throughout his life. The industrial unions had become familiar to him after several unsuccessful farming
ventures near Pasadena had forced his father into the Los Angeles labor
force. After his family moved to Berkeley to minimize the college expenses
for Carleton, Ralph attended the local public schools, visited the university
with his sibling, and followed his mother's career in local municipal and
school politics. It was in Carleton's used car that these politically activist
brothers traveled south in July 1917 into the San Joaquin Valley from San
José, headed for Bakersfield, Mojave, and Barstow. The pair crossed the
international boundary into the Republic of Mexico at Sonoyta, Sonora,
sometime in late July or early August 1917. They reached Mexico during
the final two years of the Mexican Revolution, a period of renewed military
campaigns after the temporary peace that had produced the Constitution

of 1917. Near Guaymas, where the Yaqui River drained into the Pacific Ocean, the brothers intended to work on local ranches, hoping to earn enough money for a gold expedition into the Yaqui basin.[6]

Ralph's warning that Sunday in Sonora was proved right. The two Americans with whom Ralph and Carleton had ventured into the desert approached the Yaqui for reasons that remained unclear to the brothers. They may have been searching for information that would aid them in their hunt for good land, or for directions to the alluvial beds of the area where prospectors had recently found gold. Whatever the reason, an initial greeting by the Americans to the Yaqui turned suddenly violent. The Yaqui stripped the two Americans naked and began beating them with their war clubs. "There were four screams," Carleton later wrote. "When I gazed out again, the fiends were beating the two boys to their feet with heavy clubs. They staggered into the brush."[7] The rest did not take long, Ralph recounted. Out of Beals's line of sight, the Yaqui bludgeoned the two companions to death. Carleton himself was nearly discovered by a mounted Yaqui scout, a detail Ralph fictionalized in a short story he wrote while pursuing a writing career in the United States a year later.[8] Carleton and Ralph waited until the Yaqui departed, then left for Guaymas for assistance to recover the bodies. "We found Joe's and Wolman's battered bodies," wrote Carleton, "but no Yaquis. Their tracks led straight toward a sharp cleft in the red mountains."[9] The Yaqui attack shocked Carleton and Ralph into leaving Guaymas for good. Ralph remained in the vicinity of Culiacán for the remainder of his stay in Mexico, returning to the United States several months after the armistice ending World War I. Carleton headed for Mexico City, where he remained through May 1920 before departing for Spain and Italy and beginning a career as one of America's prominent radical journalists.

Ralph began capturing the concern with modern social conflict that would characterize his later civil rights career in a rich series of fictional essays composed while trying to become a writer upon his return to the United States.[10] In those essays, he developed a political account of the escape into revolutionary Mexico that had almost ended in his death. His escape from the United States had been a protest against the brutality of the World War I battlefields. But it had also been a repudiation of industrial systems in the Western nations that he believed had ultimately caused the conflict between Germany and England. In one story, Beals transformed his criticism into a fictionalized escape into the desert by a man too troubled by modern society to endure its destructive influence on his life any longer. "Jim Reeves boasted of his narrow escapes in every desert of the southwest. Years before he had sought the bosom of the great unfolding desert to forget. Year after year he had gone out into the enfolding solitudes to dream his dreams and seek to forget."[11] In a second essay, set aboard a ship that is circulating the oceans of the world, Beals memorialized a young scientist who is intent on freeing "mankind from the struggle to produce the necessities of living." Aboard ship, the young man is taken into the confidence of a brilliant inventor whose new invention promises to end World War I. "Think of it!" the inventor tells the young man. "What a power this would place in the hands of a nation at war."[12] There was something of John Dos Passos in Beals's account of shipbound inventors riding the waves in search of answers to the destruction of modern industrial society. In another, Beals descended into Romantic escapism as he critiqued the sordidness of human society. "Let me do this alone," he wrote. "No partnership do I want but what I find in the rocks and the shrubs and the trees."[13] It was in these literary essays of isolation, the desert, and the agrarian life that Beals gave us a glimpse of the concerns with the carnage of World War I and the scope of modern industrialization that would find their ultimate expression in the career in anthropology that he pursued after 1925.

Ralph's initial answer to the wages of modern industrial society came in the form of farming rather than social science. His father had pursued farming in Kansas and Pasadena, and Ralph had written his fictional essays after spending his time in Mexico working on farms. A climax came in the high deserts of the Imperial Valley that separated California from Arizona in 1919, when Beals held a series of jobs on farms and ranches before purchasing his own land as he attempted to establish his own farm. Intent on writing fiction, however, he left the Imperial Valley to attend high school in 1921, and thereafter the University of California, Berkeley, in spring 1922. His Berkeley transcripts show early courses in English and literature, and alongside, enrollment in Berkeley's anthropology department as a fitting introduction to writing about people. "I encountered in the catalog an interesting course description—under the heading of Anthropology—[whose] subject matter seemed to offer insights into human behavior and institutions that would be more useful [than philosophy] for my ultimate goal [of becoming a novelist]," he wrote in 1982.[14] As he looked back on his career later in his life, the skills of fictional description and cultural analysis seemed complementary, not antithetical, to his goal of becoming a writer. "The games people play for fun or to rationalize, explain, or understand the universe as they see it are innumerable," he wrote in 1978. "Some pursue the illusive quark. . . . Others seek to convey insights into the human condition through the exercise of creative imagination in art and literature. . . . And some devote themselves to discovering and explicating the varied patterns of shared behavior and belief among members of groups that we call culture, and to exploring its part in forming the uniquely patterned thought and behavior of the individual."[15] Under the tutelage of anthropologist A. L. Kroeber, who had returned to Berkeley after studying with Franz Boas at Columbia University, the confluence of Romantic escapism from industrial culture and his encounter with the Yaqui people of Mexico reversed themselves. Quickly, the idea of anthropology as an adjunct to a career in writing transformed itself into the idea of writing as an adjunct to anthropology. "By the end of my freshman year I had resolved to dedicate myself to the discipline which seemed to offer so much toward understanding the nature of humankind and its condition through the discovery of alternative lifeways and belief systems, through its enlarged comprehension of human institutions and the principles by which they operated, its refreshingly new view of human history."[16]

Beals's conversion from fiction writing to social science reflected the same concerns that had propelled him toward his encounter with the Yaqui Indians. In the academic study of culture, he found new forms of social organization that stood in contrast to those of industrial America that had repelled him. In ethnography, he found an opportunity for rich description that complemented his interest in writing. And in the fieldwork he would pursue, he would immerse himself in the cultures of Mexico that had first awed him in the form of the Yaqui murders: "Despite the danger, the experience was exhilarating to a youth already stimulated by his immersion in Mexican culture. What motivated these Indians to fight so tenaciously for their lands and their divergent lifeways? How did it relate to the bloody holocaust still raging unabated in France?"[17]

Not every American who came to Mexico between 1920 and 1940 had as dramatic an introduction to the peoples of Mexico as had Ralph Leon Beals, anthropologist and founder of UCLA's Department of Anthropology in 1941. Yet whatever else he had expected to find when he decided to go there, Beals's early trip to revolutionary Mexico turned out to be the decisive moment of his life.

The Ethnos and Acculturation in Postrevolutionary Mexico

It would be natural to point to Boasian anthropology as the largest influence on a social scientific career that moved away from the moral certainties of the nineteenth century to the moral uncertainties of the twentieth. Beals's career in anthropology began immediately after Franz Boas's sweeping reconfiguration of the discipline through his 1911 *The Mind of Primitive Man*.[18] At Berkeley, Beals had even learned cultural relativism from Boas's first Columbia Ph.D. student, Alfred L. Kroeber, who was turning the Berkeley department into one of the premier anthropology centers in the nation by the advent of World War I.[19] Yet cultural relativism's influence on Beals is better understood in the context of the Yaqui attack rather than through the influence of *The Mind of Primitive Man*. Throughout the rest of his career, Beals continued to underscore the murder of his companions as the founding experience of his anthropology career. What Boas allowed Beals to do was to study dynamic cultures in Mexico whose value systems presented alternatives to those of an American society that Beals was seeking to transform. "The ideas of culture, of cultural relativism, and the diversity of cultural forms were new and highly exciting to me," allowing him to begin to understand that episode.[20] "Since then for more than 40 years I have visited many groups of American Indians in Mexico, Central America, and Ecuador, living among them for many months," he wrote in 1978. He continued:

> I sought not only to discover the adaptations by which they managed to survive in their physical and cultural environments and the varied ways by which they organized their interpersonal relationships, but to learn the values and belief systems which organized their reality and made their own lives tolerable, all following my vision of contributing something to the understanding and possibly the improvement of the human condition.[21]

Beals's study of Mexico's cultures initially sprang from Kroeber's notion of the "culture area." By the time Beals arrived at Berkeley in 1922, Kroeber was nearly finished with his synthetic survey of California's culture areas, *Handbook of the Indians of California*.[22] There, Kroeber had used Boasian theory to build a taxonomy of California's cultural systems, based on the distribution patterns he found of the cultural attributes of the discrete

Indian communities located on the Pacific Coast of North America. Kroeber had just expanded his investigations to include the cultures of northwestern Mexico, as part of a new project to map the historical relationships between California's aboriginal cultures and those of the Republic of Mexico that Manuel Gamio and Moisés Sáenz were elsewhere charting out of Mexico City. "Already Kroeber and the geographer Carl Sauer were making preliminary surveys of Northwest Mexico," Beals recalled. Beals had already lived in Sonora, and he had learned Spanish there. "A knowledge of Spanish and some experience in northwest Mexico led me in the same direction," Beals later wrote about his decision to study the culture areas of indigenous Mexico.[23] Beals's publication record began with an ethnographic study of the culture areas of the Yaqui and the Mayo populations with whom he had come into contact in northwestern Mexico in 1917. In "Aboriginal Survivals in Mayo Culture," and "Masks in the Southwest," he provided an ethnographic account of the cultural patterns of the Mayo Indians who lived in the southern regions of the state of Sonora, and a theory to explain the origin of the use of ceremonial masks by the Yaqui during religious festivals.[24] In "The Sacred Clowns of the Pueblo and Mayo-Yaqui Indians," written with Elsie Clews Parsons in 1934, meanwhile, Beals described the role of the sacred shamans in the religious culture of the Mayo and Yaqui.[25] Beals quickly broadened his work to the larger spectrum of cultural communities of Mexico that had become the subjects of the integrationist projects of the postrevolutionary Mexican state.

Ultimately, however, Beals's career concerned not Kroeber's fascination with group identification, but rather the related process of cultural transformation that had begun to occupy the attention of graduate students in anthropology in the mid-1930s. Given the great variations among the cultural systems of California and North America more generally, what happened when distinctive communities came into contact with one another? How did discrete systems of culture change, and why? If it was true that cultures were not related to one another through evolutionary scales of development, as Boas had argued in *The Mind of Primitive Man*, then an alternative explanation had to be found to explain how cultures changed. How, for example, did indigenous societies develop new forms of warfare, if not necessarily though the spontaneous generation of new weapons? When the Spanish moved north through Mexico across the Rio Grande, for example, one result of contact with the Pueblo was the introduction of the horse into North America's indigenous societies. Beals's questions flipped Kroeber's concept of the culture area on its head. To determine the presence of the culture area, Kroeber had worked to establish the traits of discrete groups by recreating characteristics of their cultures at particular moments in time, in order to itemize the features that distinguished one group from another. The Yurok Indians of California, for example, could be characterized by a particular set of practices in 1650. Beals himself had adopted this technique in his earliest studies, for it was necessary to develop a baseline definition of a cultural system before one could begin to account for the influences that had changed it. "Such a data base seemed necessary to the study of acculturation, for how else could we identify change?" he wrote.[26]

The vehicle through which Beals developed the process of cultural change was the same concept that would take him into the civil rights movement in the United States. "Acculturation" was one variant of the class of phenomena that sociologists collectively refer to as "assimilation."[27] For Beals, acculturation located the origins of cultural change in the particularities of cultural contact among previously segregated groups. Acculturation had begun evolving into a major discourse of pre–World War II anthropology after Robert Redfield, Melville J. Herskovits, and Ralph Linton published one the most heavily cited papers in the history of American anthropology in 1936.[28] Beals later recalled that the idea of acculturation had been popular among graduate students at Berkeley even before the publication of Redfield's piece. Kroeber had not especially liked Beals's heavy use of "acculturation" as a framing mechanism for his cultural analysis in Beals's first postdoctoral fellowship application in 1934, however: "Reading the first draft, Kroeber remarked, somewhat grumpily I thought, that he supposed it was necessary in such applications to include the latest 'fad' words."[29]

How groups change when they came into contact with one another became a dominant question of Beals's anthropology career. In his 1934 study of the Mayo, he attempted to chart the distinguishing characteristics of the Mayo culture as its patterns had changed under the influence of the European colonization of northern Mexico. "The 300 to 400 years of this interchange has led to a convergence of the two cultures, to some extent reducing them to a common level and wiping out the more obvious differences between them."[30] Only after World War II did Beals begin to seriously study cultural transformation in the urban environment of Southern California, as a result of the institutional growth of the UCLA department of

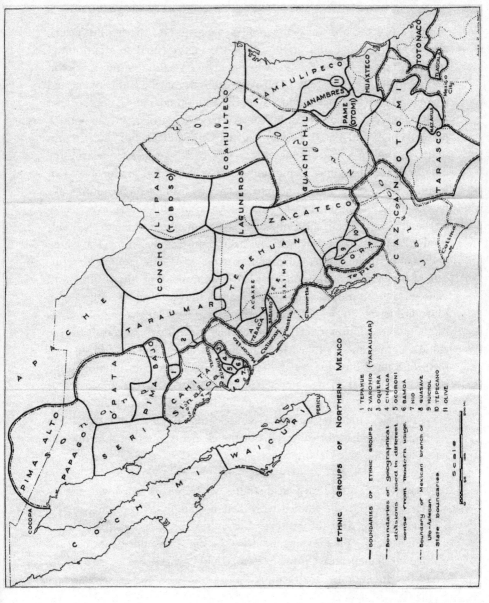

Figure 17. The ethnic groups of Northern Mexico according to Ralph Beals. Ralph L. Beals, *The Comparative Ethnology of Northern Mexico Before 1750,* Ibero-Americana 2 (Berkeley: University of California Press, 1932).

anthropology and postwar demographic change in Los Angeles. But Beals's turn to California's ethnic cultures after 1945 represented an expansion of concerns that he had developed while studying Mexican ethnic history in the late 1920s. Beals's study of what he came to call the "adjustment and adaptation between sociocultural systems" was a fundamental concept that would unite every moment of his life as a writer, a farmer, and an anthropologist. In World War I, he had fled the United States because it represented to him a sociocultural system that had managed to destroy the independence of regional communities. As a writer and graduate student in 1920s Mexico, he had come into contact with indigenous cultures like the Yaqui and Tarahumara who, in contrast to the differential experiences of Native Americans in the United States, had managed to retain their cultural structures in the face of a weaker industrial system. As a young anthropologist, his professional concerns included ethnographic description of indigenous civilizations that had been transformed by contact with new cultural communities, including Spanish transformations of the Yaqui, Mayo influences on the Pueblo communities of New Mexico, and attempts by the postrevolutionary central government in Mexico to transform the cultural communities of the Mexican republic, as we shall see. Throughout his professional life, one sees reflected in Beals's career an interest in the process of cultural change among cultural systems, whether in Mexico or the United States, that emanated from his concerns as a graduate student. "[We Berkeley students] were in varying degrees interested in intercultural relationships and historical origins of the elements entering into the system," he wrote.[31] He elaborated:

> Despite criticism of early field studies, we were concerned with the relations of groups studied with their neighbors or in placing the culture studied in the context of its culture area. In doing so, we were rejecting the idea that any tribal or subtribal culture, however many unique features it might have, could be viewed as an isolated system functioning in a vacuum.[32]

The turn to Southern California as a contemporary problematic of cultural contact would be seen in Beals's work beginning in 1943. By 1938, he had already commented on cultural transformation in the United States in the context of the Pueblo Indians of Arizona. And in 1941, he began reviewing monographs for the anthropology journals on the indigenous cultures of the American West, including the Yaqui people of Arizona and the Sho-shone of Southern California.[33] By the time of Pearl Harbor, Beals was clearly expanding the anthropological focus that he had developed in Mex-ico in the direction of the United States. In 1943, he published a review on the Apache; in 1944, meanwhile, he wrote a suggestive essay on the cultural relationships between Mesoamerica and the American Southwest, and two pieces on the folk art of New Mexico and the archaeology of Northern Arizona.[34] By the early 1950s, his interest had expanded to Mexican Ameri-cans in Southern California and the effects of urbanization on the immi-grant cultures of the Los Angeles metropolitan area. Where he had uniquely focused on the indigenous cultures of Mexico before World War II, after 1945, he now began writing about immigrant and minority cultures in the geographies of southern California.[35]

The Moral Power of the Postrevolutionary State

Beals's study of acculturation in Mexico in the 1930s did differ from his post-World War II study of acculturation in California in one respect: the moral understanding of the state. In the case of his studies of the Yaqui, it had been the distance from the state by the Yaqui that Beals had always found compelling. In his later study of California society and American civil rights, however, he supported the use of the federal state to help fash-ion new relationships between ethnic groups that had previously been kept separate from one another. The differential between these two positions was not an anomaly, but a manifestation of the ethical transformation that Mexico's postrevolutionary state had made on Beals's career.

For as long as Beals had continued to write about Mexico, the Yaqui had remained a powerful symbol of resistance to the power of the state. Neither Loyd Tireman nor George Sánchez had ever described armed uprisings as characteristics of their trips to Mexico, but for Beals, revolu-tionary violence had captured his imagination since his earliest entrance there. Episodes in revolutionary warfare were scattered among the writings that Beals and his brother left beginning with their first entry into Mexico. In Chihuahua, to the east, the Tarahumara Indians were posing problems of political control, even as Francisco "Pancho" Villa was threatening Mex-ico City with his northern armies. Carleton and Ralph remembered, too, the marauding bandits of the north central highlands of the country, who

proved stronger than the state's ability to control them.[36] Violence by the
Yaqui became a persistent feature of Beals's writing, mirroring the
nineteenth- and twentieth-century relationship between the Yaqui and
the Mexican state that scholars have charted since the 1960s. Beals wrote of
the Yaqui destruction of Mexico's railway lines, for instance, an intractable
problem that the Mexican state was never able to control. As late as 1978,
as he looked back on his professional relationship in Mexico with Elsie
Clews Parsons, Beals recalled the marauding Yaqui Indians who had gone
on the warpath in Sonora in 1930, imperiling his travel and work:

> About two weeks after the start of Lent [1930], [Elsie and I] moved
> to the Yaqui village of Estación Vicam on the railroad about fifteen
> miles north of the river and the military post at Esperanza. The
> year before, I had been thrown out of the Yaqui country by the
> military—the area was under martial law and the 1928 uprising in
> connection with the last large scale attempt at a revolution in Mex-
> ico was still fresh and there were still Yaqui living in the Sierra de
> Bacatete who had not accepted the peace terms. Trains passing
> through the area still carried an armed escort and every week two
> or three cars or trucks passing through the Yaqui country between
> Guaymas and Esperanza were ambushed and the occupants usually
> murdered.[37]

The power of the Yaqui was so extraordinary that it had captivated Beals
from the moment that he watched the death of his companions in 1917
until the end of his career there.

The ability of local cultures in Mexico to remain aloof from the power
of the state was important, for it was there that Beals found the leverage
against modern industrial growth that allowed him to reconsider the possibilities of ethnic survival within the modern nation. Beals's initial understanding of the state had been a critique of modern government as the
United States was entering World War I. He had been skeptical of the modern American state from his study alongside his family of socialism and
Marxism. In the literary isolation from the wages of modern industry and
government that he memorialized in his short stories after his return from
Mexico, meanwhile, he sought to carve out a Romantic escape away from
the imperatives of the modern social structure. But, meanwhile, the Yaqui
had continued to resist the encroachments of the Mexican military onto
their lands with great success. Not in Marxism or modernist literature did

Beals ultimately find an answer to the oppositional force that was needed to resist the encroachment of the modern state, but among the Yaqui and the remaining northwestern cultures of postrevolutionary Mexico.

Beals's respect for Yaqui resistance climaxed by rechanneling his interest in the modern state in the years after his initial ethnographic studies of Sonora's peoples. As he continued to write about Mexico's Indians, he shifted his focus to the postrevolutionary state's relationship to local communities. And as he watched the state that Mexico's theorists were constructing, he slowly grew to believe that it was developing an alternative example of government relationship to local culture different from that of the United States government. The role of the state could be something more than destructive, Beals started to believe. In George Sánchez, we witnessed praise for the Mexican state for its institutional commitment to Deweyan investigation. Loyd Tireman had imported Mexico's rural school models as a novel policy prescription for rural New Mexico, based on their attention to the relationship between experience and language. For Ralph Beals, the fragility of the Mexican state in the rural scene, as it built itself piece by piece while intervening in the life of local cultures, made it a moral alternative to be studied. It came to represent a reconstituting bureaucracy whose tenuous relationship to Mexico's broad diversity of communities provided original new possibilities for rethinking how America's social structure might be reconfigured.

Ralph Beals's transformed view of the state became evident in *The Contemporary Culture of the Cáhita Indians* and *Cherán*, two ethnographies he researched in the 1930s and published on the eve of his testimony in the American civil rights cases.[38] These texts are seminal ethnographic contributions to the twentieth-century flowering of community studies in Mexico written by Robert Redfield, Oscar Lewis, and George Foster, among others. In them, Beals captured the relationship between the state, the school, and assimilation he had formulated during his time in Mexico in the 1930s. Beals's studies did not celebrate the state as an agent of cultural diversity as enthusiastically as Sánchez had, but they did underscore its constructive use as part of the attempt to reconstitute the nation after the revolution. It is this knowledge gained that Beals implicitly brought into the desegregation cases in late 1945, as the United States was struggling with its own questions about the role of the school in integration.

The Contemporary Culture of the Cáhita Indians was an analysis of the communities of the Yaqui and Mayo people that Beals had first encountered in 1917. Estimates on the sizes of the two groups were difficult to make, but Beals gave a figure of 20,000 people for each group, located in a geographical area along the Pacific Coast of Mexico from the state of Sonora to the north to the state of Sinaloa to the south. The Yaqui were predominantly located in Sonora, with some communities scattered as far north as southern Arizona. The Mayo were largely located in Sinaloa and were more concentrated than the wider-ranging territory of the Yaqui. In the contemporary period in which he was writing, Beals found almost no cultural differences between the two groups. Both groups also remained aloof from contemporary metropolitan society, including a remoteness from the postrevolutionary state. In only one way did they differ from each other: whereas the Mayo people had no larger sense of nationalism unto themselves as a group that united them across the many communities of their people, the Yaqui had a rabid sense of nationalism manifested as aggression and a willingness to defend themselves physically against the encroachment of outsiders.

Whereas Sánchez had portrayed independent communities of rural villages in *Mexico: A Revolution by Education* that depended on the postrevolutionary state for their autonomy, Beals found the Cáhita people to be arranged in settlements that lived almost completely outside the political orbit of the Mexican state, including its institutions, economy, and schools. "Isolation" was not the word to describe the Mayo and the Yaqui, since both lived in the vicinity of white and mestizo villagers who inhabited the river valleys of Sinaloa and Sonora. Rather, what marked these indigenous villagers was the positive steps they took to reinforce their social and cultural differences from the whites and mestizos who lived nearby, and from the institutions of the federal state that was ready to incorporate them into the postrevolutionary milieu of the nation. The Mayo remained aloof not by aggression and the physical defense of their homeland, but rather by an attitude of evasion that was manifested as inwardness, a refusal to communicate with non-Mayo peoples on anything but the most general statements, and the concealment of anything considered intimate. "The Mayo live *among* whites, but he rarely lives *with* them," is how Beals made this distinction. "When whites begin to settle in a town, the Mayo moves to the outskirts; when the town becomes predominantly white, he moves into the *rancherías* in the brush."[39] The Yaqui maintained their aloofness through physical aggression that reinforced their sense of difference from those considered external to their communities, meanwhile. The Yaqui were frank in the presence of strangers, and reticent about almost nothing in their community except religion and curing techniques, reported Beals. They were also far more willing to adopt the technology of the whites and mestizos, including typewriters, tractors, irrigation pumps, plows, and wagons, since they saw little threat to their sense of peoplehood from the acquisition of machine power and farming techniques associated with outsiders. Yet just as he had found among the Mayo, the Yaqui nonetheless sought to preserve their community by maintaining clear boundaries to the outside. Aggression, wrote Beals, was the manifestation of difference that marked the attempt to maintain affiliation to the ethnic group: "The Yaqui adjustment to white culture is part of an effort to master their own destiny, conscious, selective, and aggressive."[40]

If state institutions resided alongside the Cáhita peoples, the aloofness of these indigenous citizens minimized their influence, including the school, within the orbit of the community. "Nowadays a large percentage of the children are receiving formal primary school education, available up to the fourth or sixth grade," he wrote.[41] Yet most education still came from the family, and despite what appeared to be a recent period of rapid modification in the culture, the strong cohesion of the Yaqui and Mayo peoples continued to offer stubborn resistance to the transformation of their societies. To describe the contemporary Cáhita, Beals returned to a contrast he had first written about in the 1930s. "Although in the United States similar problems may exist, they are those of a dying culture which has only minor relations with the dominant civilization. In Mexico one is dealing, not with two cultures of which one is dying, but with two cultures which are each functioning entities."[42] The continuing strength of the Yaqui left open the possibility that the Indian culture of the Cáhita would predominate in the face of acculturation pressures from the metropole: "Nor is it certain that the European culture is to be wholly dominant in the final synthesis. In content, much of the final culture of Mexico will be Euro-American. But its patterns, its habits of thought, and its organization will probably be profoundly influenced by the Indian cultures."

In *Cherán*, Beals moved far south of the Baja California coast and into the central highlands of the Mexican republic to analyze the Tarascan peoples of the state of Michoacán, some 250 miles to the west of Mexico City. Cherán numbered a population of some 5,000 people at the start of World War II, Beals estimated, and in general was an indigenous community that was highly integrated ethnically, economically, and politically into the institutions of the postrevolutionary state. "All around the edges of Tarascan territory occur villages in various degrees of assimilation to Mexican culture and with various degrees of physical mixture with the Mestizo population," he wrote in 1946.[43] Such acculturation extended to Tarascan economic activity, for example, which Beals found had largely been assimilated into the metropolitan economy of Mexico City. "Actually Tarascan economics, like the rest of Tarascan culture, is strongly influenced by European culture. . . . The long period of assimilation and reintegration that characterized all of Tarascan culture occurred also in the economic field, and the result is a hybrid."[44] Beals found an indigenous community in Cherán whose people were difficult to define culturally because of the high level of acculturation to larger Mexican society that had taken place throughout the geography in Michoacán where they lived.

The high acculturation rate of the Tarascans of Cherán was not a highly contested phenomenon. Quite the opposite was true. The Tarascans had no objection to being acculturated into the larger society, and a substantial part of the population even desired it. "Cherán residents are not averse to changes leading to more money, food, medical service, or elements increasing comfort, such as a larger and better distributed water supply," Beals wrote.[45] New industries were not resisted since they made better wages possible, and political reforms by the state received support in Cherán when the community believed it could provide more effective self-government. In short, whereas the people of the Cáhita were resistant to the state, the villagers of Cherán were favorably oriented toward it and to the national society that was being created. Given their porosity to outside influences in a wide spectrum of ways, Beals was fascinated by the persistence of what he called the "mixed" culture of the Tarascans and believed it deserved much further study. The persistence of some forms of corporate culture had not coalesced into an ideological resistance to changed patterns of life that were occurring as a result of postrevolutionary reforms. Such hybridity was bound to endure amid "the long-continued Mexican efforts to incorporate native groups more fully into the national economy," with the result that the Tarascans would continue to be increasingly integrated into the national and world economies.[46]

Beals took up the assessment of *la casa del pueblo* in the context of Cherán's highly assimilated culture. As with the Cáhita, he found that most of the education in Cherán took place outside the formal institution of the state schools. Children learned largely by imitating their parents and without coercion of any kind. Meanwhile, only 25 percent of the boys received formal education through the fourth grade, and very few parents sent their men to attend high school in the state capital of Morelia. But Beals pointed out that low attendance in Cherán was not a consequence of opposition in the community to the public school. Rather, as one would have expected in a culture that was porous to cultural influences from external society, the failure of the school stemmed from the local belief that the state had not yet molded formal education to the needs Cherán's inhabitants found important. Beals found that the public schools were driven by hard effort and sincerity, in fact. Yet they remained a failure because "they did not train children in any real sense for real life in Cherán."[47] Those who completed the standard course of training had no real advantages over those who did not, Beals argued, and those who managed to acquire some basic skills beyond farming techniques found that they needed to move out of the community to put those skills to work as a storekeeper or mill operator. "The major advantage of school training is to better equip some individuals to cope with the Mestizo world which impinges on Cherán to some extent," wrote Beals. But "insofar as the education is effective and is utilized . . . the effect is to move the individual out of the culture of Cherán." In general, the schools were making little difference in the lives of the villagers since the forms of education provided were so remote from the activities of their lives. Instead, those with formal education were forced to emigrate from the homes where they preferred to remain.

Beals concluded that residents of Cherán were predisposed to welcome the benefits of the state's new schools if the schools could provide a more instrumental education for their children. There was no ideological opposition to the school, he found, but frustration with its lack of precision. What was needed was a school with applicability to the culture of the community rather than one that required the individual to isolate himself from it. If one notices carefully, one sees that Beals had arrived at the same conclusion Sánchez had for the schools of Louisiana. "Only when [political] and similar objectives are concretely framed and the necessary decisions made can a practical program be formulated for Cherán," wrote Beals. "In other words, until the educational process is conceived of first of all from the standpoint of Cherán culture, instead of from the standpoint of national needs or theories, it will not be effective."[48] *Cherán* depicted cultural communities that were oriented toward accepting the public school rather than opposing it, implying that under the right conditions the public school could become an agent of cultural transformation welcomed by some communities in the postrevolutionary nation-in-the-making.

Figure 18. The Yaqui Indians of the state of Sonora as Ralph Beals captured them in his 1945 ethnography of their northwestern Mexico communities. A 1917 encounter with the Yaqui that had resulted in the death of his companions became the founding moment of his career-long commitment to understanding the relationship between ethnicity and the state. Ralph L. Beals, *The Contemporary Culture of the Cáhita Indians* (Washington, D.C.: Government Printing Office, 1945), 232.

Support for the state in rural Mexico varied across the various Tarascan communities Beals surveyed in *Cherán*. In some, Indians were physically hostile to government intervention. Yet in others villagers were glad to see the intervention of the government in social relations, though not without first offering their own advice to state administrators. Beals's ethnography accurately reflected the complexity of cultural change as it was being affected by the institutions of Mexico's state just after World War II. Just as other scholars have found, he was right to note that there was no absolutist answer to the question of the state's relationship to assimilation in rural Mexico.[49] For that reason, Beals came to no rigid ideological answer on the question of nationalism as it was being constructed through the schools and economic agencies in relation to indigenous Mexico. The state could function constructively in some instances, he found, and was not uniformly antithetical a priori to the interests of local cultures.

One can see the transformative role of Mexico's postrevolutionary state in shaping Beals's career in his cautious willingness to grant the state a role as a potentially constructive actor in *The Contemporary Culture of the Cáhita Indians* and *Cherán*. Rather than adopting an ideological line toward the revolutionary schools or the role of the state in local matters, he remained cautious and pragmatic, neither denying the possibility of the state for constructive social relations nor accepting its authority unquestioned. Compared to Sánchez's more enthusiastic one, Beals's posture was a more tenuous line of support for the postrevolutionary government. Yet the possibility of local support for the state's schools did reinforce earlier claims by Loyd Tireman and George Sánchez that they, too, had witnessed villages in Mexico that celebrated the work of the public school and supported its function with enthusiasm. During an ethnographic career spent watching the assimilationist projects of the Mexican state, Beals's experience in Mexico culminated in assigning to the central state a potential for progressive transformation in its relationship with the cultural enclaves of the nation. If one accepts Beals's formulation of the Mexican state as a tenuous institution its redeveloped in the two decades after 1920, then it is possible to understand the calculus that had reshaped his earlier antipathy to modern government.[50] In contrast to the corrupt American central state from which he had fled during his youth, the weaknesses of the Mexican state were tangibly evident in the form of radically distinct relationships to the nation's cultural groups. If the national government had one kind of relationship with the Tarascans, its uneven position toward local communities was mirrored in its quite different relationship to the Yaqui. Under such conditions of fluid postrevolutionary politics, Beals cautiously began assigning the possibility of progressive social transformation to the state. Beals's willingness to imagine constructive possibilities for state intervention in Mexico's rural communities in his World War II work represented a dramatic change of politics in view of the foundational hostility to the state that had characterized his career since World War I.

Beals's ethical transformation toward the possibilities of government action was never constrained by a normative definition of what social and economic goals should be pursued. In a 1934 fellowship application to the Guggenheim Foundation in which he proposed an ethnographic study of the Cora Indians of the Mexican state of Nayarit, for example, he cited

Manuel Gamio and Moisés Sáenz, not because he agreed with their institutional proposals to achieve national consolidation, but because of the cultural surveys the Mexican state was preparing as part of the project in nation building.

> It is proposed to spend about six months in field study of the Cora with headquarters in the town of Jesús María, Nayarit, Mexico, with visits to neighboring Cora towns. There are no Mexican authorities who could be expected to render assistance in the ethnographic part of the study but the problems of the contemporary description would be aided by consultation with Dr. Manuel Gamio, Moisés Sáenz, and the Ministry of Education, which is undertaking regional studies in more accessible portions of Mexico. Certain documentary researches might be necessary also in Mexico City.[51]

His attention to the work of the canonical Mexican integrationists was, in other words, less a normative institutional guide for the challenges of modern Mexican society than it was a guide toward understanding the chronology of cultural change within indigenous communities that postrevolutionary institutional transformation had worked on them. Beals relied on the institutions of the Mexican state crafted by the Mexican integrationists to understand postrevolutionary society, but he was too shrewd an analyst of culture to assert that the state's institutional projects in national consolidation were as benign as some might have asserted. He never allowed himself to become a partisan of the Mexican state as it developed its assimilationist program across the republic.

Beals's cautious approach to state action was also apparent in his attention to the destructive changes that he noticed occurring in Mexico's indigenous communities as a result of the postrevolutionary interventions in local life. He was concerned in the 1930s with the influence economic nationalism would have on the indigenous communities of Michoacán, for example. "Until very recently the [Tarascan] area was relatively inaccessible and the majority of the Tarasca lived in comparative isolation. . . . The recent opening of the heart of the Tarasca area by the highway from Mexico City to Guadalajara and by the branch highway to Uruapán makes rapid change in the near future almost certain."[52] As the Secretaría de Educación Pública was transforming its various agencies seven years later in its continuing efforts to solve the question of national integration amid cultural heterogeneity, Beals noted the changing authority structure of the SEP National Institute of Anthropology and History, the National Museum, and the National School of Anthropology.[53] Considered in isolation, as bureaucratic agencies pursuing scientific research in Mexico, these shifts were meaningless. But Beals was clearly interested in the negative effects that nationalism could have on the Tarascans of Michoacán as the Mexican state pursued its organizing goals through the instruments of the schools, the road networks, and its bureaucratic agencies.

Ultimately, however, Beals's transformed belief in the ethics of the state was reflected in three optimistic characteristics of his work. First, just as Gamio had underscored in *Forjando patria*, cultural relativism provided an antidote to the moral distress that Beals felt in the wake of America's entry into World War I. For Gamio, World War I had provided a context for questioning the civilizations of Europe amid his defense of the indigenous cultures of Mexico as vibrant cultural systems on which the Mexican nation could rely as it sought to rebuild itself. Similarly, Beals used relativism to underscore the importance of Mexico's cultures as a substantiation of social universes whose moral codes provided alternative models to those of the United States. For both Gamio and Beals, the Boasian turn to culture provided a rationale for questioning the legitimacy of moral structures that they perceived to be indefensible. Second, the cultural diversity Beals found in Mexico underscored new possibilities for understanding the limits of institutional transformation as a result of his comparison to the more rapid industrialization of the United States. In Mexico, neither the state nor industry had yet accelerated to the point of destroying the panoply of cultural communities that defined the country. For Beals, this proved to be an argument for reading the indigenous cultures of Mexico to better understand the complex changes that state policy could bring to them, in an attempt to forestall their future destruction. Third, Mexico provided Beals an opportunity to understand the redemptive possibility of state-sponsored change, by virtue of its attention to social science research as a component of transformation. This was a remarkable characteristic of Beals's experiences in Mexico, for from the perspective of his 1917 pessimism about industrial society, no one could have guessed that Beals would have found any redemptive possibilities in the operation of modern government.

Beals's longer time in Mexico made the institutional history of postrevolutionary society a more complicated narrative than it was for either Sánchez or Tireman. If for Sánchez and Tireman the Republic of Mexico provided fundamental new episodes in institutional transformation that molded their careers, Mexico's institutional projects for them were registered through narrower windows of time. They were each escorted to the rural schools they subsequently wrote about, as well, by officials of the Secretariat of Public Education. Their desire to intensify the transformational role of government in rural New Mexico could also sometimes translate itself into naive celebrations of the power of the state to effect social change. Mexico's influence on Sánchez and Tireman was no less consequential as a result of their shorter experiences with the projects of the Secretaría de Educación Pública. But their understanding of the state as an agent for both constructive and destructive purposes might have been more subtle had they spent more time among the rural communities of the Mexican countryside, as did Beals. Still, Beals's shifting appreciation for the broader role of the U.S. central state in American society emanated from the influence that the postrevolutionary Mexican state had on his understanding of industrial society. As he compiled ethnographic descriptions of Mexico's Indian communities during the late 1930s and early 1940s, he was also synthesizing the central state's work in the context of the two decades of revolutionary violence. It was postrevolutionary Mexican statecraft and social science that most transformed Beals's understanding of the possibilities of state-sponsored social change throughout North America.

Mexico's Geography of Influence

Relatively few Americans in the 1930s were studying the psychology of "experience" as the avenue toward renewed social exchanges in New Mexico, as was Loyd Tireman. Montana Hastings had devoted her career to the psychology of intelligence across New Mexico, California, and Mexico City, but the bar graphs charting her experimental results meant little to outsiders. Ralph Beals struggled with the ethics of the state as he sought to understand Yaqui resistance to the Mexican government, but few would have known what it had to do with cultural relativism. Likewise, few would have recognized what Dewey meant by "reconstruction in philosophy," or the importance of practice to theory in the universe of ideas that Sánchez had created while he walked through Zacatecas and Querétaro. Yet if Mexico's policy experiments were rarefied apertures for understanding assimilation and ethnic relations in the American West, it would be a mistake to assume that Mexico's influence remained locked away in the halls of science. The guiding philosophies of Mexico's scientific state may have remained unclear to many outside the realm of social science, but the politics of race relations to which they were tethered were clearly visible to broader circles of intellectuals, artists, and public officials whose work helped document the changing landscape of ethnic relations in the American West. The fiction writers of the West's rural communities, for instance, narrated the movement of science into the ethnic landscapes of Mexico, Texas, and Arizona. Among them were John Steinbeck, Josefina Niggli, Américo Paredes, and Mario Suárez. In Texas, meanwhile, an expanding circle of civil righters that included the Spanish-language *La Prensa*, Texas governor James Allred, and the Teachers Association of Texas popularized Mexico's scientific reforms to a working-class audience. If the Progressive Education Association and the Rosenwald Fund had already traveled to Mexico to study its state reform models, these other groups showed that Mexico's influence over American politics was not anecdotal, but a broad reform movement that became part of the cultural history of the American West.

The relationship between experience and language that spurred Loyd Tireman into Mexico is captured in institutional terms as an instrument of social reconciliation in one of the central novels of 1930s Texas, Américo Paredes's *George Washington Gómez*.[54] Throughout the novel, the ethnic and racial hierarchies of the United States and Mexico structure a social landscape of conflict that is emblematized in Paredes's repeated allusion to war. Amid such hierarchies, Mexico's peoples suffer violent upheaval via the U.S. invasion of Mexico, the War of the Reform, and the Mexican Revolution, all of which the reader encounters as episodes of dislocation and strife and never as redemption. In the United States, too, an array of national wars signals the historical claim to physical violence as the structuring rationale behind the social order. There is Custer's Last Stand in an image on the wall, repeated turns to the violence of the Civil War, and the guerrilla war fought by the Texas Rangers and Mexican Americans along the Rio Grande River. Nevertheless, how close Paredes came to theorizing the melting pot worlds Tireman and Sánchez had created becomes clear from the book's early injunction, told through the voice of George Washington Gómez's father, that his son must never be told about his father's violent death. "My son. Musn't know. Ever. No hate, no hate." The father makes his brother promise never to tell his son. It is in the context of this ethic of brotherhood that the public school of Paredes's novel acquires its significance. Where the history of Mexico and the United States had been a long narrative of war and ethnic violence, the school would help Guálinto to develop into "a great man who would help and lead his people to a better kind of life."[55] He could use the instruments of the school to become a lawyer who would help win back the lands that had been lost to the white Texans. He could become a great doctor whose art could heal the sick. Or he could become a great orator who "could convince even his greatest enemies to the rightness of his cause."

It is in the portrayal of the public school as an instrument of renewed social ethics that Paredes shows how close he came as a novelist to the universe of psychology Tireman had formulated in the ideas of Deweyan science. Guálinto Gómez could become a great orator, but to do so meant first mastering the English language that would become his adopted civic tongue. He had initially repeated the English alphabet with great facility, Paredes wrote, since his knowledge of the analogous Spanish version had been taught to him at home. Yet he had made the mistake of adding the letters "ch," "ll," and "ñ," as was conventional in his native Spanish. Paredes used these distinct alphabets to chart Guálinto's evolution to a mastery of the English language. He learned to match English syllables to letters he had learned in Spanish, before translating words to the physical experiences to which they corresponded. "Mrs. Huff began to draw a tree with green leaves and a lot of little red fruit and a boy wearing a funny-looking hat and knickers," wrote Paredes as he portrayed Guálinto's passage to literacy in English.[56] "I am surprised that his English pronunciation is so good," his teacher later remarks. "I mean, for a Latin boy his age, he did an excellent job."[57] Paredes's descriptions of Guálinto's evolution toward literacy are ones Tireman could have written himself. Both captured in their books the experiential platforms on which language is built and whose secrets Tireman struggled all his career to unlock. What they show is a novelist capturing in one of the signal novels of the 1930s social experience in Texas the same ideas being fielded in science at that very moment by Tireman in New Mexico and the cultural missionaries at Actopan, Mexico.

The political realm of integration science in Mexico's postrevolutionary state can be found in the work of John Steinbeck, Josefina Niggli, and Mario Suárez, meanwhile. Steinbeck boldly took on the subject of science and the integrating function of Mexico's public school in *The Forgotten Village*, the 1941 story of the fictional village of Santiago that was turned into a movie version in that same year.[58] The story depicts the efforts of one of Moisés

Sáenz's cultural missionaries to convince the rural villagers of Santiago that science can help them to chlorinate the polluted drinking well that is killing their children and to immunize their youth against the diseases that infect their bloodstream. In *The Pearl*, meanwhile, Steinbeck created an allegory about the limits of the Indian's potential new place in Mexico's postrevolutionary hierarchy of professional and capitalist elites.[59] If there were promises for new opportunities in the new republic, only misfortune redounds to the indigenous family of the book in the aftermath of the discovery of a precious pearl. Steinbeck does not allow the Indian family to assimilate to the national culture being created in an ascendant middle class. The Indian protagonist dreams of the public school for his newborn son, but he loses his child and friendships, a metaphor that speaks to Steinbeck's critique of the possibility of social mobility in Mexico's new society. Other works of literature similarly captured Mexico's scientific state for a reading public of the American West. Josefina Niggli's *Mexican Village* depicted village life in Mexico's northern provinces in the 1930s and 1940s, a social landscape in which the schoolteacher has been relocated from far southern Mexico to resocialize the village students of Nuevo León.[60] And in Mario Suárez's 1940s short stories, immigrant Mexican schoolchildren in Tucson's urban barrios negotiate new terrains of public schooling and ethnic cultures even as they sometimes return to Mexico for educational opportunities in Mexico's new rural schools.[61]

An analogous history of engagement with Mexican integration policy took place in the state of Texas, where the critique of American segregation was increasingly occupying the thought of public officials and social scientists in the public schools of the large cities of the Lone Star State during the 1930s. The occasion of Ramón Beteta's speech on rural education in Mexico, delivered in San Antonio in November 1935, provides one helpful way to read the descriptions of Mexico's scientific state circulating in 1930s Texas. By 1935, Mexico's national integration project had become not simply a bureaucratic project of the state, but a reflection of a state that increasingly was willing to assert its political future in North America before the dominance of the United States. Such growing confidence was in evidence in Mexico's continuing challenge to the Rockefeller oil interests in Mexico, for instance, which would end in Mexico's nationalization of its oil fields and the establishment of PEMEX. It was evident in Mexico's willingness to defend land redistribution in the Western Hemisphere amid European and U.S. concerns about the expansion of Soviet communism.[62] And it was

Figure 19. The rural school in John Steinbeck's *The Forgotten Village.* Steinbeck, *The Forgotten Village* (New York: Viking Press, 1941), 31.

evident in Mexico's staunch defense of the anti-Catholic politics of the national state, including its continuing efforts at home to keep the church away from national politics and its diplomatic efforts to counter the Vatican's anti-Mexico rhetoric.

It was against the political backdrop of Mexico's increasing assertion before the United States that Ramón Beteta, head of Mexico's Statistics Agency of the Secretariat of Industry and Commerce, embarked on a tour of the United States with stops planned for speeches to receptive audiences of academics at Williams College in Massachusetts and at San Antonio, Texas. He had trained in economics and law at UNAM and the University of Texas at Austin before becoming a professor of economics at UNAM, a member of president Lázaro Cárdenas's cabinet in the 1930s, and later a candidate for president during the election of 1952. But as he readied for his trip to the United States in 1935, it was Mexico's Six-Year Plan, the ambitious effort by President Cárdenas to accelerate the integration of the republic through public investment, that was attracting attention. "While the United States is engaged in the tremendous task of national recovery known as the 'New Deal,'" wrote the *Washington Post*, "Mexico is attempting to put into effect a vast program of social and economic reform known as the 'Sixth-year Plan.'" At the center of that plan was the rural school, Beteta told the *Post*. "The school is called 'La Casa del Pueblo'—the house of the people—and justly so, because it has been built by the men of the community in their spare time on Sundays and because it is the main center of interest in the community," he said. The Six-Year Plan had already helped to establish 1,000 new schools in the republic. But its aim was another 11,000 rural schools, which would bring the total number in Mexico to 20,000 by 1940.[63] At Williams College, Beteta described the results of the grand project in nation building on which Cárdenas and the national state were embarked. "That part of us which is growing is the mestizo. The Indian has given us a grand part of his original culture, affecting even the most Spanish of our characteristics, like language and religion. As a result, we have created a new product, neither Spanish nor Indian. We are Mexico, a country whose various races have each contributed a diversity of beliefs, colors, clothing, rituals, inhibitions, ambitions, and ideals in order to create a new nation."[64]

But it was in San Antonio that Beteta's trip created an international incident when Catholic protestors critical of the Mexican state's conduct toward the Catholic Church converged on the Teachers Association of Texas to prevent Beteta from delivering his speeches on bilingual and rural education in Mexico. "I arrived [in San Antonio] completely unaware of the public campaign against me to prevent me from speaking that a group of Catholic professors and students had organized," Beteta later wrote. "The campaign filled the local newspapers of San Antonio and had culminated in veiled threats against the teachers conference if my invitation to speak were not withdrawn," he wrote.[65] "Fortunately for me, the president of the association refused their demands, and finally, I was able to give my speeches to an assembly that consisted of 10,000 teachers who had been convened at the Municipal Auditorium." It is difficult to substantiate the figure of ten thousand teachers in attendance at Beteta's speeches in San Antonio, but there is no doubt that interest in Mexico's rural schools was large enough throughout Texas to result in Beteta's presence before the largest teachers association in the state. He had been personally invited there by association president C. N. Shaver and secretary B. B. Cobb, both of whom were interested in Mexico's bilingual education and cultural

missionary programs. Whether they knew that Loyd Tireman and George
Sánchez were at that very moment modifying Mexico's cultural missionary
program for use in New Mexico and Louisiana is something we must wonder about. But before the audience of assembled teachers, Beteta did not
refrain from talking about the subjects he had been invited to discuss. In
his first speech, he spoke of the importance of bilingual education classes
for a nation that was composed of more than two million persons who
spoke native languages other than Spanish out of a total of sixteen million.[66]
In his second speech on the cultural missionaries, Beteta reminded his audience of John Dewey's place in contemporary Mexican education.[67] As Catholics protested Beteta's speeches in San Antonio, meanwhile, the League of
United Latin American Citizens intervened via the Spanish daily newspaper
La Prensa, sending a letter to Dr. Shaver by prominent LULAC member
Alonso Perales, asking that Beteta be allowed to offer his thoughts to the
San Antonio audience. When Texas Governor Allred was invited to Mexico
City by President Cárdenas two years later, Allred reprised the Beteta incident to underscore the similarities in the national reconstruction campaigns
by the United States and Mexico. "Today in the United States, the problems
of the common and the working man, and the application of the principle
'the most good for the most people,' are being resolved under the humane
leadership of President Roosevelt," Allred said in Mexico City. "Meanwhile,
here in Mexico, the cause of the losers of history has been taken up by the
popular and much-loved President Cárdenas."[68]

Beteta's controversial appearance in San Antonio tells us very little
about how the schoolteachers of Texas subsequently used Mexico's policy
prescriptions in the 1930s, or whether they invoked John Dewey's ideas as
they studied Mexico's reforms. Similarly, what political uses of Mexico's
scientific state were made by the fiction writers of the American West will
have to await further research. It would also be important to uncover the
extent to which the League of United Latin American Citizens modeled its
integrationist platform for the American schools on policy models crafted
in Mexico. And if the Teachers Association of Texas traveled to Mexico
City and Actopan in the wake of Beteta's speech to uncover deeper policy
mechanisms to use in Texas, that too, would be important. It would represent a fundamental contribution to our understanding of Mexico's place in
the development of American nationalism after the New Deal. This would
help us to see Mexico not only as a source of aesthetics and ideas about

modern industrial society, but as a source of politics during an era of state reform that Daniel T. Rodgers has called the "age of social politics."[69]

But the reactions that Beteta's speeches garnered were further evidence that the integration policies of Mexico's scientific state had become part of the currency of public policy debate in the 1930s American West as Americans were wrestling with the meaning of American democracy. Historian Benjamin Johnson has recently shown that LULAC civil righters in 1930s Texas were well aware of Mexico's assimilation projects and reinforced their commitments to American civil rights using the metaphors of Mexico's postrevolutionary nationalism.[70] But whether it took the form of civil righters in the 1930s, writers studying Mexico's rural villages, editorial writers looking on Mexico's school reforms as a model for San Antonio and Los Angeles, or U.S. public officials trying to understand what the growth of the central state meant for ethnic communities in the modern industrial nation, these linkages to Mexico's melting pot shared a common theme. Reaching beyond clichéd constructions of the United States and Mexico as antithetical societies, they established moments of political exchange that proved fruitful to both sides of the international relationship. These connections manifested the fact that many constituencies in the American West had targeted Mexico as a province of experimentalism from which they might reframe their understanding of ethnic relations at home, beyond the American social scientists who studied in Mexico's scientific state. The wide scope of affiliations to Mexico shows that Western interest in Mexico was not quixotic and marginal, but an integral part of the national concern with interracial conflict in the mid-century United States. If George Sánchez shows us that the American West was not alone in searching for the beloved community, the career of Edwin Embree shows us that neither was the American South. John Collier and the Bureau of Indian Affairs were interested in Mexico's experiments in land distribution and Indian acculturation as they sought to formulate the Indian New Deal. And in the decade of the 1930s, the Progressive Education Association studied school reform in postrevolutionary Mexico as they continued with their experiments in rebuilding the American educational system. As all these Americans remind us, there were multiple frames of reference for thinking about Mexico's scientific state, none of which was alone in its concern with the challenges posed by ethnic difference in the modern United States.

PART III

Mexico and the Attack on *Plessy*

Chapter 6

"The Sun Has Exploded": Integration
and the California School

Mexico's bureaucracies had transformed school policy in New Mexico and Louisiana in the 1930s. But that influence continued into World War II America. Even as Mexican nationalism reached what one historian has called the most integrated moment of its twentieth-century history in the 1940s, it was shaping one of the canonical chapters of the American civil rights movement.[1] The international influences on mid-century American racial liberalism have been charted elsewhere by Mary Dudziak and other scholars.[2] But it was Mexico's scientific state that shaped the canonical desegregation campaigns in the American West. There were other factors influencing desegregation, including migration from Mexico, mobilization for war, and transformations in federal jurisprudence. The growth of the social sciences and changing conceptions of American democracy were also important. But tracing the careers of George I. Sánchez and Ralph Beals into the 1940s shows us that the international exchange with postrevolutionary Mexico's educational projects was a central component of what Jacqueline Dowd Hall has called the "long civil rights movement."[3] They show us that the history of school desegregation in the American West was an offshoot of Mexico's struggle with ethnic diversity as much as it was a domestic story of American social transformation.

How Mexico's nationalist experiments in psychology, philosophy, and anthropology became an institutional bridge to one of the central moments in the history of racial liberalism in the American West becomes evident if we examine the way Sánchez and his colleagues converged into the school desegregation cases. Through America's entry into World War II and the

emergence of the civil rights lawsuits, the Americans who had visited Actopan and Tlaxcala continued pushing the same faith they had earlier developed in pragmatism and the state to integrate the schools of the rural West.
What becomes evident is the continuity of the work that these Americans
completed between the New Deal era and World War II, across Mexico and
the United States, even as lawyers began calling on them to provide the
scientific rationale against Jim Crow in the desegregation lawsuits. The continuity of their work from earlier moments in Mexico and New Mexico
represented a parallel world of civil rights, hidden in the shadows of the
legal campaigns charted by the judges and the lawyers. In this parallel
world, Loyd Tireman continued to push Mexico within his laboratory
school as an antidote to segregation in New Mexico as late as 1948, even as
he participated in the educational lawsuits in Texas. Here, George Sánchez
continued his Mexico-descended efforts in administrative reform beyond
the Deep South, into Texas and California. And Ralph Beals continued to
study the relationship of the Mexican state to Native Americans in Sonora
and Michoacán through the 1940s, even as he participated in the legal case
that desegregated the public schools of California. These Americans continued to struggle with the challenges of the language barrier separating
English and Spanish speakers from one another, and with education systems that could not be easily modified. But they had positioned themselves
to use social science as an instrument of racial change by the advent of the
World War II school desegregation cases because they had been experimenting with questions of assimilation and integration in Mexico and the
American West for more than twenty years. It was at this moment that
they converged from the earlier moment of assimilation projects into the
campaigns of the postwar civil rights movement.

It may seem jarring to chart the influence of Mexico's rural school over
desegregation campaigns that historians have charted as a domestic story
of the American West. Yet none of the philosophical and political characteristics that had brought the American experimentalists to Mexico were
irreconcilable with the philosophical tendencies of the desegregation movements that followed World War II. Canonical to the civil rights movement,
for example, was the goal of bringing Mexican Americans and whites together in the elementary schools of Texas, Arizona, and California. Yet the
Americans profiled here had been using the school in Mexico and the
United States to fuse together the ethnic fragments of the nation into a
united whole since the 1930s. Meanwhile, if the school became a primary

location for reformulating ethnic relations after 1945, that political goal mirrored the analogous 1930s goal of using the public school to assimilate immigrants into American society.[4] Moreover, the postwar goal of bringing the federal state to bear on the question of civil rights had been antedated by these Americans in their celebration of the postrevolutionary Mexican state as an instrument of recalibrated ethnic relations. In this vein, some may have interpreted the intervention by the federal courts in the sociology of American education in the postwar United States as a monumental leap forward in American political culture. But in the context of their study of Mexico's nationalist experiments in education, these Americans saw the use of the courts as merely an incremental step forward by a state whose policies they had been critiquing for twenty years.

"The Sun Has Exploded"

It was the language of Judge Paul John McCormick's ruling that made everyone gasp. Since 1896, when the United States Supreme Court announced *Plessy v. Ferguson*, the law of the land had supported the idea that segregation of the white and black races in the United States was in keeping with the promise of equality. The history of racial conflict was decidedly unequal, everyone knew. The butchery of the American Civil War had produced a twelve-year period of hopeful social reorganization in the American South where Blacks seemed to be taking their rightful place among whites in the American union. But the white nation had returned to its ignominious history of violence and discrimination against the freedman with the end of Reconstruction. Lynchings accelerated, Jim Crow laws returned the social structure to the era of rigid separation of blacks and whites, and blacks began a slow descent into second-class citizenship that would not bottom out until the Great Depression. *Plessy v. Ferguson* was chief among the bulwarks of this new order, giving the force of law to the separation of the races that social custom and tradition had begun to make universal throughout the American South. The greatest travesty was the reasoning that lay at the heart of the Supreme Court's decision. There was nothing inherently wrong about segregation, the U.S. Supreme Court argued, since to create equal accommodations for Blacks and whites was equivalent to satisfying the conditions of equality demanded by the Reconstruction Amendments to the U.S. Constitution. If some Black Americans chose to believe that segregation was in and of itself a denial of equality in the face of equal accommodations, well, that was nothing more than a mistaken interpretation of state policy. It was this reasoning of subjectivity that Judge Paul John McCormick took aim at in *Mendez v. Westminster*, transforming the separate but equal doctrine from a subjective interpretation wrongly residing in the minds of Black Americans into a state-sanctioned structure that reinforced discrimination and inequality. "A paramount requisite in the American system of public education is social equality. It must be open to all children by unified school association regardless of lineage," he wrote in February 1946.[5]

Mendez stunned the American legal profession. It was the first time in American history that a federal judge had questioned the rationale of *Plessy v. Ferguson*, a feature that has attracted scholarly attention over the last twenty years to desegregation efforts in the American West as a previously unknown installment in the effort against segregated schooling in the Deep South. Critics at the time of *Mendez* believed that the case reflected a new moral order that was being created. One was Carey McWilliams, for example, who saw *Mendez* as a world-historical moment. At the exact moment that *Mendez* was unfolding in California, McWilliams wrote in his classic 1949 *North from Mexico*, a group of shepherds had been tending to their flock in the Jemez Mountains of New Mexico. Suddenly, the first atomic blast went off at Trinity test site near Los Alamos in the early morning hours of July 16, 1945. "It was like the sun exploded," the shepherds reported to their *gerente*. McWilliams noted that the bomb had dropped only days after the *Mendez* trial had ended, a coincidence that he turned into a metaphor for racial liberalism in America. As science had done at Los Alamos, the science of race in *Mendez* suggested that a new dawn was rising in the West for the peoples whose history in Mexico and the United States he had just finished recounting in his book.[6]

McCormick's insistence that the Fourteenth Amendment required social equality was another salvo in the demise of the separate but equal doctrine. If social rather than political equality was the basis upon which public school policy should turn, then the edifice of segregation was on borrowed time, commentators suggested. *Mendez v. Westminster* ultimately did not set a new precedent in American constitutional law. When McCormick ruled against segregation in Orange County, he was considering its legality in the absence of a state statute rather than its legality based on the statute that prescribed it. This important difference resulted in a narrowing of McCormick's decision by the Ninth District Court of Appeals based upon statutory considerations rather than a challenge to the ethics of the *Plessy* doctrine.[7] But for nearly a year, the American legal profession refused to breathe normally in view of the possibility that a legal challenge to American segregation from the Pacific Coast of California meant that *Plessy's* time to fall had come. A startled NAACP saw a legal decision in *Mendez* that could reinforce their strategy to attack public school segregation in the Deep South.[8] The ACLU called the decision remarkable. *Mendez* led Governor Earl Warren to desegregate California's schools permanently in 1947 before he later took up the question of segregation in the public schools in *Brown v. Board of Education* and provided the leadership to a fractured court in what counts among the most important legal decisions in American history. When Richard Kluger wrote his monumental history of *Brown v. Board of Education*, he added *Mendez* in the far out American West to a narrative that takes place in Kansas and the Deep South.[9]

Mendez v. Westminster represents one of the central moments in the history of race relations in the American West. In a campaign that paralleled that of the NAACP in the Deep South, tens of thousands of schoolchildren were granted access to public schools that previously had been closed to them. In *Delgado v. Bastrop*, the U.S. federal court in central Texas used McCormick's decision to declare the segregation of Mexican Americans in the public schools of Texas unconstitutional in 1948.[10] And in *Gonzales v. Sheely*, the federal court of Arizona copied McCormick's *Mendez* decision word for word to end segregation of public schools in Arizona in 1951.[11] Over a period of seven years that began with *Mendez* starting in 1944, the practice of public school segregation was destroyed as a matter of state policy in the largest states of the American West by Mexican American plaintiffs seeking to expand the privileges of American citizenship and nationalism to cultural communities that had previously been excluded. New forms of American nationalism and citizenship were opened in the American West, just as they would be opened in the American South. Like the legal campaign that included *Brown* in the American South, the legal efforts that produced *Mendez* and its progeny became one of the canonical moments in the reconstruction of postwar American nationalism.

Yet even as scholars have begun to study the links between regional desegregation struggles in the American West and the American South as a way of deepening their understanding of American civil rights, their juxtaposition has produced an unexpected irony.[12] For in pointing out the

Figure 20. U.S. postage stamp issued in 2007 in commemoration of *Mendez v. Westminster*, the 1946 decision that desegregated the public schools of California. Mendez v. Westminster © 2007 United States Postal Service. All Rights Reserved. Used with permission.

parallels between desegregation efforts in the American West and the Deep South, scholars have failed to note the important links between school desegregation in the American West and integration policies in postrevolutionary Mexico's schools. The social scientists who testified in *Mendez* and its related progeny were the same Americans who had studied Mexico's scientific state since the 1930s to rethink American ethnic relations in New Mexico and California—Ralph Beals, Marie Hughes, George Sánchez, and Loyd Tireman. Already they had used the Mexican state in the 1930s for clues about the role of government as a mediating factor in American group life. Already they had modeled policy projects in New Mexico after those of the Mexican state. And now, even as the NAACP followed *Delgado* and *Gonzales* in the American courts in the late 1940s for clues about desegregation in the Deep South, these social scientists turned back to the Mexican state for examples of school reform as they helped to desegregate the schools of the American West. If it is true that *Mendez* cannot be separated from the demise of *Plessy* and segregation in the American South, as some scholars have argued, then these Americans show us that it cannot be untethered from the history of science and state transformation in postrev-olutionary Mexico, either. Scholars should continue to study the links between *Mendez* and desegregation in the Deep South, but Mexico's role in American race relations was equally present in the borrowings these Ameri-cans continued to make from Mexico's scientific state during the American desegregation campaigns after World War II.

These links by Amercan social scientists were only one of the multiple ways in which American desegregation was linked to the postrevolutionary Mexican state. As early as 1934, for example, *Mendez* attorney David Mar-cus appears in the files of the Secretariat of Foreign Relations as a consulting attorney employed by the Mexican state to defend its citizens in the Ameri-can courts.[13] Marcus was a New Mexico-born Jewish American lawyer who had married an immigrant Mexican woman in the 1930s. For reasons that remain sketchy, Marcus had developed a legal interest in the defense of immigrant Mexicans. That interest had resulted in a contract with the Mex-ican consulate in Los Angeles to represent the Mexican state and its citizens in U.S. federal and California state courts on a variety of legal matters, mostly small. It was his record of service to the Mexican state that had first drawn the attention of the plaintiffs in *Mendez*, resulting in his representa-tion beginning in 1944 of the five families who eventually filed the desegre-gation lawsuit against Orange County.

Compelling links to Mexico resided in the social history of the *Mendez* conflict, too. Scholars have yet to explore whether the immigrant plaintiffs who filed the original complaint against the Westminster School District were supporters of Mexico's public education campaigns, but the affiliation to Mexico that the plaintiffs indicated in their earliest discussions with Orange County points in the direction of that possibility. The parents had identified themselves as primarily Mexican-born in the original 1944 peti-tion to the school districts, for example, while the court depositions show a variety of originating states in Mexico that included Chihuahua and Sonora. Given the immigrant links to the Republic of Mexico, the pursuit of a desegregation policy in the United States may have represented a political identity crafted in Mexico as the postrevolutionary state was developing its public schools in the 1930s rather than a domestic identity crafted in the United States alone. Parents could have challenged Orange County for domestic reasons in the United States alone rather than from affiliations to postrevolutionary institutions in Mexico, but the point remains understud-ied. Given the historical timing of integration projects in both the United

States and Mexico, there exists the possibility that integration in the United
States may have been a carryover from institutional identities crafted from
postrevolutionary struggles abroad rather than an acceleration of domestic
events in the United States alone.

When taken together, these discrete shapings reflect a composite pattern
of influence by the postrevolutionary Mexican state over American desegregation that was just as deep as any desegregation ties between the American
West and the American South that scholars have begun to analyze. The
Mexican state may have been a fragile state, as Beals had noted in his work
on the Cáhita and the Tarascans, but its scientific institutions had long
since molded the scientific orientation of American humanists and social
scientists by the time that those individuals began appearing in the American courts in *Mendez* and beyond. These links were not new developments,
but the results of a central state that had brought integration in the school
in Mexico after the Mexican Revolution into juxtaposition with integration
and the school in the United States beginning in the 1930s.

Mexico's connection to desegregation movements in the American
West shows that America's desegregation campaigns occurred in the context of international integration movements that transcended domestic
projects in racial liberalism at home. It suggests that desegregation in
postwar America was shaped by a continental narrative of school reform
that included Mexico's state policies as those policies radiated outward
across the American West and the Deep South. School integration policy
in postrevolutionary Mexico became an instrument that American social
scientists used to transform school segregation policy in the American
West, an effort that, in turn, shaped the NAACP legal attack on segregated
public schools in the Deep South. These linkages do not mean that the
NAACP efforts that would climax in *Brown v. Board of Education* should
be attributed to postrevolutionary integration campaigns in Mexico. But
these links do suggest the existence of an international geography of integration in which Mexican school policy provided one context for the reshaping of black-white relationships in the American South that took place
simultaneously with the desegregation campaigns of the American West.
That relationship may seem extraordinary, but it is a lineage that we can
see institutionally in Edwin Embree's interest in postrevolutionary Mexico. Embree would later play a role in the racial liberal project of American Deep South, but it was Mexican school policy that he had studied in
Mexico as early as 1928.[14]

The West's surprise attack on *Plessy* reflected the influence of integration in postrevolutionary Mexico in addition to any similarities it reflected to the desegregation struggles in the Deep South. The immigrant plaintiffs had direct ties to Mexico, not the Deep South. The communities of immigrants identified with the history of integration northward, as Carey McWilliams argued in *North from Mexico*. The consulting attorneys had been employed by the Mexican state since the early 1930s. And the American scientists who had studied in Mexico during the 1930s returned to Mexico for guidance in the integration struggles of the 1940s, finding in the scientific state reasons to fight segregation in the public schools of the United States. These ties show how the influence in the United States of Mexico's scientific state in the decade of the 1930s continued into the canonical legal battles of America's racial liberal project. Throughout the 1940s, Mexico continued to exert a deep, intense influence over one of the canonical installments of twentieth-century American racial liberalism.

The Tarascan School and School Desegregation in California

Ralph Beals underscored the continuing influence of the Mexican state on race relations in the United States when he testified in *Mendez v. Westminster* in summer 1945 that Mexican social science had been the basis for his integration work in California. Beals's renewed faith for state intervention in Mexico's rural communities in the 1930s had represented a dramatic change of politics in view of the foundational hostility to the state that had characterized his thought during World War I. He had not presented an ideological line toward the revolutionary schools or the role of the state in local matters in his ethnographic studies of Mexico's indigenous communities. Beals had been cautious, neither denying the possibility of state action in social relations nor accepting its authority unquestioned. This posture toward the school was a tenuous line of support for the role of the revolutionary state when compared with Sánchez's enthusiastic one. But the willingness to grant to the American state the possibility of a constructive role in the development of postwar social relations indicated the progressive role that Mexico's central state had had in shaping Beals's civil rights commitments in the United States.

The citrus groves of Orange County, California, out of which came one of the central court battles in the history of the American West, were not the same geography as the alluvial valleys of Sonora's Yaqui River. Here, beginning in the 1920s, immigrants from Mexico had begun to cluster in the unincorporated communities to the east of Los Angeles to work the agricultural fields that had already begun to export their produce throughout the United States. It was in four of these villages—El Modena, Garden Grove, Westminster, and Santa Ana—where a second generation of immigrant children had been born into American citizenship. Yet long-standing practices in these communities had prevented these Americans from using public schools that had been reserved by convention for white Americans only. It was here that Gonzalo Mendez organized the effort to desegregate the schools of Orange County that would become *Mendez v. Westminster*. With resources obtained from farming and from neighbors in adjoining communities anxious to aid in the effort, Mendez hired attorney David Marcus to press his claim against the public school districts of Orange County. It was on behalf of Mendez and his neighbors that Ralph Beals, charged to be head of UCLA's new anthropology department beginning in 1941, was recruited by Marcus to testify against the social effects of school segregation in Southern California. In Mexico, Beals had studied the role of the central state in shaping a new nationalism out of the peoples of Sonora and Michoacán. In the United States by 1945, Beals was now engaged in using the central state to shape a new nationalism out of the peoples of California.

Every defense that Beals gave in his *Mendez* testimony about his expertise concerning assimilation was about the relationship between local culture and the state in Mexico rather than the United States. "What has been your history or background with respect to anthropology and sociology?" attorney David Marcus asked him at the beginning of his testimony. In response, Beals described his doctoral training in anthropology before rattling off the career of work that he had completed in the Republic of Mexico since the 1920s. "I have done a great deal of research work, a very large part of it in Mexico, where I have lived for considerable periods of time." This work had been done for the National Research Council, the Smithsonian Institution, and the University of California, he reported to the court, but there had also been the School of Anthropology in Mexico City that Franz Boas had founded in 1911. When Marcus asked him to provide a list of his publications, Beals again rattled off the long list of works on ethnic cultures in Mexico. "Can I give a short précis?" he responded. "There are about 30, I believe. Perhaps those that are most pertinent here are studies of the Nahua and Maya Indians of Sonora, and the Tarascans of Michoacán, which are being published by the Smithsonian Institution," he told Judge McCormick as he testified about his work on acculturation in Mexico. "Then I have published another paper on the Nahua Indians of Yucatán, and various shorter papers about various Mexican Indian groups, as well as some Indian groups in California."[15]

It was in the context of these publications that Marcus asked Beals to present to the court the specialty in anthropology that had qualified him to testify about segregated schooling in the United States. "Aside from teaching, of course, my present personal interest is in the problems of the cultural change, as they affect the Mexican Indian in relation to the educational and social programs of the Mexican government," he replied to the court. If one looked back on his career, one would see a body of work that had been concerned from his earliest studies at Berkeley with the relationship between Mexico's indigenous groups and the growing power of the postrevolutionary state. But it was the postrevolutionary schools among the Tarascan and Yaqui peoples of Mexico that provided the more immediate context for Beals's testimony. He had just finished publishing *The Contemporary Culture of the Cáhita* and *Cherán* in Washington, D.C., both of which he alluded to in his testimony. Beals had brought Mexico's public schools into juxtaposition with the public schools of the United States as he described his specializations to the court. "In terms of the Mexican school system I have spent some time in visiting and studying Mexican schools, and also, I am familiar with the experimental work that has been done in the State of New Mexico," he told the court.[16] His own testimony in *Mendez* itself represented a juxtaposition between Mexico's schools and the public schools of Orange County. It is in these analogies that we can see how the central state's attempt to transform race relations in Southern California via the school took place in the context of the influence that the Mexican state had had on Beals's understanding of race relations and the school in postrevolutionary Mexico.

The continuity between the schools of Mexico and those of the United States was also evident in the normative definition Beals gave to assimilation in Southern California. Twenty-five years earlier, Israel Zangwill and Horace Kallen had presented two configurations of American pluralism in their canonical arguments about the American melting pot. Immigrants had been folded into a cultural ideal molded by British America against which other ethnic identities had struggled to survive. This broader question of the relationship between the ethnic group and the modern nation-state had been raised thirty years earlier by Manuel Gamio and José Vasconcelos in the context of the Mexican Revolution, as well. At the center of Mexico's melting pot discussions had been the competing visions of the nation as a collection of ethnic groups in which group cohesion predominated versus the nation as a more uniform entity characterized by peoples who shared a common series of cultural characteristics. Now, as he was pressed by the court to present his personal vision of the meaning of assimilation in 1945 Southern California, Beals registered his views of the melting pot in North America. Over and over, Beals underscored a constructive assimilation rather than a destructive one in *Mendez*, just as he had argued in *Cherán*. Loyd Tireman's model experiments at San José, he argued, had been performed in the direction of a constructive pluralism, for example. "In some of the experimental schools in New Mexico, for example, a great deal of richness has been given through the school training in emphasizing this particular thing," he told the *Mendez* court.[17] When Judge McCormick asked Beals to define what he meant by "Americanization," he concurred with McCormick that Americanization did not mean the British standard that Kallen had criticized thirty years earlier. Americanization was "supposed to be an admixture of all types of children. This is what I understand you mean by the Americanization principle. Is that it, Doctor?" McCormick asked. "Yes, that would become a part of it," replied Beals.[18] Beals suggested at the end of his testimony that assimilation was not to come at the price of ethnic particularity, as well. Rather, the proper role of the state was to push against the hierarchies of social power that produced the marginalization of some rather than others. "The advantages, properly handled, would come, then, in the breaking down of those stereotypes and in the broadening of understanding of people of different cultural backgrounds and in the understanding of different cultures."[19] The role of the state, Beals argued, was to defend a democratic concept of Americanization to which the culture of the group was necessarily intrinsic. We are used to reading more often about the destructive consequences of power in modern society for cultural affiliation rather than about attempts to harness power in the interest of protecting minority communities. For this reason, Beals's defense of a constructive pluralism usually shocks. We almost always think of Americanization as a destructive process in which the movement into the social milieu of American society destroys the cultural fabric of the immigrant group. Yet we should not have been surprised by Beals's defense of ethnic particularity given his historical admiration for the cultures of Mexico's indigenous communities. In *Cherán*, Beals had been critical of Mexico's schools for failing to preserve the social structures of Mexico's indigenous communities, just as he defended ethnic particularity in *Mendez*. In both cases, Beals had protected culture rather than uniformity as he studied assimilation in both countries.

The presence of Mexico's melting pot in the United States courtroom that Beals's testimony represented might be attributed to stereotype and ignorance. In *Mendez v. Westminster*, the court failed to distinguish the differences between the Mexican Indians in whom Beals had specialized and the mestizo schoolchildren of rural Orange County whose parents had sued the defendant school districts. As is still often done today, the court instead grouped together all the ethnic varieties of Mexico's peoples and used a nationalist label, "Mexican," to describe them. There is some evidence in the court record to support this view. No question was ever posed about the distinctions between the Yaqui of Sonora, the Tarascans of Michoacán, and the immigrant mestizos who had migrated to southern California a generation earlier, a fact that may suggest the court's ignorance of Mexico's wide ethnic geography. Yet there are reasons to be skeptical of this explanation. Beals was too careful a scholar of Mexico's cultural communities to have overlooked the differences between the Yaqui of Guaymas and the Mexican American mestizos of Los Angeles. He had spent his entire career researching Mexico's peoples, and he could not be mistaken for a colonialist administrator determined to sanitize the lives of Mexico's cultural communities, either. Beals had gone into anthropology because the Yaqui Indians had resisted the state so potently. And he had explicitly criticized the Mexican state in *Cherán* for public schools that were widening the divide between the lived cultural imperatives of the rural people of Michoacán and the industrializing economy that was placing pressures on them. Resistance to the state was an important component of culture for Beals. These factors suggest that something other than orientalism was happening in the *Mendez* courtroom when Beals made assimilation in Mexico the context for understanding integration in the United States.

A more convincing answer comes into view when we return to an analysis of Beals's court testimony on the witness stand alongside his studies of the Tarascan and Yaqui peoples. In the frontispiece to his ethnography of the Cáhita, Beals had underscored a phenomenon of history that he had first noted during his graduate career ten years earlier: *acculturation*. The

Cáhita peoples had been transforming, and had been transformed by, the cultures of Europe since the earliest entry of the Spanish invaders into Sonora. Similarly, in his *Cherán* study of Michoacán, he underscored the pressure of an industrial economy that was forcing permanent change among the Tarascans. His *Mendez* testimony shows his belief that a similar pattern of transformation was taking shape in Southern California, as well. Like Mexico's indigenous communities, Mexico's immigrant peoples in Orange County were being reshaped by the processes that had brought distinct peoples into contact with one another. It was through a discussion of Americanization that Beals took up this question of acculturation in *Mendez*.[20] "I think there is no question, with all the work that has been done with immigrant groups, not only Mexican and Spanish-speaking groups, but immigrant groups, generally, there is no question but that segregation slows up such a program of Americanization."[21] Beals added more comments after several questions by the attorneys. "In terms of making the children familiar with the whole body of customs, and so much of which is unexpressed, in our way of behavior or learning such as the attitudes of the Anglo-speaking peoples are towards various subjects or knowing what the attitudes of even children of their own age are toward various subjects, there can be no substitute, in my opinion, for actual contact with Anglo-speaking people, and rather intimate contact."[22] What Southern California shared with Mexico was a process of social change that was forcing new peoples into contact with one another. These transformational pressures were the axis around which Beals's courtroom testimony revolved, not the mistaken equivalence of distinct cultural communities across the United States and Mexico. Acculturation, and not identity, was the commonality that Beals was analogizing across the Mexican and U.S. communities that he had studied.

When he reached the top of his profession five years later, Beals used his presidential address to the American Anthropological Association to make explicit the interpretive common ground that had led him to bring cultural change in Mexico into a conversation with cultural change in the United States during the civil rights cases and elsewhere. "Within an urban area such as Los Angeles," he wrote, "characterized by rapid growth produced mainly by immigration and including a wide variety of ethnic minorities, we could find abundant material for studies which would relate to acculturation problems among American Indian groups." He continued, "As one of my colleagues put it somewhat inelegantly, 'The processes involved when a Navaho Indian is relieved of his jewelry and savings in a backstreet saloon in Gallup are essentially the same as those involved when a Mexican laborer is "rolled" in a saloon on Main Street.' " [23] He generalized his statement several remarks later:

> We believe that there are common factors which link together the processes taking place among the peoples of Yucatán, or such an Indian group as the Tarascans, the immigrant Mexicans in Southern California, the rural southern Negro or white moving into an urban setting, or the Iowa or Kansas farm family settling in the Middle Western Mecca. . . . It is our tentative hypothesis that there is a commonality of process which, if verified by empirical research, will ultimately lead to the development of a common body of concepts and generalizations to an ever-widening body of phenomena.[24]

It was here that the link he had charted between Mexico and the United States six years earlier in *Mendez* became explicit. Using the cultures of Mexico he had grown familiar with over the course of his career, he argued that the process of cultural change amid contemporary industrialization did not differ widely among geographic regions in North America. Whether it occurred among the cultures of Mexico's peoples, Blacks and whites in the South, or farmers in the American Midwest, cultural change among distinctive cultures coming into contact with one another was substantially the same everywhere. "Our ultimate agreement has been that within the framework subsumed by the concepts of urbanization and acculturation we are dealing with processes which, if not identical, at least form a related continuity of social phenomena."[25] Beals never stopped studying Mexico, but acculturation in California became increasingly important to him after 1945. Thus, even as Beals continued to study acculturation in postrevolutionary Mexico after 1950, he increasingly began to publish work on the immigrant cultures of Los Angeles.[26] His generalization of cultural change in the context of the United States had come from his theoretical study of Mexico's cultural groups.

Beals's belief in the constructive potential of the school tells us something about how remote we are from the era in which Beals operated. Seventy years living with the New Deal state in the United States and with the PRI party in Mexico has stigmatized government in both nation-states and made us skeptical of the claims to social reconstruction that its advocates proclaimed. Our skepticism has only been intensified by fifty years living in what Daniel T. Rodgers has called the "age of fracture."[27] In the hermeneutic world of culture created by Foucault, Geertz, and Gramsci, claims to the constructive regeneration of institutional power are deeply suspect. It is equally powerful to consider the current-day malaise of Cherán and so many other communities in contemporary Mexico. Rubén Martínez has recently depicted contemporary Mexican immigration to the United States from Cherán as a world of economic instability in which the immigrant is trapped in a world of fractured identities, for example.[28]

Yet many people in Michoacán and Orange County were not skeptical of the state and the school seventy years ago as they built new lives through the mechanism of the federal governments in Mexico and the United States. The intervention of the federal courts in the desegregation battles in Southern California shows the optimism ethnic Americans were developing in the American federal state at the moment that it was beginning its upward trajectory as an instrument of social transformation in American life. For the next thirty years until the protests of the Vietnam War, as Marc Simon Rodriguez has recently shown, Mexican Americans would hitch their fortunes as citizens of America to the federal state and the resources that its growth provided.[29] The federal courts would begin to integrate American public institutions. Mexican Americans would use the Wagner Act to fashion new lives of labor and social welfare. They would serve in America's armed forces in large numbers, thereby earning their claim to American citizenship. By the time John F. Kennedy would be elected president, they would vote in record numbers as members of the democratic electorate. When the *Mendez* plaintiffs originally asked the school districts of Orange County to desegregate, they argued for the assimilationist benefits of the public school as they sought to hitch themselves to an expanded definition of American nationalism. "Some of our children are soldiers in the war, all are American born and it does not appear fair nor just that our children should be segregated as a class," the *Mendez* plaintiffs had written. "This situation is not conducive to the best interests of the children nor friendliness either among the children or their parents involved, nor the eventual thorough Americanization of our children."[30] The central state would become a target of protest beginning in the late 1960s. But at the time of *Mendez*, there was only an upward slope in the belief by Mexican Americans that the state could deliver promises to them that they sought as assimilated members of a broadened American society.

Using social science as the platform to understand cultural change in Mexico, Beals had put twenty years of scholarship on the Mexican state's relationship to Mexico's Native Americans to work in the service of the Southern California civil rights movement. By the time that *Mendez v. Westminster* ended public school segregation in California in 1947, Beals had shifted his understanding of the role of government institutions in managing social change as he universalized the notion of acculturation. In contrast to his pessimistic interpretations in the late 1910s and early 1920s about the role of the state in industrial society, Beals had begun to think of the state as an agent of constructive engagements with local communities, not merely destructive ones. Beals's testimony in *Mendez* helps us to see how the shift in his thinking to a parallel engagement with the agencies of both the Mexican and American central states during his time in Mexico became central to post-World War II civil rights in the United States.

The Cultural Missionary in California

The same outreach worker in the cultural missionary system that Loyd Tireman had replicated in New Mexico after his visit to the normal school at Actopan followed Ralph Beals on the witness stand in *Mendez v. Westminster*. Marie Hughes had been hired by the Los Angeles public schools in 1941 to do the same itinerant cultural missionary labor that she had performed in Tireman's San José Project for nearly a decade. Her words on the witness stand in *Mendez* on the same day that Beals presented his work on assimilation in Mexico to the federal court showed that the history of school desegregation in California was not sui generis, but constructed on assimilation projects that had originated outside the state. Like Beals's own testimony about race relations in Mexico, her words reflected how postrevolutionary statecraft in Mexico had worked its way to ever greater circles of influence in the American West.

Fourteen years after her work in New Mexico had first begun, Marie Hughes found herself before the federal court of Paul John McCormick, in Los Angeles, California, testifying for the plaintiffs as a social science expert in the federal desegregation lawsuit that destroyed California's system of segregated public education. In the Santa Ana and Westminster communities of immigrants on whose behalf she testified in *Mendez*, the plaintiffs were Mexican American citrus workers who picked lemons and oranges for the emergent citrus industry of southern California. These Mexico-descended people were recent arrivals to California from Mexico, most first generation with children who had been born in the United States. Hughes's expertise in assimilation among the Mexico-descended peoples of California had been developed almost entirely in the context of New Mexico's mining communities and the San José Experimental School, even though her career is often associated with the desegregation lawsuits of the postwar West. She had worked among the rural villages of New Mexico between 1920 and 1940, obtaining skills that she transplanted to California after the end of Tireman's San José experiment, just as she told the court in *Mendez*. "I have worked in the State of New Mexico as principal and curricular director, and so on, for a period of some 19 years, and worked in Los Angeles County for the past 5 years," she told Judge McCormick and the *Mendez* courtroom in 1945.[31] Her later publications were similarly descended from work she had first produced in New Mexico twenty years earlier. She published her Stanford dissertation, "The English Language Facility of Mexican-American Children Living and Attending School in a Segregated Community," in 1952, for instance. But in 1932, she had already published *Teaching a Standard English Vocabulary*, while in New Mexico, and by 1935, she had published her University of Chicago master's thesis on "Rate of Acquisition of an English-Speaking Ability by Spanish-Speaking Children."[32] The role of language in Hughes's understanding of assimilation in postwar California was nothing new.

When the *Mendez* court asked her to describe her expertise in assimilation and the language acquisition capabilities of the schoolchildren of California, Hughes rattled off the long line of projects out of New Mexico that had only recently culminated in her Southern California tenure. "Have you made any special study of research to children of Mexican descent?" the court asked. "Yes," Hughes replied. "I was field worker and principal of the San José Experimental School of the University of New Mexico, where we studied the problem of the Spanish children, with the help of a graduate from the General Education Board."[33] That New Mexico and California should have been juxtaposed together in the courtroom as sites of experimental work on public schools in the postwar era is not completely surprising, though few contemporary scholars of civil rights have ever underscored New Mexico's relationship to American desegregation history that Hughes represented. But it is startling to consider that the ratio of ethnic relations work completed in those two places is exactly the reverse of the scholarly interpretation of the places where civil rights in the American West took place. It was the deep research conducted in New Mexico, with all its links to Mexican integration policy in the 1930s, that became the legal rationale for the testimony that Hughes provided to the *Mendez* court in 1945.

There were some nominal differences in Hughes's contruction of ethnic relations after her move to Southern California. In an important project report that she presented with Loyd Tireman in Santa Fe in 1943, for instance, her descriptions mimicked the idioms of the "minority rights" revolution of World War II American society. The distinctive idioms of intergroup democracy that Hughes used in her report mirrored the postwar discourses in interracial unity of national groups like the American Council on Race Relations, the American Jewish Council, and the American Civil Liberties Union, who were working to dismantle segregated public institutions. The county schools of Los Angeles, she argued, had sponsored workshops where "young people of Latin-American descent . . . explained . . . the discrimination which they have suffered and have expressed their ambitions and desires to become a real part of American life." In the same document, she argued that the Claremont Colleges had helped to organize an "intra-cultural" school in San Dimas, Orange County, whose value "lies in the community's awakening to its responsibility in bringing the citizens of Latin-American descent into full partnership with other members of the community." Those efforts had much work to do, she continued, but at the very least, some movement in the expansion of American political life had been initiated. "This next school year, it has been announced, there will be no segregated classes of Mexican pupils."[34]

Yet Hughes's turn to new terms like "discrimination," "segregation," and "minority peoples" must not be allowed to obscure the continuity of ethnic relations thought that had defined her work since the early 1920s. "In order to have the people of the United States understand one another, it is necessary for them to live together, as it were, and the public school is the one mechanism where all the children of all the people go," she told the federal court during *Mendez*.[35] This sentiment reflected her understanding in 1945 of the relationship between the public schools as pedagogical institutions and their presumed capacity for blending the peoples of America into a larger community. But that relationship was nothing new. It had characterized her work since her beginnings in the state of New Mexico in 1920. Using different idioms, Loyd Tireman had described the related social goal that Hughes had shared with him at the San José Experimental

School a decade earlier. "The bi-lingual project [of San José] has its concep-
tion in the belief that the bi-lingual tendencies that now operate as an
educational handicap to Spanish-American children in general, can be
transformed into an educational asset by the simple process of teaching
Spanish along with English in the lower grades," Tireman wrote. "For both
[Spanish-American children and English-speaking children], bilingual
classes offer a competitive field in which group advantages and disadvan-
tages are more or less equalized and in which group barriers can be effectively broken down. In a word, the project is an attempt, not only to find a
satisfactory solution of a very real educational problem, but aspires,
through educational channels, to solve the broader bi-racial problem of the
Southwest."[36] This view of the school as an agent of assimilation connected
Hughes's work in the California integration movement to the New Mexico
melting pot. One could not have guessed that Hughes's early ethics in New
Mexico would converge into the California integration movement after
World War II, but in retrospect, one can see the integrationist ethics that
defined her later career in the earliest pieces that she had published in New
Mexico. "[W]e are led to believe that in this County our objectives must
be classified as follows. . . . Knowledge of the nation's interdependence
[and] common courtesies and actions which make an organized society
possible," she had written in 1930.[37]

California society had transformed Hughes's idea of what ethnic
democracy should look like. By 1943, the Sleepy Lagoon and Zoot Suit riots
of 1942 and 1943 that had brought much attention to the role of government in stemming ethnic hostility in Southern California seemed to have
transformed her idea of assimilation. The Santa Fe report she authored with
Loyd Tireman gave broad attention to the questions of juvenile delinquency, ethnic violence, and social maladjustment that many had come to
associate with Latin American youth in Southern California. Hughes
defended Latin American youth from the perception that they were in-
ordinately predisposed toward violence, citing juvenile court records that
showed rates of delinquency in every other ethnic category compiled by the
court that were equivalent to those among Latin Americans. Yet despite her
effort to humanize these youth, her solution to ethnic violence in Los
Angeles worked by reshaping the cultures of Latin American youth to a
national culture structured by white Protestant majorities. Hughes never
defined precisely in Santa Fe what she meant by assimilation, but in the
context of heightened nationalist violence during America's war against
Germany, her description of ethnic interaction placed broad emphasis on

redirecting the characteristics of Latin American culture toward exogenous elements from the Protestant cultural groups that had been historically dominant in American history. In comparison to her New Mexico work, she placed less emphasis on pluralistic cultural relations in the American West. She focused far more on Latin Americans as the objects of transformation than she had ever had during her time in New Mexico.

Her court testimony in *Mendez v. Westminster* provided a good indication of this changed stance on assimilation. Her position initially seemed to mirror the pluralist vision that Ralph Beals had offered to the court. "In order to have the people of the United States understand one another, it is necessary for them to live together, as it were, and the public school is the one mechanism where all the children of all the people go," she said.[38] Here, her references to group differences in American life seemed porous to fluid borrowings of culture and language across groups, with no one group assumed to be more important than any other. But as the court asked her to discuss the role of the school in Americanization, Hughes tipped her hand in favor of a less pluralist position. Hughes first noted implicitly—"if we mean by Americanization, the learning of the ways of the larger group"—that there was no unanimity on what "Americanization" really meant. But if it meant "the learning of the ways of the larger group," then Americanization in the context of California's Latin Americans meant "learning the Anglo-American culture, which is the dominant culture of our country," she told the court.[39] Here, her definition coincided with Anglo Protestant culture. There was no discussion of Anglo Americans adding on the ways of the Spanish-speaking, indicating less concern with the fluid borrowings of culture within the school that George Sánchez and Ralph Beals had previously indicated in their own work. Rather, assimilation in the Southern California schools meant the movement of the Spanish-speaking into an ideal associated with white Protestant society. Conversely, segregation would result in the opposite of this assimilationist ideal. "Association with their own group mainly, the Spanish-speaking group, would tend to cement, to crystallize, to amalgamate to just the ways of that particular group, and not to add on the ways of the dominant group, or majority group," she said.[40]

In contrast to Beals's explicit references to Mexico's integration policy in *Mendez*, one is hard pressed to find Mexico's schools in Marie Hughes's court testimony, correspondence, and books. When one of the early intellectuals of the U.S.-Mexico relationship, Samuel Guy Inman, asked Hughes to write those portions of a text on Latin America that he was writing alongside University of Texas historian Carlos Castañeda, she gestured toward Mexico's integration policy by recommending that he add a chapter on Mexico's schools. "A chapter on going to school in Mexico should be included," she commented.[41] Mexico appeared in her correspondence again several months later. Hughes was having little luck finding fictional accounts of immigrant life in Southern California, but one book she did like was *Tumbleweed*, set in San Bernardino not far from the communities where she performed her missionary work for the Los Angles public schools. Still, the book was weak in one respect. "The ending is bad from my standpoint since the Mexican family returns to Mexico and the simpler life. Most families do not want to return," she wrote to George Sánchez.[42] Hughes provided only small glimpses of the Mexican state in her work. In contrast, Beals's testimony in *Mendez* pointed to direct influence of Mexican political history in postwar America. Sánchez and Tireman would also refer directly to Mexico as a context for American politics after World War II, as we shall see in our next chapter.

Yet if Hughes tended not to mention Mexico explicitly in her work, her career between her time at San José in New Mexico and the advent of the civil rights cases in California had been formed from the institutional convergence of the *misiones culturales* and the *escuela normal rural* with her educational labors in the United States. Nowhere were the vestiges of Mexico's role in her career more obvious than in the missionary pattern that she had established in the Los Angeles communities where she had replicated Mexico's policy work. In the area of Oaxtepec, Morelos, the rural communities to which Moisés Sáenz's missionaries had roamed were named Atotonilco, Jonacatepec, and Tlacotepec. It was there that the Americans had come to study school reform in postrevolutionary Mexico in the early 1930s. When Loyd Tireman replicated that system after returning to the United States from Mexico in 1932, he had tasked Marie Hughes to travel to "key schools" in the New Mexico villages of Hot Springs, Luis Lopez, and Atoka.[43] This was a labor that she continued to perform through the end of the 1930s. Louisiana's rural schoolteachers radiated outward to the communities of Kentwood, Mansfield, and Natchitoches when George Sánchez created the state's missionary system at Grambling in 1937 from the example he had studied in Mexico.[44] After the Los Angeles County schools had hired Hughes to reach out to the segregated rural communities that had been left out of Southern California's educational systems, Hughes herself itemized the rural communities to which she traveled in the effort to harness Mexico's immigrant peoples to the state's expanding school projects. San Dimas was a "rural school located in the heart of the lemon-growing section" that served "people [who] have lived pretty largely under conditions of real segregation," she wrote. At Puente, she described the rural school as "several wooden bungalows with improper light, unpainted walls, and few furnishings" for people who earned their living picking walnuts. She found that Whittier was a larger community with better school facilities, yet there, too, she indicated, "the elementary schools [had] a large problem in doing away with the practice of segregation."[45] Postrevolutionary Mexico had no monopoly on rural outreach programs in North America. But the particular ways the Mexican state had constructed such educational outreach became the central administrative model for Marie Hughes and the others who converged into the American civil rights movement. It was the more intense efforts of the Mexican state's outreach endeavors in the 1930s that had been the model for the outreach work that Hughes had performed at San José. Similarly, Tireman celebrated the outreach work of the cultural missions throughout the American West, finding in it a more intense engagement with local communities than anything he had ever seen at home.

Hughes's modest references to Mexico may best symbolize the flip side of Mexico's scientific state through the era of the civil rights cases. Across the span of her career in New Mexico and California, the one connecting thread in Hughes's work had been the magnitude of the movement of people north from Mexico into the rural communities where she had worked. Whether in Tyrone or Hurley, Doña Ana County or Albuquerque, Los Angeles or Orange County, the unending march of people northward that Carey McWilliams had captured in North from Mexico was the one constant in her life. It should not have been this way, according to the great theorists of the Mexican melting pot. Twenty years had passed since the end of the revolution, and the great textual monuments to the dreams of unification like La raza cósmica and Forjando patria were nearing thirty years in age. In Mexico, the nation was embarking on the first years of the Mexican miracle, that thirty-year span in the middle of the twentieth century when Mexico grew its middle class and financed its great universities, UNAM and the Instituto Politécnico Nacional. Amid these tangible successes of the revolutionary project, the unblemished defeat of the ancien régime and the triumph of equality that some believed had been promised by the Constitution of 1917 should have been clear. Throughout the Mexican countryside was the educational evidence of the SEP's millenarian project in nation-hood in the form of the Escuelas 123 of the republic, the Escuela Moisés Sáenz in Guanajuato, and the Escuela José Vasconcelos in Oaxaca. In Geneva, the United Nations would begin to copy Mexico's educational models throughout the world, while Mexico's ministers of education would become the directors of UNESCO. And in Mexico City, it was the begin-ning of the celebration of *lo mexicano* in word and film, that integrated cultural amalgam that writers like Octavio Paz and Samuel Ramos would elevate into a romance of political stability. Much had been gained by the postrevolutionary nation. The United States of America had been deflected as a military force not merely by World War II but by the diplomacy of President Cárdenas, who had nationalized the Rockefeller oil interests. No longer were rebel Cristeros fighting the garrisons of federal troops in Michoacán, Jalisco, and Guanajuato. These were enormous mid-century successes for the Republic of Mexico that should not be overlooked by anyone.

Yet always there was the immigrant moving northward into the isolated spaces of the American West as a testament to the limits of Mexico's melt-ing pot projects. Manuel Gamio had once dreamed of *forjando patria*, but he was implicitly forced to concede partial defeat of that great project when he wrote *Mexican Immigration to the United States* in 1930.[46] It is in the career of Marie Hughes where one could see the weakness of the tremen-dous project in unification that the Mexican federal government had set for itself in 1920. It was this same weakness that explains the people who were crashing into Marie Hughes's schools in New Mexico and California. Mon-tana Hastings could not find enough immigrants to conduct the intelligence testing she had wanted as she attempted to survey the psychology of Mexi-can immigrants across New Mexico and California in the early 1920s. Instead, she had relocated to Mexico City for twenty years. But by the time Marie Hughes was testifying in *Mendez* in 1945, there were hundreds of thousands of new immigrants from Mexico throughout the American West. They had become the subjects of the intelligence testing programs at the San José school. They had provided the initial streams of people in Doña Ana County and Tyrone, New Mexico, where Hughes had tried to convert them into Americans. And by the time of *Mendez*, they had become the immigrant manpower that picked America's oranges, lemons, nuts, and cotton in the rural communities in Arizona, Texas, and California, out of which the desegregation movement in the American West came.

The promise and the weakness of the Mexican state's melting pot as it moved through the middle decades of the twentieth century were not incongruous with one another. Beals had grown fond of the Mexican state because it was fragile, after all. Its inability to coerce the absolute submission of its people to the will of the administrative bureaucracies in Mexico City provided the space in which local cultures could continue to flourish. Beals's view of the state would come crashing down on him in the aftermath of the Vietnam War, but between 1930 and 1965, one can see his accelerating confidence in central government that nowhere manifested itself more strongly than in his participation in the American desegregation movement. Yet it was also that very weakness that could not produce enough largesse, quickly enough for many hundreds of thousands, to keep Mexico's disparate peoples at home long enough for the eventual triumph of la raza cósmica, that symbolic agglomeration of peoples of Vasconcelos's dreams. Throughout Hughes's career one could track the same weakness of the Mexican state that Beals reflected in his own career, not on the Mexican side of the international boundary, but on the American side. These were the same states, seen from two different points on the North American map. The Mexican state was the context for both of these researchers, even if Hughes had little to say about it in her work.

Amid this ambiguous legacy of the melting pot in postrevolutionary Mexico, the residues of the Mexican state were found not only in acculturation programs in Mexico, but in acculturation programs in the United States. When historian George J. Sánchez wrote his important Becoming Mexican American in 1995, he underscored the centrality of the American and the Mexican national states to acculturation programs in urban Los Angeles between 1920 and 1950.[47] He painted a portrait of two states warring for the hearts and minds of the immigrants flowing northward from Actopan and Cherán to the American West of Hoover and Roosevelt. The Mexican state helped to sponsor ethnic academies for younger students in the effort to draw them into the postrevolutionary Mexican project that had been crafted in the heart of the republic and to capture the immigrant flows of people that Gamio had documented in his 1930 Mexican Immigration to the United States.

Yet Sánchez's portrait of the Mexican state was rooted in the urban terrain of Los Angeles, close to the consulates and institutional seats of power in Southern California of the postrevolutionary Mexican republic. Immigrants could access consular officials even as consular officials performed the centripetal function of drawing back the multitudes who had peeled themselves away from the millenarian republic being created to the south. But those hits and misses took place in the middle of the city. In rural Los Angeles County where Marie Hughes worked, the power of the Mexican state was found in the minds of science rather than the embassies of the republic. There was no consulate in the rural communities of New Mexico's Rio Grande Valley where Hughes had once worked, either, just as there were no consular officials in El Modena where the lemon pickers who filed *Mendez* worked. In those places, the Mexican state was to be found in the policy models Hughes had carried in her mind from New Mexico to California. The paradox was that those models were now working in pursuit of integrationist projects in America rather than in Mexico. Hughes carried Mexico's missionary program every day in the details of her radiating work out of Los Angeles into the countryside, just as the cultural missionaries in Mexico continued to move out of Mexico City into rural Tlaxcala and Michoacán. In Mexico City, the Mexican state may still have had a chance. But in rural America it had very little chance at all. José Vasconcelos's fears had come true. That work had been co-opted by the republic to the north, just as he had feared in *La raza cósmica*. Mexico's peoples were headed north, to the former empire of the British that was stripping them away from *la patria*.

From *Integración* to Integration: Assimilation and the Legacy of Pragmatism

The world of Mexico's integration experiments in the 1930s and the world of the school desegregation movement in the 1940s United States might seem to some to be separated by their divergences rather than united by their convergences. Like their Mexican counterparts, for example, the Americans had worked on ethnic integration in the public schools from the executive branch of the state, but by the advent of the school desegregation cases they had begun to place more faith in the courts. Additionally, the distinctive institutional forms of schooling in each nation might seem to make integration in Mexico different from integration in the United States. In the rural schools of Mexico, children were often not being mixed across the racial line, while in the United States, mixture was the explicit goal.

Despite the change of venue from the executive to the judicial branch of government as the stimulus for bringing ethnic groups together, however, the pragmatist Americans never stopped making the public school the central institutional location for the transformation of social relationships. Scholars would later praise the federal courts for intervening in the structure of local communities as instruments of integration. But such appreciation for the role of the courts is narrower than the Americans had conceived of it in the 1940s. Courts, these Americans believed, were central instruments for bringing together the diverse communities of the West, and represented the activation of the central state in the direction of cultural reconstruction. But the courts were merely the gatekeepers toward a resynthesized West, not the agent of its actual creation. Reconstruction remained the work of the school, and the court merely an enabler. Theoretically, one way to understand the investment Beals and his colleagues had made in the court-centered civil rights movement of the 1940s was provided by Milton Gordon's distinction between *desegregation* and *integration*. As Gordon had pointed out, the school was amenable to a court decision for Sánchez because only the school could deliver on the promise of changing the "hearts and minds of men." To create an integrated society was a matter of individual transformation, not institutional fiat, and only the mechanism of the school, these Americans believed, was capable of steering the individual mind in a new direction of tolerance and inclusion.

Sánchez had expressed reservations about the law as the best avenue to desegregation in the American West as early as March 1945, before Beals and Hughes had offered their testimony in *Mendez v. Westminster*. "While I am convinced that the segregated school as it now exists does not meet with the law, and while I have hopes that in the future its legality will be successfully challenged, the legal approach is a tedious one and one which, in any case, will have to be supported by the expert educational evidence, a more enlightened public opinion, and fully documented evidence of various kinds," wrote Sánchez to Edwin Embree.[48] Elsewhere, Sánchez argued for the superior role of the school in the diminution of ethnic hostility. "The genius of our powers of assimilation, and of our powers of Americanization, lies largely in our public school—a school that is indeed a melting pot and a training ground for democracy," Sánchez wrote in 1947. Shortly after *Brown v. Board of Education*, in 1958, Sánchez made his most succinct case for the difference between the school and the court as the best avenue toward social reconciliation. At the heart of the matter was not the power of the court to force integration in the schools of the United States, he argued, but the transformation of bias in the human mind to achieve mutual cooperation and respect: "court rulings do not always change local customs and usages immediately, nor do they immediately change the ingrained biases of those who, in the last analysis, must do the job on the front lines."[49] Court rulings, indeed, have sometimes made the problem more intractable, argued Sánchez, causing policy reactions by school administrators in the form of gerrymandered school zones, "neighborhood schools" that were organized to keep minorities out, and transfer policies that created the same rigid forms of segregation as previous practice. "The guiding thought had been that true integration occurs only in a climate of cooperation and respect; and while those qualities may not be fully present at the outset, nothing should be done in the preliminary negotiations that might inhibit their expression and development when physical integration has been accomplished."[50] As these examples show, Sánchez had never been primarily concerned with the idea of *desegregation*—that is, access to public resources and institutions—but with *integration*, the creation of a pluralistic democracy of difference in which ethnic groups mutually celebrated their unique characteristics with one another.

For some, the distinctive institutional forms of integration in Mexico and the United States might seem to be a case of divergence rather than convergence, as well. Beals, Sánchez, and Tireman had all believed there was a clear line of institutional continuity between the school in Mexico and the school in the United States, but their comparisons skipped over an important difference. As a policy of the state, *integración* in Mexico had often not meant the placement of Mexico's diverse peoples alongside one another in the same classrooms. La Casa del Estudiante Indígena where Montana Hastings had worked in Mexico City was one institution that placed Mexico's diverse cultural communities together in the same class-rooms. But integration in Mexico had usually denoted the use of the schools for the assimilation of ethnically homogeneous communities to the political and economic projects directed by the metropole. Moisés Sáenz captured this sense of nationalism well when he wrote that the goal of the postrevolutionary state was incorporation into "that type of civilization which constitutes the Mexican nationality."[51] In the postwar United States, however, desegregation meant the placement of disparate people alongside one another in the same classrooms. When Mexican Americans challenged California education policy in *Mendez*, for example, the federal courts intervened in order to put two peoples together that previously had been kept separate from one another. This sense of assimilation through the mechanism of the classroom was different from the prevailing practice in Mexico in the postrevolutionary era. Reconciling *integración* in Mexico and desegregation in the United States given this difference is made ever more difficult by different labor and community formation histories. In the United States, public elementary schools predated the arrival of the immigrant peoples of Mexico in those communities where integration battles took place, whereas the case of Mexico witnessed concurrent school construction alongside the *integración* experiment. A second contrast included the distinctive labor histories of the United States and Mexico. Institutional separation by ethnic groups appears to have been a more rigid practice in rural Mexico because of more rigid labor patterns, whereas a higher concentration of distinct ethnicities seemed to congregate in the fields of the rural U.S. West.

But this difference between Mexico and the United States quickly disappears if we telescope outward to the larger context in which integration was occurring in the United States. For the Americans, in fact, integration did imply the assimilation of minority ethnic groups into the economic and political projects of the welfare state from which they had conventionally been kept apart, representing a de facto similarity to the integration projects of the Mexican state. One can see the similarity to Mexico at work in *Mendez v. Westminster* at the level of both the social scientists and the plaintiffs. Gonzalo Mendez has become famous as a civil rights hero in the American West for his challenge to segregation, but his life shows a clear trajectory into the farming economy and middle class lifestyle that had been a defining characteristic of the Southern California whites who controlled the local schools that Mendez fought to desegregate. From the perspective of the social scientist, meanwhile, Sánchez had argued in his 1940 *Forgotten People* that the solution for the ethnic minorities of Taos who had been bypassed by the institutions of the state was incorporation into the economic and political patterns of white America.[52] An analogy to the legal arguments against *Plessy v. Ferguson* provides an alternative way to see this de facto similarity, as well. The separate but equal doctrine had established the legality of separate schools for Blacks and whites in the face of equal funding for both constituencies of students. Funding formulas were never equal, of course, representing an inequality that became the basis for the original legal strategies adopted by Charles Hamilton Houston when the NAACP first began to attack the separate but equal doctrine in the 1930s. A generation later, Thurgood Marshall would drop the inequality argument in his *Brown v. Board of Education* arguments. Since the social space that kept ethnic groups away from one another had a power of its own that funding could never erase, equal funding in the context of segregation could never imply equality, the NAACP argued.

Yet in making the eventual case for shared social space across the color line as intrinsic to the definition of equality, the NAACP was depending on the movement of minority students into social spaces that were the province of white America. Built into the social scientific attack on the separate but equal argument was an implicit defense of the prevailing economic and political structure, in other words, since it was that structure that ethnic minorities were asking the state to enter. A contrasting position had been presented by W. E. B. Du Bois's critique of school integration as destructive to the cultural integrity of Black American communities. In Du Bois's reasoning, the closer Black America came to penetrating the institutions of white America, the faster such affiliation would erode the independence that had historically accounted for Black America's strength. *Wisconsin v. Yoder* in 1972 would bring many of these same issues to light two decades later in the case of the Amish minority of America.[53]

Nonetheless, we should not underestimate how radical a change in American race relations was being proposed by the desegregation of the schools even if it did little to destroy directly the economic platforms on which American society had been constructed. As Tim Tyson has pointed out in the case of the American South, for example, school desegregation raised violent backlash from white communities fearful that their social privilege was being eroded by federal courts moving in the direction of establishing social equality as a basis for American citizenship.[54] In the American West, Matt García and Charles Wollenberg have similarly pointed out the radical meaning of desegregation in the context of a historical past premised on hierachies of race and ethnicity.[55]

Moreover, John Dewey was deeply critical of the prevailing economic order and never anticipated the prevalence for all time of the structure of power that had reinforced deep ethnic and class tensions in American society. His criticism of American economic arrangements may have reached its fiercest moment in the 1930s, when he vehemently disagreed with the New Deal state for its built-in limitations on economic transformation. But into the era of World War II, Dewey continued to criticize the American social hierarchy, and his criticism would have held fast for Mexico, as well. The Americans likewise shared Dewey's hope for the structural transformation of economic and cultural relations as they fought to integrate American society. Like him, they looked forward to the future reorganization of America's economic structures as a follow-on consequence of new affiliations among America's ethnic groups. Intimate sharing across ethnic lines via the school would produce a revolution to the prevailing structure of power, the pragmatists believed, without sacrificing the cultural integrity of the groups in question. Perhaps their optimism would be proved wrong beginning in the late 1950s, in the aftermath of the reactions to the American civil rights movement. But as they continued to look to Mexico for inspiration for their political projects at home into the 1940s, that optimism for a richer, more spacious nation was alive and well.

Chapter 7

Texas and the Parallel Worlds of Civil Rights

The world of civil rights operating in the shadow of Mexico's state was manifested in the careers of George Sánchez and Loyd Tireman, as well. Like the parallel world of integration that Ralph Beals created between the Tarascans and the Californians, these assimilationist Americans who had studied in Mexico in the 1930s continued to turn to the Mexican state in the 1940s as they fought in the campaigns that destroyed Jim Crow in Texas. Sánchez and Tireman had traveled to Mexico in the 1930s and imported into the United States those models of education that they found particularly useful for assimilationist policy in Louisiana and New Mexico. But as they continued hoping for the expansion of the state into the realm of interethnic relations, they continued looking at education in Mexico as a parallel universe of integration policy to be studied for its effects on building a pluralistic democracy in the United States. Through World War II and beyond, they used Mexico's state policy in education to measure that of the American West, maintained their contacts with Mexico's social theorists, and continued experimenting with models of education that reflected Mexico's rural schools. Other Americans were using Cold War civil rights to construct integration policy in the United States, but these Americans continued with the study of Mexico that they had first started fifteen years earlier.

Mexico had not stopped experimenting with education through the 1940s, meanwhile, despite the new international concerns raised by World War II. In spite of important transformations in the Mexican educational experiment, Mexico continued to field its cultural missionaries and continued the experiments in rural education that it had embarked upon twenty years earlier. Thus, even as the court-centered desegregation movement accelerated in the United States, Sánchez and Tireman continued to study Mexico's administrative bureaucracies. For them, Mexico's assimilation projects remained the premier model of educational reform through which they understood integration into the civil rights era. The Mexican state's experiments continued to be a laboratory against which they measured change in rural communities. They established schools of the type they had first seen in Mexico. Even as the federal courts became the dominant institution for integration in the United States throughout the 1940s, Mexico continued to inform a parallel track of assimilation against which they evaluated their own political projects in the United States.

For George Sánchez, the Mexican state became the epitome of successful national reconciliation at the very moment that the legal desegregation movement was emerging in the United States. Never again would he maintain as close a relationship to the Mexican central state as he would during the 1940s. He would travel to Mexico City and Monterrey for educational conferences, become an unofficial diplomat for the Mexican state for his strong defense of public education in Mexico, and defend Mexico's national government in the face of the conservative shift in national politics that threatened the previous twenty years of SEP experimentalism. For Loyd Tireman, meanwhile, Mexico would become the primary model of the public school in New Mexico. He would rebuild the San José school in the guise of the Nambé Laboratory School, where he would produce important results in experience-based education that he would incorporate into the school desegregation cases. It was Mexico's rural school that would guide him in this new endeavor. Tireman would continue to hold up Mexico's public school as an example throughout the desegregation lawsuits of Texas and Arizona in the 1940s.

Sánchez and the Mexican State in American Civil Rights

Although *Mendez v. Westminster* later proved to be one of the canonical cases in the history of the American West, nobody had seen it coming. When he learned of the decision in late 1946, Roy Wilkins fired off a memo to the public relations department of the NAACP wanting to know why nobody seemed to know that the case had been going on.[1] All of a sudden, on the American Pacific Coast where no one was looking, a legal decision pressed by immigrants from the Republic of Mexico seemed to presage the end of the U.S. Supreme Court's separate but equal doctrine. Reaction to *Mendez v. Westminster* by the NAACP and its legal allies was swift in the immediate months after the decision. The NAACP sent its lawyers to California, where they tracked the decision through the appellate courts and awaited the possibility that the decision would rise to the Supreme Court. At Harvard and Yale law schools, professors debated McCormick's decision and tried to make sense of the possible demise of *Plessy*. Carl Murphy, who had long supported the NAACP as president of the prominent chain of Black newspapers, Afro-American Newspapers, was surprised to learn that *Mendez* had become the site of new arguments against *Plessy* within the American federal courts. "The attack upon the Supreme Court's theory that the 14th Amendment to the Constitution permits separation when facilities are equal is the first I can recall in this matter," he wrote to Thurgood Marshall. "Do you know of any other?"[2] But in Texas, where more immigrant Mexicans were still arriving than to any other state, George Sánchez, too, was unaware that *Mendez* had unfolded in the courts. There, Sánchez was in the beginning stages of a career in American civil rights that complemented the desegregation efforts of the NAACP. By 1943, he had taken money from the American Civil Liberties Union for desegregation lawsuits in Texas, and he would shortly become a liaison to the NAACP on Black desegregation lawsuits in the American West. Sánchez had left the Rosenwald Fund and assumed a professorship of Latin American education at the University of Texas at Austin, a position from which he would become one of the leading champions of school integration in the country. These were the early stages of George Sánchez's desegregation career, coinciding with the shift to the public elementary school as the focus of legal efforts in the American West as contrasted to his earlier focus in New Mexico on administrative reform from within the New Mexico state government.

Yet these years were most noteworthy for Sánchez's emphasis on integration in Mexico as the best educational model in the hemisphere. Indeed, at the very moment between 1940 and 1948 that Sánchez was helping to align the cadres of civil rights workers who would help to desegregate the public school in Texas and Arizona in the aftermath of *Mendez*, Sánchez's attention to Mexico reached the highest point in his life. Sánchez's study of Mexican integration policy at the same time that he was beginning his integration career in Texas was not accidental. Sánchez had remained close to the Mexican schools through World War II, including the years that

Mendez had been gestating in the lemon grove communities of Orange County. Although nearly all his publications in the 1930s had been about education in the United States, the majority of his work in the decade after his Rosenwald appointment in 1936 was about the Mexican schools. He published short pieces on Mexico for general audiences.[3] There were scientific articles for the American Academy of Political and Social Science.[4] He had published his synthetic study of Mexico's public schools for the Rosenwald Fund in 1936, yet he had followed up in 1944 with another synthetic study of Mexico's education system, *The Development of Higher Education in Mexico*.[5] Sánchez's attachment to Mexican education during this time tells us something about the context and chain of events from which the American civil rights movement took its cues in the postwar years. At the same time that Sánchez was beginning his involvement in the desegregation lawsuits, his writings reflected the continuous juxtaposition that he was making between the public education system in Mexico and that in the United States. Those comparisons show that Mexico functioned as a parallel universe of integration ideas against which he tested similar concerns in the United States, revealing his thoughts on the assimilation question in the United States just as much as they revealed his thoughts on assimilation in Mexico. Just as Ralph Beals had reflected in his *Mendez* testimony, Mexico's schools had remained the primary model from which Sánchez had attempted to desegregate the American schools during the years in which the American integration campaigns were launched in California and Texas.

Sánchez was clearly enthralled by the shadow Mexican education had cast over American schooling as he entered his career in integration in Texas. He had been permanently changed by his direct connections to Mexico's struggles with ethnic diversity, and for the rest of his career he would never forget the influence Mexico's experiments had on his understanding of education. But Sánchez's sense of Mexico's influence on the United States was predicated, as well, on the broad institutional contributions that Mexico had made to schools in New Mexico, Louisiana, and Washington, D.C., since 1935. "The spectacular developments in education that have taken place in Mexico during the past twenty years have been the subject of great interest to educators in many parts of the world," he wrote in 1943. "In the United States not only has this interest been expressed through the writing of visitors to Mexico but some of our efforts in developing community schools, the education of rural teachers, and Indian education have been influenced by ideas and procedures Mexico has applied to related problems with resounding success."[6] In a short article published at the moment he was cementing his ties to the ACLU in 1943, Sánchez revealed how deeply impressed he remained at the rapid transformation that Mexico had made in its schools. "These evidences of widespread appreciation of recent Mexican educational endeavor has led students of the problem to marvel that, in the course of less than one generation, the Mexican nation should have been able to attain such success in education as to become the focus of international professional attention."[7]

An Albuquerque speech a year later revealed the depth of Sánchez's acclaim for Mexico. At a jointly sponsored conference by the Universities of Texas and New Mexico in February 1944 entitled "Mexico's Role in International Intellectual Cooperation," a handful of Mexico's most prominent intellectuals were feted for their contributions to postrevolutionary society. The list included Alfonso Caso, considered among the leading archaeologists of his day, former minister of education Jaime Torres Bodet, and Rodulfo Brito Foucher, president of UNAM. This was a group of Mexico's most eminent humanists, all of whom were celebrated by state university presidents, historian Carlos Castañeda, and scholars across the disciplines from both the United States and Mexico. It was in front of this audience that Sánchez indicated the dimensions of Mexico's educational experimentation in relation to that with which he was involved in Texas. "The leading position in modern education on the North American continent belongs to Mexico," Sánchez told the guests as he introduced Torres Bodet at the celebration dinner. "From the time that the incomparable Fray Pedro de Gante established a grand school in 1523 to our contemporary epoch today, when illustrious educators from Mexico are establishing cultural missions, establishing rural medicine academies, and are embarked on a cultural revolution over the entirety of Mexico's people and Mexico's national territory, Mexico stands out as the preeminent example in the entire continent for its advanced ideas on the function of education."[8] This was no extemporaneous attempt to praise foreign guests with decorum of World War II partnerships. Sánchez had been a persuasive critic of public education in the American West for twenty years, with affiliations reaching into the American South, Washington, D.C., and Latin America. Many might have chafed at the strength of his conviction, yet few critics anywhere in the United States were positioned to challenge his belief that Mexico had done a better job of educating its people than had the United States. We may not agree with his decision, but Sánchez's belief is an artifact of history that tells something about the many ways that the civil rights movement emerged: at the same time that Sánchez was developing his ties to the ACLU, it was the Mexican education system that was guiding Sánchez's hopes for new race relations in the United States. Why did Mexico continue to have such a powerful hold on his politics at the moment that he was helping to build the American desegregation movement, and what difference did it make to his view of desegregation in the United States?

Nothing was more important in Sánchez's calculus of the Mexican schools than the rural political economy in which Mexico's integration programs continued to take shape. If historians have frequently noted that the American West to which immigrants from Mexico were moving in the 1930s and 1940s was a predominantly agrarian West, they have not noted that the desegregation struggles of the public school took place uniformly in local communities where a rural economy predominated. The rural economy as a site of struggle for the school still deserves much more attention than it has received—why, for instance, did local conditions permit the more rigid segregation patterns found less often in the urban American West?—but it is even more critical to consider that solving the problem of segregation meant looking for integration models that were specifically set in the rural context. This was a fundamental axiom of the Americans who turned to Mexico for inspiration, for the use of pragmatism as an instrument of social reconstruction implied the search for education models specifically tailored to the unique conditions of the rural community in the United States. The rural community was one in which few progressive school experiments had ever been designed, however, a fact that necessitated a greater field of view than that of the United States alone. As early as 1936, one can detect Sánchez's increasing shift toward an analysis of the rural scene as the unique circumstance for a consideration of the work of the school in assimilation and integration. His Louisiana publications in 1936 were precisely a consideration of this phenomenon, serving as the bridge over which he switched back and forth between the American West, Mexico, and Louisiana during his tenure with the Rosenwald Foundation.

By the time that Sánchez had entered into his career at the University of Texas in 1940, he had firmly begun a celebration of the Mexican state for its strong presence in Mexico's rural scene. "This responsiveness of Mexico's great educators to the agrarian folk cultures of her peoples constitutes the outstanding contribution of the nation to the theory of education," he wrote in 1940. "The desire and hope to develop an 'integral

Figure 21. George I. Sánchez with Mexico's humanists at the University of New Mexico in 1944. Simultaneously, he was beginning his desegregation career in Texas. Seated at far right is Sánchez, next to UNAM president Rodolfo Brito Foucher. *Mexico's Role in International Intellectual Cooperation: Proceedings of Conference Held in Albuquerque, February 24–25, 1944* (Albuquerque: University of New Mexico Press, 1945), 28.

education'—an education adapted to the total cultural situation—had long motivated the efforts of many of Mexico's humanitarian leaders, even though it has been given a clear-cut expression only recently." Sánchez then described the dramatic change that had occurred in Mexico's rural provinces. "The organization of a system of rural schools was seriously undertaken only after 1920 and has progressed apace since that time," he argued. "It is in the development of that program that Mexico has made its greatest contribution to educational theory and practice." Such an expansion was the great creative gift of the revolution to the nation. "In meeting the problem of education for the rural masses, the 'men of the Revolution' have shown a creativeness and a sense of fitness that has received the acclaim of the world."[9] Sánchez continually repeated his sentiments about rural education in Mexico through the start of his desegregation career, including contributions to the *Encyclopedia of Modern Education* (1943), *The Educational Forum* (1943), and *Educación Nacional* (1944) in Mexico City.[10]

A second basis for Sánchez's defense of Mexico's schools came out of his immersion in pragmatism. The presidency of Manuel Ávila Camacho between 1940 and 1946 had marked a decided rightward tilt in national politics, in part because Ávila Camacho was a professed Catholic who denied the post-1920 anticlerical policies of the national state during his time in office. It was in this context that Catholic leaders began a campaign to move back the educational reforms of the Secretariat of Public Education, an effort that succeeded in raising the concern of educational leaders abroad. Among Sánchez's strongest writings at the moment he began his desegregation career in Texas was a defense of the Mexican state against Mexico's new conservatism, an argument he conducted in the language of pragmatism. The renewal of debates after 1940 about the proper role of the school in postrevolutionary society, wrote Sánchez, was a partisan affair alone, responding to the Church's historical antipathy to the post-Juárez Mexican state rather than to any defensible lapses of the postrevolutionary schools. "To the disinterested spectator of these events, is seems clear that justification for the attack upon the modern Mexican school on the grounds [of the weaknesses in the nation's present program of public education] is not to be found in Mexico's history of education," Sánchez wrote in 1942. "It would appear, from this distance, that such attacks arise out of the still unsettled education phase of the State-Church question, a matter which has little to do with the validity or nationality of the fundamental principles of Mexican education."[11]

What Sánchez found most disturbing was the conservative argument that Mexico's schools of action were not native to the Mexican experience. "The contention that the Mexican school of action is a product of principles foreign to Mexican culture or alien to its Catholic heritage is not in keeping with the facts of history," he argued. Here, Sánchez turned to the colonial education system of the Catholic mendicant orders once more, just as he had in his 1936 Rosenwald book. "Almost a century before Comenius and Bacon's *Novum Organum*, Gante and Quiroga were operating schools of experience and were showing that their interest was not in knowledge per se but as a tool for the utilization of the forces of nature in the interests of human welfare—precursors of the scientific method and of pragmatism," he argued. "Even as the Protestant Revolt was in its initial stages, Mexican education had cast away the outmoded ties of the old educational order, and, in close harmony with the vital features of Mexican life, set out to carve a new, a native pattern." Indeed, argued Sánchez, the sixteenth century was the precursor of the modern pragmatist school in Mexico, since that "century, beyond any doubt, anticipated the modern Mexican school in its social philosophy of education and, in some respects, set up goals and demonstrated practices which make modern, progressive schools, in Mexico and elsewhere, seem conservative." The work of Fray Pedro de Gante, Bishop Vasco de Quiroga, and Viceroy Antonio de Mendoza "stand as a monument to a social philosophy of education and as the cornerstone of Mexican culture," wrote Sánchez. "Their pragmatism, their intelligent fusion of spiritual goals with social action, and their devotion to the cause of redemption of the masses through realistic education can certainly not be regarded as giving rise to a conservative tradition."[12]

It was in light of this history that Sánchez defended the post-1940 Mexican schools as the epitome of enlightened political thought in the twentieth century. There was no denying the errors committed by the Mexican schools, but the program that the Mexican state had set into motion after the revolution had brought attention from all around the world for its progressive politics. "The rural teacher, the Cultural Mission, the Indian school, reached out militantly to unshackle the Mexican from the fetters of ignorance and filth, of hunger and oppression," he wrote. "In twenty short years, the revolutionary administrations of the nation did a remarkable job of channeling the expression of nationalism along Mexican ways, in the interests of Mexicans, and for the enhancement of Mexican culture." At the root of this success, and of the acclaim that the world had given to Mexican education, was the liberation of local identity. "The schools of the Republic attracted the admiration of the world by their intelligent application of principles of acculturation and by the fervor and determination with which they dedicated themselves to the task of 'cultivating culture' at the grassroots of the nation."[13]

Sánchez did not refrain from criticizing Mexico's educational system as he considered its integration ideas for application in the United States. Chief among Sánchez's criticisms of post-1940 education in Mexico was the slow development of a professional corps of teachers who could saturate Mexico's communities, both rural and urban, as part of a revolutionary mandate to rebuild the nation. Teachers were too often part-time employees of the state, and they sometimes functioned at multiple institutions rather than permanently within a single community. The rapid transition from Church-centered schools to public ones after 1920 had been too precipitous, resulting in an ad hoc system of instruction rather than a planned structure whose resources could match the optimism of the revolution's ideology. Much of the problem could, of course, be attributed to the challenge of constructing an economy that could absorb the new professionals imagined by the state, Sánchez observed, and by the understandable rise of new vested interests who benefitted from the per-contract wage system of the schools, as low as that pay may have been.[14] In a system of education whose principles placed enormous responsibility on the educator, what was at risk was the progressive transformation of a society that had been stabilizing itself for two decades. "This general practice . . . is an obvious handicap both to the pursuit of a professional career by teachers as well as to the development of the educational institutions," he wrote in 1943.[15]

Sánchez also criticized the politics of personalism that had infected the upper administrative structures of the Secretaría de Educación Pública, a development that compromised the social ethics of the postrevolutionary commitment to the communities of the nation and narrowed the philosophical importance of wide intellectual debate in the very ministry charged with transforming the quality of educational practice in the republic. "Educational policy in Mexico is quite often simply an expression of the personal point of view of the Secretary of Education then in office," he wrote. "Quite often the personal views of this individual make themselves felt even in such matters as the very content of the textbooks." The effects of such policy predilection were devastating for pedagogy on the ground; "coeducation may be very 'Mexican' and 'revolutionary' under one Secretary and, in a few months, anathema under another," he commented, before taking aim at Vasconcelos, Puig Casauranc, and their successors for failure to stabilize the content of the schools. "The Greek classics are just the thing under one administration, but the next administration rules that children's literature must be more vital, contemporary, and realistic. And so it goes, the very spirit of the educational program being left at the mercies of sincere, honest, and otherwise able cabinet members—but too often to cabinet members who view education with non-professional eyes and whose opinions, therefore, respond not to educational principles but rather to personal bias."[16]

What may have been most striking about Sánchez's ongoing engagement with Mexico's educational system as he was developing his desegregation career was how little direct experience with Mexico's rural schools he actually had in comparison to his work in the 1930s. Nearly everything he wrote as he began his desegregation career in the 1940s was outside the orbit of the work being done in Mexico's small rural schools, in contrast to the analysis he had performed in the decade of the 1930s. His 1944 monograph on Mexican higher education was a historical interpretation of the university system, while his articles on the Mexican educational miracle were positive assessments of the expansion of educational programming that extended his 1930s conclusions without reevaluating them. There was certainly enough variety in Mexico's school programming that Sánchez would have found plenty of evidence for a celebration of continuing experimentation in Mexico's attempts to rebuild the national culture, as scholars have shown.[17] But Sánchez was flying too high above the rural schools as he was establishing a career at the University of Texas to make us completely confident of his assessments. Sánchez had been there in the 1930s, but he was now surveying Mexico from afar rather than studying it up close. He had been critical of Mexico's schools, but the difference in his orientation toward the Mexican state project in the 1940s from that of a decade earlier was significant. Whereas he had devoted much of his earlier analysis to the relationship between the school and the student, by early 1940 he was celebrating the central state as the enabling instrument of education almost exclusively and spending almost no time studying the function of the teacher, pedagogy, or philosophy of learning in the classroom. Sánchez himself recognized this difference: when asked to write a new contribution on Latin America to Columbia University's *The Yearbook of Education*, a task he had done regularly over the previous years, he demurred. "For the past several years I have been very much out of touch with what we have been doing in Latin America," Sánchez responded.[18] It was the first time he had deferred any project whatsoever about Mexico and Latin America since his first trip there in 1935.

In view of this unpragmatic approach to Mexico in the 1940s, an offer Sánchez made to Professor Isaac Leon Kandel of Columbia University to speak at the University of Texas in 1947 provided the sharpest insight for understanding why Sánchez believed Mexico remained the premier example of education in the hemisphere at the very moment he was deepening his involvement in desegregation in the American West. Kandel was the leading comparative education researcher in the country, and had recently been involved in efforts to survey educational trends in Latin America after similar studies documenting educational transformations in Europe and Asia. Sánchez had known Kandel personally for some time as a result of mutual work they had done on education surveys across the globe. But on this occasion, simultaneous with his accelerating work with the legal suits of the American West after *Mendez v. Westminster*, Sánchez invited Kandel to speak on Latin American education at the University of Texas at Austin Institute of Latin American Studies. "We would consider ourselves fortunate if we could persuade you to come here during March to deliver one or two prepared lectures on Latin American education or other intellectual developments," he wrote to Kandel.[19] When Kandel later published his University of Texas at Austin address—"Dr. Kandel gave us two exceedingly interesting and valuable lectures," Sánchez wrote to a colleague—his analysis drew attention to a central feature of Latin American education Sánchez had begun to focus on.[20] "If many of the weaknesses in education in the United States are due to extreme localization, many of the weaknesses of education in the Latin American countries arise from extreme centralization," Kandel argued.

> In the early stages of building up an educational system in countries with great distances to be covered, with sparse means of communication, and with populations scattered in small and isolated groups, the only way of laying the foundations for an educational system at all was through the central government. Centralization in itself is not an evil provided that the financial support of education is separated from its control in every detail. The only safeguard against rigidity of control lies in an alert public. Generally, however, the public has not been taken into partnership by the governments in determining the progress of education.[21]

What Kandel had described to the Latin Americanists at Austin as one of the fundamental flaws of Latin America's new educational systems was the one characteristic Sánchez celebrated about Mexico through the 1940s, as he was fighting the authority of local school districts in Texas using the new power of the American central state to desegregate the schools of the American West. Throughout the 1940s, as Sánchez increasingly became involved in the desegregation movement in Texas, the strong central state was a characteristic element of Mexico's education programs that Sánchez underscored again and again. In his 1940 *Annals* article, for example, he argued that the strength of the Mexican state had finally made good on the promise of educational programming for the variety of people across the nation.[22] Similarly, in 1943, he argued that the national government's efforts to create a national education system had been the basis for the widespread international acclaim that Mexico had garnered.[23] He reiterated the same point later in 1943 by detailing the logistical success of the Secretariat of Public Education after the revolution, down to the number of schools that had been established, the number of teachers that had been placed into the field, and the annual expenditures for education by the state. "Since its establishment in 1921," he wrote, "the SEP has gradually taken over most of the burden in elementary and secondary education in the nation."[24] It is telling that Sánchez had invited Kandel to speak at Austin in 1946, only months after the federal court in *Mendez* had outlawed segregation of Mexican Americans in California. The use of the U.S. central state to integrate the public schools of the American West was for Sánchez, in fact, a deeply held tenet of progressive social transformation that one could best read in Sánchez's work on the Republic of Mexico. What we see in the 1940s compared to his earlier work in the 1930s was a symbolic celebration of the state as an agent of social transformation rather than a focus on the school as the instrument of experimentalist regeneration.

In view of the politics of the central state that had become more important to him by the early 1940s, we should not be surprised that Sánchez involved himself in a project with the very high state builders in Mexico who had built the Secretariat of Public Education and written the literary classics that would come to occupy that nationalist genre known as "lo mexicano," the essentializing aesthetic whose analogue would come to the United States in the 1950s in the form of the myth-and-symbol and national character schools. It was 1943, and together with Samuel Ramos, Sánchez had embarked on a plan to document the grand projects of Mexico's education builders with the support of the University of Texas at Austin.[25] In the letter they signed together, Sánchez and Ramos explained the purpose of their project. "In view that the international exchange between the U.S. and Mexico is of utmost importance, the preparation of a directory of Mexico's educators is of utmost utility," they wrote. "The University of Texas and the Secretariat of Public Education have therefore jointly proposed a collaborative project, the *Directory of Mexican Educators*. We believe that it will be of great utility for those continuing studies that are taking place in the United States and in Mexico and to further the international exchange between our two countries."[26]

Ramos was only five years removed from the publication of his *El perfil del hombre y la cultura en México*, whose argument for an inferiority complex as the psychological feature that united all Mexico's peoples made it one of the great masterpieces in twentieth-century Mexican letters and, simultaneously, one of the ignominious installments in the essentialist typologies of Mexico that would later receive scathing indictments by scholars in both the United States and Mexico.[27] Yet here was Sánchez working alongside Ramos in 1943, trying to organize all of Mexican education after the revolution in the form of a directory that would map the treetops of Mexico's national renascence. Among the many who responded to the call by Sánchez and Ramos were the great educators of the SEP's project in national integration. Ezequiel Chávez, who had appeared in the *Lemon Grove* report prepared by the Secretaría de Relaciones Exteriores (Secretariat of Foreign Relations) in 1931, responded with a lavish thirty-two-page recapitulation of his life. There was Rafael Ramírez, too, whose pedagogy had become the basis for instruction at Actopan and the other normal schools of the republic. "Attached please find the bibliographic citations for the educational work that have recently appeared in Mexico, my fine friend and respected gentleman," Ramírez wrote to Sánchez.[28] There were others that no scholar today would leave out of Mexico's pantheon of great humanists: Alfonso Reyes, Lucio Mendieta, Juan Comas, and Francisco Santamaría. Among the last that came in was a contribution from José Vasconcelos himself, whose *raza cósmica* project had been among the originary platforms for the millenarianism of the revolutionary schools. Considered as a whole, it was a spectacular assemblage of the nationalist project that was represented in the survey that Sánchez had gathered on his desktop in Austin, like a chessboard of knights who had done battle against the forces of Porfirian philosophy and won.

It was 1943, the same year in which Sánchez first reached out to the American Civil Liberties Union to carry out the desegregation of the American West, and the two projects were not unrelated. Sánchez was embarking on a political career in civil rights whose history would include the American courts that would help to end segregation in the West. Sánchez did not know this yet, and it must have been an uncertain moment for him. The war was raging in Europe and in Asia. Nazis were destroying the Jews in one part of the world, and in America the United States was interning Japanese Americans in the West, incarcerating zoot-suited Mexican Americans in California, and lynching Blacks in the American South. It was at that moment that Sánchez was more focused on the Mexican state than he ever would be again, romanticizing its exponents and celebrating its successes. Mexico was his model, the example that gave him hope for the United States, the central state that had long ago begun to do what America at home still refused to consider. Mexico kept him going, just as it had for the last decade, and just as it would continue to do through the end of his life.

Mexico's Rural School in America

Pragmatism was under assault as Sánchez was launching his desegregation career. Claiming that a historicist ethics could not be a sufficient platform for a critical reading of culture, metaphysicians like Mortimer Adler accused pragmatism of making possible such extremist politics as the rise of the fascist state in Germany.[29] It was as antithetical an approach as could be formulated to Dewey's own vision of philosophy as an instrument of social reconstruction, but the criticism would stick. By the end of World War II, the emigration of European intellectuals from Vienna would accelerate the death of American pragmatism. In the guise of logical positivism and analytic philosophy, American philosophy would drive pragmatism underground until the 1970s, when it would surface again not among philosophers, but among literary theorists and historians. Hammered on one side by those who thought pragmatism was not scientific enough and on the other by those who thought pragmatism was too scientific, Dewey was fast becoming the one social critic with whom no philosopher wanted to deal.

But even as philosophy departments were supplanting one set of ideas with another, school theorists persisted in attempting new models of the school as an instrument of pluralistic community. For them, pragmatism's approach to social unification could not be erased so precipitously. Institutions took time to build, and the education professors and psychologists still found themselves putting into practice the theory of knowledge to which Dewey's school had committed itself.[30] One was Loyd Tireman in New Mexico. Sánchez would pull him into the Texas school desegregation movement after the *Mendez* decision in spring 1947, a moment when Tireman had returned to the principles of Mexico's rural schools to create one of the last manifestations of Deweyan pragmatism in education, the community school. As his desegregation career in Texas accelerated after 1940, Sánchez had found Mexico's state bureaucracies more instructive for his work than its rural schools. Tireman moved in the opposite direction. He returned to pragmatist first principles, abandoning the weaknesses of the

San José approach to experience in the immediate environment as the means by which to construct knowledge. By returning to the more intense example of experience-based education he had first seen in Mexico's rural schools in 1931, he built a new school in New Mexico whose successes became central to the Texas desegregation movement *Mendez* had helped foster.

Tireman's unease with San José had been surprising on one level. The San José model had become a promising way to attack the challenges of social conflict and cultural difference for educators in neighboring states struggling to understand the arrival of immigrants from Mexico, for example. The Arizona Normal College wrote to the General Education Board in 1935 that it was taking control of a Flagstaff school in order to replicate the San José model for the state of Arizona. "As I see the thing right now," wrote college president Thomas Tormey, "we could use the techniques you used from the first to the sixth grades, improving such checks on mental ability of achievement as you are using in your control school."[31] The Key School program Tireman had built had even worked itself out of a job, meanwhile. The state department of education had found Tireman's importation of Mexico's cultural missionary program so successful that it had implemented an itinerant supervision program of its own.[32] The system of the Key Schools "has aided in selling the idea of supervision to the state," he wrote. "It has demonstrated the value of good supervision, and undoubtedly facilitated the work of the State Department of Education in providing state supervisors as it is now doing."[33] Tireman lamented that the Key Schools program would have to be eliminated to avoid duplication. But Tireman was satisfied that the state's new efforts at outreach and supervision were directly attributable to the implementation of practices he had modified from the postrevolutionary models he had copied from the Republic of Mexico. Meanwhile, Tireman's San José teachers were being recruited by top universities, including Marie Hughes, who left for graduate work at the University of Chicago in 1935.

But it was the relationship between experience in the world and the development of social ethics that Tireman had always been most concerned with. And on this level he remained uneasy. Despite San José's successes, Tireman's experiments with language had never yielded the results he had hoped to see. "San José has reason to be deeply concerned over the fact that with all of the effort put forth and with all of the emphasis on reading the grades above the second are below norm," he wrote in his five-year report to the GEB in 1936. "San José must strive not only to retain the place won by the early grade but also to bring the other grades up to the norm."[34] He had invested three years work to establish the San José School, and an additional five to bring the European- and Latin American-descended cultures of New Mexico into a unified community of cooperation via the development of his experiments in language. He had learned new techniques in rural pedagogy in postrevolutionary Mexico, hired new teachers to serve the rural communities of New Mexico, and overcome state bureaucracies that had questioned his project. Across the United States, he had sought advice from government officials, university professors, and local communities. Yet three years after traveling to postrevolutionary Mexico in 1931, he admitted his attempt to solve the language problems and harmonize the cultural enclaves of New Mexico into a single whole was failing. "I feel sincerely that we must have three more years to validate our work," Tireman wrote to the GEB in November 1934. "I should feel that education in general would have a perfect right to put a great question mark after all of our statements in regard to the performance of the Spanish-speaking child."[35] It was to these failing results in language that he later attributed the sudden transformation of the San José project.

The transformation was dramatic. By 1938, Tireman had abandoned the San José School and the city of Albuquerque altogether and relocated his project to the rural community of Nambé, New Mexico, eighteen miles north of Santa Fe and one hundred miles from the University of New Mexico. In Albuquerque, he had had a school that had grown to more than 800 pupils, in an environment that bordered an urban core. In Nambé, the school comprised a handful of small rooms, with a student population of 180, "at the end of a dirt road that followed the Nambé River over the hills beyond the highway" that bisected the state. In Albuquerque, increasing enrollment had made students anonymous to Tireman, but at Nambé, he developed a tight relationship with the people who made up the smaller institutional scale of a rural community. Nambé "consists of three crude adobe structures in one of which pre-kindergarten instruction is given; in another, kindergarten training; and in the third and largest, the higher grades," reported the GEB during a 1937 site visit. "The children are drawn from a radius of several miles in the valley from homes of Spanish speech."[36] Over the span of twenty-four months, Tireman had completely transformed San José into a new configuration that differed in almost every respect from what he originally implemented in Albuquerque in 1930.

Tireman's isolated agricultural village matched the one-room schoolhouses of Iowa where he had been raised. He had always had a career interest in one-room schools, an interest that his move to New Mexico in 1927 had only reinforced. Tireman romanticized the village and school in Nambé to which he had now moved. "The shallow Nambé River winds through the fields and by the houses," he wrote in a later 1943 project report. "Instead of one or two broad fields there are dozens of little fields, symmetrically marked off and planted in alfalfa, beans, corn, potatoes, peas, and chili."[37]

But if Iowa had a distant place in his mind, the more immediate context for the move to Nambé had been Mexico. Tireman left his own record of Mexico's role in the creation of Nambé in his project reports, but that role was best captured by Tireman's San José protégé Frank Angel, Jr., "Mexico was pioneering in the education of its indigenous population and the Community School idea was being tried," wrote Angel in 1959, as he looked back on Tireman's career in the American West: "Tireman's imagination was fired by what he observed. Later he put these ideas into practice in the Nambé School."[38] Mexico's influence on the Nambé school dramatized the continuing influence of pragmatism across Mexico and the United States that had shaped Tireman's career. And it left little doubt that Tireman came closer to replicating the Mexican rural school that he had studied during his 1931 trip to Mexico than any other model. It also showed us what we have already seen in the careers of Beals and Sánchez before him: at the moment that these Americans were embarking on the desegregation of the American schools, they were simultaneously turning to Mexico as the premiere example of progressive social transformation for the United States.

As early as 1931, Tireman had considered the possibility of reordering the San José School along the experience-based models of pedagogy of Mexico's rural experiments. In the wake of his return from Mexico, Tireman had initially channeled his enthusiasm for Mexico's rural schools into new possibilities for the one-room schoolhouses in New Mexico. In his first meeting with the San José board that had authorized him to travel to Mexico, he was so enthusiastic about experience in Mexico's rural schools that Tireman had to cajole his board members from immediately establishing a one-room schoolhouse in the mountains near Albuquerque. Rather than establishing a new school "where we could demonstrate the possibilities in community leadership and also give our visiting teachers instruction in exactly the same environment in which they are teaching," Tireman satisfied his enthusiasm by establishing a close relationship with an apprentice

teacher from Cedro, a small village in the mountains outside Albuquerque.[39] Jennie Gonzáles became one of his favorite teachers as he invited her
to talk about her rural village to conferences across the state. Her description of the challenges that confronted her as an educator, in the isolation
of her community in New Mexico, was among the most vivid ever produced by the San José project.[40]

> My community is twenty-three miles from the city of Albuquerque
> and is situated in the midst of a National Forest. It is on a Federal
> Highway, that is, all but one mile AND HEREIN LIES THE
> THORN. It takes a brave man to venture on this road when it rains,
> and rain seems to be the rule rather than the exception. . . . I wish
> you could see my village with my eyes—sympathetic and uncritical.
> Tall pines and noble cedars form a beautiful background and right
> now patches of crimson sumac give a vivid contrast to the bright
> green of the pine trees.[41]

To transform San José into Nambé beginning in 1937, Tireman
returned to pragmatism's cardinal idea that there was no transcendent reason why the school should be arranged in any particular way. There was no
ultimate moral sanction why the common school had been built as it had,
any more than there were any moral reasons why the school in New Mexico
should now subscribe to any dominant archetype. Instead, like knowledge
itself, schools were instrumental institutions whose reason for being derived
from the social outcomes their organizers had set out for them in advance.
"It is axiomatic that the method of doing a thing is determined by the
purpose in mind," Tireman wrote in his Nambé retrospective.[42] Sánchez
had said this same thing in his 1932 dissertation.[43] There were no warrants
for doing anything at all, except the political outcomes one wanted to
achieve.

This instrumental logic gave Tireman the opening he needed to reconsider the tradition of the school in New Mexico. Those schools had never
been organized according to the needs of the Spanish-speaking people of
New Mexico who were expected to use them, he wrote. Looking back on a
line of logic he had first used in 1932 as he tried to explain the impression
Mexico's rural schools had made on him, Tireman pluralized the communities of the American republic in order to destroy the legitimacy of the
conventional village school. "The curriculum now followed in New Mexico

was originally designed for English-speaking children of the Atlantic sea-coast," he argued. "When the settlers from the East and Middle West came to make their homes in the Southwest, they brought their school along as naturally as they brought the right to worship as they pleased." Tireman maintained his critique of the American school in the idioms of the progressive educators as he considered two centuries of education from colonial New England to twentieth-century New Mexico. "Accordingly, the curriculum stressed academic requirements. One must learn to read not primarily to form intelligent opinions but to understand the history and literature courses. One learned to figure in order to do compound interest and complicated problems in algebra and geometry, not to fulfill the simple needs of everyday life." The move would have been recognized by any pragmatist educator. An entire corpus of learning had been thrust on a people for reasons that had nothing to contribute to their patterns of life. Schooling in New Mexico was foreign, extraneous, inorganic, inflexible, unstrategic. Tireman chastised the federal government for its role in this clash of civilizations: "They have sent teachers, doctors, and sanitation experts [elsewhere], but in New Mexico the two different ideologies were permitted to run into each other headlong and nature allowed to take its course."[44] This was a survival of the fittest model, not the leveling model of the pragmatists.

The solution was a redesigned school built philosophically for the needs and aspirations of the people of New Mexico, as they had historically led their lives. "If New Mexico has problems which differ from the problems of New England, then the curriculum of the common school should be designed to aid New Mexico in the solution of its problems," wrote Tireman.[45] It was the responsibility of the educator not to mold the people to the school, but to mold the school to the people. "Only one answer was natural: to the victor belong the spoils. The Spanish-speaking people were expected to adjust themselves to the American pattern," he wrote. "They must learn English, they must learn to help run the government, they must educate their children because democracy rests upon a literate electorate." But this answer would not suffice in the face of pragmatism's philosophy of education. The school should be the center of the community, an organizer for experience, one that supported students to engage in the activities of life so that they might think in pursuit of their own priorities. As Tireman himself indicated, this design for the school was a radical one. It placed the rural community of New Mexico at the core of the school, not the mandates of schools that had been designed for the Eastern seaboard. It insisted that the problems and needs of the rural way of life, as it had unfolded in the West, were to be the locus for educating the child. "We propose to keep in mind what Nambé needed even if it was somewhat different from Santa Fe or other parts of the state," he argued. "The program must stay close to this locality," he continued. "Now we were getting somewhere. If boys and girls can learn to think they will be prepared for life, no matter whether they spend it on the farm, at a desk, or before a machine."[46] In his original prospectus for Nambé, Tireman listed the principles that were to function as the guiding tenets of the redesigned curriculum. Among others, Nambé would center on the needs of the community. It would use the immediate environment, built and natural, as its laboratory. All learning would radiate from the village to the world: "the pupil may go to the furthest point of the earth but he must follow the plan of going from something that is familiar and well known to something that is over the horizon." The school would attempt to teach English and Spanish. And children were to be given "sufficient time for planning, discussing, experimenting, thinking."[47]

Of the pragmatist philosophy Tireman announced for Nambé, nothing became more important to culture and politics than Tireman's renewal of the concept of "experience." At the level of language, "experience" was the practical working out of the concept that resided in the word, the signified of the signifier. But this was not the poststructuralist 1960s yet. It was 1930s New Mexico, where children raised in Spanish and children raised in English had to live with one another. Spanish was the currency of life, English of politics, and in this environment, "experience" was the difference between fitting the two to one another or widening a history of conflict. "Experience" meant something else, too. For Tireman, it meant the practicalities of the life along the arroyos of New Mexico. Indeed, there was nothing else on which one could build the platform for learning in rural New Mexico. The only available resources were the village itself and the life its people had built for themselves through time. Learning could not be coerced via models imported from the Eastern seaboard. It had to unfold from within itself, to grow only from within the resources it had assimilated to itself. The third meaning of "experience" may have been the most important for Tireman. Looking back on what he had valued about learning, "experience" meant the thrill of discovery. At Nambé, Tireman put the thrill this way: "Until Spanish-speaking people can be interested in schools, they will continue to be slow in supporting them." The thrill of learning meant the difference between bringing students into the classroom with the support of their parents and students who remained distant from the possibilities offered by the school: "When the Spanish-speaking parent can see some immediate value coming to his child from attendance in schools, he makes the necessary sacrifices to keep the child there." In Tireman, the thrill was not marginal. It was the ingredient that brought students to the class and activated the relationship between action in the world and the word that described it.[48]

If the entire run of Nambé was about intensifying "experience" to eliminate the failures at San José, nothing showed this more than the parallel that Tireman made between his new school, the schools that Dewey had once showcased in *Schools of Tomorrow*, and the Secretaría de Educación Pública's images of rural schooling in postrevolutionary Mexico.[49] Leafing through Tireman's analysis of Nambé is like adding a chapter to the list of vanguard schools Dewey had captured in *Schools of Tomorrow*. If *Democracy and Education* had captured the philosophical theory of experimentalism, it was *Schools of Tomorrow* that had shown the principles of experience at work in the institution of the school.[50] "Experience," said Dewey in *Democracy and Education*, was the foundation of meaning, for things gained meaning by being used in a certain way. "[The sound and the thing] acquire the same meaning because they are used in a common experience by both."[51] It was in "experience" that the child acquired the relationship between action and meaning, and only through so doing could she master the environment in the attempt to transform it. It was in *Schools of Tomorrow* where Dewey had shown these principles in action, via an examination through text and image of ten leading laboratory schools Dewey believed were articulating the pragmatist philosophy of education that was under development. Among them was the Laboratory School at Columbia University, which had become a working example for Gamio and Sáenz while they had studied in New York City. There were also the Francis Parkman School of Chicago, the Fairhope School of Alabama, Public School 26 of Indianapolis, and the Cottage School of Riverside, Illinois.

Dewey had also been impressed with the University School of the University of Missouri, where Tireman had trained twenty years earlier, especially for Junius Merriam's belief there that the natural development of the child was an excellent guide for the school curriculum. "We learned to say, 'Please Mamma, give me a drink,' when we wanted a drink. We did not practice on such words at nine o'clock each morning," wrote Dewey when he depicted the University School in *Schools of Tomorrow*. The University School had bracketed off the day into a successive chain of observation, exercise and play, stories, and handwork. Children selected for themselves a topic for study during observation, whether it took a day or a month. Instruction was individualized, to give the child time to reflect on her approach to the topic, and to allow for the formulation of a response that widened the relationship between the student and the community. Gymnastics and free play stressed interaction with the environment, while story development allowed children to create stories rather than read them straight out of primers. "Some stories they tell by acting them out, others by drawing," wrote Dewey.[52] Meanwhile, the use of crafts and handwork developed creativity, dexterity, and knowledge of social relationships. "The child has learned the meaning of the immediate objects he sees about him, their relation to himself and his friends, and he is ready to go on and enlarge this knowledge so as to take in things he cannot see, processes and reasons, and the relations that embrace the whole community, or more communities, and finally, the whole world."

Dewey's school models had been an influence on Loyd Tireman throughout his career in New Mexico. Yet ultimately it was not Merriam's school in Missouri that Tireman cited as the model for New Mexico as the school desegregation cases were emerging in California and Texas. *Mendez* had taken place in 1946, at a time when Tireman was assessing the relationship between the word and the world the Nambé experiment had helped him reformulate beginning in 1938. Sánchez was in Texas, looking to extend the effects of *Mendez* by attacking segregation in the public schools that bordered on Austin. As Sánchez reached out to Tireman in New Mexico in 1947, Tireman underscored Mexico's rural school as the primary example for schools in the American West. "Much can be learned from a study of the rural schools of Mexico, often called the 'people's houses,'" he wrote in 1948. Tireman quoted Rafael Ramírez's description of schooling in Mexico, concentrating on those portions of Mexico's philosophy of education that mirrored the descent into "experience" that Tireman had put to work at Nambé. "At one time or other," Tireman wrote, quoting Ramírez, "I saw in some rural school all of the following things being done: Making rubber raincoats . . . tanning leather; carving objects from wood . . . making lacework and embroidery of all kinds, making blackboards, cultivating flower gardens, wheat fields, corn fields, rice fields, and banana fields; raising poultry, and breeding rabbits." It was "experience" that had made Mexico's rural school the primary model for Nambé in the United States. Ramírez had adequately conveyed the millenarianism that Mexico's state intellectuals had attached to the two decades of institutional growth after 1920 in the description that Tireman had repeated. "Little by little, without being aware of it, the teachers have come to realize that the rural school had ceased to be a place where children and adults learn the alphabet, and had been converted into a broader thing of transcendent social importance which embraces the entire community—young and old, men and women—and which teaches all people not only the rudiments of knowledge, but also . . . to lead a better life."[53]

Tireman would never have used the term "transcendent," since nothing beyond the terrestrial could serve as the guide to social ethics. But Tireman had copied Ramírez's words because he had found Mexico's methods for activating "experience" easily adaptable to the case of the Nambé investigations he conducted between 1938 and 1946. The explorations that characterized Mexico's public schools had become the model for work and play Tireman sought for the rural schools of New Mexico. The rural scene was similar to that of Mexico, as was the Spanish language. The religion was Catholic, and the distance from the national authority equally great. Under such parallel conditions, Tireman found that Mexico's instruments of "experience" could easily be modified to the moral ends he sought for the United States at the moment that the desegregation movement was accelerating in the American West. Conditions did not have to be perfectly symmetrical. What was needed was an example, and nothing was closer to Nambé than what Tireman had seen in Mexico. "The program must minister to the real needs of the community," wrote Tireman. "The acceptance of this principle may lead the school to develop a curriculum which is quite different in Spanish-speaking communities from that developed in an English-speaking community, which more or less already meets the needs of that community."[54]

Mexico's continuing influence on Tireman's development of rural schooling beginning in 1938 and extending through the desegregation movement after 1946 has remained obscured by his scattered references to the SEP experiments. Sánchez had sought out Samuel Ramos and José Vasconcelos and traveled to Monterrey and Mexico City in celebration of Mexico's federal state during the 1940s. His movements into Mexico thus left easy footprints in the form of photographs, letters of invitation, and correspondence back and forth from the University of Texas to UNAM and beyond. But as Tireman locked himself away in his new experimental school, seeking the secrets to language that had confounded him since his move to New Mexico in 1927, he left references to Mexico only in short, scattered strokes. There were references to Mexico's rural school in his project reports to GEB officials, for example, but they were easy to overlook. The intertextuality of his work made it easy for scholars to miss Mexico's continuing influence on Tireman's career as well. There is not a single reference to the Mexican state or its schools in his project report on Nambé, published in 1943 and republished in 1948. The references to Mexico's schools are locked away in Tireman's 1948 *Teaching Spanish-Speaking Children*, an early attempt to systematize through experimentalist philosophy the same questions of culture and politics that today fall under the categories of "bilingual education" or "English as a second language." Few people have read Tireman's 1948 text, yet there, Mexico's schools act as the supreme example of experimentation via experience and as the institutional catalyst for the philosophy of language that Tireman was resynthesizing at Nambé at the moment American public schools were beginning to desegregate in California and Texas.

Hold up Tireman's *La Comunidad* study of Nambé alongside the Secretaría de Educación Pública reports on the rural school in Mexico meanwhile, and the experiment Tireman created in experience across New Mexico and Mexico is clear. In each, children learn about the physical environment by tending to rows of flowers and vegetables. Parents are invited to help repair schools and roads with their sons and the assistance of soil conservation officials. The grasses and rocks of Nambé and Actopan provide the occasion to move from local conditions to the expanse of the national community. Mothers are invited to learn new techniques for improving the health of their children. Tireman could have placed his photographs of Nambé in Dewey's *Schools of Tomorrow* and no one would have known the difference. He could have put his photos in the SEP reports on mestizo communities in Mexico and no one would have known the difference, either. Nambé manifested the loop in Dewey Mexican and American progressives shared across the United States and Mexico.

The rural school at Nambé is central to American civil rights for another reason, as we shall see in our next section. At Nambé, Tireman's intensification of "experience" worked. Tireman had never raised test scores at San José. In five years of experimentalism there, he had not been able to show

Figure 22. Nambé School in New Mexico, 1943. Loyd Tireman followed Mexico's rural school model in this last incarnation of the Dewey laboratory school in the United States. From it would stem his conclusions about language in the school segregation cases. Loyd Tireman and Mary Watson, *La Comunidad: Report of the Nambé Community School, 1937–1942* (Albuquerque: University of New Mexico Press, 1943), 6.

that Spanish-speaking children were every bit as prepared to learn, to live, and to transform their environment as were the children of the English seaboard. But at Nambé, Tireman's test scores soared. At San José, reading had not improved, but at Nambé, "reading comprehension is close to, or above, the normal expectation of the first five grades." There had been no formal instruction in arithmetic in the lower grades, yet the children did "well on arithmetic reasoning." Although Nambé had not been academic in orientation, its students had learned as much natural science as any at the other schools. Attendance had always been a concern for Tireman, but at Nambé it jumped 30 percent. "One of the outstanding accomplishments was the increased interest in education on the part of both parents and children."[55]

In view of these results, Tireman made a recommendation that the federal courts adopted when they relied on his testimony to desegregate the public schools of Texas in the wake of *Mendez*. "These years of work at Nambé reinforce our opinion that it is wrong to make special categories for Spanish-speaking people as though they were quite different from all other groups," he wrote. "It is true that language makes a complication; that past generations make for different social customs—but in the essentials of life people are pretty much alike anywhere you find them. As we place children in equally favorable environments they tend to react very much alike. Improve the economic level of rural New Mexico, give boys and girls schooling that will help them solve their own problems, and by so doing we build a better state."[56] In his Nambé project reports, Tireman had reached back to Franz Boas's *The Mind of Primitive Man* to describe theoretically what he had now done at Nambé in practice. "The conclusions arrived at by certain investigators regarding 'racial inferiority' do not agree with the beliefs of anthropologists," Tireman had written in his reports.[57] Tireman had always believed Boas was right, but he had never been able to show it empirically. "Anthropology holds that all groups of people are equal as far as innate hereditary abilities are concerned," he had written. "Differences are due to environment." But through Dewey and Mexico's experience-based practices, now he had shown it at Nambé. It had taken twenty years and the revolution in progressive education to show that Boas had been right, and it funneled Tireman into the central recommendation about segregation he gave to the American federal court in Texas in 1948, as we shall see. Children could not be separated from one another in the schools based on presumptions of inferiority, for such inferiority did not exist naturally among human beings. And if schools paid closer attention to the students they served, the language barrier that divided them could be overcome.

Delgado v. Bastrop and the Desegregation of Texas

More than the fragility of *Plessy* was at stake for George Sánchez when the "sun exploded" in Paul John McCormick's courtroom in 1946, as Carey McWilliams put it. Sánchez did not learn about Judge McCormick's attack on the logic of the separate but equal doctrine in *Mendez* until spring 1947, but when he did, he immediately recognized that the judicial branch of the American government had poised itself to help reshape ethnic pluralism in the American West via the schools. When a federal appeals court in San Francisco upheld McCormick's decision just one month after Isaac Kandel had argued at the University of Texas at Austin about strong central state power in Latin America, Sánchez's hope for the American state must have been doubly underscored. Suddenly, something for which Sánchez and his colleagues had been turning to Mexico for twenty years seemed to be happening. For them, the American state seemed ready to unleash the power of the school as an arbiter of ethnic relations.

Sánchez wasted no time in reacting to the indications that the central state was moving in the same direction of race relations that the Mexican state had been doing since 1920. Looking backward to the community of intellectuals with whom he had worked in New Mexico for a decade before his move to Texas, Sánchez sent letters to Loyd Tireman and Marie Hughes, proposing that they join him in an effort to do something they had been trying to do mutually since 1935: to place children of varying ethnicities together in the public schools of the West. They would do so this time, however, by extending the *Mendez* decision to other states in the American West. "A suit exactly like the *Mendez* case is being initiated in Texas," Sánchez wrote to his erstwhile colleague Hughes in late 1947. "If necessary, we will ask several of those authorities, among them yourself, to come here and testify in person."[58] Tireman was busy updating his project report on Nambé when he received Sánchez's letter in Bolivia. His success with experience-based education had taken him to South America, where he was now analyzing Bolivia's public schools at the invitation of a government that had been as impressed with Mexico's school reforms as he had.[59] Sánchez continued to bask in Mexico's educational successes at the same moment, meanwhile, celebrating José Santos Valdés's leftist treatment of democracy and education in Mexico, *La batalla por la cultura*, and planning a large anthology in which he would publish the extensive work on education in Mexico he had written since 1935.[60] The details that had made Sánchez's organizing work possible are well known. In 1943, Sánchez had initiated contact with the American Civil Liberties Union in New York, which had subsequently sent him a substantial sum of money to initiate desegregation test cases in Texas.[61] It was out of these relationships that looked backward to New Mexico and forward to the era of the NAACP and the ACLU that Sánchez helped guide the federal lawsuit that desegregated Texas in 1948, *Delgado v. Bastrop*, through the courts.

Delgado remains the least studied school desegregation struggle of the three landmark decisions beginning with *Mendez* that changed the history of racial liberalism in the American West after World War II. Located on the outskirts of San Antonio and Austin along a northeasterly axis that divides the hill country of central Texas from the coastal flats that move toward the Caribbean, Bastrop and its immediate neighbor counties had historically supplied the economy with cotton and lumber. Corn, cattle, and grain production became more important by 1930, with an acceleration of production that began with the onset of World War II. Minerva Delgado and her children and grandchildren had been long-standing citizens of the United States, having migrated to Texas not after the Mexican Revolution but two generations before. Yet they had represented a numerical minority of Bastrop and surrounding counties, rarely accounting for more than 25 percent of a population that traced its roots largely to mid-nineteenth-century German immigrants to Texas. School accommodations in the area mirrored the rigid labor segregation patterns that had developed from the culture of slavery that had predominated through the Civil War and the cotton-growing labor conflicts captured by Neil Foley in his important work on Texas labor culture. With the assistance of returning World War II servicemen, including prominent civil rights lawyer Hector Garcia, Minerva Delgado sued the state of Texas in 1947 in the aftermath of *Mendez* to integrate Mexican American and white European-descended pupils in the schools of Texas.

For Sánchez, the *Delgado* lawsuit was something more than the second of a triptych of cases built on McCormick's attack on *Plessy* or the outcome of Sánchez's personal investment in the relationship of assimilation to the public schools. His correspondence with his former New Mexico colleagues shows us that the desegregation of the schools in the American West was an extension of the assimilation narrative that Sánchez, Hughes, and Tireman had projected across New Mexico and Mexico since the 1930s. The work of these scientists in the school desegregation cases has often appeared tangential amid the consequent turn toward the courts by the lawyers and citrus workers who integrated the public schools of the American West. But their work in desegregating the schools was more than an interesting aside to more important labors by attorneys and judges. Instead, as Sánchez's letters asking Tireman and Hughes to join him in *Delgado* reflect, that work represented the convergence into the desegregation cases of the social science rooted in pragmatism that these Americans had tested in New Mexico and Mexico since the early 1930s. These Mexico-inspired intellectuals had remained close between the end of their New Mexico careers in the late 1930s and the emergence of the social protest movements during World War II, a relationship in ideas whose cohesion out of the 1930s became central to the desegregation cases that followed *Mendez*.

The wider influence this community of social scientists would have over desegregation politics in California, Texas, and Arizona had already become apparent when Marie Hughes left New Mexico in 1941 to work in the Los Angeles Public Schools office out of which she testified in *Mendez*. There, Hughes began her itinerant outreach work to the rural communities of Los Angeles County, much as she had done in rural New Mexico. Sánchez and Tireman had continued their work in assimilation from within the government agencies of the state of New Mexico as late as 1939. They, too, however, had moved to new academic posts by 1940, effectively dispersing this circle of colleagues across the breadth of the American West. Sánchez had resigned from his post at the University of New Mexico and accepted the professorship in the Institute of Latin American Studies at the University of Texas that he rode to prominence.[62] Beals had never had an institutional platform for his political work, but with his appointment to the UCLA Department of Anthropology beginning in 1941, he developed a political career in civil rights that would include the public school desegregation cases and the Sleepy Lagoon defense trial of World War II Los Angeles. Physical distance now may have separated Sánchez, Tireman, and Hughes, but they kept alive the set of ideas that helped transform ethnic relations in the American West through books and conferences. Sánchez and Hughes jointly contributed to Carlos Castañeda's 1942 manuscript series on Latin

America's relationship to the United States, and continued to publish together through the 1950s on ethnic relations in Western American social history. In the middle of the discussions about the Castañeda project, meanwhile, Sánchez congratulated Hughes on the success of the Southern California workshops she had established to expand the assimilationist role of the public school in the American West. "I congratulate you on a job very well done. . . . It is my opinion that this procedure is one of the indispensable avenues that must be followed if we are ever to obtain a solution to the problem of acculturation of this or any other minority group."[63] These books and conferences could not have been as exciting as earlier trips to Actopan. Yet it was through these instruments that this political circle held fast as they worked geographically away from one another across the tier of states that bordered the Mexican republic.

Delgado was argued before the court on June 15, 1948, and a decision rendered that same day based on evidence and arguments presented over the prior two months. Sánchez had searched for a test case in Texas for two years when he contacted Tireman and Hughes after McCormick's *Mendez* decision. He had searched throughout central Texas for the best possible location for a suit, in conjunction with the legal advice of Hector Garcia, the private attorney who took the legal lead on behalf of the plaintiffs. By late 1947, Sánchez and Garcia had arranged to sue a collection of school districts in the vicinity of Austin. At issue was the segregation of schoolchildren of Mexican descent in the public schools of Texas in the absence of a specific state statute that permitted their separation. "Upon my advice a suit has been filed in the Federal District Court, here in Austin by a large group of children against several school systems to prevent those systems from practicing segregation. . . . You will note that this is almost an identical case with the one which was decided favorably by the Federal Court in California," Sánchez wrote to Tireman in January 1948.[64] To Hughes he wrote the same thing: "This suit has received very careful preparation and, in addition to the points tested in the *Mendez* case, will include certain features that I have always deemed essential in such cases."[65] Among the details of the lawsuit was the presence of citizens of Mexico as plaintiffs against the defendant school districts, a characteristic that had not been a feature of the *Mendez* case three years earlier. While most of the plaintiffs were U.S.-born children and their parents, Desiderio Gutiérrez of Bastrop, Guadalupe Montemayor of Elgin, and Enrique Martínez of Colorado, all parents of segregated schoolchildren, were citizens of the Republic of Mexico.[66]

At question, everyone agreed, was the administrative practice of segregation in the absence of a legal statute that gave specific statutory authority to the schools to separate children who were considered different from one another. As in *Mendez*, the school districts had engaged in a practice of rigid segregation of Mexican children from those who were not. Separate buildings were kept in grades one to seven in Bastrop, for example, while in Elgin, separate facilities were kept for grades one through five. There was an inequality of programs for Latin American youth as well, including sports and recreational programming, though the equality issue was not pressed by the plaintiffs. Instead, they questioned the prevailing practice of segregating Spanish-speaking youth on the grounds of language deficiencies when no scientific tests had ever been performed to determine the language capacities of the children in question. The question of race quickly came up and was dismissed just as easily. Neither the children nor the schools argued that racial segregation accounted for the school district practices, since everyone agreed, in consonance with Texas law, that citizens of Texas who were Mexico-descended were considered part of the white race rather than the colored race.[67] What was at issue was the separation of two groups of white children, one of Mexican heritage and the other of European, for reasons that seemed arbitrary and without foundation in state statute. The court relied on the decision in the *Mendez* appeal to declare that Mexico-descended children in Bastrop had been illegally separated from those of European descent because no law permitted the practice. In two separate orders issued statewide, in 1948 and 1950, the state educational agency subsequently ordered an end to the practice of segregating Mexican Americans and European Americans.

It was in their work surrounding *Delgado* that Sánchez and Tireman left their visions for assimilation and race relations in the post-*Delgado* West. Tireman offered no normative definition of assimilation, but the description he elsewhere gave of Nambé and the role of the school in social ethics moved in a direction opposite to that which Marie Hughes had presented in *Mendez*. Where Hughes had placed an emphasis on changing Latin Americans to Protestant majorities to achieve assimilation in California, Tireman emphasized remolding the school to the contours of the ethnic community in the effort to preserve local lifeways. Tireman had located his school in Nambé, not in Albuquerque, for example, and had created a curriculum whose elements fit the social and economic characteristics of the people who used it. Natural science training emphasized the land and animal husbandry that was characteristic of the community. Parents and adults participated in the construction and maintenance of school facilities that were used at night as well as during the day. Teachers had been imported to serve the needs of a demonstration project designed to adapt the New Mexico education agency to the particularities of rural New Mexico. Assimilation toward the larger American community remained one of Tireman's primary goals as he participated in *Delgado*, but his strategy for reaching it rested on preserving rather than destroying the elements of culture in rural New Mexico. This was a more malleable assimilation than what Hughes had presented in the *Mendez* courtroom. Assimilation for Tireman moved in the direction of activating rather than eroding Spanish-speaking culture as part of a transformed society. "We shall try to find out what is most needed in the lives of the people of the community and minister to that before all else," he had written.[68]

George Sánchez came closer to describing a normative position for assimilation via a strong defense of the cosmopolitanist vision most often associated with Randolph Bourne, meanwhile. Sánchez had always hewn close to a cosmopolitanist ethic, including the mythic melting pot that he had provided in his 1934 dissertation. There, he had defended the melting pot on the grounds that the public school had historically made possible the "amalgamation" of many distinct peoples into a single harmonious blend. Ten years of work in the agencies of the state of New Mexico had strengthened his theoretical position on the normative character of pluralism to which the state should aim its efforts. Now, as the desegregation lawsuits in California and Texas attempted to transform race relations in the 1940s West, it was this same cosmopolitanist definition that he defended. "National culture," he told a convention of social scientists in Texas in 1941, "represents a pageant wherein the variegated colors of many tongues and races have been fused into a unity that is greater than the sum of its parts."[69] Oblivious to what the U.S. Civil War and the Immigration Act of 1924 said about American race relations, Sánchez provided a history of peace among distinctive peoples that had resulted in the creation of an orderly, democratic society marked by pluralism that was celebrated by the members of the nation. This was historically suspect, of course, but Sánchez was defining what he was trying to create, looking forward in America rather than the dirtier ambiguities of the American experience that became obvious by looking backward. "The very essence of Americanism lies in the freedom of heterogeneous social groups and individuals to contribute from their respective cultural wealth to the welfare of the mass," he wrote. "This freedom to contribute represents the potential energy of the American nation to grow culturally. Therein lies a fundamental aspect of American democracy."[70] Sánchez also outlined the defense of cosmopolitanism that became a hallmark of his definition of American national identity throughout the period of the desegregation lawsuits. "Examination convinces us that much of what we call American democracy is grounded upon the right and duty of the peoples of this country to contribute from their respective cultural resources that which might enhance the total culture," he wrote.[71] There was no defense of the single ethnic group in his description, nor a presumed purity of Anglo Protestant culture that had typified Hughes's definition of the American cultural ideal. Assimilation in America was to be defined by the mixing of cultural traits from the diversity of peoples that made up the nation, Sánchez argued. The fellow students of the American child "and his neighbors, have cultural gifts which he can have for the asking," he wrote. "He, in turn, can share with them those cultural assets with which his forbears and his social group have endowed him. All can glory in this boundless social and intellectual freedom and in this virtually limitless cultural wealth."[72]

These visions by Tireman and Sánchez of an enlarged pluralism that defined their view of school integration in the 1940s was tested by an unexpected disagreement from Tireman's world of language. As Tireman looked on Sánchez's correspondence to him while he was still in Bolivia, Tireman pointed to a conundrum that the *Delgado* court would have to resolve. The Nambé school had been a watershed moment for its experimentalist proof that children learned at the same rate regardless of their cultural particularity. If the pragmatist tenets of experience were activated in the right environment, it did not matter whether children came from a culture in Mexico, the United States, or elsewhere. Children learned at the same rate everywhere, despite their origin points. Nambé had shown empirically that children could not be distinguished from one another based on a presumed biological propensity for knowledge. It was in view of this experimentalism that Tireman threw a surprise at Sánchez in the middle of their *Delgado* correspondence. "I do not know of any evidence which indicates the extent of progress of a group of non-English-speaking children who have been introduced directly into a room where there is a large proportion of English-speaking children and where the program of the room is planned in accordance with the abilities of the English-speaking group," Tireman wrote to Sánchez in February 1948.[73]

It was not an elegant syllogism. But Tireman had pointed out something fundamental. Nambé had shown that students taught in Spanish could advance normally through school. But Spanish speakers who had been integrated into a classroom that was taught in the experience of English had never advanced as expected. The history of San José and Nambé showed that Tireman was exactly right. San José had never overcome the reading lag of Spanish-speaking students who had been integrated into the English-speaking classroom. That had been San José's Achilles heel. No matter how hard Tireman had tried, test scores had never risen in such a context. Test scores had risen normally at Nambé, meanwhile, but the language of experience there had been Spanish, not English. As one compared classroom techniques at San José with those at Nambé, one could see that there was no overlap between them. This was the problem for the court, Tireman warned Sánchez. No one had ever shown that Spanish-speaking children who were integrated into an English-speaking classroom that had been organized for English speakers could succeed in conventional language-acquisition patterns. For this reason, Tireman argued that he could not agree with the legal strategy Sánchez had proposed in *Delgado*. Given what he had learned at Nambé and San José, there was simply not enough science to justify Sánchez's argument that language deficiency among Spanish-speakers should not result in separate classes. At stake in the arcana of these psychology experiments was a moral race to avoid two large sources of inferiority among immigrant children joining American society. On the one hand, to integrate children into a classroom that was English-speaking alone risked opening them to the inferiority produced by the inability to converse with the larger group. On the other hand, to separate the children into a classroom that was Spanish-speaking alone risked opening them up to the inferiority produced by the physical separation from the English speakers. Which was worse? Which was better? Which inferiority outcome should be risked as part of the court's ethical attempt to create a synthetic American culture?

The federal court reconciled the difference in *Delgado* by integrating Tireman's empirical answer into the court's orders to the State of Texas. From Bolivia, Tireman had proposed to Sánchez a working solution based on his work at San José and Nambé. "I do believe that children who do not speak English should be grouped in separate classes within the same building from those who do speak English until they have acquired an English vocabulary of from three to five hundred words," he wrote. "Then I favor their incorporation in the regular classes of the school."[74] The *Delgado* court followed Tireman's logic by adopting Tireman's theory of segregation for the first year of school. "The defendants . . . are hereby permanently restrained and enjoined from segregating pupils of Mexican or other Latin American descent in separate schools or classes within the respective school districts; provided, however, that this injunction shall not prevent said . . . districts from providing . . . separate classes on the same campus in the first grade only, and solely for instructional purposes, for pupils in their initial scholastic year who . . . clearly demonstrate . . . that they do not a possess a sufficient familiarity with the English language to understand classroom instruction in first-grade subject matters."[75] The court's policy decision, if one looks historically, had been based on experimentation in Mexico that Tireman had used to reconstruct the Nambé experiment. Experience in Mexico had overturned Tireman's understanding of learning in the American school, and that conversion had led to a series of policy results on which the *Delgado* court now acted.

Contrary to what some scholars have recently argued, I have found little evidence that whiteness was the assimilationist norm on which Tireman and Sánchez believed the culture of America should be constructed.[76] Prior to 1945 and the advent of the school segregation cases, none of the individuals profiled here had resorted to phenotype as a descriptor for group difference in American life. Beals sometimes described the varying color tones of the Indians of Mexico, but his was an attempt to measure the historical operation of skin color in the Mexican social hierarchy rather to ascribe cultural features to particular individuals. Tireman described "skin pigmentation" in his 1948 *Teaching Spanish-Speaking Children* as one factor that might account for Anglo intolerance of Mexican Americans in the American West, but it was environmental factors that he underscored for the operation of the social hierarchy.[77] George Sánchez sometimes referred to the people of New Mexico as Spanish Americans—a common substitute for "white" in the history of New Mexico race relations—but a look at his work before 1945 reveals that he called himself a "mestizo" and a Mexican American just as often. After 1946 and the need to marshal evidence for the federal courts in *Mendez* and its progeny, meanwhile, one is struck again by the absence of a reference to phenotype. Never once did the question of color come up in the court records by the American social scientists whose lives I have examined across Mexico and the United States. Nothing has been more striking to me than to contrast the use of whiteness discourse among many intellectuals of the League of United Latin American Citizens in the 1930s with its absence among the social scientists profiled here. They were each involved in the desegregation cases, yet their difference from LULAC concerning phenotype is clear and unambiguous.

There is a good explanation for the absence of a discourse of whiteness among these scientists. Simply put, they could not have been committed to pragmatist analysis while simultaneously maintaining allegiance to the idea that color was deterministic over social relations. Since at least Boas's *The Mind of Primitive Man* in 1911, the idea that color carried with it particular traits for particular people had come under sustained attack.[78] Likewise, the psychology of the mind upon which pragmatist philosophy was based placed the balance of the social hierarchy on people's perceptions that color made a difference rather than on the idea that color actually did. Pragmatist analysis resided in the equivalence of biological aptitudes across the spectrum of human communities, and if a social hierarchy emerged, it emerged from specifically social causes rather than predetermined natural ones. This does not mean that culture could not become the equivalent of biology as a deterministic explanation for perceived differences among people. But here, too, there is relatively little evidence that the social scientists whose careers are measured here ever thought of culture as impermeable to social change and thus deterministic on life outcomes. Quite the contrary was true. In 1959, for example, Sánchez criticized his old colleague at the University of Texas, Lewis Hanke, for Hanke's adoption of the "black legend" in the reading materials they recommended for their students. "'Hispanic culture,' indeed! So the sophisticates down there cannot run a threshing machine or a combine—whoinell can! Just think of a combine operating in the Otomí country, or along the Orinoco! Or maybe, at Cuzco. When you are between a rock and a hard place, you don't inaugurate a technological survey—you pray!"[79] Change was central to their understanding of social life, and determinism anathema to their conceptions of human societies. When *Delgado* did make mention of race, whiteness emerged as a courtroom strategy of the lawyers in the attempt to take advantage of legal statutes as they existed on the books. Whether the lawyer who argued on behalf of the children in *Delgado* harbored real conceptions of the determinism of race, or whether he was making mere instrumental use of racial distinctions that had been codified in law in order to win a judgment for his clients, is a question that deserves much more scrutiny. But nowhere in the court records or the related documents they continued to produce in their professional careers was there a use of racial categories to defend hierarchies of people. The social scientists who help shepherd *Delgado* through the courts were students of "culture" whose understandings of human societies was little based on outdated notions of biology.

When *Delgado* had come to a close, Sánchez received a letter from the Mexican state thanking him for steering the case through the courts. "I have been ordered by the Mexican embassy in Washington D.C. to send you the heartiest congratulations and sincere appreciation for your intelligent and active intervention in the court case moved through the courts by Minerva Delgado et al. challenging the school officials who were responsible for school segregation [in Texas]," wrote San Antonio consul Miguel Calderón.[80] Given Sánchez's long relationship with Calderón, Calderón's warm message might reasonably be interpreted as a pro forma diplomatic cable from one colleague to another. But the deep relationship Sánchez had created with the Mexican state by 1948 shows that the message was something more. By 1948, Sánchez had become the foremost champion of Mexican education in the United States. He was regularly serving as an honorary spokesperson for Mexico's schools. He was on the short list of every invitation from the Mexican government celebrating the accomplishments of the Mexican schools. In this context, Calderón was not merely feting a colleague, but extending an admiring hand to a tested convert of Mexico's postrevolutionary federal state. His words meant more than formal pleasantries. They were the words of a functionary of the Mexican state to an informal cultural ambassador whom the Mexican government had come to trust and respect by the advent of the segregation cases in the United States that had the large potential to alter the school careers of immigrants from Mexico to the United States. It was a reflection of Sánchez's respect for the Mexican state's educational crusade at home. "My government was frequently informed of the technical assistance that you provided in this case, which without a doubt will constitute one of the most transcendent and historical cases in the history of the drive to stamp out school segregation, which is the most deplorable form of discrimination anywhere," wrote Calderón. "It is for this reason that I am happy to lend my personal acknowledgment to that which the Embassy of Mexico wishes to send you."[81] Sánchez had become one of the foremost champions of the desegregation cases, indeed, and the Mexican state knew that he was still relying on their schools as he searched for the meaning of integration in the context of postwar America.

Historicism in the Arizona Civil Rights Movement

In 1951, Judge David Ling of the federal district court of Arizona used *Mendez* to desegregate the public schools of Arizona. As in *Mendez* and *Delgado*, segregation in Tolleson, Arizona had been based on a local district policy that assumed the lack of English proficiency by the Mexico-descended communities of the rural village. Arizona law did not permit such segregation, however, and a naturalized U.S. citizen from the state of Chihuahua, Mexico, with children in the local schools, Porfirio Gonzales, filed a lawsuit to end the segregation of his children from those who were considered white. Thus was Mexico's influence on civil rights manifested in the third canonical installment in the desegregation history of the American West.

Located ten miles west of downtown Phoenix, Arizona, Tolleson was a cotton-growing rural community that also supported cultivation of onions. It was the home of immigrants from Mexico who had begun to settle in Arizona during the two decades that preceded America's entry into World War II. Unlike both the Orange County and Texas communities that had spawned the earlier desegregation cases, Tolleson's recent immigrant population identified closely with the Catholic Church, including the construction of neighborhoods around a central plaza where the church resided and the presence of religious altars on the front lawns of family homes. Beginning in 1950 with the assistance of the local fraternal organization, the Alianza Hispano-Americana, Porfirio Gonzales began an organizing effort to desegregate the public schools of the rural community. Mexican American schoolchildren had been forced to attend a separate public school located away from the main public schools of the community that white children of European extraction attended. In the courtroom during the proceedings were representatives of the NAACP, whose attorneys were preparing for the lawsuits in the American Deep South and Kansas that would be consolidated by the federal courts into *Brown v. Board of Education*.[82]

Gonzales v. Sheely was a truncated version of the *Mendez* and *Delgado* cases. By 1951, the political results of McCormick's decision were becoming plainer across the American West, even as school districts found it increasingly difficult to defend policies based on few scientific criteria. During a trial that lasted fifteen days, Ling ruled that Arizona's defense of segregation, like those of Orange and Bastrop Counties in the earlier two cases, was spurious. The school district had not provided any means of determining whether students were proficient in English. Students from Mexico's ethnic communities who had been born in the United States were simply assumed to be foreign born. Students of white and Mexican extraction routinely socialized in other locations of the community, yet only in the schools were they kept separate. Judge Ling found the features of segregation patterns in Arizona so close to the segregation patterns in Orange County, California, that he copied Judge McCormick's ruling in *Mendez* word for word. A preeminent concern of education in the United States was to create social equality, not merely political equality. The defendant school districts were obliged to provide equal accommodations to children of Mexican extraction based on their capabilities, not on presumptions haphazardly assigned by the defendant school officials. By the end of 1953, Judge Ling's central conclusions had precipitated the desegregation of Arizona's entire public school system. It was the final installment in a remarkable series of three federal lawsuits that resulted in the desegregation of the American public schools from California to Texas between 1945 and 1953.

Except for the echoes of a *Mendez* decision that was still expanding throughout the American West, the direct links between "experience" in Mexico and *Gonzales v. Sheely* were not so obvious. Sánchez had tried hard to involve himself in the case, for example, but the local attorney fought a more independent legal battle than had taken place in California and Texas. In California, Beals had explicitly juxtaposed integration in Mexico with integration in the United States in his testimony to the *Mendez* court. Hughes had shown the continuing influence of Mexico on civil rights by the itinerant way that she had continued to perform her labors in the rural communities of Los Angeles County. In New Mexico, Tireman had used experience in Mexico as the way to fashion results in his laboratory school that he subsequently incorporated into the desegregation lawsuits in Texas. In each of these ways, these integrationist Americans had continued to reflect the policy influence that Mexico's schools had continued to have on American education as late as the early 1950s. In *Gonzales*, the evidence of the policy links to Mexico's schools had begun to recede from direct view.

Instead, Mexico's struggles for justice left their imprint in the worlds of social history and the arts that Arizona's Mexican American peoples had created. At the time of *Gonzales*, for example, writer Mario Suárez was describing the world of culture that recent immigrants from Mexico were crafting in the communities of Phoenix and Tucson from which the desegregation lawsuits had come. His oeuvre remains largely unknown, but it depicts the institutions of postrevolutionary Mexico as an important

shaping force in the development of the political and social history of the
Arizona neighborhoods where the desegregation struggles took place. In
"Señor Garza," for example, a young elementary school student successfully argues to his American teachers that he should be placed in the third
grade since he had already attended the public schools of postrevolutionary
Mexico. In the context of the chronology that Suárez depicts, the young
student would have been in school in Mexico in 1923, corresponding to
the opening years of the SEP school campaigns in Mexico. The young boy's
argument to his teachers reflects a political context for immigrant Mexicans
to Arizona that included Mexico's postrevolutionary schools rather than
those of the United States alone.[83]

Suárez also captured civil rights in World War II Arizona in ironic
tones. In "Los Coyotes," two expatriates from revolutionary Mexico, one
claiming to have been a general in the Mexican army, have taken up the
struggle for immigrant civil rights in Arizona. "There will come a day
when the forces of truth and justice will carry the day," one says to the
other. "Great forces," he adds. But the story is not a triumphant one.
Instead, the expatriates see the organizing efforts of the Mexican Americans who pressed the desegregation campaigns in Arizona as an opportunity to defraud immigrant Mexicans of their money. While pretending to
raise money for civil rights, the expatriates agree to steal immigrant
money as a way to enrich themselves rather than the community. Here,
the history of revolutionary Mexico left a record of its influence on American school integration in the form of a tale of thievery and deception.[84]
Suárez's work captures nationalizing Mexico's influence in other ways, as
well. The Mexican residents of Suárez's fictionalized community provide
food, candy, and wine to the troops of Mexico's postrevolutionary army.[85]
Mexico City becomes the framework for a celebration of bullfighting
among residents of the community who look back on Mexico with nostal-
gia.[86] "Cuco has come from his job at Feldman's Furniture Store to converse of the beauty of Mexico and the comfort of the United States,"
writes Suárez in "Señor Garza." Taken collectively, Suárez's accounts of
the Mexican American communities of Arizona show a political world
that was grounded in institutional connections that reached backward
to Mexico's schools, the postrevolutionary army, the Mexican Catholic
Church, and the cultural celebrations of Mexico City in ways that have
been left out of the historical accounts of integration in Arizona. The
institutional presence of postrevolutionary Mexico extended to life

abroad, just as it had among the American social scientists who had studied Mexico's schools for clues about American integration at home.

Mexico's politics as a central context for *Gonzales* was also captured in the monthly news report produced by the Alianza Hispano-Americana, the long-standing fraternal organization connecting the worlds of Mexico to the worlds of the United States, under whose auspices attorney Ralph Estrada had attacked segregation in the Tolleson schools. In the aftermath of *Gonzales*, the Alianza's magazine, *Alianza*, became the primary publicity outlet for the desegregation efforts that expanded in Arizona after 1951. After winning the *Gonzales* decision, for example, Estrada joined forces with George Sánchez and the ACLU of Southern California to fight segregation in the schools of Glendale, Arizona. In January 1954, *Alianza* published an account of a new attack, this time against segregation in Winslow. And in the immediate aftermath of the U.S. Supreme Court's decision in *Brown v. Board of Education* in May 1954, *Alianza* announced that it had joined forces with the NAACP to eradicate segregation in the public schools of El Centro, California. Such efforts mirrored the regional connections between the American South and the American West that had occurred in *Mendez*. But just as *Mendez* reflected Mexico's history with race and nationalism as much as it did racial conflict in the American South, so too did *Alianza*. The July 1954 issue celebrated the Fourth of July with a portrait of George Washington and an acknowledgment of the *Brown* decision, for example. Two months later, however, it published a portrait, this time of Mexican independence hero Miguel Hidalgo. In its summer 1956 issue, meanwhile, *Alianza* proudly reported that its members in the United States had traveled to Guaymas, Mexico, to celebrate the expansion of the Alianza Hispano-America into the Republic of Mexico. Here in the same city where Ralph Beals had encountered the Yaqui Indians forty years earlier, the Alianza saw fit to recognize the connections of history to the Republic of Mexico from which its original founders had come.[87]

These links between Mexico and the Arizona civil rights struggle were also recorded in the public lore of Tolleson, Arizona. In a display of public history that was later celebrated by the community, a group of high school students emblazoned the tennis courts of Tolleson High School with an enormous muralistic representation of ethnic regeneration that the *Gonzales v. Sheely* lawsuit has come to represent for the community. In the middle of the mural is Tolleson Public Elementary School, just behind a rainbow that points skyward. The school radiates light from its front doors, memorializing the school in a blaze of fire but also celebrating the arrival of two sets of students to its halls. The first group is the Mexican American children of Tolleson; the second is the European-descended community. It was in 1951 that the Tolleson School District, in the very school depicted in the mural, desegregated the public elementary schools of Arizona. As a narration of civil rights, the mural became a symbol of Tolleson's moral rebirth in the wake of *Gonzales*.

As in the Diego Rivera murals in Mexico City with which we began our book, the Tolleson mural deliberately displays an ethic of state-centered reform in which the school is held up as the institution of political rebirth. The state and the school are celebrated as agents of social regeneration whose ethical success rests on preserving ethnic diversity in Arizona. Flight into the desert by cultural communities from points east and south once implied social conflict, but the state transformed difference into communal strength via the work of the public school. The artistic treatment of the themes in the Tolleson mural is radically different from that in the integrationist murals of the Mexican Revolution, but the moral tale of ethnic reconciliation is analogous to that depicted in Diego Rivera's artwork. Like the depiction of the state and the school as mediators of ethnic difference in the Mexico City murals, the Tolleson mural captures the role of the public school as an agent of social regeneration in the rural countryside. One can like or not like this depiction. But the mural captures the desegregation story as a narrative of the state as much as of the ethnic community.

The mural also elevates immigration to a central position in the moral plot of Tolleson's rebirth. To the left of the public school is a historical narrative of immigration from Mexico that climaxes in a family of five arriving in the United States. There is a Catholic church, and the wide vistas of the Sonoran desertscape that frame the environmental geography of the transit northward from the Mexican republic. As one moves forward through time, the territorial institutions of the community come into focus, including a train depot and a small school. To the right of the mural's sun-filled public school stands a portrayal of the history of European American immigration to Arizona, also portrayed backward through time. There is a Conestoga wagon of pioneer immigrants crossing the Great Plains, Union soldiers from the American Civil War, and a Model T Ford of the Depression years. Americans from points east are depicted as arriving to Arizona in historical stages represented by westward movement across the continent, just as immigrants from Mexico are depicted to the left as moving north in historical stages.

The symmetrical attention to immigration frames the desegregation history of Arizona not as a stepping-stone to *Brown v. Board of Education*, as has become a central theme in recent historiography of desegregation in the American West, but as a self-standing reconciliation narrative of Arizona's Mexico- and Europe-descended ethnic communities. The mural depicts the transformation of immigrants into citizens of the nation through means of the public school, focusing one's attention on the role of the state as the instrument of social rebirth in the American West. But such assimilation in the United States was nothing new, the mural suggests. A mounted don and a mestizo on a wagon move outward from the Mexican past, subtly capturing a process of assimilation among discrete ethnic communities in Mexico that are depicted in the form of Spanish colonial and indigenous communities presented next to one another. A field of cotton depicts the rural origins from which the immigrants came north to the United States, meanwhile, reminding us of the agrarian political context in which assimilation occurred. In these discrete frames of history, the mural represents Mexico as a political terrain whose ethnic history carried over into the integration history of the United States. In capturing an international story rather than a domestic story alone, the mural reflects the international context of assimilation across Mexico and the United States in which the desegregation of Arizona's public school occurred. We should not deny the connections between *Brown v. Board of Education* and the civil rights history of the American West that recent scholarship has pointed to in the effort to understand the links to postrevolutionary Mexico that formed the context for desegregation in Arizona. But it is Mexico that the community of Tolleson underscored in its mural, not the civil rights history of the American South. It is a historicity coming out of Mexico's past that pervades the mural, not a forward-looking historicity that underscores the links to race relations outside the American West. It is the amalgamation story reaching backward into Mexico that Tolleson's community history restores to a place in our understanding of the West's political history, just as the careers of our social scientists do. The context in which desegregation occurred cannot be separated from Mexico's own assimilationist history, the mural suggests, just as the careers of our social scientists have reflected.

Had they been around to see it, Sánchez and Beals might have emphasized the mural's subtle reminder of pragmatism's role in shaping the integration history of Mexico and the United States. Many years ago, Morton White pointed out a feature of the American social scientists who helped desegregate the public schools of the American West. Pragmatism, wrote

Figure 23. The school depicted as a meeting place of culture in the Tolleson mural. Here, the school creates a new society from the ethnic communities that have come from points south and east. Mexican immigration from the south and white immigration from the east are depicted at left and right. At the center, the distinct ethnic communities of Tolleson embrace one another and enter a rainbow of light that radiates from the community's public school. The scales of justice are adjacent to the rainbow, signifying the federal courts of the American central state that desegregated Arizona's public schools in 1951. Located at the Tolleson City Complex, Tolleson, Arizona. Personal collection of the author.

White, was one of a number of interpretive models in the twentieth-century social sciences that had turned to history as an instrument for reconceptualizing the social hierarchies academics had once accepted as natural to the social universe.[88] Gone with the advent of these new models was the nineteenth-century faith in the revealed word of God and the sophistries of philosophers whose truth models could not be validated empirically. This was the rupture that Henry May later called the "end of American innocence."[89] In the aftermath of that rupture, social scientists had lost faith in transcendent standards of ethics. In place of transcendent morality, social scientists had now begun to rely on the accumulated record of human achievement as a source of possibility from which to reassess the ethical codes that governed social relationships.

Jurist Oliver Wendell Holmes had captured this new sensibility when he argued that experience, not logic, had been the path of the law. "You will hear some text writers telling you that [law] is something different from what is decided by the courts of Massachusetts or England, that it is a system of reason, that it is a deduction from principles of ethics or admitted axioms or what not, which may or may not coincide with decisions," he had famously written.[90] Many still believed that law was a distillation of a transcendent code of universal morality, but in fact law was nothing more than a mortal history of the choices jurists had made about social conflicts over time. Transcendence was ultimately unknowable, a criticism Holmes captured in the form of a metaphoric criminal. "But if we take the view of our friend the bad man we shall find that he does not care two straws for the axioms of deductions, but that he does want to know what the Massachusetts or English courts are likely to do in fact," Holmes had written. "The prophecies of what the courts will do in fact, and nothing more pretentious, are what I mean by the law." It was the resort to history as the method of inquiry that the legal analysis of Oliver Wendell Holmes shared with the pragmatism of Dewey.[91]

The resort to history as a means of social regeneration is clearly reflected in the Tolleson mural. At the center of the mural is the school as the pragmatist social scientists had reformulated it. Using Dewey, they had reconceptualized the school as an instrument of social transformation rather than an instrument of social hierarchy. They had believed in Mexico and the United States as manifestations of unique histories whose respective pasts could be reconciled by the pragmatist understandings of man and society that Dewey and Boas had helped to pioneer. And just as the mural depicts the possibility of ethical reconciliation from within the accumulation of history, so, too, had the Americans placed their faith for social transformation in the record of what had come before. These social scientists had reached out to the past to refashion the future, just as the mural narrates. There was no other way for them, since on either side of the international boundary that separated the United States and Mexico, they had put away God and biology as agents of moral regeneration.

Epilogue. Pragmatism
and the Decline of Dewey

The Spanish philosopher George Santayana had enshrined one of the enduring images into American philosophical history in the same year that Mexico's revolutionary armies had mobilized against Porfirio Díaz in 1911.[1] Speaking before the Philosophical Union at the University of California, Berkeley, he argued that California, like the eastern United States, was a new society. Yet amid its newness, it had somehow managed to create a tradition of philosophical investigation of its own. Some of that tradition had emerged from the Calvinist traditions that had come from Europe to America through the Puritans, whose strict doctrines of life had become the foundational system of American thought. Calvinism in America was "an old wine in new bottles," the transplantation of European philosophy to a new continent. But America had been unexpected. Its materialism had created an aggressive spirit of achievement that had left behind the ascetic philosophy of the Calvinists, necessitating a new philosophy to replace the old wine that had been forgotten in the wake of continental expansion. What America now needed was a philosophy that could reconcile the old systems of the fathers with the experience of change that was hurtling the new nation forward into the twentieth century. A new wine that many would call America's only original contribution to philosophy, pragmatism, was being formulated at that very moment, ironically. It was fitting for that reason that Santayana was speaking at Berkeley, since it was there in 1898 that William James had become the first person to use the term "pragmatism" for the philosophical system that he, Charles Peirce, and John Dewey were then developing.[2]

Twenty-four years later, in 1935, José Vasconcelos surveyed the state of philosophy and education in postrevolutionary Mexico and found that his countrymen had grown drunk on the new wine that James and Dewey had expanded across North America.[3] "Once we have emerged from the drunken stupor of this bad wine, let us return to the fruitful wine of our own tradition. In that manner, we will resuscitate Odysseus from the dead, in order to oppose him to the simplistic formulations of the Robinson Crusoes that surround us."[4] For Vasconcelos, Homer's Odysseus represented the good wine of philosophy to which Mexico had to return, and Robinson the bad wine that had poisoned the postrevolutionary republic as the new Mexican state had risen from the ashes of war. "Robinsonism, empiricism, the philosophy of the travelogue, it is necessary for us to complement these other philosophies with the theory of final ends, with the metaphysics of happy disinterest, and with the supremacy of the absolute." Nothing better captured the disagreement between pragmatism and idealism than the contrast that Vasconcelos here set up in the signifiers of Robinson and Odysseus. To Dewey's criticism that ends had to reside in social consensus, Vasconcelos counterposed the superhuman of the absolute. To Dewey's experience and experimentalism as the method for consensual truth, Vasconcelos counterposed the closed universe of the ultimate end. To Robinson Crusoe's rudimentary adaptations to the island of Juan Fernández that Vasconcelos believed pragmatism represented, Vasconcelos counterposed the sublime seafaring and noble resourcefulness of Odysseus.

Dewey had become a shaping influence on Mexico's public schools between the time of Santayana's speech and the time of Vasconcelos's attack. There were thousands of new schoolhouses between 1920 and 1950 where previously there had been none, and in them labored teachers who had received their instruction from the Deweyites Moisés Sáenz and Rafael Ramírez. "It is in so much vogue today throughout Latin America and its colonial antecedents," Vasconcelos had written of Dewey in Mexico and Latin America before excoriating pragmatism for its undue influence over the minds of the young students of the nation.[5] "The importation of the Deweyan system among our countrymen is an aberrant case, with graver consequences than the opium and alcohol trades which other colonized people had been subjected to," Vasconcelos had also written.[6] Scholars in the United States would similarly note the deep imprint that Dewey had left on the Mexican schools, especially after World War II. Ralph Beals noted Dewey's influence in a 1957 piece, and within four years so too would the eminent historian of Mexico, Ramón Eduardo Ruiz.[7]

For the pragmatist civil righters, Mexico and the United States shared a common language of pragmatist philosophy taken from Columbia University from which they took their politics. Mexico and the United States shared a commitment to an enlarged federal government as an instrument of social balance in a world that had been undone by industrial capital. Mexico and the United States shared large territorial bases whose political histories depended on ethnic communities so dissimilar that achieving a nation seemed only a dream. There was no transcendent answer to what "achieving a nation" meant in these worlds of plurality, but merely a spectrum of terrestrial possibilities. There were no borderlands of sharing in which cultures from the North entered into a mythic union with cultures from the South in an answer to the problems of conflict. There was one society to the north whose universities struggled to make sense of capital and labor, ethnicity and identity, without having any of the essential answers. And there was another society to the south whose universities were trying to do the same, and they did not have all the answers either. Americans and Mexicans alike could have chosen the race relations cycle of Chicago's Robert Park as the answer for their search to national integration. Their politics might have started with the ethics of Aquinas or More, just as some philosophers were doing. They might have turned to the existential universe of Sartre later in the century. Likewise, they might have chosen Bolshevik Communism, Trotskyite Marxism, or the social democracy of Denmark as the political platforms on which to build their work. But they chose none of these other available options. In a world of available philosophies and politics, they looked to a small cluster of ideas born in the U.S. northeast at the end of the nineteenth century for inspiration about politics in the twentieth.

These reformers believed in pragmatism because its method addressed the epistemological understandings of knowledge they had come to share. Pragmatism offered them a way out of the transcendent morals of the social hierarchies against which they had rebelled, including the Catholic Church in the case of Mexico and the American genteel tradition in the case of the United States.[8] It allowed them to escape the established hierarchies of the Porfirian era on the one hand and the biological determinism of social Darwinism of early twentieth-century America on the other. But pragmatism also mattered to them practically, beyond its attack on nineteenth-century philosophy. It justified the importance of real-world, local experience to the nation in the context of the multiethnic society, with all the complicated and muddled diversity such experience implied. It gave Loyd Tireman a way to fashion programs of study in New Mexico for rural schoolchildren whose Spanish-rooted culture had never been accounted for by English-language schools. It gave Sánchez the defense for local conditions in the face of institutional systems that wanted to destroy local culture. It shared with cultural relativism the flexibility that had transformed Beals's attitude toward the state. It gave Moisés Sáenz and Manuel Gamio new ways to rethink the Mexican state's troubled relationship to its indigenous communities instead of merely ignoring them. The practical and epistemological merits of pragmatism did not mean that the ethical dilemmas of the modern nation-state were any easier to answer. Depending on the choices that one made, pragmatism could be used to destroy local culture just as easily as it could be used to fortify it. But within the universe of questions in which these social scientists operated, pragmatism made it more difficult to craft the relationship of the local to the national with a foregone conclusion.

The Mexicans and Americans also shared economic and political similarities with one another. They were each concerned with the relationship of rural ethnic cultures to the industrializing bases of the nation that had become economically hegemonic, for example, hoping that the instrument of the school could become the mediator for reconciling the local to the national without destroying the vibrancy of the former. They were concerned with maintaining vibrant ethnic cultures within the nation-state as the solution to the question of unity. And they shared the presence of an enlarging federal state whose resources were being marshaled to re-create the national culture.

The new wine the Mexicans and Americans shared continued to shape the political ideas and international links that the civil righters maintained to Mexico and Latin America through the late 1950s. Loyd Tireman would continue to study language acquisition among the Mexican immigrants of New Mexico, culminating in his 1948 *Teaching Spanish-Speaking Children*, a synthesis of twenty-five years of pragmatism-inspired work in psychology.[9] Like the experimentalist attitude that had always marked his career, what characterized Tireman's text was the same uncertainty about language and experience that had been a feature of his work since 1927. "What is our position [about language through the intermediate grades]," he asked. "The truth cannot be determined by armchair philosophy," he replied. "That is the type of problem which can only be solved experimentally;

yet there is too little scientific accumulation of experimental data." It was remarkable. Twenty years after he had begun his studies, he was still trying to fashion the necessary science to determine the answers to his questions. "Experimentation and research must continue whenever possible, and every helpful point should be tried out." Tireman was self-conscious, and even embarrassed, by the dearth of results. Yet he held fast. "The writer is fearful that some reader may think he is dodging the question by refusing to give dogmatic 'solutions' to these problems. Let him remind you how science has advanced. Each successive generation of scientists has patiently built upon the findings of the previous generation. Opinions and facts have been altered or reversed as new techniques and new instruments of research have been discovered. What was accepted as 'truth' in one decade has been found to be only a partial truth or erroneous in the next."[10]

Tireman carried the experimentalist spirit of pragmatism to Bolivia in 1948, when he argued for a Deweyan analysis of Bolivia's public schools as part of that nation's state-centered attempts to remold its democracy. The historicism that marked pragmatist analysis was the starting point of his report to the Bolivian state. "To study the educational system of a nation requires that we first understand its geographic and historical influences, its human communities and its economic development," he argued. Those conditions existed in a dialectic with the system, the one affecting the other and vice versa. Such a perspective lent itself to an understanding of the school as an instrument for the state to accomplish its goals, which could be good or bad.[11] From the contextual and organic analysis of the school, Tireman turned to the psychology that had marked his career. "I differ with that psychology built on the idea that the mind of the child is a type of vessel into which thoughts are deposited," he argued. "According to this theory, children are thought to be passive receptors of ideas. This is a psychology that readily lends itself to the dictatorial regime, since it creates compliant technocrats rather than learned men." To this outdated notion of education Tireman counter-posed the psychology of the pragmatists. "The psychology of a democracy is different. In this case, one presupposes that a child develops his faculties by learning to put them into practice. It is for this reason that I recommend the reduction in the number of hours spent on lectures in the classroom and a corresponding increase in the number of hours spent in the laboratory and in the library. There, the child will be taught to learn through his own efforts."[12]

Ralph Beals would continue to study Mexico's native cultures in their environmental settings into the 1970s, out of which he would produce *The Peasant Marketing System of Oaxaca, Mexico*, one of the major contributions to an understanding of the economic systems of Mexico's Native Americans in the face of the postrevolutionary industrializing economy.[13] But it was his 1957 *No Frontier to Learning: The Mexican Student in the United States* that would most closely continue the line of acculturation concerns that had marked his work during the 1930s and 1940s.[14] *No Frontier to Learning* marked an empirical movement in the direction of his 1951 presidential address to the American Anthropological Association, where he had optimistically juxtaposed the cultures of Mexico and the United States as social structures connected by common factors of change in the context of industrialization. With the Rockefeller, Ford, and Carnegie Foundations behind him, he would study the middle- and upper-class Mexican students who traveled to the United States for temporary study in American universities and colleges before they returned home for professional careers in Mexico. What values and attitudes characterized this subset of the Mexican peoples, and how did study in the United States change the hierarchy of priorities that they associated with U.S. and Mexican societies? Did the United States make a difference in how change was occurring in Mexico, meanwhile, and if so, how? The results were considerably more complicated than he might have hoped for. One could register the effects of changes on the value systems of individuals rather precisely, he concluded, but how such changes produced new forms of social organization in Mexico was too complex a question for his data to support. That his interviews had come from the middle sectors of Mexico's new social classes was also challenging, for they did not share the characteristics of the immigrants who had migrated to the United States permanently. The larger project in charting the universal principles, it seemed, would have to wait.

More interesting were the glimmers of analysis about the comparative melting pots that were being shaped on either side of the international boundary as two states continued wrestling with the meaning of social integration into the Cold War period. Beals's overview of culture and society in Mexico was striking, for example, for his depiction of the state's role in cultural transformation since 1920. The Mexican state now included a professional corps of politicians and a growing bureaucracy, but among its most noteworthy features was the greater influence of intellectuals on governance than was the case in the United States. The revolutionary movement had also emphasized paintings and art as part of the creation of Mexican nationalism, just as Rivera's murals had long since indicated. Beals also noted the role of education in the postrevolutionary period. "Mass education has developed since the revolution," Beals noted. "Its character is strongly influenced by the pragmatic philosophy of John Dewey."[15]

Beals's attention to the proportionality of social transformation was also illuminating. If cultural change and social transformation was happening in Mexico, it was happening not in the context of the nation's Indian communities only, but in the context of the much larger mestizo base of the country. Such attention to the wide spectrum of cultural communities in Mexico whose fortunes were being transformed by the creation of the post-revolutionary economy and new politics was an important reminder that Mexico's melting pot project was an expansive, deep-seated transformation of the country, for which no easy summarizing statement was possible. Within the discipline of anthropology, Beals recounted, there were few general studies of the Mexican culture that was being created and almost none at all on the urban middle classes from which Mexico's students to the United States had come. "We know a great deal about the Indian village, but very little about the other 80 percent of Mexico and virtually nothing about the city."[16] Mexico, Beals reminded his reader, was a heterogeneous culture when considered from the perspective of class, region, and the rural-urban divide. Such extreme differences made it difficult to define the themes, values, and attitudes of Mexico's groups during the forty years following the end of the revolution, especially in light of the destruction of the traditional elite that had once ruled Mexico but whose power had been supplanted by that of the emergent middle sectors who lived in the cities. It was no wonder, then, that Mexico was characterized by enormous contradictions in the 1950s. "As in thirty years much of Mexico has moved from pack train to motor truck and airplane, so Mexican society has moved from a feudal society toward an industrial society," he wrote.[17] Such contradictions were captured in the differential rates of change for the various communities of Mexican society, from the Native Americans who continued to challemge state-led transformation to the growing number of middle-class students leaving Mexico City to study at UCLA and Northwestern.

George Sánchez would carry on an explicitly comparative history project in the Americas through his relationship at the University of Texas at Austin with one of the great comparative historians of the United States and Latin America, Lewis Hanke. No one in Latin America or the United

States spent more intellectual capital attempting to understand the idea of the comparative history of the Americas Herbert Bolton had spawned than Hanke, who carried on his project through the directorship of the University of Texas's Institute for Latin American Studies (ILAS) in the 1950s. It was there that he came into contact with George Sánchez, whose original appointment at UT Austin in 1940 had come through ILAS and who served as a member of the ILAS board during much of his career in Texas. For the entire decade of the 1950s, Hanke and Sánchez collaborated on what became the most prominent research center in the United States for the study of the Americas. Hanke, Sánchez, and ILAS would conduct the largest exchanges of scholars from Latin America and the United States during the rise of the area study centers in the academy, international research from the University of Texas at Austin on Latin America, and a continuing examination of the relationship between the American West and Mexico. It was from his base at ILAS that Sánchez completed his work on Mexico during the 1940s and 1950s.

The legacy of Sánchez's own work on Mexico would continue through the work of his graduate students, whose work on Mexico's postrevolutionary education system elaborated the lifetime of analysis that Sánchez had completed on the Secretaría de Educación Pública. James Van Patten's 1962 "Education in the United Mexican States" updated the reform programs of the Mexican state through the Vietnam era, providing an analysis of the twenty-year period after 1940 when Mexico entered the fastest period of economic development in the history of the republic.[18] Albert Villareal's 1954 "The Cultural Missions of Mexico" provided a synthesis of the successive reorganizations of one of the Mexican state's fundamental platforms for postrevolutionary education in the era of *Brown v. Board of Education*.[19] The most interesting study may have been Louise Schoenhals's 1962 seminar paper for Sánchez, "Problems of Acculturation for the Mexican-American and the Indian of Mexico," in which she returned to a theme that had been at the center of Ralph Beals's own analysis of Mexico.[20] "The same factors of material innovation, education, governmental policy are responsible for a good deal of the acculturation which is taking place between the Mexican Indian and mestizo society," she concluded near the end of her paper.[21] It was a process similar to, if not exactly a replica of, acculturation processes occurring in the United States.

In his spare time, Sánchez managed to produce several books on Mexico on his own. There was *Mexico* for the Ginn Company, a short text introducing Mexico to the American audience.[22] None of what he wrote there was different from his earlier work, but it did reinforce the standard model of cultural pluralism through which he had always understood the postrevolutionary republic. The people of Mexico were not products of just one culture, but the products of many different cultures, just as was the United States, he wrote. The most fascinating was *Arithmetic in Maya*, a short treatise on the numerical system of the Maya Indians of Mexico, in which Sánchez reached outside the usual social universe of Texas in which he operated.[23] The Maya, Sánchez wrote, had pioneered the use of the number zero in their mathematical models. That use had come from the history of the culture, whose way of life was complemented by sign systems that others had not found so necessary. Sánchez's turn to the Maya would seem strange only to those unfamiliar with his lifelong engagement with Mexico. But for Sánchez it was a return to the same themes about Mexico he had always emphasized. Mexico's people were not one, but culturally distinctive, and each ethnic group had produced creatively throughout its history. Sánchez never forgot the influence of Mexico and the Mexican state on his thinking as he aged.

Pragmatism was going into steep decline amid these comparative history projects and studies of Mexico and the American West in the late 1950s. In the United States, Dewey was going underground across the departments of the university, a casualty of analytic philosophy and the counterattack against the civil rights movement. Even in education, Dewey and pragmatism were beginning a decline amid post-Sputnik observers of Soviet success. Dewey may have been a victim of his own system, in one sense, since the pluralisms on which he founded his philosophy produced students who could not agree on a common platform for educational change in the 1950s. The reformers knew they wanted change, meanwhile, but it was difficult for them to articulate a clear vision of what they wanted to create in place of the old. Deweyans and the progressives never answered the challenge of the extreme pressures that progressive education models placed on the talents of teachers. And as America turned increasingly conservative during the Cold War, progressive education found itself attacked by those who thought it had placed too much emphasis on the child and not enough on the system.[24] "The fact is that postwar America was a very different nation from the one that had given birth to progressive education," wrote Lawrence Cremin. "The great immigrations were over, and a flow of publications by David Riesman, William Whyte, Jr., Will Herberg, and others wrestled insistently with a redefinition of community. The search for *Gemeinschaft* of the nineties had become the quest for pluralism of the fifties, while the rampant individualism that Dewey so earnestly feared was now widely applauded as nonconformity."[25]

In Mexico, meanwhile, Dewey would be remembered more for his defense of Leon Trotsky in Mexico City in 1937 than for the policy reforms that his students had initiated through the cultural missions and the rural normal schools. Pragmatism had never circulated widely outside the Secretariat of Public Education, and within it, it had competed with communist-inspired agrarian reformers, French-inspired theorists trained in Montessori, and Spanish philosophers who had fled Franco after 1936. In Mexico's universities, it had struggled to compete with UNAM's renowned humanistic philosophers, and after 1950, with existentialism. In only one arena outside the SEP did Dewey's ideas remain vibrant, and even then their influence continued to be limited. At the prestigious Colegio de México, founded in 1938 by the exile philosophers from Franco's Spain, the eminent Spanish philosopher José Gaos embarked in the early 1950s on a multiyear translation of some of Dewey's most important work. Gaos would reissue Dewey's *Experience and Nature* in Spanish in 1948 as part of an oeuvre that recent scholarship sees as Gaos's attempt to bridge Heidegger and Dewey.[26] Similarly at the Colegio de México, the Mexican sociologist José Medina Echavarría would bring attention to Dewey a decade later as part of the effort at the Center for the Social Sciences there to better understand the role of the University of Chicago in the development of the twentieth-century social sciences.[27] Yet, Dewey's influence at the SEP and the Colegio de México notwithstanding, not until the work of Gregory Pappas, Guillermo Hurtado Pérez, and Ramón del Castillo in 2010 would scholarship in Mexico and the United States begin to examine the question of Dewey's synthetic influence in twentieth-century Mexican philosophy and politics.[28] Vasconcelos ultimately had nothing to worry about from within Mexico's postrevolutionary universities, including the prestigious UNAM, since Dewey remained universally tangential to the idea systems of the humanistic traditions in Mexican scholarship.[29]

Loyd Tireman died in New Mexico in 1959, and, so, too, did Rafael Ramírez, one of the architects of the cultural missions and the person who would go down in Mexican history as the *maestro de las Américas*—"the teacher of the Americas." Catholic melting pot theorist and architect of the Secretaría de Educación Pública José Vasconcelos died in Mexico City in that same year. Moisés Sáenz had died long before, in Lima, Peru, of pneumonia in 1941. But by the late 1950s, it was the emergence of critical anthropology in Mexico that was raising new questions about the role of the state in the transformation of Mexico's Indian communities. In the United States, George Sánchez remained steadfast in his support for the courts and the schools as instruments of social change, but he had grown weary of the constant attention it required. A disagreement with Lewis Hanke in 1959 exposed his shortening temper with old intellectual battles and his growing unease with the fight.[30] To a younger colleague in Texas, he similarly revealed his frustration: "Don't expect an oldtimer like myself to hold your hand; I've fought, bled, and died in this game. Go out and fight your own fight."[31] Sputnik had blasted into space in 1957, precipitating a counteroffensive against progressive models of schooling, and in the American South the resistance movement to civil rights was beginning to harden. Dewey himself had died in 1952, and within a decade books that would win the Pulitzer Prize were attacking him for his role in the decline of the American school.[32]

As Dewey was in full retreat in Mexico and the United States, one last episode in the career of pragmatism symbolized the work that it had done in the American West between the New Deal and the civil rights movement. In December 1958, George Sánchez received his latest newsletter from the John Dewey Society. The society had been founded in 1935 to keep alive the ideas of this American pragmatist and would continue to be a primary advocate for his work across the twentieth century. "Good news!" wrote acting president William Van Till, "Your society has initiated a national observance of the John Dewey Centennial year, 1959."[33] It was one hundred years since the birth of John Dewey, and in his honor, thirty-eight members of the John Dewey Society had undertaken to sponsor thirty-eight society meetings across the nation. The University of Texas had agreed to sponsor one visit, and George Sánchez gladly took over arrangements for the conference. Sánchez had underlined item three in the margins of his newsletter in bold black ink: "Oscar Handlin, Pulitzer Prize-winning Harvard historian and author of 'Rejoinder to the Critics of John Dewey' (*New York Times Magazine*, June 15, 1958), will deliver the second John Dewey Society Lecture before the National Society of College Teachers of Education at Chicago, on Friday, February 13th at 9:00 a.m." Within a month, Sánchez was corresponding with Handlin, trying to arrange the details of a March visit to the University of Texas at Austin to celebrate the Dewey centennial. Handlin agreed to deliver two lectures on theories of elementary education to teachers in training, and he would deliver one paper on John Dewey to an after-dinner audience of graduate students and faculty. "This meeting

[will] be called to commemorate the centennial of John Dewey . . . and we would like an after-dinner paper on John Dewey, one that I hope you will give us first chance at publishing in one of our academic journals," Sánchez wrote to Handlin.[34]

For Sánchez, the meetings with Handlin were one more opportunity to underscore the relationship between the pragmatism of John Dewey and the melting pot that he believed was represented in the culture of the United States. Handlin was only eight years removed from his 1951 *The Uprooted*, his classic sociological study of the movement of immigrants from Europe into the fabric of American life.[35] The movement from Europe to the United States had been an injurious one, he had written, resulting in the loss of the home culture amid the shock of the new home in America. Immigrants were stripped bare of their cultural trappings once they arrived in the United States, but quickly, the ways of the old world were replaced with the ways of the new one. From this world of transformation captured in his book, Handlin diverged into the defense of Dewey that the *New York Times* had published earlier that year. What marked the world that the immigrant was moving into was change, Handlin had written in the *New York Times*. "Society was changing rapidly [in the 1890s] under the impact of urbanization and industrialization, and not always for the better," Handlin wrote in the *Times*. "But the teacher ought not to pretend therefore that his pupils still walked along the lanes of an eighteenth-century village back to a rustic farmhouse. He had to take account of the city streets and of the American home as it actually was."[36] Handlin now switched gears, defending Dewey in the language of psychology that had been the currency of Tireman's understanding of Dewey. "The realm of the classroom was totally set off from the experience of the child who inhabited it. . . . Learning consisted of the tedious memorization of data without meanings immediately clear to the pupil." The answer for Dewey, wrote Handlin, was to end the isolation of the school from the experience of the student by pulling it into a closer relationship with the family and the community. By recognizing the unity of the child's experience, the school could communicate more directly with him or her and at the same time break down the pernicious "division into cultured people and workers." Handlin returned to "experience" one last time. "Instruction, under such conditions, could be carried forward as a succession of direct experiences on the child's part."

Here is where Handlin may have best captured the meaning Dewey had had for Sánchez and his cohort across Mexico and the American West amid the decline of Dewey in the academy and the schools. In contrast to those who were criticizing Dewey, wrote Handlin, Dewey's ideas had become one of the most important influences on the development of the schools in America. "In the last fifteen years, there had been a growing tendency to lay the blame for the failures of American education to a single cause. Johnny's inability to read, juvenile delinquency, the high divorce rate. . . . There is, it is charged, a simple explanation to all our difficulties. John Dewey, one of those vague professors—and a philosopher at that—devised some abstract, and therefore unrealistic, theories." But in truth, wrote Handlin, Dewey had had a profound effect on American education. "Despite the occasional errors in their application to practice and despite the distortions by uncritical enthusiasts, our schools have profited immensely from his influence. . . . Our schools are more adequate now than they were sixty years ago. The task of making them fully adequate is nevertheless far from complete. But it is more likely to be pushed forward by extending rather than by narrowing Dewey's visions of freedom in which to learn to live in the modern world."[37]

One wonders what José Vasconcelos must have thought about Handlin's defense. For his own part, George Sánchez was pleased. He had used Dewey alongside his colleagues in the American West and Mexico in ways that had made the school more accessible, and more instrumental, to thousands of young minds across the arc that stretched from Texas to California. It was in the spirit of that work that he looked forward to Handlin's lecture with relish. "I am anticipating an outstanding lecture by this eminent historian and scholarly interpreter of John Dewey," Sánchez told his colleague in the University of Texas History Department, A. R. Lewis.[38] To Handlin, meanwhile, Sánchez was solicitous. "Please let me know [the] time of [your] arrival, and airline, as I would like to meet you at the airport."[39] The philosophy that had sustained these Americans across Mexico and the United States was quickly being forgotten, but for Sánchez and Handlin both, there was time for one final hurrah in the face of the new politics that was washing Dewey away.

Notes

Introduction

1. The term "melting pot" is most often associated with Israel Zangwill's play of the same name, first performed in 1908 and published a year later as Israel Zangwill, *The Melting-Pot, Drama in Four Acts* (New York: Macmillan, 1909). Throughout the text, however, my use of "melting pot" mirrors that of sociologist Milton Gordon, *Assimilation in American Life* (New York: Oxford University Press, 1964) rather than Zangwill's. Like Gordon, I mean to suggest that the term "melting pot" represents a series of different assimilationist possibilities rather than any single one, in Mexico as in the United States. For the range of these possibilities, see, for example, Gonzalo Aguirre Beltrán, *El proceso de aculturación* (Mexico City: UNAM, 1957); Mary K. Coffey, "The 'Mexican Problem': Nation and 'Native' in Mexican Muralism and Cultural Discourse," in *The Social and the Real: Political Art of the 1930s in the Western Hemisphere*, ed. Alejandro Anreus, Diana L. Linden, and Jonathan Weinberg (University Park: Pennsylvania State University Press, 2006); and Estelle Tarica, *The Inner Life of Mestizo Nationalism* (Minneapolis: University of Minnesota Press, 2008).

2. Manuel Gamio, *Forjando patria* (Mexico City: Porrúa, 1916); José Vasconcelos, *La raza cósmica* (Madrid: Agencia Mundial de Librería, 1925); Moisés Sáenz, *México íntegro* (1939; Mexico City: Consejo Nacional para la Cultura y las Artes, 2006).

3. For *sinfonía de culturas*, see Sáenz, *Mexico íntegro*, 42; for *crisol de razas y culturas*, see Miguel Othón de Mendizábal, "Esbozos etnográficos," in *Obras completas*, vol. 4 (Mexico City: Talleres Gráficos de la Nación, 1946), 154; for *mosaico de razas*, see Carlos A. Echánove Trujillo, *Sociología mexicana* (Mexico City: Porrúa, 1946), 229, emphasis original. Sáenz used *crisol* at *México íntegro*, 57. All translations to English from the original Spanish sources are by the author.

4. For the classical formulation of the "antiformalist" revolution, see Morton White, *Social Thought in America: The Revolt Against Formalism* (Cambridge, Mass.: Harvard University Press, 1957). I shall maintain my focus throughout my text on the two strains of that thought known as pragmatism and cultural relativism.

5. For my definition of discourse I depend on David A. Hollinger, "Historians and the Discourse of Intellectuals," in *In the American Province: Studies in the History and Historiography of Ideas* (Baltimore: Johns Hopkins University Press, 1985), 132.

Hollinger stresses the importance of shared questions to discursive conversations as much as are shared values or shared concepts.

6. See Carlin Romano, *America the Philosophical* (New York: Knopf, 2012) for a recent book on the history of philosophy that analyzes the importance of John Dewey and the pragmatist tradition to American culture.

7. For the relationship between pragmatism and political action in the 1930s, see Arthur Schlesinger, Jr., *The Crisis of the Old Order, 1919–1933* (Boston: Houghton Mifflin, 1957), especially chaps. 17 and 18; and Alfred Kazin, *On Native Grounds: An Interpretation of Modern American Prose Literature* (New York: Reynal and Hitchcock, 1942), especially chap. 5. Kazin was a scholar of literature, but he understood the rise of modernist social science to be a part of the same movement that had produced modernist literature.

8. See, for example, Mary Kay Vaughan, *Cultural Politics in Revolution: Teachers, Peasants, and Schools in Mexico, 1930–1940* (Tucson: University of Arizona Press, 1997).

9. Sáenz, *México íntegro*, 102–5.

10. Ralph Beals, *Mendez v. Westminster*, 64 F. Supp. 544 (C. D. Cal. 1946), *Reporter's Transcript of Proceedings*, 662.

11. See, for example, Paul S. Taylor, *Mexican Labor in the United States* (Berkeley: University of California Press, 1928–34).

12. For a recent argument in the context of Latin America that criticizes the separation of practice from theory as Dewey understood it, see Raymond Craib and Mark Overmyer-Velázquez, "Migration and Labor in the Americas: Praxis, Knowledge, and Nations," *Hispanic American Historical Review* 92, 2 (2012): 248–49. Craib and Overmyer-Velásquez rely on the work of Paulo Freire, but the similarity to Dewey is not accidental. Both Dewey and Freire understood schools to be institutions for social transformation rather than social control.

13. John Higham, "The Cult of the 'American Consensus,'" *Commentary* 27 (1959): 98.

14. Ibid., 100.

15. See George I. Sánchez, *Mexico: A Revolution by Education* (New York: Viking, 1936).

16. John Dewey, *Democracy and Education* (New York: Macmillan, 1916).

17. Gamio, *Forjando patria*.

18. Sánchez, *Mexico: A Revolution by Education*.

19. Ibid., 95.

20. Ibid., 134.

21. Ibid., 95.

22. See, for example, George I. Sánchez, "Education in Mexico," *Annals of the American Academy of Political and Social Science* 208 (1940); Sánchez, "Mexico in Transition," *Proceedings of the Conference on Latin America in Social and Economic Transition* (Albuquerque: University of New Mexico Press, 1943); Sánchez, "Education

in Mexico," *Encyclopedia of Modern Education* (New York: American Association on Indian Affairs, 1944); Sánchez, *The Development of Higher Education in Mexico* (New York: Kings Crown Press, 1944); Sánchez, *Mexico* (Boston: Ginn, 1966).

23. George I. Sánchez, as quoted in "Southwest Spanish-Americans Prepare to Challenge Power-Structure Forcing Second-Class Citizenship," *The Southwesterner*, December 1966, on file in the Sánchez Vertical File, Center for Southwest Research, University of New Mexico.

24. Sánchez, *Mexico*, 7.

25. Loyd S. Tireman, *The Rural Schools of Mexico*, University of New Mexico Bulletin, Training School Series 2, 1, Whole no. 205 (Albuquerque: University of New Mexico Press, 1931).

26. Loyd Tireman, "Mi Amigo el Hispano," address delivered at the Rural Conference of the Colorado State Teachers College, January 1932, 11, on file at the General Education Board Collection, Box 599, Folder 6361, Rockefeller Archival Center, Tarrytown, New York.

27. See Robert R. Alvarez, Jr., "The Lemon Grove Incident: The Nation's First Successful Desegregation Court Case," *Journal of San Diego History* 32, 2 (Spring 1986).

28. Sánchez's relationship to Rosenwald is documented in the Julius Rosenwald Fund Archives, Special Collections and Archives, Franklin Library, Fisk University, Nashville, Tennessee (hereafter cited as JRFA).

29. John Collier, "Mexico: A Challenge," *Progressive Education* 9 (1932).

30. John Dewey, "Mexico's Educational Renaissance," *New Republic* 48 (1927): 4, emphasis original. Mexico's Secretaría de Educación Pública published Dewey's essay as *What Mr. John Dewey Thinks of the Educational Policies of Mexico* (Mexico City: Talleres Gráficos de la Nación, 1926).

31. Benedict Anderson, *Imagined Communities: Reflections on the Origin and Spread of Nationalism* (London: Verso/NLB, 1983); and John Dewey, *The Public and Its Problems* (New York: Holt, 1927).

32. See Randolph Bourne, "Trans-National America," *Atlantic Monthly* 118 (July 1916). For historical uses of "beloved community," see Ninian Smart, "The Later Royce and the Beloved Community," *Inquiry: An Interdisciplinary Journal of Philosophy* 12, 1–4 (1969); and Casey Blake, *Beloved Community: The Cultural Criticism of Randolph Bourne, Van Wyck Brooks, Waldo Frank, and Lewis Mumford* (Chapel Hill: University of North Carolina Press, 1990). In the U.S. Congress, Rep. John Lewis of Georgia has recently referred to the "beloved community" as the object of his search for equality in the United States since his first moments in the civil rights movement in the 1960s. See, for example, his public address "Building the Beloved Community," delivered at Dalton State College, Dalton, Georgia, April 30, 2012.

33. The history of the state amid national consolidation could also be paradoxical and contradictory. See, for example, Margot Canaday, *The Straight State: Sexuality and Citizenship in Twentieth-Century America* (Princeton, N.J.: Princeton University Press,

2009) in the case of the United States; and Grace Peña Delgado, *Making the Chinese Mexican: Global Migration, Localism, and Exclusion in the U.S.-Mexico Borderlands* (Stanford, Calif.: Stanford University Press, 2012) in the case of Mexico.

34. For studies that place the growth of the American state in a European context, see Daniel T. Rodgers, *Atlantic Crossings: Social Politics in a Progressive Age* (Cambridge, Mass.: Belknap Press of Harvard University Press, 1998); James T. Kloppenberg, *Uncertain Victory: Social Democracy and Progressivism in European and American Thought, 1870–1920* (New York: Oxford University Press, 1986); Leslie Butler, *Critical Americans: Victorian Intellectuals and Transatlantic Liberal Reform* (Chapel Hill: University of North Carolina Press, 2007); and Canaday, *The Straight State.*

35. See, for example, Ramón Eduardo Ruiz, *Mexico: The Challenge of Poverty and Illiteracy* (San Marino, Calif.: Huntington Library, 1963).

36. Jacquelyn Dowd Hall, "The Long Civil Rights Movement and the Political Uses of the Past," *Journal of American History* 91, 4 (March 2005): 1233–63.

37. For the influence of the legal segregation cases in the American West on those of the American South, see Philippa Strum, *Mendez v. Westminster: School Desegregation and Mexican-American Rights* (Lawrence: University Press of Kansas, 2010); and Jeanne M. Powers and Lirio Patton, "Between *Mendez* and *Brown*: *Gonzales v. Sheely* (1951) and the Legal Campaign Against Segregation," *Law and Social Inquiry* 33, 1 (March 2008): 127–71. For a recent book that places Mexican American civil rights in the larger context of California civil rights, see Mark Brilliant, *The Color of America has Changed: How Racial Diversity Shaped Civil Rights Reform in California, 1941–1978* (New York: Oxford University Press, 2010).

38. For two recent analyses of racial conflict in the American West against which these Americans were struggling, see Katherine Benton-Cohen, *Borderline Americans: Racial Division and Labor War in the Arizona Borderlands* (Cambridge, Mass.: Harvard University Press, 2009); and Anthony Mora, *Border Dilemmas: Racial and National Uncertainties in New Mexico, 1848–1912* (Durham, N.C.: Duke University Press, 2011). A classic installment to these debates in the field of whiteness studies is Neil Foley, *The White Scourge: Mexicans, Blacks, and Poor Whites in Texas Cotton Culture* (Berkeley: University of California Press, 1997).

39. Mary Dudziak, *Cold War Civil Rights: Race and the Image of American Democracy* (Princeton, N.J.: Princeton University Press, 2000); Timothy B. Tyson, *Radio Free Dixie: Robert F. Williams and the Roots of Black Power* (Chapel Hill: University of North Carolina Press, 1999); and Mary Dudziak, *Exporting American Dreams: Thurgood Marshall's African Journey* (New York: Oxford University Press, 2008).

40. For other texts that emphasize the border as a site of difference rather than one of convergence, see Rachel St. John, *Line in the Sand: A History of the Western U.S-Mexico Border* (Princeton, N.J.: Princeton University Press, 2011); Mora, *Border Dilemmas*; and Andrés Reséndez, *Changing National Identities at the Frontier: Texas and New Mexico, 1800–1850* (New York: Cambridge University Press, 2005).

41. In this sense, the social scientists I have studied reflected a sense of international history that Rob Kroes has described as seeing "the United States as just another nation among nations, without any messianic destiny or exceptionalist aspirations." See Kroes, "American Empire and Cultural Imperialism: A View from the Receiving End," in *Rethinking American History in a Global Age*, ed. Thomas Bender (Berkeley: University of California Press, 2002), 296.

42. Leo Marx, "Believing in America: An Intellectual Project and a National Ideal," *Boston Review*, December 2003/January 2004; and C. Vann Woodward, *The Strange Career of Jim Crow* (New York: Oxford University Press, 1955).

43. Ralph L. Beals, "Anthropological Research Problems with Reference to the Contemporary Peoples of Mexico and Guatemala," *American Anthropologist* n.s. 45 (January–March 1943): 2.

Chapter 1. A Symphony of Cultures

1. Daniel T. Rodgers, *Atlantic Crossings: Social Politics in a Progressive Age* (Cambridge, Mass.: Belknap Press of Harvard University Press, 1998), 5.

2. For a recent example of such orientalisms, see Jason Ruiz, *Americans in the Treasure House: Travel to Porfirian Mexico and the Cultural Politics of Empire* (Austin: University of Texas Press, 2014).

3. See "Forjando patria" in Manuel Gamio, *Forjando patria* (Mexico City: Porrúa, 1916).

4. See Gamio, "Resumen," in *Forjando patria*.

5. See George I. Sánchez to Edwin Embree, June 10, 1935, on file at JRFA, Box 542, Folder 14.

6. Sánchez to Embree, August 21, 1935, JRFA, Box 542, Folder 14.

7. George I. Sánchez, *Mexico: A Revolution by Education* (New York: Viking, 1936), 60.

8. George I. Sánchez, *Mexico* (Boston: Ginn, 1966), 7.

9. Edwin Embree, "Schools in Mexico: A Report to the Trustees of the Julius Rosenwald Fund," 8, JRFA, Box 537, Folder 4.

10. Ibid., 7.

11. W. E. B. Du Bois, *The Souls of Black Folk* (Chicago: McClurg, 1903).

12. Madison Grant, *The Passing of the Great Race: or the Racial Basis of European History* (New York: Scribner, 1919).

13. Franz Boas, *The Mind of Primitive Man* (New York: Macmillan, 1911).

14. Horace Kallen, "Democracy Versus the Melting-Pot: A Study of American Nationality," *The Nation* (February 25, 1915).

15. Israel Zangwill, *The Melting-Pot, Drama in Four Acts* (New York: Macmillan, 1909).

16. Kallen, "Democracy Versus the Melting-Pot."

17. Randolph Bourne, "Trans-National America," *Atlantic Monthly* 118 (July 1916).

18. See Carey McWilliams, *North from Mexico: The Spanish-Speaking People of the United States* (Philadelphia: Lippincott, 1949), 209–12. McWilliams adopted Gamio's notion of "cultural fusion" as Gamio had articulated it in his 1916 *Forjando patria* to describe social relationships between Mexican Americans and Mexican immigrants in Southern California. In borrowing from Gamio, McWilliams was using ideas produced in the context of ethnic relations in Mexico to describe the history of ethnic relations in the United States.

19. Lincoln Steffens, for example, had called Mexico's war the first social revolution of the twentieth century, while John Reed had traveled with Pancho Villa on horseback in Chihuahua before heading for Russia to write *Ten Days That Shook the World* (New York: Boni & Liveright, 1919).

20. Gamio, *Forjando patria*, 4–5.

21. Ibid., 6.

22. Ibid., 190.

23. Vasconcelos is so prominent among U.S. scholars that his image of the Latin American melting pot has even become a cliché. Among others, see the treatment of his *raza cósmica* vision in Gloria Anzaldúa, *Borderlands: The New Mestiza = La Frontera* (San Francisco: Spinsters/Aunt Lute, 1987); Richard Rodriguez, *Brown: The Last Discovery of America* (New York: Viking, 2002); and Neil Foley, *The Quest for Equality: The Failed Promise of Black-Brown Solidarity* (Cambridge, Mass.: Harvard University Press, 2010). U.S. scholars are right to note the importance of Vasconcelos, but the alternative visions of fusion offered by other Mexican thinkers deserve equal attention. For more on Vasconcelos, see Ilan Stavans, *José Vasconcelos: The Prophet of Race* (New Brunswick, N.J.: Rutgers University Press, 2011).

24. Park's collection of articles on race relations were later published as Robert Park, *Race and Culture* (Glencoe, Ill.: Free Press, 1950).

25. José Vasconcelos, *La raza cósmica* (Madrid: Agencia Mundial de Librería, 1925).

26. Critics often miss Vasconcelos's argument that British America, too, and not just Spanish America, was a melting pot. As Vasconcelos put it, "other mixtures created Hellenic culture," which subsequently expanded into Western Europe and became, among others, the Spanish and English. See *La raza cósmica*, Part I.

27. Vasconcelos, *La raza cósmica*, Part I.

28. Piña Mora's mural, entitled *La Profecía de la Raza Cósmica* (1979), is in the Posada Tierra Blanca Hotel in Ciudad Chihuahua, Chihuahua, Mexico.

29. Moisés Sáenz, "Contraste," in *México íntegro* (1939; Mexico City: Consejo Nacional para la Cultura y las Artes, 2006), 35.

30. Sáenz, *México íntegro*. The literal translation would be *Integral Mexico*, based on the word *íntegro*, which means "whole," "entire," or "completed." Sáenz wrote of the institutional mechanisms for consolidating the nation-state politically and culturally, and thus I have chosen to emphasize the importance he attached to the idea of unity. Sáenz himself defined the term *íntegro* as "completed," though his argument

that twentieth-century Mexican society was "fluid, and still in the process of being formed," argues for a title more like *A Unifying Mexico*. See *México íntegro*, 44–45, 51.

31. Ibid., 42.

32. Ibid., 58.

33. Ibid., 44.

34. See Lesley Byrd Simpson, *Many Mexicos* (New York: Putnam, 1941).

35. George I. Sánchez, "The United Mexican States," 2, in Box 72, Folder 19, George I. Sánchez Papers, 1919–1986, Benson Manuscripts Collection, Benson Latin American Collection, University of Texas at Austin, Austin, Texas (hereafter GSP).

36. Carlos A. Echánove Trujillo, *Sociología mexicana* (Mexico City: Porrúa, 1946), 229, emphasis original.

37. For the "one-drop rule," see David Hollinger, *Postethnic America: Beyond Multiculturalism* (New York: Basic Books, 1995).

38. Katherine Benton-Cohen, *Borderline Americans: Racial Division and Labor War in the Arizona Borderlands* (Cambridge, Mass.: Harvard University Press, 2009) has recently contrasted *mestizaje* to *miscegenation*, for example, arguing that Mexicans in Arizona had different notions of race from U.S. citizens. Gregory Rodriguez's recent *Mongrels, Bastards, Orphans, and Vagabonds: Mexican Immigration and the Future of Race in America* (New York: Pantheon, 2007) positions *mestizaje* in a vanguard slot, arguing that the racial ambiguities that have been historically present in Mexican society have positioned Mexican immigrants as the leading edge of the accelerating movement in the United States toward increased racial crossings. Other interlocutors have included Gloria Anzaldúa and Richard Rodriguez, both of whom have signaled hybridity as an ethical platform from which to reformulate ethnic relations in the United States. See Anzaldúa, *Borderlands*; and R. Rodriguez, *Brown: The Last Discovery of America*.

39. For contrasts and comparisons between U.S. and Latin American conceptions of race, see, for example, Peter Wade, *Race and Ethnicity in Latin America* (London: Pluto, 1997).

40. On mosaic, mariachi, and choir, see Sáenz, *México íntegro*, 41, 43–44, 58.

41. See Sánchez, *Mexico: A Revolution by Education*, 95, 134.

42. On state funding rather than private largesse, see Embree, "Schools in Mexico: A Report to the Trustees of the Julius Rosenwald Fund."

43. Luis Villoro, *Los grandes momentos del indigenismo en México* (Mexico City: El Colegio de México, 1950). Alan Knight agrees; see Knight, "Race, Revolution, and Indigenismo, 1910–1940," in *The Idea of Race in Latin America, 1870–1940*, ed. Richard Graham (Austin: University of Texas Press, 1990), 77.

44. Villoro, *Los grandes momentos del indigenismo en México*.

45. Ibid., 170–71.

46. Francisco Pimentel, *Memoria sobre las causas que han originado la situación actual de la raza indígena de México y medios para remediarla* (Mexico City: Andrade

y Escalante, 1864), 217, as quoted in Villoro, *Los grandes momentos del indigenismo*, 168–69.

47. Alan Knight argued, for instance, that the destruction of local fiefdoms at the hands of the central government did not necessarily mean transfer of power to the central state from the peasants, proletarians, and church supporters on whom the former cacique system had rested. Just as important, he argued that the postrevolutionary state often encountered stiff opposition in its goals and sometimes failed, even as the government began successfully to reproduce itself. See Alan Knight, "State Power and Political Stability in Mexico," in *Mexico: Dilemmas of Transition*, ed. Neil Harvey (London: British Academic Press, 1993), 49. See also Alan Knight, "Cardenismo: Juggernaut or Jalopy?" *Journal of Latin American Studies* 26, 1 (February 1994): 73–107. For earlier arguments about the strength of the Leviathan state, see, for example, Arnaldo Córdova, *La ideología de la revolución mexicana: la formación del nuevo régimen* (Mexico City: Ediciones Era, 1973).

48. See Knight, "Race, Revolution, and Indigenismo, 1910–1940," 83.

49. Hollinger, *Postethnic America*.

50. For a contemporary text that refers to Mexico's social triptych, see Guillermo Bonfil Batalla, *México profundo: una civilización negada* (Mexico City: SEP, 1987).

51. Andrés Molina Enríquez, *Los grandes problemas nacionales* (Mexico City: Carranza e Hijos, 1909), 197. Though precise figures for the Mexican population have never been determined, social theorists conventionally agreed that Mexico's population on the eve of the Mexican Revolution was fourteen or fifteen million. Gamio, *Forjando patria*, and Moisés Sáenz, "Integrating Mexico Through Education," in *Some Mexican Problems: Lectures on the Harris Foundation 1926* (Chicago: University of Chicago Press, 1926), both cited a figure of fourteen million, while Miguel Othón de Mendizábal cited 15.1 million. See Mendizábal, "La antropología y el problema indígena," in *Obras completas*, vol. 4 (Mexico City: Talleres Gráficos de la Nación, 1946), 168. That figure does not seem out of place with later statistics. Mendizábal reported that the 1930 census revealed a total of 16.5 million persons in Mexico, for instance. See Mendizábal, "La antropología y el problema indígena," 163.

52. Molina Enríquez, *Los grandes problemas nacionales*.

53. Mendizábal, "Los problemas indígenas y su más urgente tratamiento," in *Obras completas*, vol. 4 (Mexico City: Talleres Gráficos de la Nación, 1946), 9

54. See Milton Gordon, *Assimilation in American Life* (New York: Oxford University Press, 1955), chap. 3.

55. See, for example, Alan Dawley, *Struggles for Justice* (Cambridge, Mass.: Belknap Press of Harvard University Press, 1991).

56. *New York Times*, March 25, 1926.

57. Gamio, *Forjando patria*, chap. 5. Gamio cites Boas, *The Mind of Primitive Man*.

58. Moisés Sáenz and Herbert Priestly, *Some Mexican Problems: Lectures on the Harris Foundation 1926* (Chicago: University of Chicago Press, 1926), 78. Sáenz cites John Dewey, *The School and Society* (Chicago: University of Chicago Press, 1899).

59. Sáenz, *México íntegro*, 148.

60. For "experience" in Deweyan philosophy, see Gregory Pappas, *John Dewey's Ethics: Democracy as Experience* (Bloomington: Indiana University Press, 2008).

61. Moisés Sáenz, *Carapan: Bosquejo de una experiencia* (Lima: Librería e Imprenta Gil, 1936).

62. Sáenz, *Carapan*, 126–27.

63. For the influence of John Dewey on Ramírez, see Gonzalo Aguirre Beltrán, Introducción to Rafael Ramírez, *La escuela rural mexicana* (Mexico City: SEP, 1976).

64. See the records of the Progressive Education Association's correspondence with the SEP in the SEP's Mexico City archives for 1932, for example, located at Sección Subsecretaría, Box 6, Folder 21, Archivo Histórico de la Secretaría de Educación Pública, Mexico City.

65. For a recent discussion of the relationship between Boas and Gamio, for example, see Quetzil E. Castañeda, "Stocking's Historiography of Influence: The 'Story of Boas,' Gamio, and Redfield at the Cross-'Road to Light,'" *Critique of Anthropology* 23, 3 (2003): 235–63.

66. John Dewey, *Democracy and Education* (New York: Macmillan, 1916); and John Dewey, *How We Think* (Boston: Heath, 1910).

67. The standard account of the social scientific thought these thinkers shared, "antiformalism," remains Morton White, *Social Thought in America: The Revolt Against Formalism* (Boston: Beacon, 1957). White based his argument on the disciplines of law, economics, psychology, and history, but George Stocking, Jr., later cited White to show that the principles of antiformalism could be extended to include cultural relativism in anthropology as well. See Stocking, "Franz Boas and the Culture Concept in Historical Perspective," *American Anthropologist* n.s. 68 (August 1960): 880. Stocking also cited H. Stuart Hughes, *Consciousness and Society: The Reorientation of European Social Thought, 1890–1930* (New York: Knopf, 1958).

68. See Arthur Schlesinger, Jr., *The Crisis of the Old Order, 1919–1933* (Boston: Houghton Mifflin, 1957); and Rexford Tugwell, *The Battle for Democracy* (New York: Columbia University Press, 1935).

69. Rafael Ramírez, foreword to Sánchez, *Mexico: A Revolution by Education*, vii.

70. On the turn to history and context, see White, *Social Thought in America*.

71. Loyd Tireman, *The Rural Schools of Mexico*, University of New Mexico Bulletin, 2, 1, Training School Series, Whole no. 205 (Albuquerque: University of New Mexico Press, 1931).

72. Ralph L. Beals, "Anthropological Research Problems with Reference to the Contemporary Peoples of Mexico and Guatemala," *American Anthropologist* n.s. 45 (January–March 1943): 2.

73. Sánchez, *Mexico: A Revolution by Education*, 71, 73.

74. John Dewey, *Impressions of Soviet Russia and the Revolutionary World, Mexico-China-Turkey* (New York: New Republic, 1929), 158.

75. On Deweyan philosophy as an instrument for ameliorating the condition of man, see Pappas, *John Dewey's Ethics*, especially Part One, "Moral Theory and Experience."

76. For the transatlantic discourses in ideas, see James T. Kloppenberg, *Uncertain Victory: Social Democracy and Progressivism in European and American Thought, 1870–1920* (New York: Oxford University Press, 1986); Rodgers, *Atlantic Crossings*; and Leslie Butler, *Critical Americans: Victorian Intellectuals and Transatlantic Liberal Reform* (Chapel Hill: University of North Carolina Press, 2007).

77. For the imperial relationships between the United States and Mexico during this time, see, for example, Gilbert M. Joseph et al., eds., *Close Encounters of Empire: Writing the Cultural History of U.S.-Latin American Relations* (Durham, N.C.: Duke University Press, 1998).

78. On contingent possibilities in history, see Rodgers, *Atlantic Crossings* in the context of United States progressivism and Gil Joseph and Daniel Nugent, eds., *Everyday Forms of State Formation: Revolution and the Negotiation of Rule in Modern Mexico* (Durham, N.C.: Duke University Press, 1994) in the context of revolutionary Mexico. For examples of other convergences that scholars have charted between the United States and Mexico, see Grace Peña Delgado, *Making the Chinese Mexican: Global Migration, Localism, and Exclusion in the U.S.-Mexico Borderlands* (Stanford, Calif.: Stanford University Press, 2012); and Henry Louis Gates, Jr., *Black in Latin America* (New York: New York University Press, 2011). For the United States and Brazil, see Greg Grandin, *Fordlandia: The Rise and Fall of Henry Ford's Forgotten Jungle City* (New York: Metropolitan, 2009).

79. For *sinfonía de culturas*, see Sáenz, *México íntegro*, 42. One scholar who has noted the resemblance between Sáenz and Kallen is José Antonio Aguilar Rivera, "Moisés Sáenz y la escuela de la patria mexicana," in Sáenz, *México íntegro*, 15–22."

80. See Villoro, *Los grandes momentos del indigenismo en México*, chap. 12

81. Gonzalo Aguirre Beltrán, *El proceso de aculturación* (Mexico City: UNAM, 1957); and Russell Kazal, "Revisiting Assimilation: The Rise, Fall, and Reappraisal of a Concept in American Ethnic History," *American Historical Review* 100, 2 (April 1995): 437–71.

82. For example, the SEP juxtaposed integration in Mexico and the United States in *Memoria de la Secretaría de Relaciones Exteriores de agosto de 1930 a julio de 1931*, vol. 2 (Mexico City: Secretaría de Relaciones Exteriores, 1931), 1784–1801.

Chapter 2. Shock Troops

1. Some impressive recent work detailing these processes includes Alicia Hernández Chávez, *México, breve historia contemporánea* (Mexico City: Fondo de Cultura Económica, 2000); Jocelyn Olcott, Mary K. Vaughan, and Gabriela Cano, eds., *Sex in Revolution: Gender, Politics, and Power in Modern Mexico* (Durham, N.C.: Duke University Press, 2007); and Rick López, *Crafting Mexico: Intellectuals, Artisans, and the State After the Revolution* (Durham, N.C.: Duke University Press, 2010).

2. José Vasconcelos, *La raza cósmica* (Madrid: Agencia Mundial de Librería, 1925).

3. The best essay on Sáenz remains John Britton, "Moisés Sáenz: nacionalista mexicano," *Estudios Mexicanos* 22 (1972), though large gaps remain in Britton's account of his life.

4. John Dewey, "Mexico's Educational Renaissance," *New Republic* 48 (September 22, 1926): 116–18, emphasis original. The SEP published Dewey's essay as *What Mr. John Dewey Thinks of the Educational Policies of Mexico* (Mexico City: Talleres Gráficos de la Nación, 1926).

5. Daniel T. Rodgers, "An Age of Social Politics," in *Rethinking American History in a Global Age*, ed. Thomas Bender (Berkeley: University of California Press, 2002).

6. Thirteen other normal academies had been established across the republic in addition to Actopan, including institutions in the states of Tamaulipas, Nuevo León, Sonora, Baja California, Michoacán, San Luis Potosí, Morelos, Campeche, Oaxaca, Guerrero, Nayarit, Puebla, and Tlaxcala.

7. For threats to the teachers, see Moisés Sáenz, *Carapan: Bosquejo de una experiencia* (Lima: Libreria e Imprenta Gil, 1939), 260. For bodies dumped on the outskirts of the Tarascan villages of Michoacán, see Paul Friedrich, *The Princes of Naranja: An Essay in Anthrohistorical Method* (Austin: University of Texas Press, 1986).

8. Audit Report of the Oaxtepec Normal School by Higinio Vázquez Santa Ana, Year 1932, Sección Dirección de Misiones Culturales, Serie Escuelas Normales Rurales, Box 57, Folder 18 (Oaxtepec), Archivo Histórico de la Secretaría de Educación Pública, Mexico City (hereafter AHSEP).

9. Ibid.

10. Ibid.

11. See George Sánchez letter to Edwin Embree, June 10, 1935, JRFA, Box 542, Folder 14, for a record of his first trip to Oaxtepec.

12. See Sánchez's descriptions and photograph of Morelos and the volcanoes at George I. Sánchez, *Mexico: A Revolution by Education* (New York: Viking, 1936), 8, 192.

13. See George Sánchez letter to Edwin Embree, August 21, 1935, JRFA, Box 542, Folder 14, for a record of his August trip to Mexico's north.

14. Elsie Rockwell, *Hacer escuela, hacer estado: La educación posrevolucionaria vista desde Tlaxcala* (Zamora: Colegio de Michoacán, 2007).

15. Josefina Zoraida Vázquez, *Nacionalismo y educación en México* (Mexico City: Colegio de México, 1970).

16. For nascent pluralism in Mexico, see Alexander Dawson, *Indian and Nation in Revolutionary Mexico* (Tucson: University of Arizona Press, 2004).

17. See the forthcoming book by Todd Shepard of Johns Hopkins University for an analysis of the French state's use of postrevolutionary Mexican policy to redress discrimination after the Algerian Revolution.

18. *New York Times*, September 26, 1926.

19. Primitivo Alvarez, as quoted in *El sistema de escuelas rurales en México* (Mexico City: SEP, 1927), 231.

20. James Gouinlock, "Introduction" to *John Dewey: The Later Works, 1925–1953*, vol. 2, ed. Jo Ann Boydston (Carbondale: Southern Illinois University Press, 1984), xxii. The heavy burdens that Dewey placed on the state given its capacity for the destruction of local conditions in industrial society has been recently taken up by philosophers for the specific case of postrevolutionary Mexico. See the important essays by Nathan Crick and David Tarvin, "A Pedagogy of Freedom: John Dewey and Experimental Rural Education"; Kyle Greenwalt "John Dewey in Mexico: Nation-Building, Schooling, and the State"; and Deron Boyles, "John Dewey's Influence in Mexico: Rural Schooling, 'Community,' and the Vitality of Context," in *Inter-American Journal of Philosophy* 3, 2 (Fall 2012).

21. Which is not to say that they altogether avoided romantic assessments of postrevolutionary Mexico. As Daniel Rodgers has observed, the field of social politics across nations during the Progressive era was always subject to "perception, misperception, translation, transformation, co-optation, preemption, and contestation." See Rodgers, "An Age of Social Politics," in *Rethinking American History in a Global Age*, ed. Thomas Bender (Berkeley: University of California Press, 2002), 260.

22. For a recent discussion of contingent possibilities in the context of contemporary Latin America, see Raymond Craib and Mark Overmyer-Velázquez, "Migration and Labor in the Americas: Praxis, Knowledge, and Nations," *Hispanic American Historical Review* 92, 2 (2012).

23. "Tema desarrollada por Félix Gómez en su examen recepcional: la octava y décima cláusulas del Decálogo del Maestro Rural," Sección Dirección de Misiones Culturales, Serie Escuelas Normales Rurales, Box 48, Folder 4 (Michoacán), AHSEP.

24. Salvador León y Ortiz, "El método de proyectos," Sección Dirección de Misiones Culturales, Serie Escuelas Normales Rurales, Box 48, Folder 4 (Michoacán), AHSEP.

25. María Chávez, "La obra de Don Vasco de Quiroga en relación con la escuela rural," Sección Dirección de Misiones Culturales, Serie Escuelas Normales Rurales, Box 48, Folder 4 (Michoacán), AHSEP.

26. J. Jesús Soto, "Máximas," in *Alma Tarasca*, Sección Dirección de Misiones Culturales, Serie Escuelas Normales Rurales, Box 77, Folder 11 (Michoacán), AHSEP.

27. "Valor del interés en la educación del niño," in *Nueva Luz: Periódico Mensual*, Sección Dirección de Misiones Culturales, Serie Escuelas Normales Rurales, Box 26, Folder 4 (Tlaxcala), AHSEP.

28. María Chávez, "La obra de Don Vasco de Quiroga en relación con la escuela rural."

29. Agripina Magaña J., "Cómo procederé para mejorar la cultura de los habitantes de una comunidad?" Sección Dirección de Misiones Culturales, Serie Escuelas Normales Rurales, Box 48, Folder 4 (Michoacán), AHSEP.

30. Catalina Medina César, "Cómo debo organizar una escuela," Sección Dirección de Misiones Culturales, Serie Escuelas Normales Rurales, Box 48, Folder 4 (Michoacán), AHSEP.

31. See Mary Kay Vaughan, *Cultural Politics in Revolution: Teachers, Peasants, and Schools in Mexico, 1930–1940* (Tucson: University of Arizona Press, 1997); Vázquez, *Nacionalismo y educación*; and Susana Quintanilla, *Escuela y sociedad en el periodo cardenista* (Mexico City: Fondo de Cultura Económica, 1997).

32. Dawson, *Indian and Nation in Revolutionary Mexico*, xviii.

33. For an example of such cultural relativism at work in the field in postrevolutionary Mexico, see Rafael Ramírez, *La escuela rural mexicana* (Mexico City: CONAFE, 1981), 59.

34. Rockwell, *Hacer escuela, hacer estado*, 149.

35. See the beginning chapters of John Dewey, *Art as Experience* (New York: Minton, Balch, 1934) for a sense of how he used psychology to understand the process of knowledge creation in the effort to destroy social hierarchies in human communities. His use of psychology as an instrument of liberation in *Art as Experience* is a potent reminder of his career-long project to increase freedom in human society.

36. See the discussion of experiential learning in Brazil at the height of John Dewey's influence over education in Greg Grandin, *Fordlandia: The Rise and Fall of Henry Ford's Forgotten Jungle City* (New York: Metropolitan, 2009), 62–65.

37. For two examples of the psychology of learning that attracted the Americans to Mexico's rural schools, see Rafael Ramírez, "La educación activa y la funcional," and "Los nuevos rumbos de la didáctica," both in Ramírez, *La escuela rural mexicana* (Mexico City: CONAFE, 1981).

38. John Dewey and Evelyn Dewey, *Schools of Tomorrow* (New York: Dutton, 1915).

39. As Estelle Tarica has argued, *indigenismo* is the parent discourse out of which mestizo nationalism springs. Historically, it has referred to the relationship between Native Americans and Spanish settlers over the entire expanse of five centuries of conflict since the arrival of Spanish explorers to the Americas. In the specific context of Mexican history, *mestizaje* is a twentieth-century discourse that has emphasized biological and cultural mixing across distinctive ethnic groups to create a single nationalist citizenry. As such, it represents a single particular form of the broader set of interethnic relations with which *indigenismo* has been historically concerned. *Indigenismo* receives far less attention in the context of the American West than does *mestizaje*, but it is fundamental to an understanding of race relations in Latin America. See Estelle Tarica, *The Inner Life of Mestizo Nationalism* (Minneapolis: University of Minnesota Press, 2008), xiv.

40. Ibid., xi–xiii.

41. Tarica points out, for example, that early twentieth-century *indigenismo* represented the revolutionary spirit of twentieth-century modernism even though it became a hegemonic project of the state after 1960; see *The Inner Life of Mestizo Nationalism*,

xv. The revolutionary fervor of early twentieth-century *indigenismo* was mirrored in the United States in the revolution in antiformalist thought charted by Morton White and Alfred Kazin.

42. Martin S. Stabb, "Indigenism and Racism in Mexican Thought: 1858–1911," *Journal of Inter-American Studies* 1, 4 (1959): 405.

43. Tarica, *The Inner Life of Mestizo Nationalism*, xx.

44. Rosario Castellanos, *Balún-Canán* (Mexico City: Fondo de Cultura Económica, 1957); Rosario Castellanos, *The Nine Guardians*, trans. Irene Nicholson (New York: Vanguard, 1960).

45. Tarica, *The Inner Life of Mestizo Nationalism*, 183.

46. Ibid., 194.

47. Gregory F. Pappas, *John Dewey's Ethics: Democracy as Experience* (Bloomington: Indiana University Press, 2008).

48. Ibid., 70. For a recent discussion of the possibilities and difficulties of such transformation from within Latin Americanist scholarship, see Craib and Overmyer-Velázquez, "Migration and Labor in the Americas: Praxis, Knowledge, and Nations," esp. 248–49.

49. John Dewey, *Experience and Education* (New York: Kappa Delta Pi, 1938).

50. Dawson, *Indian and Nation in Revolutionary Mexico*, xviii.

51. Ibid., 16.

52. Ibid., 33. For pluralism as a contingent possibility in postrevolutionary Mexico, see also José Antonio Aguilar Rivera, "Moisés Sáenz y la escuela de la patria mexicana," in Moisés Sáenz, *México íntegro* (Mexico City: Consejo Nacional para la Cultura y las Artes, 2006).

53. Dawson, *Indian and Nation in Revolutionary Mexico*, 53.

54. I thank my colleague Guillermo Hurtado Pérez for bringing Fernando Benítez, *Los indios de México* (Mexico City: Ediciones Era, 1967) to my attention. See also Francisco Rojas González, *El diosero* (Mexico City: Fondo de Cultura Económica, 1952).

55. On this point, see Henry May, *The End of American Innocence: A Study of the First Years of Our Own Time, 1912–1917* (New York: Columbia University Press, 1959); and Arthur Schlesinger, Jr., *The Crisis of the Old Order, 1919–1933* (Boston: Houghton Mifflin, 1957). May and Schlesinger noted many years ago that populist rural Americans and the antiformalist social science thinkers of America's metropolitan universities had a common political criticism revolving around their outsider status in early twentieth-century society. Like the outsiders portrayed by May and Schlesinger, the Americans in the West saw themselves as outsiders to an economic system whose resources and politics marginalized the communities to which they claimed allegiance. In the realm of the public school, see Paula Fass, *Outside In: Minorities and the Transformation of American Education* (New York: Oxford University Press, 1989) for a similar view of the subjectivities of Americans who sought to reform the institutions of U.S. society from outside the institutional structures to which they sought access.

56. Mariano Azuela, *Los de abajo* (1915; Mexico City: Fondo de Cultura Económica, 1958); George I. Sánchez, *Forgotten People: A Study of New Mexicans* (Albuquerque: University of New Mexico Press, 1940); and Sherwood Anderson, *Winesburg, Ohio* (New York: Huebsch, 1919). My claim is that Azuela, Sánchez, and Anderson were all equally critical at the same time of the political and economic systems of their respective nations for neglecting the cultural communities to which they claimed allegiance.

Chapter 3. The Language of Experience

1. On science as a means of inquiry that was complementary rather than antithetical to art, see Gregory F. Pappas, *John Dewey's Ethics: Democracy as Experience* (Bloomington: Indiana University Press, 2008), 7–13, 19–20.

2. *Memoria de la Secretaría de Relaciones Exteriores de agosto de 1930 a julio de 1931*, vol. 2 (Mexico City: Imprenta de la Secretaría de Relaciones Exteriores, 1931), 1784.

3. Ibid., 1791.

4. Ibid.,1791–94.

5. Ibid., 1795–56.

6. Ibid., 1797–98.

7. Ibid., 1799–1801.

8. Ibid., 1792.

9. Montana Hastings, *The Organization of the State Child Welfare Work*, New Mexico Child Welfare Service Bulletin 1 (Santa Fe, N.M.: State Department of Education, 1920), 5.

10. Lawrence Cremin, *The Transformation of the School: Progressivism in American Education, 1876–1957* (New York: Knopf, 1961), especially 179–239.

11. Montana Hastings, *Clasificación y estudio estadístico de 3,719 alumnos, la mayoría de primer año de enseñanza secundaria de la ciudad de México por medio del examen Beta y la prueba Otis* (Mexico City: Secretaría de Educación Pública, 1929), 29.

12. Ibid.

13. Hastings's SEP employment history is available in her SEP personnel file in Mexico City. See Montana Hastings Folder, Dirección General de Administración de Personal del Sector Central, Serie 4.3, Referencia D 131, Folder 3418, Archivo Histórico de la Secretaría de Educación Pública, Mexico City (archives of the Secretaría de Educación Pública (hereafter cited as AHSEP). For the correspondence to Vasconcelos, see Antonio Caso to José Vasconcelos, April 11, 1923, Montana Hastings Folder, AHSEP. See José Vasconcelos's recollection of Hastings in Mexico also in Claude Fell, *José Vasconcelos: los años del águila, 1920–1925: educación, cultura e iberoamericanismo en el México postrevolucionario* (Mexico City: UNAM, 1989).

14. For the exchanges between the United States and Mexico, see, for example, Helen Delpar, *The Enormous Vogue of Things Mexican: Cultural Relations Between the United States and Mexico, 1920–1935* (Tuscaloosa: University of Alabama Press, 1992);

and Gilbert M. Joseph, Catherine LeGrand, and Ricardo Salvatore, eds., *Close Encounters of Empire: Writing the Cultural History of U.S.-Latin American Relations* (Durham, N.C.: Duke University Press, 1998).

15. For the year 1938, see the internal memo by Enrique Beltrán, dated October 10, 1938, Montana Hastings Folder, AHSEP.

16. On the history of Mexican psychology, see Rogelio Díaz-Guerrero, "Transference of Psychological Knowledge and Its Impact on Mexico," *International Journal of Psychology* 19 (1984): 123–24. See also Lucy María Reidl Martínez and María de Lourdes Echeveste García, eds., *La facultad de psicología de la Universidad Nacional Autónoma de México: Treinta años a la vanguardia* (Mexico City: UNAM, 2004).

17. Hastings, *Clasificación y estudio estadístico*, 128.

18. Ibid., xvi.

19. Hastings used the term "tribes" in her essay, ibid., 158.

20. See SEP, *El sistema de escuelas rurales en México* (Mexico City: Talleres Gráficos de la Nación, 1927), which lists the new schools by state.

21. For example, see the records of normal school labors at Cerro Hueco, Chihuahua, at AHSEP Sección Dirección de Misiones Culturales, Serie Escuelas Normales Rurales, Box 34, Folders 1–2 (Cerro Hueco, Chihuahua).

22. Carlos Kevin Blanton, "From Intellectual Deficiency to Cultural Deficiency: Mexican Americans, Testing, and Public School Policy in the American Southwest, 1920–1940," *Pacific Historical Review* 72, 1 (February 2003): 39–62.

23. Ibid., 56.

24. For Dewey's version of this process, see John Dewey, *Democracy and Education* (New York: Macmillan, 1916), chap. 5, "Preparation, Unfolding, and Formal Discipline."

25. Dewey profiled Missouri's University School in John Dewey and Evelyn Dewey, *Schools of Tomorrow* (New York: Dutton, 1915), chap. 3, "Four Factors in Natural Growth." As Lawrence Cremin has argued, *Schools of Tomorrow* is as important to an understanding of Dewey's philosophy as is *Democracy and Education*. Whereas the latter theorized a model of social reconstruction that could be implemented through the institution of the public school, the former provided institutional examples of such reconstruction in action. See Lawrence Cremin, "John Dewey and the Progressive-Education Movement, 1915–1952," *School Review* 67, 2 (1959): 160–73.

26. The relationship between Tireman and Horn can be partly traced through Frances Jordan Stein, "Ernest Horn's Ideas on Education Within the Context of the Progressive Education Movement in America" (Ph.D. dissertation, University of Iowa, 1973); and Stephen Kaufman, "Choosing the Middle Way: Ernest Horn's Contribution to the Commission on the Social Studies in the Schools" (Ph.D. dissertation, University of Iowa, 1983).

27. Loyd Tireman rarely used "San José" to designate the name of his laboratory school or the neighborhood where it was located. He dropped the accent mark and

used the name "San Jose." Out of historical accuracy and to avoid confusion, I shall use "San José" throughout the text to designate the name of the school and neighborhood.

28. Loyd S. Tireman Papers, MSS 573 BC, Box 1, Folder 17, Center for Southwest Research, University of New Mexico, Albuquerque (hereafter LTP). Tireman was citing George F. Nardin and O. C. Whitney, "The New Viewpoint in Reading," *Education Progress* 5, 1 (October 1925): 2–3.

29. Nardin and Whitney, "The New Viewpoint in Reading," 11.

30. Ibid., emphasis original.

31. Emmett A. Betts, *Is It Progressive to Use Basic Reading Materials?* (Evanston, Ill.: Harper, Row, 1938), 7.

32. Loyd Tireman, "The Immigration Problem" (Fayette: Upper Iowa State University, n.d.), as cited in Alice Marple, *Iowa Authors and Their Works: A Contribution Toward a Bibliography* (Des Moines: Historical Department of Iowa, 1918), 294. On immigration flows to Iowa, see Dorothy Schwieder, *Iowa: The Middle Land* (Ames: Iowa State University Press, 1996); Steven D. Reschly, *The Amish on the Iowa Prairie, 1840 to 1910* (Baltimore: Johns Hopkins University Press, 2000); and Cherilyn A. Walley, *The Welsh in Iowa* (Cardiff: University of Wales Press, 2009).

33. See Stephen G. Bloom, *Postville: A Clash of Cultures in Heartland America* (New York: Harcourt, 2000).

34. For Tireman's reference to Baghdad, see Tireman, "Mi amigo el hispano," address delivered at the Rural Conference of the Colorado State Teachers College, January 1932, 8–9, contained in General Education Board Collection, Box 599, Folder 6361, Rockefeller Archival Center, Tarrytown, New York (hereafter GEB). In a similar vein, Carey McWilliams once called New Mexico the "Quebec" of the United States. See Carey McWilliams, *North from Mexico: The Spanish-Speaking People of the United States* (Philadelphia: Lippincott, 1949), 207–8.

35. For Zimmerman's life, see Faculty Senate of the University of New Mexico, "In Memory of James Fulton Zimmerman, 1887–1944, President of the University of New Mexico, 1927–1944" (Albuquerque: University of New Mexico Press, 1944), GEB Box 598, Folder 6356.

36. GEB Box 598, Folders 6349–58 document the role at the University of New Mexico of Hill and Zimmerman.

37. See GEB Board Dockets, Board Meeting, April 16, 1931, 65.

38. Loyd Tireman, Mela Saltillo Brewster, and Lolita Pooler, "The San Jose Project," *New Mexico Quarterly* 3 (November 1933): 214.

39. Tireman to George I. Sánchez, dated February 3, 1948, GSP, Box 35, Folder 2.

40. See George Counts's famous 1932 address to the Progressive Education Association, arguing that teachers should be the primary shapers of the nation's political future, reprinted as George Counts, *Dare the School Build a New Social Order?* (New York: John Day, 1932).

41. On the contrast between Dewey and Thorndike on how the mind operates, see Stephen Tomlinson, "Edward Lee Thorndike and John Dewey on the Science of Education," *Oxford Review of Education* 23 (September 1997): 365–83; Ellen Condliffe Lagemann, "The Plural Worlds of Educational Research," *History of Education Quarterly* 29 (Summer 1989): 185–214; and Robert L. Church, "Educational Psychology and Social Reform in the Progressive Era," *History of Education Quarterly* 11 (Winter 1971): 390–405.

42. On Kilpatrick's project method, see John A. Beineke, *And There Were Giants in the Land: The Life of William Heard Kilpatrick* (New York: Lang, 1998). See Dewey's dissent in John Dewey, *Experience and Education* (New York: Kappa Delta Pi, 1938).

43. See Herbert M. Kliebard, *The Struggle for the American Curriculum, 1893–1958* (London: Routledge, 1991).

44. LTP Box 2, Folder 7. Tireman was quoting John Dewey, *How We Think* (Boston: Heath, 1910).

45. County superintendent to Leo Favrot, December 23, 1930, GEB Box 598, Folder 6358.

46. Tireman to Leo Favrot, January 6, 1931, GEB Box 598, Folder 6358.

47. Loyd Tireman, "First Annual Report of the San Jose Training School," GEB Box 599, Folder 6361.

48. Ibid., 17.

49. Tireman to Favrot, July 14, December 12, 1931, GEB Box 598, Folder 6358.

50. Loyd S. Tireman, *Teaching Spanish-Speaking Children* (Albuquerque, University of New Mexico Press, 1948), 19.

51. Leo Favrot to M. F. Cain, July 20, 1931, GEB Box 598, Folder 6358.

52. Tireman to Leo Favrot, July 14, 1931, GEB Box 598, Folder 6358.

53. The timing of Tireman's trip depends on an educated guess that reconciles the discrepancies noted in the following sources: David Bachelor, *Educational Reform in New Mexico: Tireman, San José, and Nambé* (Albuquerque: University of New Mexico Press, 1991), 30, 40; GEB archives between July 1931 and February 1932; Tireman, "Mi amigo el hispano"; and Loyd S. Tireman, *The Rural Schools of Mexico*, University of New Mexico Bulletin, Training School Series 2, 1, Whole no. 205 (Albuquerque: University of New Mexico Press, 1931), 3.

54. Tireman to Leo Favrot, February 3, 1933, GEB Box 599, Folder 6362.

55. Tireman, *The Rural Schools of Mexico*.

56. Ibid., 5, 15, 17, 19, 22, 24–25.

57. Ibid., 16.

58. Ibid., 15.

59. Ibid., 17 and 25.

60. On the missions, see ibid., 17–24. Quote is at 24.

61. Ibid., 8, 11–13

62. See Rafael Ramírez's description of this effort in his "La incorporación de los indígenas por medio del idioma castellano," in *La escuela rural mexicana* (Mexico City: Fondo de Cultura Económica, 1981).

63. Tireman, *The Rural Schools of Mexico*, 19 and 22.

64. Rafael Ramírez to Catherine Vesta Sturges, July 10, 1928, AHSEP, Sección Dirección de Misiones Culturales, Serie Misiones Permanentes, Misión Permanente en Actopan, Hidalgo, Box 45, Folder 10.

65. All references are from Catherine Vesta Sturges, "The Shadow of an Airplane over Bathi Baji," *Progressive Education* 9, 2 (February 1932): 112–16.

66. Vesta Sturges to Rafael Ramírez, November 22, 1928, AHSEP, Sección Dirección de Misiones Culturales, Serie Misiones Permanentes, Misión Permanente en Actopan, Hidalgo, Box 45, Folder 11.

67. Ibid.

68. Ibid. Sturges's words closely mirror Dewey's in *How We Think* as Tireman recorded them in his notes. See note 44 above. It is important to underscore, however, that Sturges did not reference Dewey's work in her correspondence with Ramírez. She attributed her quote to the work of her SEP colleague, teacher José de la Vega, as he had expressed it in the May 1928 issue of the SEP monthly report, *Boletín de la Secretaría de Educación Pública* (May 1928): 2159.

69. Sturges to Rafael Ramírez.

70. Tireman, *The Rural Schools of Mexico*, 17.

71. For local support of the state, see Paul Friedrich, *The Princes of Naranja: An Essay in Anthrohistorical Method* (Austin: University of Texas Press, 1986). Friedrich details the internecine conflicts in the rural communities of Michoacán as they formed new relationships to the national government. See also Alexander Dawson, *Indian and Nation in Revolutionary Mexico* (Tucson: University of Arizona Press, 2004).

72. Tireman, *The Rural Schools of Mexico*, 13.

73. Tireman, *Teaching Spanish-Speaking Children*, 200.

74. Ibid.; Tireman quoted from Rafael Ramírez, "Establishing the 'People's Houses,'" *Progressive Education* 13 (February 1936): 112–13.

75. Leo Favrot to Loyd Tireman, January 26, 1932, GEB Box 598, Folder 6358.

76. Tireman, "Mi amigo el hispano," 11.

77. Frank Angel, Jr., "Dr. Loyd S. Tireman and Public Education in New Mexico," public address, November 13, 1959, Phi Delta Kappa, Albuquerque, reprinted in *Phi Delta Kappa Yearbook, 1959–60* (Albuquerque: Phi Delta Kappa, Beta Rho Chapter, 1960), 2. Angel was wrong about the sponsor of Tireman's trip to Mexico. The GEB, not the U.S. government, had sponsored his trip. Angel's reference to the "Mission School Movement" referred to the cultural missions Vasconcelos and Sáenz had designed, which were now nearing a decade in operation.

78. Tireman to Favrot, January 22, 1932, GEB Box 598, Folder 6358.

79. Tireman, "Mi amigo el hispano," 2.

80. Tireman to Leo Favrot, December 3, 1931, GEB Box 598, Folder 6358.

81. Tireman to Leo Favrot, January 22, 1932, GEB Box 598, Folder 6358.

82. See Loyd Tireman and Marie M. Hughes, "The County Extension Program of the San Jose Project," GEB Box 599, Folder 6361.

83. Ibid., 2.

84. Ibid., 3.

85. Loyd Tireman, introduction to ibid.

86. Tireman and Hughes, "The County Extension Program of the San Jose Project," 3, GEB Box 599, Folder 6361.

87. Tireman, Brewster, and Pooler, "The San Jose Project," 215–16.

88. Tireman and Hughes, "The County Extension Program of the San Jose Project."

89. The SEP map was published in Secretaría de Educación Pública, *Las misiones culturales en 1927* (Mexico City: SEP, 1928), 306.

90. Tireman to Leo Favrot, January 22, 1932, GEB Box 598, Folder 6358.

91. Marie Hughes in *Mendez v. Westminster*, 64 F. Supp. 544 (C. D. Cal. 1946), *Reporter's Transcript of Proceedings*, 688, July 11, 1945.

92. Ibid., 688.

93. See, for example, Bachelor, *Educational Reform in New Mexico*; and Lynne Marie Getz, *Schools of Their Own: The Education of Hispanos in New Mexico, 1850–1940* (Albuquerque: University of New Mexico Press, 1997); neither recognizes Mexico's place in the thought of Tireman or Hughes.

94. Tireman and Hughes, "The County Extension Program of the San Jose Project," 1.

95. See, for example, John Dewey, *The School and Society* (Chicago: University of Chicago Press, 1899).

96. Hughes's working conditions are described in Tireman and Hughes, "The County Extension Program of the San Jose Project."

97. John Dewey and Evelyn Dewey, *Schools of Tomorrow* (New York: Dutton, 1915).

Chapter 4. The School and Society

1. Georgia L. Lusk to GEB, March 6, 1931, GEB, Box 100, Folder 900.

2. Leo Favrot to President Zimmerman, March 13, 1935, GEB, Box 100, Folder 901.

3. The record of Sánchez's early professional career is preserved in the GEB archives. See especially GEB, Box 100, Folder 900, "NM 1 Division of Information and Statistics 1931–33," and GEB, Box 100, Folder 901, "NM 1 Division of Information and Statistics 1934–35."

4. For Hart and Swift, see "Programme for the Final Examination for the Degree of Doctor of Education of George Isidore Sánchez," published by the Graduate Division, University of California, Berkeley, April 30, 1934, and included in the manuscript version of Sánchez's dissertation; and electronic biographies of Hart and Swift kept by

the University of California, Berkeley, at http://sunsite.berkeley.edu/uchistory/
archives_exhibits/in_memoriam/index4.html. See also Frank William Hart, *Oil for the
Light of the World* (New York: Vantage, 1956); and Fletcher Harper Swift, *The Most
Beautiful Thing in the World* (New York: Dutton, 1905).

5. George I. Sánchez, "The Education of Bilinguals in a State School System"
(Ed.D. dissertation, University of California, Berkeley, 1934), hereafter cited as
"Bilinguals."

6. Ibid., 110–61.

7. See, for example, Gladys Leff, "George I. Sánchez: Don Quixote of the Southwest" (Ph.D. dissertation, University of North Texas State University, 1976).

8. See George I. Sánchez, "A Study of the Scores of Spanish-Speaking Children
on Repeated Tests" (master's thesis, University of Texas, Austin, 1931).

9. The inclusive pages are "Bilinguals," chap. 2 (6–14) and chap. 4 (27–38). Chapter 3 (15–26) is a literature review.

10. Ibid., 6.

11. "Amalgamation" cannot stand alone conceptually without an analysis of what
cultural groups are amalgamating to. Many of Sánchez's generation took for granted
that the outcome of such synthesis was "Anglo Protestant culture." But succeeding
generations of scholars have pointed to panethnic labor culture and "whiteness,"
among others, as alternative social outcomes, as well. For an entry to the literature, see
Russell Kazal, "Revisiting Assimilation: The Rise, Fall, and Reappraisal of a Concept in
American Ethnic History," *American Historical Review* 100 (April 1995): 437–71.

12. Sánchez, "Bilinguals," 7. See Carey McWilliams's treatment of the "Mexican
problem" in *North from Mexico: The Spanish-Speaking People of the United States*
(Philadelphia: Lippincott, 1949), chap. 11.

13. Sánchez, "Bilinguals," 7.

14. Ibid., 10.

15. Manuel Gamio, *Mexican Immigration to the United States* (Chicago: University
of Chicago Press, 1930).

16. George I. Sánchez, *Forgotten People: A Study of New Mexicans* (Albuquerque:
University of New Mexico Press, 1940).

17. Ibid., 13.

18. See Jesus Chavarría, "On Chicano History," and Juan Gómez-Quiñones,
"Three Intellectuals," in *Humanidad: Essays in Honor of George I. Sánchez*, ed. Américo
Paredes (Los Angeles: UCLA Chicano Studies Center, 1977).

19. Sánchez's footnote references to progressive education and educators are
prominent in "Bilinguals," chaps. 2, 3, and 4, 6–38. He cites, for example, George S.
Counts, *The American Road to Culture* (New York: John Day, 1932); and G. Stanley
Hall, *Aspects of Child Life and Education* (New York: Ginn, 1907). For an introduction
to the contours of progressive education sympathetic to both its promises and pitfalls,
see Diane Ravitch, *The Troubled Crusade: American Education, 1945–1980* (New York:

Basic Books, 1983). Ravitch is primarily concerned with a thematic analysis of American education since World War II, but her study is predicated on a survey of progressive education beginning with its genesis in the progressive movement and ending with the demise of its second- and third-generation educators in the late 1940s. See Paula Fass, *Outside In: Minorities and the Transformation of American Education* (New York: Oxford University Press, 1989), 255–57, for a helpful survey of the historiography of progressive education based on the 1950–90 literature.

20. Sánchez, "Bilinguals," 24, emphasis original.

21. Ibid., 28–30.

22. Ibid., 29.

23. John Dewey, *Democracy and Education* (New York: Macmillan, 1916). For the context of Dewey in Sánchez's dissertation, see Sánchez, "Bilinguals," 28–32.

24. John Dewey, *Reconstruction in Philosophy* (Boston: Beacon Press, 1920).

25. Sánchez, "Bilinguals," 29.

26. Dewey, *Reconstruction in Philosophy*.

27. See Chapter 2, n. 19.

28. Sánchez, "Bilinguals," 30.

29. See George I. Sánchez, "Rural Community Programs: The Community School in the Rural Scene," in *The Community School*, ed. Samuel Everett (New York: Appleton-Century, 1938).

30. It is only recently that scholars have begun to recognize the influence of Dewey's ideas on Sánchez's political formation. See, for example, the mention of Dewey in Luisa Durán, "The Life and Legacy of New Mexico's Own: Dr. George I. Sánchez, A Belated Tribute," public address delivered at the 40th Annual Conference of the New Mexico Association for Bilingual Education, Albuquerque, New Mexico, April 25, 2013.

31. Frank Angel, Jr., "Dr. Loyd S. Tireman and Public Education in New Mexico," public address, November 13, 1959, Phi Delta Kappa, Albuquerque, reprinted in *Phi Delta Kappa Yearbook, 1959–60* (Albuquerque: Phi Delta Kappa, Beta Rho Chapter, 1960), 3.

32. John Dewey, "The Relation of Science and Philosophy as the Basis of Education," paper read at National Society for the Study of Education, February 26, 1938, *School and Society* 48 (1938). In *Democracy and Education*, Dewey phrased the dialectic this way: "Science represents the office of intelligence, its projection and control of new experiences, pursued systematically, intentionally, and on a scale due to freedom from limitations of habit. It is the sole instrumentality of conscious, as distinct from accidental, progress. And if its generality, its remoteness from individual conditions, confer upon it a certain technicality and aloofness, these qualities are very different from those of merely speculative theorizing. The latter are in permanent dislocation from practice; the former are temporarily detached for the sake of wider and freer application in later concerted action. There is a kind of idle theory which is antithetical to practice; but genuinely scientific theory falls within practice as the agency of its

expansion and its direction to new possibilities." Dewey, *Democracy and Education*, chap. 17, "Science in the Course of Study."

33. George I. Sánchez, "Theory and Practice in Rural Education," *Progressive Education* 13, 8 (December 1936): 590.

34. See, for example, George I. Sánchez, "Ask Chairman Why He Picks on School Men," *New Mexico State Tribune*, October 14, 1932, 1.

35. George I. Sánchez to Leo Favrot, March 23, 1937, GEB, Box 286, Folder 2983.

36. Edwin Embree to Leo Favrot, March 7, 1935, JRFA, Box 542, Folder 13.

37. Edwin Embree, "Schools in Mexico: A Report to the Trustees of the Julius Rosenwald Fund," May 1928, JRFA, Box 537, Folder 4.

38. Edwin Embree to Aarón Sáenz, June 14, 1928, JRFA, Box 297, Folder 11.

39. Edwin Embree, "Appendix to Report on Mexico: Memorandum of Remarks Made by Edwin R. Embree, President of the Julius Rosenwald Fund, at the Luncheon Given at the United States Embassy," May 28, 1928, 1, JRFA, Box 537, Folder 4.

40. Embree, "Schools in Mexico," 20.

41. Ibid., 21.

42. Edwin Embree, "Memorandum on Rural School Explorations," 1, GEB, Box 212, Folder 2042.

43. Ibid., 1.

44. Charles A. Hale, "Frank Tannenbaum and the Mexican Revolution," *Hispanic American Historical Review* 75, 2 (May 1995): 215.

45. Frank Tannenbaum, *The Mexican Agrarian Revolution* (New York: Macmillan, 1929); and Frank Tannenbaum, *Peace by Revolution: An Interpretation of Mexico* (New York: Columbia University Press, 1933).

46. Frank Tannenbaum, *Darker Phases of the South* (New York: Putnam, 1924).

47. For Sánchez's nine-month assignment, see George I. Sánchez to Walter B. Hill, March 19, 1935, GEB Box 100, Folder 901.

48. For the dangers of misreading unrelated sequences of events in the Latin American past as a single stream of history, see Nancy P. Applebaum, "Reading the Past on the Mountainsides of Colombia: Mid-Nineteenth-Century Patriotic Geology, Archaeology, and Historiography," *Hispanic American Historical Review* 93, 3 (August 2013): 347–76.

49. George Sánchez, *Mexico: A Revolution by Education* (New York: Viking, 1936), 6.

50. Ibid., 3.

51. Ibid., 5.

52. Ibid., 9, 12, 15.

53. Ibid., 10.

54. Ibid., 12–14.

55. Ibid., 15–16.

56. Ibid., 36.

57. Ibid.

58. Ibid., 42.

59. Ibid., 40.

60. Ibid., 37–38.

61. Ibid., 53.

62. Ibid., 16.

63. Ibid., 10.

64. Ibid., 47.

65. Ibid., 49.

66. Ibid.,52.

67. Mariano Azuela, *Los de abajo* (Mexico City: Fondo de Cultura Económica, 1958 [1915]).

68. Sánchez, *Mexico: A Revolution by Education*, 52.

69. Ibid., 52–53.

70. Ibid., 57–62.

71. Ibid., 57.

72. Ibid., 58.

73. Ibid., 18.

74. Ibid., 58.

75. Ibid., 62.

76. See prominent examples of Deweyan laboratory schools in the United States in John Dewey and Evelyn Dewey, *Schools of Tomorrow* (New York: Dutton, 1915).

77. Sánchez, *Mexico: A Revolution by Education*, 95; emphasis mine.

78. Sánchez, "Bilinguals," 7.

79. Sánchez, *Mexico: A Revolution by Education*, 95.

80. Ibid., 38.

81. Ibid.,134.

82. Ibid.

83. Ibid.,95.

84. These include Moisés Sáenz, *Carapan: Bosquejo de una experiencia* (Lima: Librería e Imprenta Gil, 1936); Sáenz, *Sobre el indio ecuatoriano y su incorporación al medio nacional* (Mexico City: Secretaría de Educación Pública, 1933); and Sáenz, *Sobre el indio peruano y su incorporación al medio nacional* (Mexico City: Secretaría de Educación Pública, 1933).

85. George I. Sánchez, "The New Education in Mexico," 6–7, GEB, Box 212, Folder 2042.

86. Rafael Ramírez, *La escuela de la acción dentro de la enseñanza rural* (Mexico City: SEP, 1924); and Ramírez, *El pragmatismo y la escuela de la acción* (Mexico City: SEP, 1924).

87. Sánchez, Foreword, *Mexico: A Revolution by Education*.

88. Ibid., v–vi.

89. Morton White, *Social Thought in America: The Revolt Against Formalism* (Boston: Beacon Press, 1957).

90. Manuel Gamio, *Forjando patria* (Mexico City: Porrúa, 1916) and Manuel Gamio, *La población del Valle de Teotihuacán, el medio en que se ha desarrollado; su evolución étnica y social; iniciativas para procurar su mejoramiento* (Mexico City: Talleres Gráficos de la Nación, 1922).

91. George I. Sánchez, "Educational Crisis in Mexico," *Butrava: Annual Bulletin of the Bureau of University Travel* 6 (February 1942): 6–7.

92. George I. Sánchez, "Fundamental Problems in Education in Mexico," *Educational Forum* 7, 4 (1943): 321.

93. Oscar Handlin, *John Dewey's Challenge to Education: Historical Perspectives on the Cultural Context* (New York: Harper, 1959).

94. George I. Sánchez, "Southwest Spanish-Americans Prepare to Challenge Power-Structure Forcing Second-Class Citizenship," *Southwesterner*, December 1966, on file in the Sánchez Vertical File, Center for Southwest Research, University of New Mexico.

95. See, for example, George I. Sánchez, "Education in Mexico," *Annals of the American Academy of Political and Social Science* 208 (March 1940); Sánchez, "Mexico in Transition," *Proceedings of the Conference on Latin America in Social and Economic Transition* (Albuquerque: University of New Mexico Press, 1943); Sánchez, "Education in Mexico," *Encyclopedia of Modern Education* (New York: American Association on Indian Affairs, 1944); Sánchez, *The Development of Higher Education in Mexico* (New York: Kings Crown, 1944); Sánchez, *Mexico* (Boston: Ginn, 1966).

96. See George I. Sánchez, "Theory and Practice in Rural Education," *Progressive Education* 13, 8 (December 1936): 590–96.

97. Ibid., 591.

98. Ibid.

99. Ibid., 593.

100. Ibid., 594.

101. Ibid.

102. See George I. Sánchez, "Child Development in the Rural Environment," in Progressive Education Association (U.S.), *Growth and Development: The Basis for Educational Programs* (New York: Progressive Education Association, 1936), 112–18.

103. Ibid., 112–13.

104. Ibid., 112.

105. Ibid., 113.

106. Ibid.

107. Ibid., 114.

108. Ibid.

109. Ibid., 154.

110. See Jane E. McAllister, "A Venture in Rural-Teacher Education Among Negroes in Louisiana," *Journal of Negro Education* 7, 2 (Spring 1938): 135.

111. See Edwin Embree on Sánchez's role in the Deep South in Edwin Embree and Julia Waxman, *Investment in People: The Story of the Julius Rosenwald Fund* (New

York: Harper, 1949). Sánchez also appears by name in the context of the Louisiana rural missions in Minns Sledge Roberton, *Public Education in Louisiana after 1898* (Baton Rouge: LSU Bureau of Educational Materials and Research, 1952), 136.

112. Sánchez, "Rural Community Programs."

113. Ibid., 164.

114. Ibid., 165.

115. Ibid., 184- 85.

116. Ibid., 172.

117. Ibid., 171.

Chapter 5. The Yaqui Way of Life

1. Ralph L. Beals, "Problems of Mexican Indian Folklore," *Journal of American Folklore* 56, 219 (January–March 1943): 11.

2. Ibid.

3. Compare the version in Carleton Beals, *Brimstone and Chili: A Book of Personal Experiences in the Southwest and in Mexico* (New York: Knopf, 1927), to Ralph's version of events in Ralph L. Beals, "Fifty Years in Anthropology," *Annual Review of Anthropology* 11 (1982): 1–23; and Ralph L. Beals, "Anthropologist and Educator," Oral History Transcript, Oral History Collection, Department of Special Collections, UCLA University Library, 1977. Carleton argues that Ralph was not present for the encounter, while Ralph argues the opposite. In his later fictional account, Ralph wrote of a prospector whose three companions had been murdered by Yaqui. It is not easy to reconcile these disparate accounts, though they agree on the general details.

4. Carlos Castaneda, *The Teachings of Don Juan: A Yaqui Way of Knowledge* (New York: Simon and Schuster, 1972).

5. Manuel Gamio, Forjando patria (Mexico City: Porrúa, 1916).

6. C. Beals, *Brimstone and Chili*.

7. Ibid., 173.

8. Ralph L. Beals, Essay 6 ("Fictionalization of Incident in Mexico, 1919"), Ralph Leon Beals Papers 1919–1970, National Anthropological Archives, Smithsonian Institution, Washington, D.C., Box 86, File "1919, 1922–27." (References to the Beals Papers are hereafter cited as NAA, followed by the box and file number.)

9. C. Beals, *Brimstone and Chili*, 175.

10. Ralph L. Beals's fictional essays are contained in NAA, Box 86. I use them alongside his academic accounts discussing his youth and travels in Mexico to understand his decision to become a social scientist and his attraction to the indigenous societies that became the subject of his life's work. Beals detailed his early life in Ralph L. Beals, "Sonoran Fantasy or Coming of Age?" *American Anthropologist* n.s. 80, 2 (June 1978): 355–62; R. Beals, "Fifty Years in Anthropology"; and R. Beals, "Anthropologist and Educator."

11. R. Beals, Essay 3 ("The Seeker"), NAA, 86, File "1919, 1922–27," at 1.

12. R. Beals, Essay 1 (Untitled), NAA, 86, File "1919, 1922–27," 5, 6, 10.

13. R. Beals, "Brief Survey Pieces," NAA, 86, File "1919, 1922–27."

14. R. Beals, "Fifty Years in Anthropology," 1.

15. R. Beals, "Sonoran Fantasy or Coming of Age?" 356.

16. Ibid., 355.

17. Ibid.

18. Franz Boas, *The Mind of Primitive Man* (New York: Macmillan, 1911).

19. The literature on Kroeber is extensive, but one recent piece on his relationship to Boas is Ira Jacknis, "The First Boasian: Alfred Kroeber and Franz Boas, 1896–1905," *American Anthropologist* 104, 2 (June 2002): 520–32.

20. R. Beals, "Fifty Years in Anthropology," 2.

21. R. Beals, "Sonoran Fantasy or Coming of Age?" 355.

22. Alfred L. Kroeber, *Handbook of the Indians of California* (Washington, D.C.: Smithsonian Institution, 1925).

23. R. Beals, "Fifty Years in Anthropology," 7–8.

24. Ralph. L. Beals, "Aboriginal Survivals in Mayo Culture," and "Masks in the Southwest," *American Anthropologist* n.s. 34, 1 (January–March 1932): 28–39, 166–69.

25. Elsie Clews Parsons and Ralph L. Beals, "The Sacred Clowns of the Pueblo and Mayo-Yaqui Indians," *American Anthropologist* n.s. 36, 4 (October–December 1934): 491–514.

26. R. Beals, "Fifty Years in Anthropology," 8.

27. See acculturation as one form of assimilation among others in Milton Gordon, *Assimilation in American Life: The Role of Race, Religion, and National Origins* (New York: Oxford University Press, 1964).

28. Robert Redfield, Melville J. Herskovits, and Ralph Linton, "Memorandum for the Study of Acculturation," *American Anthropologist* n.s. 38, 1 (January–March 1936): 149–52.

29. R. Beals, "Fifty Years in Anthropology," 8.

30. R. Beals, "Aboriginal Survivals in Mayo Culture," 28.

31. R. Beals, "Fifty Years in Anthropology," 7.

32. Ibid.

33. See Ralph L. Beals, "Remarks on the History of Pueblo Social Organization," *American Anthropologist* n.s. 40, 2 (April–June 1938): 340–41; R. Beals, review of *Pascua: A Yaqui Village in Arizona*, by Edward H. Spicer, *American Anthropologist* n.s. 43, 3, Part 1 (July–September 1941): 440–42; and R. Beals, review of *Shoshonean Days: Recollections of a Residence of Five Years Among the Indians of Southern California, 1885–1889*, by G. Hazen Shinn, *Pacific Historical Review* 10, 3 (September 1941): 388.

34. See Ralph L. Beals, review of *An Apache Life-Way*, by Morris Opler, *Journal of American Folklore* 56, n.s. 220 (April–June 1943): 151–52; R. Beals, review of *The Social Organization of the Western Apache*, by Grenville Goodwin, *Journal of American Folklore* 56 n.s. 220 (April–June 1943): 151–52; R. Beals, "Relations Between Meso-America and the Southwest," *Proceedings, Third Annual Round Table of the Sociedad Mexicana de Antropología* (Mexico City: Sociedad Mexicana de Antropología, 1944),

245–52; and R. Beals, review of *Santos: The Religious Folk Art of New Mexico*, by Mitchell A. Wilder, *California Folklore Quarterly* 3, 3 (July 1944): 257–58.

35. Beals's anthropology colleague Walter Goldschmidt noted the turn toward the United States and Los Angeles after building a career that had focused on the cultures of postrevolutionary Mexico. See Goldschmidt's review of Beals's life: Walter Goldschmidt, "Ralph Leon Beals (1901–1985)," *American Anthropologist* n.s. 88, 4 (December 1986): 947–53.

36. For these recollections, see Beals, *Brimstone and Chili*, passim.

37. Ralph L. Beals to Professor Peter N. Hare, July 31, 1978, NAA, 3, File "Correspondence 1965–1968."

38. Ralph Beals, *The Contemporary Culture of the Cáhita Indians* (Washington, D.C.: Government Printing Office, 1945) and Ralph Beals, *Cherán: A Sierra Tarascan Village* (Washington, D.C.: Government Printing Office, 1946).

39. R. Beals, *The Contemporary Culture of the Cáhita Indians*, 210.

40. Ibid., 211.

41. Ibid., 58.

42. Ibid., ix.

43. R. Beals, *Cherán*, 5.

44. Ibid., 58.

45. Ibid., 211.

46. Ibid., 58.

47. Ibid., 175.

48. Ibid., 176.

49. See, for example, Matthew Butler, *Popular Piety and Political Identity in Mexico's Cristero Rebellion: Michoacán, 1927–29* (New York: Oxford University Press, 2004), who charts the widely different relationship to the church and state of Michoacán's agrarian villages during the era of Mexico's religious wars of the 1920s. See also Ethelia Ruiz Medrano, *Mexico's Indigenous Communities: Their Lands and Histories, 1500–2010*, trans. Russ Davidson (Boulder: University Press of Colorado, 2010). Ruiz charts the complicated relationship between Mexico's Indians and the colonial and national states as Indians used schools, the law courts, and maps to reclaim and protect their shifting land bases and corporate identities.

50. For two views of the state, see Alan Knight, "Cardenismo: Juggernaut or Jalopy?" *Journal of Latin American Studies* 26, 1 (February 1994): 73–107; and Rick López, *Crafting Mexico: Intellectuals, Artisans, and the State After the Revolution* (Durham, N.C.: Duke University Press, 2010).

51. 1934 Guggenheim Memorial Foundation Application, Ralph L. Beals, dated October 27, 1933, NAA, 3, File "Correspondence 1928–1947."

52. Daniel Rubín de la Borbolla and Ralph L. Beals, "The Tarasca Project: A Cooperative Enterprise of the National Polytechnic Institute, Mexican Bureau-Indian Affairs, and the University of California," *American Anthropologist* n.s. 42, 4 (October–December 1940): 708.

53. Ralph L. Beals, review of *Anales del Museo Nacional de Arqueología, Historia y Etnografía, Años 1936, 1937, 1938*; and *Anales del Instituto Nacional de Antropología e Historia, Años 1939–1940, American Anthropologist* n.s. 49, 2 (April–June 1947): 291–92.

54. Américo Paredes, *George Washington Gómez* (Houston: Arte Publico Press, 1990). Paredes wrote the novel in 1937.

55. Ibid., 125.

56. Ibid., 132.

57. Ibid., 133.

58. John Steinbeck, *The Forgotten Village* (New York: Viking, 1941).

59. John Steinbeck, *The Pearl* (New York: Viking, 1947). On Steinbeck's book as an allegory of ethnic relations in postrevolutionary Mexico, see Julia Tunon, "Femininity, *Indigenismo*, and Nation: Film Representation by Emilio 'El Indio' Fernandez," in *Sex in Revolution: Gender, Politics, and Power in Modern Mexico*, ed. Jocelyn Olcott, Mary K. Vaughan, and Gabriela Cano (Durham, N.C.: Duke University Press, 2006).

60. Josephina Niggli, *Mexican Village* (Chapel Hill: University of North Carolina Press, 1945).

61. Mario Suárez, *Chicano Sketches: Short Stories* (Tucson: University of Arizona Press, 2004).

62. See, for example, the concern about socialism in the *New York Times*, "Cárdenas Seeks to Cast Mexico in a New Mold: His Seizure of Oil Lands Is One More Step Toward an Indian State Based on Socialism," April 10, 1938.

63. *Washington Post*, July 14, 1935.

64. See Ramón Beteta, "Lo que podemos aprender de México," 50–51, reprinted in R. Beteta, *En defensa de la revolución* (Mexico City: Departamento Autónomo de Prensa y Propaganda, 1937).

65. See Beteta's recollection of the incident in *Memoria de la Secretaría de Relaciones Exteriores de septiembre de 1936 a agosto de 1937*, vol. 2 (Mexico City: Departamento Autónomo de Prensa y Propaganda, 1937), 211–13.

66. See Ramón Beteta, "Por que se debe enseñar el español," reprinted in *En defensa de la revolución*.

67. See Ramón Beteta, "La educación rural en el México de nuestros días," reprinted in *En defensa de la revolución*.

68. See Allred's speech in *Memoria de la Secretaría de Relaciones Exteriores de septiembre de 1936 a agosto de 1937* (Mexico City: Departamento Autónomo de Prensa y Propaganda, 1937), 209–11.

69. Daniel T. Rodgers, "An Age of Social Politics," in *Rethinking American History in a Global Age*, ed. Thomas Bender (Berkeley: University of California Press, 2002).

70. See Benjamin H. Johnson, "The Cosmic Race in Texas: Racial Fusion, White Supremacy, and Civil Rights Politics," *Journal of American History* 98, 2 (September 2011): 404–19.

Chapter 6. "The Sun Has Exploded": Integration and the California School

1. Rick López, *Crafting Mexico: Intellectuals, Artisans, and the State After the Revolution* (Durham, N.C.: Duke University Press, 2010).

2. Mary Dudziak, *Cold War Civil Rights: Race and the Image of American Democracy* (Princeton, N.J.: Princeton University Press, 2000).

3. Jacquelyn Dowd Hall, "The Long Civil Rights Movement and the Political Uses of the Past," *Journal of American History* 91, 4 (March 2005): 1233–63.

4. As I argued in note 1 of my Introduction, assimilation implies a variety of potential outcomes rather than any single one. For the Americans who had studied in Mexico, assimilation implied cultural pluralism rather than convergence into a Protestant, white cultural ideal associated with the British- and German-descended peoples of the United States. It was this ethic of diversity that connected their institutional labors in the 1930s to the civil rights movement that followed World War II, as we shall see.

5. *Mendez v. Westminster*, 64 F. Supp. 544 (C. D. Cal. 1946), *Final Judgment*.

6. Carey McWilliams, *North from Mexico: The Spanish-Speaking People of the United States* (Philadelphia: Lippincott, 1949), 304.

7. For the appeal, see *Westminster v. Mendez*, 161 F.2d 774 (9th Circuit Court of Appeals, 1947).

8. See the recollections of former NAACP attorneys Constance Baker Motley and Robert L. Carter of the relationship between *Mendez* and the NAACP decision to begin attacking segregated schooling directly in the elementary schools of the Deep South, in Constance Baker Motley, *Equal Justice Under Law: An Autobiography* (New York: Farrar, Straus, and Giroux, 1998); and Robert L. Carter, *A Matter of Law: A Memoir of Struggle in the Cause of Equal Rights* (New York: New Press, 2005).

9. Richard Kluger called Judge McCormick's decision "surprising" in *Simple Justice: The History of Brown v. Board of Education and Black America's Struggle for Equality* (New York: Knopf, 2004 [1975]), 400.

10. Civil 388 (Western District Texas, 1948).

11. F. Supp. 1004 (1951).

12. For the influence of the legal segregation cases in the American West on those of the American South, see Philippa Strum, *Mendez v. Westminster: School Desegregation and Mexican-American Rights* (Lawrence: University Press of Kansas, 2010); and Jeanne M. Powers and Lirio Patton, "Between *Mendez* and *Brown*: *Gonzales v. Sheely* (1951) and the Legal Campaign Against Segregation," *Law and Social Inquiry* 33, 1 (March 2008): 127–71.

13. Marcus appears in *Informe de la Secretaría de Relaciones Exteriores de agosto de 1934 a agosto 1 de 1935* (Mexico City: Imprenta de la Secretaría de Relaciones Exteriores, 1935), 463.

14. In visual terms, these continental borrowings happening across Mexico, the American West, and the Deep South were captured in a 1932 mural by Mexican

muralist painter José Clemente Orozco at John Dewey's New School for Social Research. In *The Table of Brotherhood*, Orozco flanked the sides of a square table with representatives from the world's great cultural communities, including ones from the Chinese civilization, others from India, and some from Europe. At the head of a square table, however, Orozco arranged the figure of a Mexican peasant, a Harlem Negro, and an American Jew. These were the representatives of the great communities that had been left out of the democratic experience in North America. Although there was no depiction of the Mexican American in the American West, it is not hard to imagine how Orozco might have included him in his depiction of North American cultural communities working toward a balance of social cooperation in the context of two neighbor republics undergoing rapid industrialization and political strife.

15. See the testimony of Ralph Beals at *Mendez v. Westminster, Reporter's Transcript of Proceedings*, 660–87, July 11, 1945. The court reporter transcribed the term "Maya" into the record, but this was probably a mistaken descriptor for the cultural community of Sonora called the "Mayo."

16. Ibid., 663–64.

17. Ibid., 676.

18. Ibid., 672.

19. Ibid., 676.

20. For Americanization as a form of acculturation, see Milton Gordon, *Assimilation in American Life: The Role of Race, Religion, and National Origins* (New York: Oxford University Press, 1964).

21. *Mendez v. Westminster, Reporter's Transcript of Proceedings*, 668–69.

22. Ibid., 671.

23. Ralph L. Beals, "Urbanism, Urbanization, and Acculturation," *American Anthropologist* n.s. 53, 1 (January–March 1951): 6.

24. Ibid.

25. Ibid.

26. A 1951 paper, for example, analyzed the cultural systems of Mexican Americans living in Los Angeles. See Ralph L. Beals, "Culture Patterns of Mexican-American Life," in *Proceedings, Fifth Annual Conference, Southwest Council on the Education of Spanish-Speaking People* (Los Angeles: Pepperdine College, 1951), 5–13. See also Beals, "A Trial Formulation of the History of Mexican Indian Acculturation," *Filosofía y letras* (1943): 6; and Beals, "The History of Acculturation in Mexico," in *Homenaje al Doctor Alfonso Caso* (Mexico City: Imprenta Nuevo Mundo, 1951), 73–82.

27. Daniel T. Rodgers, *Age of Fracture* (Cambridge, Mass.: Belknap Press of Harvard University Press, 2011).

28. Rubén Martínez, *Crossing Over: A Mexican Family on the Migrant Trail* (New York: Metropolitan Books, 2001).

29. Marc Simon Rodriguez, *The Tejano Diaspora: Mexican Americanism and Ethnic Politics in Texas and Wisconsin* (Chapel Hill: University of North Carolina Press, 2011). Rodriguez shows that the school integration movement that was enabled by

the federal courts became a central platform for democratic politics among Mexican Americans into the 1960s.

30. Original petition of plaintiff families to Louis Conrady, clerk of the Board of Education, dated September 8, 1944. A copy of the petition is in the hands of the author.

31. See the testimony of Marie Hughes at *Mendez v. Westminster*, 688–703, July 11, 1945.

32. Marie Morrison Hughes, "The English Language Facility of Mexican-American Children Living and Attending School in a Segregated Community" (Ed.D. dissertation, Stanford University School of Education, 1952); Marie Morrison Hughes, "Rate of Acquisition of an English-Speaking Vocabulary by Spanish-Speaking Children" (master's thesis, University of Chicago Department of Education, 1935); Marie Morrison Hughes, *Teaching a Standard English Vocabulary* (Santa Fe, N.M: State Department of Education, 1932).

33. *Mendez v. Westminster*, 688–89.

34. Marie M. Hughes, "Statement of Southern California's Educational and Community Projects Related to the Latin Americans," Office of the Coordinator of Inter-American Affairs, University of New Mexico, and New Mexico Highlands University, Santa Fe, 1943, 1–2. A copy is located GSP, Box 85.

35. *Mendez v. Westminster*, 699.

36. Loyd Tireman, Mela Saltillo Brewster, and Lolita Pooler, "The San Jose Project," *New Mexico Quarterly* 3 (November 1933): 214.

37. Marie M. Hughes, *Doña Ana County: Teacher's Manual* (Las Cruces, N.M.: Doña Ana County Public Schools, 1930), 7.

38. *Mendez v. Westminster*, 699.

39. Ibid., 696.

40. Ibid., 696–97.

41. Hughes to George Sánchez, November 23, 1942, GSP, Box 19, Folder 17.

42. Hughes to George Sánchez, May 3, 1948, GSP, Box 19, Folder 17.

43. For these communities, see Loyd Tireman and Marie M. Hughes, "The County Extension Program of the San Jose Project," GEB, Box 599, Folder 6361.

44. Mildred Bernice Gallot mentions the operation of the Grambling field agent system in these communities in Mildred B. Gallot, "Grambling State University: A History, 1901–1977" (Ed.D. dissertation, Louisiana State University, 1982), 78–79.

45. For these communities, see Hughes, "Statement of Southern California's Educational and Community Projects Related to the Latin Americans."

46. Manuel Gamio, *Mexican Immigration to the United States* (Chicago: University of Chicago Press, 1930).

47. George J. Sánchez, *Becoming Mexican American* (New York: Oxford University Press, 1995).

48. See Sánchez to Embree, March 12, 1945, GSP, Box 12, Folder 28.

49. George I. Sánchez, "School Integration and Americans of Mexican Descent," 1958, 10, GSP, Box 71, Folder 32.

50. Ibid., 11.

51. Moisés Sáenz, "Integrating Mexico through Education," in Sáenz and Herbert I. Priestley, *Some Mexican Problems: Lectures on the Harris Foundation 1926* (Chicago: University of Chicago Press, 1926), 72.

52. George I. Sánchez, *Forgotten People: A Study of New Mexicans* (Albuquerque: University of New Mexico Press, 1940).

53. See *Wisconsin v. Yoder* 406 U.S. 205 (1972).

54. Timothy B. Tyson, *Radio Free Dixie: Robert F. Williams and the Roots of Black Power* (Chapel Hill: University of North Carolina Press, 1999).

55. Charles Wollenberg, *All Deliberate Speed: Segregation and Exclusion in California Schools, 1855–1975* (Berkeley: University of California Press, 1978); and Matt García, *A World of Its Own: Race, Labor, and Citrus in the Making of Greater Los Angeles, 1900–1970* (Chapel Hill: University of North Carolina Press, 2001).

Chapter 7. Texas and the Parallel Worlds of Civil Rights

1. See Roy Wilkins to Ferle Hoffman, December 18, 1946, NAACP Papers of the NAACP, Part 3, Series B.

2. Carl Murphy to Thurgood Marshall, December 5, 1946, Papers of the NAACP, Part 3, Series B.

3. See, for example, George I. Sánchez, "Educational Crisis in Mexico," *Butrava: Annual Bulletin of the Bureau of University Travel* 6 (February 1942): 4–12.

4. George I. Sánchez, "Education in Mexico," *Annals of the American Academy of Political and Social Science* 208 (1940): 142–52.

5. George I. Sánchez, *The Development of Higher Education in Mexico* (New York: King's Crown, 1944).

6. George I. Sánchez, "Fundamental Problems in Education in Mexico," *Educational Forum* 7, 4 (May 1943): 321.

7. Ibid.

8. George I. Sánchez, "General Information," in *Mexico's Role in International Intellectual Cooperation: Proceedings of Conference Held in Albuquerque, February 24–25, 1944* (Albuquerque: University of New Mexico Press, 1945), 50–51, original in Spanish.

9. Sánchez, "Education in Mexico," *Annals*.

10. George I. Sánchez, "Los problemas fundamentales de la educación en México," *Educación Nacional: Revista Mensual* 1, 1 (February 1944): 56–60; George I. Sánchez, "Education in Mexico," in *Encyclopedia of Modern Education*, ed. Harry N. Rivlin (New York: Philosophical Library, 1943), 492–95; and Sánchez, "Fundamental Problems in Education in Mexico," 321–27.

11. Sánchez, "Educational Crisis in Mexico," 7.

12. Ibid., 6–7.

13. Ibid., 7.

14. These problems are rehearsed in Sánchez, "Fundamental Problems in Education in Mexico," 321–27.

15. Ibid., 322–23.

16. Ibid., 324.

17. See, for example, Alexander Dawson, *Indian and Nation in Revolutionary Mexico* (Tucson: University of Arizona Press, 2004). Dawson found significant differences among the rural schools of the nation in the 1940s.

18. George I. Sánchez to Isaac Kandel, September 24, 1947, GSP, Box 21, Folder 12.

19. George Sánchez to Isaac Kandel, November 1, 1946, GSP, Box 21, Folder 12.

20. George Sánchez to Norwood Baker, April 14, 1947, GSP, Box 21, Folder 12.

21. Kandel's speech was published as Isaac Kandel, "Education in Latin America," *Hispania*, May 1947, 163–74.

22. Sánchez, "Education in Mexico," *Annals*.

23. See Sánchez, "Fundamental Problems in Education in Mexico," 321.

24. Sánchez, "Education in Mexico," *Encyclopedia of Modern Education*, 494.

25. The original project notes for the Directory of Mexican Education can be found at GSP, Box 54, Folder 3.

26. Solicitation letter from George I. Sánchez and Samuel Ramos, July 2, 1943, GSP, Box 54, Folder 3.

27. Samuel Ramos, *El perfil del hombre y la cultura en México* (Mexico City: Imprenta Mundial, 1934). For an important critique of the literature of national identity, see Roger Bartra, *The Cage of Melancholy: Identity and Metamorphosis in the Mexican Character*, trans. Christopher J. Hall (New Brunswick, N.J.: Rutgers University Press, 1992).

28. Rafael Ramírez to George I. Sánchez, September 23, 1943, GSP, Box 54, Folder 3.

29. For these attacks on Dewey, see, for example, Mortimer J. Adler, *The Revolution in Education* (Chicago: University of Chicago Press, 1958).

30. For the ongoing relevance of Dewey and progressive education into the 1950s despite changes in American politics and philosophy, see Lawrence Cremin, *The Transformation of the School: Progressivism in American Education, 1876–1957* (New York: Knopf, 1961), esp. 352–353.

31. Tormey to Tireman, as quoted in Tireman to Leo Favrot, February 15, 1935, GEB, Box 598, Folder 6358. See also Jackson Davis interview report, GEB, September 2–3, 1940, GEB, Box 599, Folder 6359, which reported that the University of Arizona had recently copied Tireman's bilingual education techniques.

32. See *Digest of the Stenographic Report of the Minutes of the Fourth Annual Meeting of the Board of Directors of the San Jose Project*, June 19, 1934, GEB, Box 598,

Folder 6358; and Tireman, "Preliminary Report for the First Four Years of the San Jose Experimental School," GEB, Box 599, Folder 6361.

33. *Digest of the Stenographic Report of the Minutes of the Fourth Annual Meeting*; and Tireman, "Preliminary Report for the First Four Years of the San Jose Experimental School."

34. Loyd S. Tireman, *We Learn English: A Preliminary Report of the Achievement of Spanish-Speaking Pupils in New Mexico* (Albuquerque: San Jose Experimental School, 1936), 32–33, GEB, Box 599, Folder 6361.

35. Tireman to Favrot, November 7, 1934, GEB, Box 598, Folder 6358.

36. GEB Interview Report, University of New Mexico, January 25, 1938, GEB, Box 599, Folder 6359.

37. Loyd S. Tireman and Mary Watson, *La Comunidad: Report of the Nambé Community School, 1937–1942* (Albuquerque: University of New Mexico Press, 1943), 1.

38. Frank Angel, Jr., "Dr. Loyd S. Tireman and Public Education in New Mexico," public address, November 13, 1959, Phi Delta Kappa, Albuquerque, New Mexico, reprinted in *Phi Delta Kappa Yearbook, 1959–60* (Albuquerque: Phi Delta Kappa, Beta Rho Chapter, 1960), 3.

39. Tireman to Favrot, December 3, 1931, GEB, Box 598, Folder 6358.

40. Jennie Gonzales, "What I Hope to Accomplish," November 2, 1932, GEB, Box 599, Folder 6361.

41. Ibid.

42. Tireman and Watson, *La Comunidad*, 15.

43. George I. Sánchez, "The Education of Bilinguals in a State School System" (Ed.D. dissertation, University of California, Berkeley, 1934), 29: "The aims of education in a democracy arise within the process itself and by so doing are sanctioned and become the measure of the educative process."

44. Tireman and Watson, *La Comunidad*, 11–13.

45. Ibid., 13.

46. Ibid., 15–16.

47. See the guiding principles of the Nambé school in *Nambé: A Community School*, project booklet on file at GEB, Box 599, Folder 6361.

48. Loyd Tireman, *Teaching Spanish-Speaking Children* (Albuquerque: University of New Mexico Press, 1948), 192.

49. John Dewey and Evelyn Dewey, *Schools of Tomorrow* (New York: Dutton, 1915).

50. John Dewey, *Democracy and Education* (New York: Macmillan, 1916).

51. John Dewey, "Education as Social Function," chap. 2 in *Democracy and Education*.

52. Dewey and Dewey, "Four Factors in Natural Growth," chap. 3 in *Schools of Tomorrow*.

53. All quotes are from Tireman, *Teaching Spanish-Speaking Children*, 200–201. Tireman quoted from Rafael Ramírez, "Establishing the 'People's Houses,'" *Progressive Education* 13 (February 1936): 112–13.

54. Tireman, *Teaching Spanish-Speaking Children*, 195.

55. See a recapitulation of the improved learning outcomes in Loyd Tireman and Mary Watson, *A Community School in a Spanish-Speaking Village* (Albuquerque: University of New Mexico Press, 1948), 132–64.

56. Ibid., 169.

57. Tireman, *Teaching Spanish-Speaking Children*, 37.

58. George Sánchez to Marie Hughes, November 13, 1947, GSP, Box 19, Folder 17.

59. For Tireman in La Paz, Bolivia, see GSP, Box 35, Folder 2.

60. José Santos Valdés, *La batalla por la cultura* (Mexico City: Ediciones Morelos, 1937). For Sánchez's planned anthology on Mexico, see Sánchez to Edwin Embree, September 23, 1948, GSP, Box 12, Folder 28. For his reading of *La batalla por la cultura*, see Sánchez to Rafael Alfaro Cervera, March 8, 1946, GSP, Box 54, Folder 12.

61. The relationships are complex but a partial record of Sánchez's relationship with Roger Baldwin of the ACLU is on file at the GSP, Box 34, Folder 1, entitled "Texas Civil Rights Fund, 1943–1947." The best documentary account of their relationships remains the ACLU Papers, located at the Seeley Mudd Library, Princeton University, Princeton, New Jersey.

62. See Sánchez's recollection of his original hire at the University of Texas in George I. Sánchez to John P. Harrison, January 3, 1964, at GSP, Box 52, Folder 14.

63. George Sánchez to Marie Hughes, February 13, 1943, GSP, Box 19, Folder 17.

64. George Sánchez to Loyd Tireman, January 30, 1948, GSP, Box 35, Folder 2.

65. George Sánchez to Marie Hughes, November 13, 1947, GSP, Box 19, Folder 17.

66. See the schedule of plaintiffs in the *Delgado* lawsuit Sánchez compiled at GSP, Box 79, Folder 3. Whether the public schools in Mexico had played an ideological role among the plaintiffs in the desegregation lawsuit remains unknown, as is the case with *Mendez*.

67. "Memorandum of Points and Authorities in Support of Plaintiffs' Application for Injunction Pendente Lite," 3, GSP, Box 79, Folder 4. *Plessy* had involved children of different races, the court agreed, whereas in Texas, *Salazar v. State* in 1946 had ruled "that Mexicans are of the same race as the white race."

68. Tireman and Watson, *La Comunidad*, 16.

69. George I. Sánchez, "North of the Border," in *Proceedings and Transactions of the Texas Academy of Science 1941* (Austin: Texas Academy of Science, 1942), 77.

70. Ibid.

71. Ibid., 84–85.

72. Ibid., 85. On immigrants as benefactors of culture in the United States rather than as beneficiaries, see Diana Selig, *Americans All: The Cultural Gifts Movement* (Cambridge, Mass.: Harvard University Press, 2008).

73. Tireman to Sánchez, February 3, 1948, GSP, Box 35, Folder 2.

74. Ibid.

75. "Final Judgment, *Delgado v. Bastrop*, Number 388 Civil, District Court of the United States, Western District of Texas," 3, GSP, Box 79, Folder 5.

76. For an entry into the debates about the operation of whiteness among this generation of civil righters, see Lisa Ramos, "Not Similar Enough: Mexican American and African American Civil Rights Struggles in the 1940s," in *The Struggle in Black and Brown: African American and Mexican American Relations During the Civil Rights Era*, ed. Brian D. Behnken (Lincoln: University of Nebraska Press, 2011).

77. Tireman, *Teaching Spanish-Speaking Children*, 12–13.

78. Franz Boas, *The Mind of Primitive Man* (New York: Macmillan, 1911).

79. George I. Sánchez to Lewis Hanke, March 20, 1959, GSP, Box 52, Folder 16.

80. Miguel Calderón to Sánchez, June 29, 1948, GSP, Box 9, Folder 3.

81. Ibid.

82. For some of the links between the American West and the NAACP, see Jeanne M. Powers and Lirio Patton, "Between *Mendez* and *Brown: Gonzales v. Sheely* (1951) and the Legal Campaign Against Segregation," *Law and Social Inquiry* 33, 1 (March 2008): 127–71.

83. Mario Suárez, "Señor Garza," in *Chicano Sketches: Short Stories* (Tucson: University of Arizona Press, 2004).

84. Suárez, "Los Coyotes," in *Chicano Sketches*.

85. Suárez, "El Hoyo," in *Chicano Sketches*.

86. For the bullfights in Mexico, see Suárez, "Señor Garza" and "Cuco Goes to a Party," in *Chicano Sketches*.

87. Whether the members of the group who traveled to Mexico understood the relationship between the US and Mexico as one that transcended nationalism is a question that deserves more attention. In contrast to my argument that the backroads pragmatists heightened the sense of nationalism in both the United States and Mexico, Geraldo L. Cadava has underscored international affiliations among border residents in Arizona and Sonora. See Geraldo L. Cadava, *Standing on Common Ground: The Making of a Sunbelt Borderland* (Cambridge, Mass.: Harvard University Press, 2013).

88. See Morton White, *Social Thought in America: The Revolt Against Formalism* (Cambridge, Mass.: Harvard University Press, 1957).

89. Henry May, *The End of American Innocence: A Study of the First Years of Our Own Time, 1912–1917* (New York: Knopf, 1959).

90. Oliver Wendell Holmes, Jr., "The Path of the Law," *Harvard Law Review* 10 (1897): 457.

91. White, *Social Thought in America*.

Epilogue. Pragmatism and the Decline of Dewey

1. See George Santayana, "The Genteel Tradition in American Philosophy," address before the Philosophical Union of the University of California, August 25, 1911, reprinted in George Santayana, *Winds of Doctrine: Studies in Contemporary Opinion* (New York: Scribner's, 1913).

2. For the term "pragmatism," see William James, "Philosophical Conceptions and Practical Results," *University Chronicle* 1, 4 (September 1898): 287–310.

3. José Vasconcelos, *De Robinsón a Odiseo: Pedagogía estructurativa* (Madrid: M. Aguilar, 1935).

4. Ibid., "Preliminar."

5. Ibid., chap. 2.

6. Ibid.

7. Ralph Beals, *No Frontier to Learning: The Mexican Student in the United States* (Minneapolis: University of Minnesota Press, 1957), 13, and Ramón E. Ruiz, *Mexico: The Challenge of Poverty and Illiteracy* (San Marino, Calif.: Huntington Library, 1961), 29.

8. On the genteel tradition, see Henry May, *The End of American Innocence: A Study of the First Years of Our Own Time, 1912–1917* (New York: Knopf, 1959).

9. Loyd Tireman, *Teaching Spanish-Speaking Children* (Albuquerque: University of New Mexico Press, 1948).

10. Ibid., 38–39.

11. Loyd Tireman, *Apuntes en torno a la educación boliviana* (La Paz: Ministerio de Educación, Bellas Artes y Asuntos Indígenas, 1948), 45.

12. Ibid., 55–56.

13. Ralph Beals, *The Peasant Marketing System of Oaxaca, Mexico* (Berkeley: University of California Press, 1975).

14. Beals, *No Frontier to Learning*.

15. Ibid., 13.

16. Ibid., 9.

17. Ibid., 10.

18. James Van Patten, "Education in the United Mexican States" (Ph.D. dissertation, University of Texas at Austin, 1962).

19. Albert Villareal, "The Cultural Missions of Mexico" (MA thesis, University of Texas at Austin, 1954).

20. Louise Schoenhals, "Problems of Acculturation for the Mexican-American and the Indian of Mexico," 1962 seminar paper for George I. Sánchez. A copy is located at GSP, Boxes 89 and 90.

21. Schoenhals, "Problems of Acculturation," 46.

22. George I. Sánchez, *Mexico* (New York: Ginn, 1966).

23. George I. Sánchez, *Arithmetic in Maya* (Austin: University of Texas Press, 1961).

24. Lawrence Cremin, *The Transformation of the School: Progressivism in American Education, 1876–1957* (New York: Knopf, 1961), esp. 329–53.

25. Ibid., 351.

26. John Dewey, *Experience and Nature* (Chicago: Open Court, 1926). For the translation into Spanish by José Gaos, see John Dewey, *La experiencia y la naturaleza*, ed. José Gaos (Mexico City: Fondo de Cultura Económica, 1948). See Santiago Rey,

"Hermeneutic Migrations: José Gaos on Dewey and Heidegger," paper presented at the Dewey in Mexico International Conference, UNAM, Mexico City, January 12–14, 2012, for the recent attempt to bring Heidegger and Dewey into conversation with one another.

27. For Dewey in the work of José Medina Echavarría, see José Medina Echavarría, *Sociología: Teoría y técnica* (Mexico City: Fondo de Cultura Económica, 1940); and José Medina Echavarría, *Responsabilidad de la inteligencia: Estudios sobre nuestro tiempo* (Mexico City: Fondo de Cultura Económica, 1943). A recent paper that emphasizes the influence of Dewey on the thought of Medina Echavarría is María Angélica Moya, "José Medina Echavarría and John Dewey in Mexico: Sociology as a Concrete Social Science, 1939–1946," presented at Dewey in Mexico International Conference, UNAM, Mexico City, January 12–14, 2012.

28. See, for example, Gregory Pappas, ed., *Pragmatism in the Americas* (New York: Fordham University Press, 2011). Pappas, Hurtado Pérez, and del Castillo convened the January 2012 conference at UNAM in Mexico City on the subject of Dewey's influence in twentieth-century Mexico. The proceedings were published in the *Inter-American Journal of Philosophy* 3, 2 (Fall 2012).

29. See Guillermo Hurtado Pérez, *El búho y la serpiente: Ensayos sobre la filosofía en México en el siglo XX* (Mexico City: UNAM, 2007), for one recent treatment of the history of philosophy in twentieth-century Mexico.

30. Sánchez to Lewis Hanke, March 20, 1959, GSP, Box 52, Folder 16.

31. Sánchez to Manuel Salas, February 16, 1965, GSP, Box 31, Folder 19.

32. See, for example, Richard Hofstadter, *Anti-Intellectualism in American Life* (New York: Knopf, 1963).

33. See John Dewey Society for the Study of Education and Culture, *Newsletter*, December 22, 1958, 1. A copy is on file at GSP, Box 49, Folder 8.

34. Sánchez to Handlin, January 26, 1959, GSP, Box 49, Folder 8.

35. Oscar Handlin, *The Uprooted: The Epic Story of the Great Migrations That Made the American People* (Boston: Little, Brown, 1951).

36. Oscar Handlin, "Rejoinder to the Critics of John Dewey," *New York Times*, June 15, 1958.

37. Ibid. For a like-minded view of Dewey's fundamental contributions to the rethinking of education in twentieth-century industrial society, see Cremin, *The Transformation of the School*, esp. 352–53.

38. Sánchez to A. R. Lewis, March 16, 1959, GSP, Box 49, Folder 8.

39. Sánchez to Handlin, March 24, 1959, GSP, Box 49, Folder 8.

Index

Acculturation, 95, 177, 205, 233, 293; form of assimilation, 184; and George I. Sánchez, 248, 270; in Michoacán, 191–92; and Ralph Beals, 182–87, 291; in southern California, 219–25

Actopan, 62–65, 115, 124, 264, 270; "experience" at, 121–22; Tireman visits, 117

Afro-American Newspapers, 242

Albuquerque, 57, 115–16, 118–19, 126–28, 132–33, 138, 231, 244, 246, 256–58; San José Experimental School, 107–10

Alfabetización: Aprendiendo a leer, 26, 28. *See also* Diego Rivera

Alianza, 281

Alianza Hispano-Americana, 278, 281

Allred, James, 199, 204

Alvarez, Primitivo, 76, 146

Amalgamation, 8, 40, 50, 140, 147–48, 161–63, 272, 283; in New Mexico, 143–45; potential outcomes of, 319n11

American Academy of Political and Social Science, 243

American Anthropological Association, 222, 291

American Civil Liberties Union (ACLU), 8, 13, 213, 244–45, 281

American Council on Race Relations, 227

American dilemma, 10, 152, 167

American Jewish Congress, 13

American Jewish Council, 227

American Samoa, 152

American South, 22, 57, 125, 152–55, 171–75, 211, 213–14, 216, 238, 281, 283, 296

Americanization, 98, 229, 235; form of acculturation, 329n20; in *Mendez v. Westminster*, 220–24

Amish, 238

Analytic philosophy, 254, 294

Angel, Frank, Jr., 125, 148, 257

Anthropology, 3, 5, 42, 44–45, 95, 209, 266, 292, 295; Beals at Berkeley, 180–87; cultural relativism as a form of antiformalism, 307n67; in the segregation cases, 218–21

Antiformalism, 3, 165, 283–84, 307n67; defined by Morton White, 299n4

Anzaldúa, Gloria: on *mestizaje*, 305n38; on Vasconcelos, 304n23

Applebaum, Nancy P., 321n48

Aquinas, Thomas, 288

Arithmetic in Maya, 294

Arizona, 14, 39, 96, 111, 138, 142, 180, 186–87, 190, 199, 210, 213, 232, 241, 242, 255, 269; desegregation of public schools, 278–85

Arizona Normal College, 255

Assimilation, 2, 5, 30, 42, 45, 98, 105, 107, 109, 129, 135, 170, 176, 184, 189, 192, 194–95, 198, 205, 210, 218–24, 235–37, 241, 243, 245, 268–76, 271–72, 283; in California segregation cases, 218–29; courts versus schools, 235–37; in New Mexico, 112–13; relationship to the melting pot, 299n1; in Texas segregation cases, 268–76; varieties of, 40. *See also* Milton Gordon

Atoka, New Mexico, 230

Atotonilco, Morelos, 230

Austin, Texas, 151, 262, 268, 270

Aztecs, 34, 39, 156, 158

Backroads pragmatists, 11

Balún-Canán, 86–87

Nambé, New Mexico, 256–257, 260, 264–65, 271
Natchitoches, Louisiana, 230
National Association for the Advancement of Colored People (NAACP), 8, 13, 213–14, 216, 237–38, 241–42, 268, 278, 281, 328n8
National Research Council, 218
Nayarit, 195–96, 309n6
New Deal, 3–4, 8, 12, 25, 36, 47, 64, 95, 134–35, 155, 163, 173, 203–4, 210, 223, 238, 296
New England, 259
New Mexico, 4, 7–10, 12–14, 20–21, 23, 25, 54, 57, 61, 63, 69–71, 83, 99–100, 104–5, 107–15, 117–20, 123, 125–35, 137–39, 141–51, 161–64, 166–68, 172, 186–87, 189, 198, 200, 204, 209–10, 212, 214–15, 219–20, 225–32, 234, 240–44, 246, 254–60, 262–69, 272, 275, 279, 289, 295
New Mexico Highlands University, 125
New psychology, 107–11, 116, 290
New Republic, 11, 75
New York Times, 41, 75–76, 296–97
Niggli, Josefina, 199–201
No Frontier to Learning: The Mexican Student in the United States, 291. *See also* Ralph Beals
North from Mexico, 25, 212, 217, 231, 304n18. *See also* Carey McWilliams
Northwestern University, 292
Novum Organum, 166, 247

Oaxtepec, Morelos, 65–68, 117, 120, 230
One-drop rule, 34–35
Orange County, 5, 133, 212, 215, 217–19, 221–22, 224, 227, 231, 243, 278–79
Organization of the State Child Welfare, The, 99. *See also* Montana Hastings
Orientalism, 19, 89, 221, 303n2
Orozco, José Clemente, 26, 328n14. *See also* Murals
Otomí people, 39, 64, 117, 276

Pappas, Gregory, 43, 95, 295; Dewey in Mexico conference, 337n28; ethics of amelioration, 87–91, 308n75; "experience" in Dewey, 43, 307n60; science complements art, 313n1
Paredes, Américo, 199–200
Park, Robert, 30, 288

Parsons, Elsie Clews, 183, 188
Passing of the Great Race, The, 23
Paz, Octavio, 232
Peace by Revolution, 155. *See also* Frank Tannenbaum
Peasant Marketing System of Oaxaca, Mexico, The, 291. *See also* Ralph Beals
Peirce, Charles, 286
PEMEX, 201
Perales, Alonso, 204
Perfil del hombre y la cultura en México, El, 252
Peru, 87, 164, 295; pragmatism in 322n84
Phelps Dodge Corporation, 132
Phenotype, 39; whiteness, 275–77
Philosophical Union, University of California, Berkeley, 286
Philosophy, 6, 42, 46, 48, 60, 61, 81, 86, 89, 99, 118, 135, 144, 146, 149, 156, 165, 167, 168, 170, 254, 264, 294–95, 300n6, 310n20; idealism, 174, 287; old wine in new bottles, 286–87. *See also* pragmatism
Plessy v. Ferguson, 211–13, 236–38
Pluralism, 1, 6, 11, 25, 31, 50, 52, 72, 84, 107, 144, 161, 170, 174, 219–20, 272–73, 294, 309n16, 312n52; contrasted with cosmopolitanism, 24. *See also* Horace Kallen
Postville, Iowa, 110
Pragmatism, 3, 41–49, 54, 59, 72, 74, 76, 83, 171–72, 247–48, 254, 257–59, 283–85, 286–90, 294, 296–97; convergence with *indigenismo*, 84–91; defined, 6, 42–43; in Mexico, 161–68; in New Mexico, 143–49. *See also* Philosophy
Prensa, La, 199, 204
PRI party, 38, 223
Profecía de la Raza Cósmica, La, 31, 304n28. *See also* Murals
Progressive education, 9, 12, 48, 58, 72, 103–4, 114, 118, 139, 168, 170–72, 266, 294, 319n19, 332n30
Progressive Education, 168–71, 317n65
Progressive Education Association, 45, 74, 120–21, 152, 170–74, 205, 307n64, 315n40
Project method, 113, 122
Psychology, 44, 67, 77, 95–106, 107–15, 116, 118, 119–20, 123, 144, 198, 199–200, 209, 232, 274, 276, 289–90, 297, 307n67, 311n35, 314n16
Public School 26 (Indianapolis), 261

Acknowledgments

Secretly I have hoped that this book would never come to a close because of the joy I have had on the way to its completion. Putting it to rest, however, does allow me to thank the people whose support I have long needed to acknowledge. I begin with colleagues in Mexico whose interest and insight has been a great inspiration to me. Claudia Salas Rodríguez, Claudia Argueta Sánchez, and Fabiola María Luisa Hernández Díaz were patient and solicitous as I navigated my way through the Archivo General de la Nación and the Archivo Histórico de la Secretaría de Educación Pública. I am especially indebted to Roberto Pérez Aguilar, whose many years of experience at the SEP archives allowed me to look beyond the limits of the established indices, and to María Inés Ortiz Caballero and Rebeca Agramonte Rosales for making it possible to document the photographic record of John Dewey's 1926 trip to Mexico after many years of searching. I thank my friend and colleague Guillermo Hurtado Pérez of the Universidad Nacional Autónoma de México Instituto de Investigaciones Filosóficas, whose interest in my work brought me in contact with the faculties of philosophy and history at UNAM and enabled me to present my ideas before sympathetic audiences in Mexico City. At the Centro de Investigaciones sobre América Latina y el Caribe, Adalberto Santana was deeply supportive at an early stage, as was Virginia Guedea Rincón Gallardo of the Instituto de Investigaciones Históricas. I thank Marco Antonio Calderón Molgora and Philippe Shauffhauser Mizzi of the Colegio de Michoacán for their suggestions and advice as my manuscript was underway.

Especially important in the United States were a number of researchers and bibliographers whose dedication helped me to analyze manuscript collections whose obscure items seemed forgotten but proved essential to the story I have tried to narrate. At the Rockefeller Archive Center, Thomas Rosenbaum and Camilla Harris led me though the massive files of the General Education Board. At Fisk University, I am indebted to Beth Howse,

Aisha Johnson, and Vanessa Smith for guiding me through the papers of the Julius Rosenwald Fund. I thank the staff members of the Center for Southwest Research at the University of New Mexico for their assistance with the Loyd Tireman Papers, and to Susan Tiano and Vickie Madrid Nelson at UNM's Latin American and Iberian Institute for their assistance at a late stage of my manuscript. At the National Anthropological Archives, Robert Leopold assisted me with the Ralph Beals Papers. I appreciate the support of the Regional Oral History Office at the Bancroft Library and its director, Richard Candida Smith, as I tried to understand UC Berkeley's role in my narrative. Shannon Davis of the Lewis Memorial Library at Grambling State University helped to track down various references that otherwise would have remained unknown. The Benson Latin American Collection at the University of Texas at Austin remains one of the highlights of my work on Latin America, and I especially thank Michael Hironymous and Margo Gutiérrez for their assistance there.

Financial support was critical to my thinking and writing. The Institute for Historical Studies at UT Austin allowed me a year's time to reorganize my argument and to underscore it with the holdings of the Perry-Castaneda Library. I am especially indebted to Julie Hardwick for her guidance and leadership, and to the faculty of the UT Department of History for their questions and comments on my work. A special note of thanks goes to my friend and colleague Anne Martinez for her many observations and advice as my book progressed. I thank fellow IHS scholars-in-residence Dave Kinkela, Ebru Turan, Matt Childs, Jim Sweet, and Nancy Applebaum for their support and comments. At the National Academy of Education and the Spencer Foundation, the dedication and knowledge of colleagues provided an unparalleled source of support and inspiration that continues to guide my thought and questions. I especially thank Adam Laats for his friendship and support. I also thank Maris Vinovskis, William Reece, Carl Kaestle, Marilyn Cochran-Smith, Kris Gutiérrez, Barbara Rogoff, and John Meyer for their feedback and suggestions at various moments along the way and for encouragement throughout. At the Clements Center for Southwest Studies at Southern Methodist University, Andrew Graybill and Ruth Ann Elmore facilitated my writing and research as I completed my book. I thank John Chavez, Bill Tsū/sui, Ed Countryman, Crista DeLuzio, Ken Hamilton, Kathleen Wellman, and Sherry Smith for their comments on my work. I must give a special note of thanks to Neil Foley, now at Southern Methodist University but formerly at UT Austin, for his support throughout the years.

At various stages, Neil has never wavered in his support of my book and has facilitated my efforts to reach southward across the continent for a better understanding of American politics and culture. I thank the Clements Center and SMU, as well, for arranging critiques of my manuscript by Ben Johnson and Alexander Dawson that resulted in sharpening my focus and streamlining my prose.

At the University of Kansas, a network of supportive colleagues prepared the ground for my project many years ago and helped steer me through the publishing landscape through the very end. I especially thank Victor Bailey, Kathy Porsche, and Sally Utech at the Hall Center for the Humanities for their expertise in negotiating the humanities landscape and their sponsorship of proposal writing workshops, fellowship review boards, and application services that strengthened my book. Likewise at the Hall Center, senior faculty members Betsy Kuznesof and Brian Donovan critiqued early versions of my project with the assistance of faculty colleagues Megan Greene, Tanya Golash Boza, Stephanie Fitzgerald, Margot Versteeg, Ebenezer Obadare, and Tamara Falicov. At the Office of International Programs, Juliet Kaarbo was supportive intellectually and financially, as was KU's Office of Research and Graduate Studies and the Dean's Office at the College of Liberal Arts and Sciences. I thank the Center for Latin American and Caribbean Studies for travel and moral support, as well, including Jill Kuhnheim and Judy Farmer. Cheryl Lester and Henry Bial of the American Studies Department supported my research away from campus, for which I am grateful. Finally, I thank a larger group of faculty colleagues for their intellectual and moral support, including Sherrie Tucker, Robert Antonio, Ann Schofield, Norm Yetman, David Katzman, Bill Tuttle, Jeff Moran, Shawn Alexander, Randal Jelks, Danny Anderson, Marta Caminero-Santangelo, Tanya Golash Boza, Jennifer Hamer, Clarence Lang, Luis Corteguera, Marta Vicente, Peter Herlihy, Laura Herlihy, Chris Brown, Greg Cushman, Santa Arias, Stuart Day, Jorge Perez, Jonathan Earle, Leslie Tuttle, John Rury, Lisa Wolf-Wendel, Susan Harris, Ludwin Molina, David Johnson, and Omri Gillath. I owe a special debt of gratitude to Jacob Dorman, Ben Chappell, Tanya Hart, and Tanya Golash Boza for their camaraderie and support.

It has been my great fortune to have come in contact with Gregory Pappas during the writing of my book. If anyone is more interested in Dewey's career in Latin America than Greg, I do not know who it is, and his zeal spurred me to understand the depths of American pragmatism.

Greg is a gracious and generous scholar, and one result of his commitment to the study of ethics has been the chance to broaden my work alongside colleagues in the United States and Latin America who share my belief that ideas matter philosophically and as instruments of politics. It was through Greg that I returned to the work of John McDermott, and that I also found myself attempting to close the divide that separates the United States and Latin America, alongside Larry Hickman, Richard Bernstein, and the devoted members of the Society for the Advancement of American Philosophy. It has been a pleasure to study Greg's work in Mexico and the United States, and I hope to continue to broaden a path that he, Guillermo Hurtado Pérez, and Ramón del Castillo have jointly embarked on establishing.

David A. Hollinger and William B. Taylor were guides for me in ways of which they were not always aware, including their respect for subtlety in logic and conviction in argumentation. Time and again they reminded me that people in all their human capacities and contradictions must be at the center of historical writing. They also share the idea that good writing is an art to be continually improved. I thank them, too, for their patience and willingness to let me make mistakes. Nothing in my career would ever have been possible without the example of Suzanne A. Marchand, meanwhile. More than anyone else, Suzanne showed me that history could be fun, and I am proud to call her my mentor and my friend. Suzanne's joy for history changed my life forever, and I am thankful and happy to have been her student. Along the way I have benefited from conversations with Robin Einhorn, Kerwin Klein, James Kettner, Jon Gjerde, Paula Fass, Estelle Tarica, Waldo Martin, Margaret Chowning, Richard Candida Smith, Mark Brilliant, Harry Scheiber, Daniel T. Rodgers, Christine Stansell, Sean Wilentz, and Jeremy Adelman. I thank, too, the Princeton Institute for International and Regional Studies, the Townsend Center for the Humanities at the University of California at Berkeley, the Bancroft Library, the DeGoyler Library at SMU, the Centro de Investigaciones sobre América Latina y el Caribe, Instituto de Investigaciones Filosóficas, and Instituto de Investigaciones Históricas at UNAM, the Society for the Advancement of American Philosophy, the National Academy of Education, and the Hall Center at the University of Kansas for the opportunity to defend my work before receptive audiences. I also thank Paddy Riley, Kevin Schultz, Molly Oshatz, Susan Haskell, Dan Geary, Andrew Jewett, and Jennifer Burns for their example and many comments over the years. At the University of Pennsylvania Press, I cannot say enough about Robert Lockhart. He has been a direct and clear editor throughout the writing process, and he was uniformly supportive of a project that reached across national borders.

I owe a special debt of gratitude to my family for many years of encouragement. I thank Artemio and María Trinidad Flores for their love and commitment to my education, and Renee Flores and María de Lourdes Camacho for standing beside me even when we were far apart. I also thank Howard and Carol Newman, and Amy Newman and Brent Noorda, for helping me in so many ways through the years.

I am not sure what to say to my wife and partner, Leslie Faith Newman. In my lonely times I sometimes quipped that she would receive an acknowledgment rather than a dedication. But the truth has always been clear. Alone of all those I have known, it was Leslie who brought me out of my room and helped me to believe that writing was something that I, too, could do. That was an act of courage that speaks to her faith in people and willingness to believe in possibilities rather than sure bets. Such courage and faith also brought us to Jacob Daniel Flores and Zachary Isaiah Flores, who lighten my load every day and help me to see the beauty of the world. Without Leslie, none of this would have been possible. As we move away from one another and yet find each other anew, amid the crush of the everyday and the confusions from which inspiration must be created, I am happy that our lives together have made me a more fulfilled human being. My book is done, and I will be forever grateful to her for the chance she made possible to press myself toward the pleasure of words and the meaning with which we imbue them.

CPSIA information can be obtained
at www.ICGtesting.com
Printed in the USA
BVOW08s0723260118
506148BV00003B/4/P